GOETHE:

The Story of A Man

OTHER WORKS OF LUDWIG LEWISOHN

Criticism
- THE MODERN DRAMA
- THE SPIRIT OF MODERN GERMAN LITERATURE
- THE POETS OF MODERN FRANCE
- THE DRAMA AND THE STAGE
- THE CREATIVE LIFE
- CITIES AND MEN
- EXPRESSION IN AMERICA
- THIRTY-ONE POEMS BY RAINER MARIA RILKE

Autobiography and Philosophy
- UPSTREAM
- ISRAEL
- MID-CHANNEL
- THE PERMANENT HORIZON
- THE ANSWER

Fiction
- THE BROKEN SNARE
- DON JUAN
- ROMAN SUMMER
- THE CASE OF MR. CRUMP
- THE ISLAND WITHIN
- STEPHEN ESCOTT (THE VEHEMENT FLAME)
- THE LAST DAYS OF SHYLOCK
- THE GOLDEN VASE
- THIS PEOPLE
- AN ALTAR IN THE FIELDS
- TRUMPET OF JUBILEE
- FOREVER WILT THOU LOVE
- RENEGADE
- BREATHE UPON THESE
- ANNIVERSARY

Drama
- ADAM: A DRAMATIC HISTORY

Goethe in 1817. Drawing by Ferdinand Jagemann.

GOETHE:

The Story of A Man

BEING THE LIFE OF *Johann Wolfgang Goethe*
AS TOLD IN HIS OWN WORDS AND THE WORDS
OF HIS CONTEMPORARIES

Volume Two

By LUDWIG LEWISOHN

Farrar, Straus and Company

NEW YORK

Manufactured in the U.S.A. by
The Colonial Press Inc., Clinton, Massachusetts
Designed by Stefan Salter

CONTENTS

Book Five

THE HOME AND THE WORLD

1788-1805
(Continued)

1797

January 11, 1797

To Schiller

Here I am back after a two weeks' absence. The trip was satisfactory. Some pleasant things occurred and nothing unpleasant. . . . Of poetical results the journey was barren, except that I have outlined the rest of the narrative poem.

Early January, 1797

Charlotte to Goethe

My best thanks, dear Privy Councillor, for the charming books which were brought me by August, my little favorite, who continues to make his way ever more deeply in my heart. While thanking you for your intellectual gifts, I must not fail to thank you for those edible ones which arrived during your absence. I hope soon to say this to you in person.

January 17, 1797

From a Friend to Körner

Whenever Goethe is in Jena he is the only one who sees much of Schiller. He comes in every afternoon around 4 and stays till after supper. As a rule he enters silently, sits down, rests his head on his hand or takes up a book or else a pencil and sketches. This silent scene is interrupted by one of the wild Schiller children. The boy will have a whip and strike out at Goethe with it. The latter jumps up and shakes the child and rumples his hair and swears that one of these days he'll play ninepins with his head. This little incident mobilizes him. In any event he begins to thaw out when tea is served, of which he brews himself a kind of punch with a lemon and a glass of arrack.

Schiller walks, nay, one might better say runs uninterruptedly up and down the room. He dare not sit down. Often he betrays his physical sufferings, especially when he is overtaken by extreme short-

ness of breath. When it gets too bad he leaves the room for a moment
and uses a palliative.

January 17, 1797

Schiller to Goethe

I'm quitting work for the day and herewith bid you a good evening
before I put the pen aside. Your last visit, brief as it was, melted my
stagnation and gave me new courage. . . .
What delighted me especially was the vividness of your impulse toward a continued poetical activity. A newer and more beautiful life
thus opens up for you. . . . I am inclined to believe that the development of your mind and character symbolizes a certain necessary
procedure in human nature. You must have undergone a rather
lengthy period which I would call your analytical one, in which you
strove out of division and distractedness toward integration, in
which your nature was, as it were, at odds with itself and sought to
reconstitute its oneness through art and science. Now it would seem
to me that, fully formed and ripe, you are recapturing your youth
and are combining the season of the flower and the fruit. . . .

January 31, 1797

Schiller to Goethe

. . . *Hermann and Dorothea* is bound to have a brilliant sale. It is
only fair, however, that the publisher make no profit on books of
this character, but let the honor of publishing them suffice him. Let
him grow rich on the bad books. . . .

February 1, 1797

To Schiller

As a roof in Weimar my garden house is entirely at your disposal.
Alas, it is fit only for summer and for a very few persons. Since I
lived there so long and since I know your way of life, I am sorry to
have to say that you couldn't live there. I have had both the laundry
and the woodshed removed, both of which are indispensable to a
household. . . .

February 4, 1797

To Schiller

Henriette Karoline Jagemann, 1777-1848, actress and operatic singer at the Weimar Theatre.

My prospect of paying you a longish visit is put off again and again. I had to be here on account of the engagement of the Jagemann and her introduction to our theatre. But I shall let nothing keep me from coming to see you on the 12th of this month. It will be full moon and we won't have to be nervous on our return over the disrepair of the valley road.

February 18, 1797

To Schiller

I venture finally to send you the first three cantos of my little epic. Have the kindness to read them attentively and to communicate your observations to me. I request the same friendly service of Herr von Humboldt. Neither of you is to let anyone else see the manuscript. I am now working at the fourth canto. . . .

February 22, 1797

Christiane to Goethe

I am sending you the things you want, the watch, the book and the six bottles of wine. I will also send you money. I have taken money out of the drawer because the upholsterer wants 14 to 15 thaler for horsehair, linen, yarn, nails and wages for the chairs and the sofa. I went over his accounts and the things will cost us less than the other ones did. I hope you'll be visited by fine moods which will help you to work at your poem.
Farewell and love your "little child of nature."

Jena, February 27, 1797

To Schiller

I am housebound; I sit by the warm stove and shiver within. My head is dull and my poor mind wouldn't be able to think enough to produce a worm. I owe my existence to spirits of ammonia and licorice juice, things of a most revolting taste. Let us hope that we will arise once more from the humiliation of these sordid circumstances to the glory of poetic creation.

Jena, March 1, 1797

To Schiller

The catarrh is on the way out, but I'm still confined to my room which is beginning to grow bearable through habit. . . . Tell your dear wife that I am being punished for my dislike of tea by having to drink horrible herbal brews.

Jena, March 3, 1797

To Schiller

I am happy to tell you that the poem is making good progress. If the thread does not snap, it may well be completed. Thus the Muses seem not to reject the anaesthetic condition which my illness induces; perhaps it is even favorable to their influences.

Jena, March 28, 1797

To Knebel

When you see my poem which is nearly complete and which has been worked through twice, you will be able to judge whether I was idle these four weeks. Then, too, the sympathy with which I follow the activity of my friends takes some of my time. Schiller is busy with his *Wallenstein,* Humboldt is working at his translation of the *Agamemnon* of Aeschylus . . . and so, while I have every reason to reflect on the nature of narrative poetry, I am induced at the same time to pay attention to the character of tragedy. . . .

April 4, 1797

Schiller to Goethe

As I reflect more and more concerning my own business and, in that connection, on the Greek treatment of tragedy, it is borne in upon me that the cardinal point of the matter lies in the invention of a poetic fable. The modern writer has to fight his miserable and fearful way through the accidental and the second rate. In his effort to get close to reality he is burdened with the empty and the insignificant and runs the danger of missing that deep inner truth which constitutes the essence of all poetry. He would so like to delineate an event in reality and forgets that poetic representation, being absolute in its truth, can never coincide with the crude facts of life.

April 19, 1797

To Schiller

I want to make a very special observation to you. There are a number of lines in Homer which the critics declare to be spurious and late. Well, they happen to be of the very same kind as several lines which I myself recently interpolated in my own poem, in order to make the story clearer and easier to grasp and in order to foreshadow certain future events. . . .

April 22, 1797

To Schiller

. . . Of a good narrative poem and its action the reader not only can but must know the outcome. The interest must be fixed wholly on the execution. Curiosity has nothing to do with a work of this character. Its purpose is concentrated within every point of its development.

April 28, 1797

To Johann Erichson

A student of theology at Jena who later became Professor of Aesthetics at the University of Erlangen.

I am returning the poems you entrusted to me. As you asked me to do, I add a few observations. You seem to me to labor under the error which I have remarked in several other young men, namely, that one must yield exclusively to an inclination for poetry, once it is felt. Consider that even he whom nature seems to have destined to be a poet must first derive from life and knowledge the substance without which his efforts will always be empty. In my opinion you will neglect nothing by dedicating yourself either to active life or to

the pursuit of knowledge, for only when you have mastered the difficulties in either of these spheres, will you have any assurance of your
talent. If your impulse powerfully integrates within itself all your
garnered experience and knowledge and fuses the most alien elements into oneness—then, and then only, the phenomenon which
you seem to desire will truly have appeared. There is no other way.
If, on the contrary, it were to appear that your inclination toward
the art of poetry does not stand this test, you would still be in possession of the fruits of your other efforts. Nor need anyone, though
his path lie in another direction, regret having made himself acquainted with the techniques of the poetic art.

Late April, 1797

Wilhelm von Humboldt to His Wife

Goethe is extremely kind and friendly and this intimacy with him is
delightful. In Jena I usually saw him only in the evening, but these
evenings were charming. He was very confidential and talked with
great ease of the things nearest his heart. Then he would grow warm
and show that blending of modesty and faith in himself which is so
characteristic of him.

May 13, 1797

To Schiller

I shall be busy here another week. In that time several things will
come to a head. I'm very eager to pass some time in your company
again; I've fallen back into that condition of indecision in which I
can accomplish nothing and have no impulse to do so.

May 17, 1797

To Schiller

I'm doing my best to get clear in order to earn a few free weeks and
get back into the mood to finish my poem. I have said a final farewell
to our respected contemporary literature. Criticism is exclusively
dictated by good will or ill will toward the author and I find the
grimace of faction more revolting than any other kind of caricature.

Jena, May 23, 1797

To Schiller

I am sending you at once a little poem which I do hope will truly please you. I feel wonderful. . . .

ECHO OF LOVE

When the bloom our vineyard graces,
In the vats the new wines shiver;
When the roses lift their faces
Wherefore am I troubled so?

Tears at break of dawn awake me,
What I do or dream soever;
Subtle griefs will not forsake me
That within my bosom glow.

Till at last it is my duty
To confess without a quiver,
That in days of just such beauty
Doris loved me long ago.

May 23, 1797

Schiller to Goethe

Thank you for your dear note and the poem. It is so inimitably lovely and rounded and perfect. It makes me feel how a small thing that is complete and a simple idea can, through the perfection of its execution, give one the enjoyment of the highest art.

June 5, 1797

Elisabeth Goethe to Her Son

Goethe was planning a long journey and wanted to assure the financial security of Christiane and August in case of his death.

Dear Son, Whatever I can do to give you peace of mind I will do with all my heart—irrespective of the fact that I know absolutely that God will not let me live to see your—no, I can't write the word. So

I will formally renounce my rights as your heir and do everything you desire in the matter, in order that you may set out on your journey without anxiety and, whether in Italy or in Weimar, enjoy life forty years from now.—I am deeply happy at the prospect of seeing you again. But I do beg you to let me know a week in advance and whether you are bringing one or two servants. . . . You see, I have to rent a servants' room from my landlord. My dwelling is unique by its favorable situation, but I haven't got the space which I had in our old house.

June 6, 1797

To Karl August

. . . As I see others move about, the desire stirs in me, too, to take a look at the world once more. I count on your permission. Early in July I would like to visit my mother and get a real insight into our financial situation. By the promise of higher interest and other advantages she was persuaded to invest considerable capital in foreign loans and I am not satisfied to have the greater part of our fortune permanently in such securities. Meyer isn't very well in Florence and I expect that he will go to Switzerland which did him good before. I might want to spend some time with him on the Lake of Zürich. The atmosphere there agreed with Wieland, too.

June 12, 1797

To Karl August

Frederick August Hervey, Lord Bishop of Bristol, 1730-1803, visited Goethe and upbraided him on the immorality of his *Werther* and other writings.

Your reproach, my dear Lord, concerning my laziness in writing letters which was conveyed to me by Councillor Voigt is, alas, not wholly undeserved. My reluctance to use pen and paper increases daily. . . . Night before last I had a very curious conversation with the Bishop of Bristol. He was here on his way from Karlsbad and since he asked me to come to see him, I went. He at once made a few solemn but quite rude remarks and so put me quite at my ease. Luckily I was in good humor and had, so to speak, my French day, so I gave him as good as I got. After we had discoursed and disputed and also insulted each other—though now and then the conversation was sensible enough—we said goodbye to each other very courteously and contentedly. It amused me to see this queer and original character, about whom there has been so much gossip, with my own eyes at last. . . .

Since everything here goes its accustomed way, there isn't much to add.

To Schiller   June 22, 1797

Since it is necessary that I set myself a task in my present restless condition, I have decided to start at my *Faust* and, at least, to make some real progress, even if I can't finish it. I am taking what has been printed and divided it and grouped it in larger fragments with what has since been finished or imagined in addition. Thus I prepare myself for the execution of the plan which, in reality, exists only as an idea. Now I have taken this idea up again and its delineation as well and have arrived at definite conclusions. What I would like is that you have the kindness to think the whole thing through once more in some sleepless night and to submit to me the demands which you would make upon the whole poem. Next, like a true prophet, you might relate and interpret my own dreams to me.

Since the various parts of the poem can be treated separately in respect of the mood of each, provided they be kept subordinate to the spirit and tone of the entire poem and since, moreover, the entire work is a subjective one, it is clear that I can work at it during isolated moments, which means that I can add to it now, too.

To Schiller   June 24, 1797

Thank you for your first words on the revival of *Faust.* . . . But it's really a matter of prudence that I take up this work now. In view of Meyer's state of health I suppose I will have to undergo another Northern winter. Since I don't want the irritation of my disappointment to make me a nuisance to my friends I am preparing a place of refuge for myself within that Faustian world of symbols and ideas and Northern mist. . . .

July 1, 1797

To Schiller

In the matter of outline and general grasp I have made very rapid progress with *Faust*. . . . If I could just be sure of one tranquil month, this work would ooze from the earth like a great plantation of mushrooms to everyone's horror and amazement. If the journey is definitely off, I place my whole reliance in these drolleries. I am having what has been printed copied but divided into its component parts, so that the new may the more easily be grafted on the old.

Weimar, July 9, 1797

From the Diaries

Burned letters. The flame had a lovely green color when the burning paper was near to the fire screen.

July 11, 1797

To Schiller

I am making all preparations for my journey, so that I can leave right after the Duke's arrival. For an hundred reasons, then, it would be excellent if you could come to Weimar for a few days. I would visit you once more in any event, but that could be for but a few hours and there is so much that we ought to discuss.

July 19, 1797

To Schiller

Nothing could have been more delightful or wholesome for me prior to my departure than your stay here during the past week. I'm sure I don't deceive myself in my belief that our being together was extremely fruitful. Much was developed for the present and prepared for the future. I am leaving much more contentedly with the hope that I may be productive during my journey and with the prospect of your sympathy upon my return.

July 21, 1797

Schiller to Heinrich Meyer

We have not been inactive here, as you know; least of all our friend, who has surpassed himself in recent years. Doubtless you have read *Hermann and Dorothea* and you will admit that it represents a culmination of his own and of all modern art. I saw it arise and admired its way of coming to be almost as much as the work itself. While we others must carefully collect and test our material in order to produce something tolerable, he need but gently shake the tree and the luscious fruits, ripe and heavy, fall into his hands. It is incredible with what ease he now brings home the harvest of a well-used life and a continuous cultivation, how significant and assured is each step he takes, how his knowledge of himself and of the world save him from all vain striving and groping. . . . When you see him you will agree with me that on the height which he has reached, he must apply himself rather to bring forth the beauty of form he has attained, than to look about for new subjects; in brief, he ought from now on to devote himself wholly to creative productivity.

July 25, 1797

Elisabeth Goethe to Her Son

Dear Son, The notice of the arrival of your trunk gave me great pleasure. I'll take good care of it. But I beg to be excused from any thought of its having to be returned again without your coming. I haven't forgotten how I hung out of the window two years ago and peered at every postchaise for two long weeks. I won't touch a thing; I'm leaving everything as it is—until you write me: I am leaving on such and such a day and I expect to be with you on such and such a day. Ghosts, however beautiful, are only ghosts, and that's that.

July 27, 1797

To an Officer in the Ducal Chancellery

Goethe set out on his journey to Switzerland on July 30. Christiane and August accompanied him to Frankfurt where Goethe remained until

August 25. It was the last time that mother and son were to see each other.

For the purpose of my journey to Frankfurt and Switzerland I desire that a passport be issued me by the Ducal government. There will be no difficulty about that. But since I purpose to take my little family with me as far as Frankfurt and since, more especially, it will lack my protection on the way back here alone, I would request that a special passport be issued for both mother and son. I leave it to Your Honor whether you would consider it harmless to have the passport made out in the name of, let us say, Frau Vulpius and her son. Use whatever formula seems proper and effective to yourself. P.S. May I request that the deputation which is to call for my last will and testament appear at my house at 11 o'clock this forenoon.

Frankfurt, August 9, 1797

To Schiller

Very happily and well and without any untoward incident I arrived in Frankfurt. In a tranquil and serene house I am now considering what it means to go out into the world at my age. . . .
I am making a very curious observation on the character of the public of a great city. It lives in a constant nightmare of earning and consuming; what we call mood neither arises nor can it be communicated. All entertainments, even the theatre, are meant to distract merely; the lively taste of readers for newspapers and novels arises because the former always and the latter usually aim to distract people from their state of distractedness.
In view of these circumstances I am not surprised to have observed a kind of shyness in the face of poetical productions, insofar as they are truly such. Poetry, creative literature, demands concentration and isolates man against his will. It will have its way and in this broad world (not to say in this great world) is as annoying as a faithful mistress.

Frankfurt, August 10, 1797

To Knebel

I got your dear letter in Frankfurt, being now a traveler like yourself. . . . I am coming to see more and more that a man should stick seriously to his craft alone and take everything else in good humor. A few lines of verse which I want to write interest me far more than more important things, upon which I am not permitted to have any influence. If everybody were to follow this example, it would be well for the cities and houses of men. . . .

I have no desire to go to Italy now. I don't care to observe the caterpillars and chrysalises of liberty; I would much rather see the full-fledged butterflies of France.

August 24, 1797

Elisabeth Goethe to Christiane

Christiane and August had returned home from Frankfurt on August 9.

Dear Friend, The pleasure I enjoyed in your dear and intimate presence still delights me. I am obliged to my son for having introduced you to me. Brief as our meeting was, yet it was gay and cordial, and I look forward with delight to having you with me some day for a longer period. Now that we know each other, it will make our future happier and better. Remember me affectionately and be assured that I reciprocate.

Frankfurt, August 24, 1797

To Christiane

First of all, my dear child, I must ask you to have no anxiety concerning my traveling and not to ruin the pleasant day which you can have. You saw with your own eyes that I couldn't possibly work in Frankfurt and what else is there to do, since I have seen the city and have no specific relationship to it, nor desire to have. Anyhow, you know and have seen for yourself on our journey that I am very careful and very prudent. You may be quite sure that I won't take any risks and I can promise you that I won't go to Italy this time. But don't say this to anybody. Let people gossip as they like. You know how they all are—they would rather harass you and stir you up than console and encourage you. Take good care of the house and arrange things so that you either are ready to receive me or, perhaps, join me again somewhere. But you did see how that family of yours carried on during your brief absence and what arrangements you would have to make, if you were to stay away longer. Be sure to take good

care of the child and consult the doctor as to what should be done
in future on journeys to prevent his being indisposed. . . .
The good mama sends you a beautiful cup and sweets for the child
and yourself. In return, let your brother, if you yourself can't find
it, look in my library for Hufeland's *Treatise on Longevity* and send
it to her with a grateful and cheerful letter. Let the little one write,
too, for her attitude to you both is a most kindly one.

Tübingen, September 11, 1797

To Schiller

I have been here since the 7th. During the fine weather of my first
days I saw the surroundings with pleasure. A pleasant society now
cheats a rainy period of its melancholy. I have a lovely room in the
house of Herr Cotta between the old church and the university
building with an agreeable though narrow view of the valley of the
Neckar. . . .
I like Cotta better as I get to know him. Considering his ambitious
and enterprising business dealings, there is much that is moderate
and gentle and self-controlled about him. . . .
I was surprised by a little book of Kant's that I found here, the
tractate concerning perpetual peace among men. It is a most estimable example of his well-known opinions; like everything from his pen
it contains magnificent passages, but its composition and style are
more Kantian than Kant.

Tübingen, September 12, 1797

To Christiane

Although I am slowly increasing the distance between us, I write you
the more quickly that you may never lack news of me. . . .
I am well taken care of at Herr Cotta's house. The town is abominable, but a short walk takes you into the most beautiful countryside.
. . . P.S. I just hear through Privy Councillor Voigt that you had
a double scare and worry during the past few days, because the child
was ill and fire consumed the barn beyond the Erfurt Gate. I can
imagine how you suffered and how you wished me back home an
hundred times. I also hear to my comfort that the child is recovering.
Give him my love and take the best care of him. Let his tutor just
play with him and amuse him until he has completely recovered.

September 23, 1797

Elisabeth Goethe to Christiane

Dear Friend, I owe you double and threefold thanks for the volumes of Hufeland and for the extraordinarily handsome and well-made stockings which are just the right size and which will protect me from the cold this winter, and finally that you give me a gleam of light concerning my son, for I dare say you know where he is. He left here four weeks ago and I haven't had a line from him yet. Letters that came in my care after his departure are lying on my table. Since I don't know where he is, I can't possibly forward them. . . . Remember me to dear August and kiss him for his lovely letter. May God keep him well for the sake of all of us and guide him to tread in his father's footsteps. Amen.

Stafa, Switzerland, September 23, 1797

To Christiane

. . . Councillor Schiller writes me that the child is perfectly well again. Since his letter was sent on September 7, my mind is put at ease, since I can now assume that your letters were delayed quite by accident. . . .
If all goes as I now think it will, we may be back in Frankfurt by the end of October. I know that that will make you happy. Make all your preparations promptly. As a reward, since I am in the country where muslin is made, a pretty frock of this material will be bought for you. . . . Now I'll stop dictating and add in my own handwriting that I love you very dearly and tenderly and that I deeply desire that your love of me remain ever the same. I don't think I'll do much more traveling unless I can take you along. For at this very moment I'd rather be back home and say good night and good morning to you in our green alcove and have you bring me my breakfast. . . . Tell nobody about my plans. Leave people in uncertainty about the date of my return. Think of me and don't flirt too much or, rather, don't flirt at all. I haven't either on my whole trip. I think of you only and the beautiful dress of muslin is now being bargained for.

Stafa, Switzerland, September 24, 1797
To Schiller

Tell me in your next letter what your arrangements for the coming winter are: whether you intend to get the garden or the house or come to Weimar. I want to be sure that you are thoroughly comfortable, in order that the inclemencies of the weather be not added to your other ills.

I do thank you for your news that my little son is well again. . . . My anxiety over him darkened many a moment. . . .

Stafa, Switzerland, October 14, 1797
To Schiller

. . . I can truly say that so far I have been well content with the results of this journey. . . . From the barren peaks of St. Gotthard to the magnificent works of art which Meyer brought back from Italy, a labyrinthine path leads one through the interesting and intricate objects which this curious land contains.

October 20, 1797
Schiller to Goethe

A few days ago I received two beautiful copies of your *Hermann and Dorothea.* It is out in the world now and we shall see how the voice of a Homeric bard will seem in this political and rhetorical period. . . . Quite recently I also reread *Meister;* it struck me all over again how significant its form is. . . . Nor can I say how much this new reading enriched and vivified and charmed me. . . .

Zürich, October 25, 1797
To Christiane

. . You need have only a little more patience. I'll be back soon. . . Give my love to the little one and thank him for his letters which gave me much pleasure. Since I am not returning by way of

Frankfurt, I don't know yet what I'll bring home for him. If I go by
way of Nürnberg I'll be sure to find something both useful and agreeable. There is better provision here for women. I have that beautiful
muslin frock for you and a flowered one for your sister, as well as
neck kerchiefs and all kinds of lace so that you can give presents to
your aunt and the others. I have bought some neck kerchiefs for
myself, too, but I dare say you will pilfer them, because they can be
used as head kerchiefs. Everything is in the latest style, especially
your frock, which wasn't cheap either. . . . It was really difficult to
make a choice among the various designs, but Meyer and I agreed at
last.

Tübingen, October 30, 1797

To Schiller

I'm so glad that *Hermann* is in your hands and holds up. I understand all that you say about *Meister;* it is most true. Its very imperfection gave me most trouble. A pure form helps and holds one up,
an impure one hinders and tugs. Be this as it may, I shall not easily
be tempted again to make a wrong choice of subject and of form.
Let us await what will inspire us in the autumn of life.

Tübingen, October 30, 1797

To Christiane

We have given up going to Basle and have come from Zürich directly here. We did well, too, because the weather is depressing, the
roads bad and the prices incredibly high. . . . We ought to be home
by the middle of November. I'm sure you won't mind seeing your
friend again so soon. I can truly say that I am coming back only for
your sake and the child's. You alone need me; the rest of the world
can do without me.

November 25, 1797

To Schiller

I appreciate your sending both the letter and the package. I hasten
to say at once and without much reflection that I not only agree with
you but go much farther. All poetical subjects should be rhythmically
treated! Such is my conviction. That people could think of intro-

ducing what they call poetic prose shows only that they had wholly
missed the distinction between prose and poetry. It makes no more
sense than though one were to order a dry pool in one's park and
as though the landscape architect tried to execute this commission
by producing a swamp. These mixed genres are for dilettantes and
tyros, just as swamps are for amphibious creatures. The evil has
become so prevalent that no one pays any more attention. People
are like those Swiss who are afflicted with goitre and consider a
healthy neck a punishment from God. . . . What we must do under
all circumstances is to forget this age in which we live, and work
exclusively according to our own convictions.

November 28, 1797

To Schiller

I haven't a thing to tell you, because these last few days I have
lived amid the things of the outer world and have neither thought
nor done anything that could interest either one of us. . . . I feel
at this moment as though I had never written a poem nor would
ever write one again.

December 4, 1797

Elisabeth Goethe to Her Son

Dear Son, The first thing for which I want to thank you was that you
gave me sundry weeks of your time this summer, during which I so
deeply rejoiced in your presence and in your extraordinarily excellent appearance. Also I thank you for bringing your dear ones here
and letting me make their acquaintance. May God watch over you
all, as He has done hitherto, and to Him be all praise and thanks.
Amen. That you did not visit me on your return journey hurt me in
one way. Yet it is true that I would rather have you with me in spring
or summer, when I have space enough. For to have you lodge anywhere else—that is a thing I could not bear. . . . The things you
left here would have been returned before, had I not desired to take
the occasion to include my Christmas gifts in the same box. . . . If
the present I picked for my dear daughter were not to please her—
since I completely forgot what we agreed upon when you were here—
just send it back and I'll pick out something else. It appealed to me,
but it doesn't follow that it need please her for whom it is meant.

. . . What a sensation *Hermann and Dorothea* made here—of that I have already written my dear daughter.

December 6, 1797

To Schiller

I am glad indeed that you are convinced that the winter will be better for both your health and your work in Jena, since I shall be obliged to be there right after New Year in order to recover any kind of concentration and balance. And Jena would seem strange to me indeed, if you were not there. . . .

And so let us pursue our appointed way. . . . We can also count on the sympathy of the public. Though we are right to abuse it as a whole, yet there are cultivated individuals in its ranks who are able to value a writer's earnest and honest efforts. Meanwhile let old Wieland, *laudator temporis acti* [*that praiser of past time*], wax melancholy over these lees of the 18th century. The Muse is sure to pour us as much clear wine as we need.

December 9, 1797

To Schiller

Our actors are much depressed by the fact that you will not be in Weimar this winter. They had quite made up their minds to live in your reflected glory. . . . I can quite imagine the conditions necessary for your work. I, too, have never succeeded in the creative use of any tragic situation without a vivid pathological interest. Hence I have preferred to avoid them. Perhaps it is another of the advantages of the ancients that to them the highest pathos was but an aesthetic game, while we must seek the truth of nature if we want to produce a tragic work. I don't know myself well enough to say whether I could write a genuine tragedy. But the thought of the mere attempt frightens me and, I am almost convinced, might destroy me. . . .

I'm not taking Meyer to Jena with me. I have found out again that I can produce only in absolute solitariness. Not only the conversation but the mere sense of the presence even of people whom I love and esteem dries up my poetic source completely. I would fall into a kind of despair, seeing that every trace of productive impulse seems to have left me, were I not certain to recover myself in Jena in a single week.

December 16, 1797

To Schiller

I'm no good for either big or little things. To keep in some contact with what is good I read Herodotus and Thucydides and read them for the first time with pure delight, because I read entirely for the sake of form and not of content.

December 23, 1797

To Schiller

It just occurred to me again how it comes about that modern writers are so inclined to confuse the genres and seem, in fact, no longer able to distinguish between them. It seems to me to be so, because artists, who ought to produce their works within the pure conditions of their kind, yield to the desire of the audience that everything be felt to be real. . . . Thus novels in the form of letters are completely dramatic; quite properly may one insert formal dialogues in them, as Richardson has done; narrative novels mixed with dialogue would be more questionable. . . . But who can separate his ship from the very waves that bear it, and against the current and the wind no great distances can be measured.

December 30, 1797

To Schiller

I was so sorry that your dear wife had to hurry home and couldn't even come to see our new art treasures. The high hopes you entertain for our operatic performances would have been satisfied to a great degree by our recent production of *Don Giovanni*. Of course, this composition is quite unique and Mozart's death has rendered vain any expectation of a thing to equal it.

According to Lotte Schiller

The Körners told me that on one occasion Goethe was trying to persuade the Prussian Ambassador in Dresden to get married. The question was flashed back: Why don't you get married yourself? He replied: I am married, only *un*-ceremoniously.

1798

January 3, 1798

To Schiller

If we poets were like jugglers and wanted to make sure that no one find out how our tricks are produced—our game would be easily won. He is sure to have luck who is willing to make a fool of the public by swimming with the current. Now, at least as far as subject matter is concerned, I have for once, in *Hermann and Dorothea,* given the public something it wanted, and it is well satisfied. This makes me wonder whether in this way a play could not be written which would be played on all stages and universally applauded, without the author considering it good at all.

January 5, 1798

Knebel to Goethe

To the horror of his sister and of all female society in Weimar, Knebel had decided to marry his mistress, the opera singer, Luise Rudorff.

Most frightful is the behavior of the female fools of Weimar. Men are so indulgent and so ill-represented in such matters, especially at Court, that these Weimar women in a very frenzy of arrogance dare to darken the days of a good and just man. These absurd and tyrannical female bachelors seem to want to set up a law that one dare not live without their approval, although they contribute nothing to the happiness of human life and, like the old aunts in Fielding's *Tom Jones,* condemn every pleasing young woman before their abominable bar of judgment and in their rage seek to destroy every germ of life. And, of course, the feeble and equivocal attitude of most of the Weimar gentlemen gives support to their malice. Even Herder and his wife have acted the weaklings and the hypocrites in this matter.

January 12, 1798

To Knebel

I wish you all happiness in the matter of your decision. In cases of this kind one must decide in the end to make the one sacrifice or the

other. And that decision can be made only by those most closely concerned. Do not therefore be too censorious of those mere onlookers,
some of whom opposed you violently and some of whom were doubtful as to how they ought to cooperate with you. They all, according
to their way of thinking, desired your welfare—in their own special
way, to be sure—and nothing can better justify your decision than
your future happiness.

January 31, 1798

To Schiller

Business affairs and distractions seem to beget more of their own
kind, so that I have almost decided to run over to you for a couple
of days, since I see no really tranquil period ahead. . . .
I'm sending you the curious announcement that the last descendant
of one of the old *Meistersänger* is going to publish a selection of
his own poems. I've seen some of them and regret not to have met the
man himself in Nürnberg. Some of his things are very natural and
humorous. . . . We'll get the book through Knebel so soon as it
appears. That friend of ours has returned to Ilmenau. *His* lovely
friend will arrive in a few days to place the yoke of marriage on his
stiff old neck. Since I am so very fond of him, I hope that this undertaking will have the happiest results.

February 1, 1798

To Knebel

Welcome to the snows of Ilmenau, in which I wish you very happy
days, until spring comes and revives us again. May the tight bond
which you are knotting into your fate bring all the good desired. Let
me hear from time to time how you are and wherewith I can give
you any pleasure.

February 3, 1798

To Schiller

I have half a dozen fairy tales and stories in mind. . . . In addition
I am thinking ever more seriously of *Faust,* and so I foresee my occupation for the entire year.

February 14, 1798

To Schiller

We dwellers in Central Europe are, indeed, charmed by the Odyssey; yet it is only the moral aspect of the poem which affects us; our imagination grasps the descriptive parts imperfectly and poorly. How radiantly did this work arise before me, when I read its verses in Naples and Sicily. . . . I confess that it ceased to be a poem to me; it seemed a work of nature itself, a circumstance all the more necessary to the ancients, since their poems were recited in nature's very presence. How many of our poems would stand the test of being read aloud on the market place or anywhere under the open sky?

February 20, 1798

Schiller to Goethe

> *Wallenstein,* Schiller's dramatic trilogy and his most powerful and eloquent work.

Unger writes me from Berlin that the theatre there would pay me any price I asked for *Wallenstein,* if I were to send him the manuscript. I wish it were finished! I'm working a bit again but my head is still dull. My wife is coming over to Weimar tomorrow to hear *The Magic Flute,* but since she is returning the same night she'll hardly be able to see you. Do come over soon again. We miss our lovely evenings.

February 28, 1798

To Schiller

> The *Luise* of J. H. Voss inaugurated the kind of writing which culminated in *Hermann and Dorothea.* It was imitated in English by Longfellow and Arthur Hugh Clough.

According to the news I get Voss is not as well pleased with my poem as I was with his. I remember so clearly the purity of my enthusiasm; how often I read it to my friends, so that I still know long passages by heart. And this enthusiasm of mind finally became productive and persuaded me to try the genre and so produce *Hermann.* That Voss enjoys my poem only despite himself hurts me for him. What

does all the little poetry writing we do amount to, if it doesn't stir
us to the point of appreciation for whatever is well done? Would to
God that I could start all over again and leave all I have done behind
me like the outworn shoes of my childhood and write something
better.

March 10, 1798

To Schiller

All that was lacking was that sundry hides of land be introduced into
the tenth house of my horoscope, in order to render my life a bit
more complicated. Yet it is so. I have finally acquired the estate at
Oberrössla, after the present lessor and his lawyer have bedeviled me
for two years. Yet I am contented to possess it, as well as with the
price, for land may now be likened to the sibylline books. Everybody
hesitates to buy during this rise in prices, the while the prices continue to rise. Moreover my purchase has a purity rarely seen. I have
never laid eyes on either the farm or the buildings. I'm going tomorrow to look at it all.

March 12, 1798

Elisabeth Goethe to Christiane

The pleasure your letter gave me demands an appreciative word.
. . . That you are all enjoying the approaching spring in your
garden, in the healthy fresh air, is very well done. On every fair day
this season I shall be thinking of you and rejoicing with you. . . .
Dear Son, everybody is reading *Hermann and Dorothea*—tailors,
seamstresses, servant maids—and everyone finds something in it that
corresponds to his feelings. . . . Dear Grandchild, Many thanks for
your fine description of the many four-footed animals and handsome
birds you saw. . . . That you remembered it all so clearly and wrote
about it so that your grandmother could actually see it—that deserves great praise.

April 21, 1798

To Lotte Schiller

During these last few days *Faust* has continued to grow, which is a
good preparation and presage. What held me back from it all these
long years was the difficulty of melting down the rigid old material

and making it fluid again. Now I have adopted the method of Cellini. I have melted down a mass of old pewter by using a goodly quantity of hard, dry wood. I trust that the fluidity will continue.

FAUST: PROLOGUE ON THE STAGE

The Poet's Defense

When Nature the unending thread devises,
Upon indifferent whirling spools to spin,
When from all creatures' clashing mass arises
A sullen and discordant din—
Who cleaves the dull monotonous gyration
And into living rhythms divides the whole,
Who calls the singular to general consecration
Wherein the chords accordant nobly roll,
Who shapes the storm as symbol of our passion,
In thoughtful souls lets sunset glow be red,
Who rifles all the floral spring to fashion
A path for the beloved's tread,
Who plucks the green leaves without form or meaning
To be as crowns of human honor sealed,
Unites the gods from safe Olympus leaning?—
Man's power in the poet's soul revealed.

FAUST: BEYOND THE CITY GATE

Farewell to the Sun

He stirs, recedes; fordone the fading day,
But he sets forth new fruitfulness to waken.
Oh that no wing uplifts me on that way
To follow him forever unforsaken!
Then would I by eternal beams behold
A silent sunset world beneath me glowing,
Tranquil the vales, the heights a ruddy gold,
The silver stream with fiery billows flowing.
Naught then could curb that course's godlike speed,
Nor lofty mountain gorges bid me tarry;
Even now the sea with each warm estuary
Before the dazzled eye were freed.
At last the orb divine sinks past my seeing,

But a new impulse gathers might:
To drink the eternal radiance onward fleeing,
The day before me and behind the night,
The heaven above my head, the waves deep under.
Beautiful dream the while he fades from me!
Not lightly to the spirit's wing will be
Added of corporeal wing the wonder.
Yet 'tis among man's inborn graces
That upward, forward his emotions throng,
When far above us lost in azure spaces
The lark intones its vibrant song,
When over rugged pine-clad highlands
The eagle floats on pinions twain,
And over plains and lakes and islands
On to his homeland flies the crane.

April 27, 1798

Schiller to Goethe

I am sending you Cotta's answer in the matter of the publication of your short treatises. As you can see he is far too interested in being your publisher to be perfectly frank with you in regard to his attitude to this particular work. It is clear, however, that, the contents being of a highly technical nature, he fears that it will appeal to a very limited public and hence wishes it were of more general interest. I can't say that I blame him entirely. Since, on the other hand, your works must be published in the right order, I would propose that you give him the refusal of your next creative work, say of *Faust,* or, in fact, engage yourself definitely to let him have it. If I were to make a suggestion, I would say: for the theoretical writings, printed more or less like *Meister,* ask four louis d'or per sheet and for *Faust* ask eight. If you think that Unger or some other publisher would pay more, why, Cotta will pay as much. All I want you to do is to formulate a demand. I'll communicate it to Cotta at once.

May 7, 1798

Elisabeth Goethe to Christiane

Many thanks for your dear letter. . . . News from Weimar is the only thing that interests me and keeps me bright and happy. . . .

The months of May and June are the worst for me. Butter is churned for the whole year and the supply of wood comes and the big washing must be done, so that I can't read properly nor play the clavichord nor make lace. . . . But when I get such a nice letter from Weimar, then all goes well again.

May 9, 1798

To Schiller

People like ourselves have a melancholy time at social gatherings. You are told a lot and you learn nothing. And the thing that we need most, nay, uniquely, namely, the right mood, is not given us but destroyed.

May 16, 1798

To Schiller

I was reading the *Iliad* as your letter came. The study of that poem never fails to fill me with rapture, hope, insight and despair.
I am more than ever convinced of the oneness and indivisibility of the poem and that there lives no man nor will one ever be born capable of passing judgment upon it. . . . Meanwhile my first *aperçu* concerning the possibility of a poem about Achilles was correct. . . . Such an Achilleis would be tragic in character, yet the subject matter is of purely personal and private interest, while the *Iliad* involves the fate of nations, of continents, of earth and heaven.

May 18, 1798

Schiller to Goethe

I'll tell you about Cotta when I see you. What pleased me especially was his report on the enormous popularity of *Hermann and Dorothea.* . . . Cotta is of the opinion that a cheap edition should be issued for Swabia alone. Several thousand copies will be sold at once.

Jena, May 25, 1798

To Christiane

I am so glad that you keep active during my absence and that you are happy in that situation in life in which you find yourself and

which can be agreeable to us both only insofar as you keep everything in good order and thus can spend your spare time freely and
devoid of care. I have used the few days in Jena very profitably both
for the present and for the future. . . .
The matter of my bodily nourishment is better taken care of now.
The cook prepares the asparagus acceptably, as well as an occasional
omelet. The Schillers supply me with roast meats and the oil you
sent makes the salad tasty. Thus my dinners are taken care of. I
spend the evenings with Schiller in his garden where we have read
and discussed many interesting things. Of course, the walk home is
troublesome. It takes quite half an hour. . . .
I am adding a letter for the little one. I will send the soap in good
time. . . . I am also sending you a haunch of venison and desire
that you all enjoy it in good spirits.

Jena, June 18, 1798

To a Chamberlain of the Ducal Court

Although I have always been determined to let the public have no
say, whether positive or negative, in respect of our actors in the
theatre, because I know the public's whims and variability and extravagance only too well, nevertheless there are circumstances which
might well cause us to engage the artist you speak of. You have
set forth these circumstances very well and I am inclined to agree to
your proposal. Therefore I am willing to have you draw up a contract for eighteen months, but make sure that the man will be satisfied with 8 thaler a week. . . . Don't let us forget, whatever comes
or goes, that in each group the public desires to have a scapegoat on
which it can wreak its own irritations and vulgarities. If there were
none to be found in a given group, one would have to engage one
for the express purpose of taking over this pleasant function.

Oberrössla, June 22, 1798

To Wieland

My dear brother in Apollo and comrade in the service of Ceres, I beg
to inform you cordially that I have arrived in this place in order to
take possession of my land and of whatever goes with it. Delighted
by our being neighbors now, I would most courteously request that,

toward noon tomorrow, you descend from your palace to our hut and deign to partake of an economical and frugal meal and thus give us the opportunity of a happy meeting after so long an interval. Your dear wife, as well as any other member of your family who would desire to give us the pleasure of his company, is cordially invited.

June 24, 1798

To Schiller

So soon as I leave Jena another polarity activates me and holds me down for a while. There were a number of reasons why I had to return to Weimar. I am now waiting for the Duke's arrival and then for a while I will try to put various things in order. Yet I hope to be with you once again a week from now.

July 14, 1798

To Schiller

I am returning the poem you submitted. It has a curious sort of emptiness. These young men learn to make verses the way a grocer makes paper bags. But they forget to put the spices in. . . .
The sketch of the new theatre building now definitely exists and next week work on it will be begun.

July 21, 1798

To Schiller

I do wish with all my heart that you soon recover the mood for poetical productivity. . . . You know, poets should be treated the way the Dukes of Saxony treated Luther. They should be picked up on the street and locked up in a castle on the top of a mountain. I wish they would begin with me. . . .

July 28, 1798

To Schiller

Your letter today was badly delayed. Insist that the woman who is paid to carry the letters do so herself. These people sometimes take things too easy and give the letters to small boys who arrive too late.

Jena, August 5, 1798

To Christiane

With my best wishes for your birthday I am sending you some fruit
which I want you and August to eat, the while you remember my
love of you. . . . See to it that everything is in proper order and
then go to Oberrössla and take pleasure in your pastoral occupations
there. It would be well if you familiarize yourself with all the details.
Don't be depressed by what people think or say. That's the way they
treat each other in great affairs and small. Remember that I love
you and that my chief care is to assure your independence. I have
succeeded in more difficult matters.

August 28, 1798

To Schiller

It was so good of you to remember my birthday and to think of coming to see me. For me the day passed distractedly and fruitlessly and
I hope to recover concentration of mind in your neighborhood quite
soon now. . . . It rather pleases me that the gentlemen you mention
are having a good time indulging in illicit love affairs. It would
amuse me even more if I were to live to see Matthisson go in for the
same sort of thing.

September 6, 1798

To Schiller

We were expecting you most eagerly. As far as a cold in the head is
concerned, you know the Duke's well-tested theory that the best
thing for it is exposure to the open air.
It's the building of the theatre and the various arrangements concerning it that keep me here from day to day. Otherwise I would
have seen you long ere this. . . .
I've looked through all my papers and find nothing suitable for you
to print in the *Almanach*. And whence am I to get the mood for
productivity?! To be sure, our friend Jean Paul Richter tried to
enlighten me the other day. He assured me (modestly enough and
in his own peculiar way) that this having to be in the right mood
was a lot of nonsense. All he had to do was to drink coffee to spout

forth things on the instant which were the delight of all Christendom.

October 1, 1798

Lotte Schiller to Fritz von Stein

The influence of his presence on Schiller's soul is astonishing. . . . I am personally very fond of Goethe but even more so for Schiller's sake. But when he is in Jena he is a different man; the influence of this place on him is curious. He is so stiff and reserved in Weimar. If I hadn't got to know him here, much would have escaped me; I would never have seen him clearly. I am bound to believe that it is his domestic situation which is so unsuitable to the world of Weimar, to which his behavior there is to be traced. Here he loses the sense of the weight of the opinion of society and so gains a freer idea of his own existence.

October 6, 1798

To Schiller

> Goethe was both director and stage manager of *Wallenstein* with which the new theatre was to be opened. Schiller's famous prologue to the *Wallenstein* trilogy was written for this occasion.

. . . Now everything is developing toward the final intensity and all that keeps me on my feet is the hope that the crucial evening will soon be here and equally soon be behind us.

October 17, 1798

To Cotta

Our theatre has now been opened and I expect to send you all the documents concerning the event by Friday. Assuredly Schiller's dramatic treatment of the Wallenstein story should be universally known and appreciated. It will give me pleasure to become a frequent contributor to your newspaper. But I hope that the paper will preserve at least the appearance of impartiality. . . . In France and England the case is different. There the journalists may well work in the interest of their parties. Here we had better learn that it is not well for us to do so.

October 27, 1798

To Schiller

I wouldn't mind getting the honorarium for my contribution to the *Muses' Almanach* here in Weimar, though it amounts to the same thing, since Cotta owes me payments which must be remitted sooner or later.

I have a letter from the theatrical manager in Hamburg. I suppose he means to be friendly and polite, but his way of expression is incredibly dry and withered. It is my impression that he won't come here this winter nor probably the next. I am just as well satisfied to be sure of this and so to have us continue on our accustomed way. Hoping and waiting are not in my line.

November 7, 1798

To Schiller

I congratulate you on moving into town. When all is said and done the city, especially in winter, does make things livelier and communication easier.

Jena, November 20, 1798

To Christiane

For a change I'll write you in my own hand in order to tell you more warmly that I love you and am glad that you and the child are well. The doctor should be consulted sometime about the headaches of which August complains. My work begins to move along, though more slowly than is usual. I therefore beg you not to come here unexpectedly. I've got to go on in my accustomed way and work as continuously as I can. Then we'll celebrate a gay reunion. There are no flirts here at all. The old ones are dead and no new ones have grown up.

Late November, 1798

Christiane to Goethe

Christiane's spelling cannot be imitated in another language; her punctuation has been preserved.

Now the delights of winter begin with us and I wont let nothing spoil them for me. The Weimarers would like to do it but I pay attention to nothing I love you and you alone take care of my little boy and work and my housekeeping to have order and make merry. But they cant leave a person in peace day before yesterday at the play comes Meissel [*the actress Corona Schröter*] and asks me without making any bones about it if it was true that you were going to get married you were already buying a carriage and horses I got so mad the very instant that I gave her a hell of an answer and I am convinced that one wont ask me anything again but I do keep thinking of it so I dreamed of it last night that was an evil dream which I must tell you when you come I cried and shrieked so loud that Ernestine waked me up and there was my whole pillow wet I am very glad it was nothing but a dream. and your dear letter makes me happy and contented again. The ice is very good now and I will go sleighing across the river I Ernestine and two girl friends, and afterwards our friends will go to Jena and we to Weimar: we are looking forward with pleasure to the big ball if you were here it would be nicer to be sure but as I hear that your work is getting along well that is better than all the pleasures of a ball because I know when your work goes all right you come back very gaily and then we will be happy together.

November 30, 1798

Schiller to Goethe

I've gotten so used to your coming in every evening to set the clock of my mind and to wind it that it seems very strange to be left to myself after my day's work is done.

December 1, 1798

To Schiller

How different is the echo of our tranquil conversations in your letter from the tumult that begins to surround me here during the few days of my presence. . . . Remember me to your dear wife and do you both think of me as you eat the roast which I am sending over.

December, 1798

Schiller to Cotta

Goethe still has a lot of work to do before *Faust* is finished. I nag
him all I can to get it done and it is, indeed, his intention to do so
by next summer. It is, I assure you, a very precious undertaking. It
will be a longish book and he wants illustrations. He counts on a
considerable honorarium. I am quite sure that he will let you publish
the work if you meet his terms, for his attitude to you is a friendly
one.

December 19, 1798

To Voigt

I am returning the volume of Kant's *Anthropology* with double
thanks, seeing that your wife renounced the pleasure of reading the
book for my sake. . . . Granting all that is excellent, penetrating,
precious in our old teacher's balanced writing, yet it seems to me
that in many passages he is narrow-minded and in many more quite
illiberal. A wise man should not use the word fool so freely, especially one who so objects to arrogance in others. He sweeps all genius
and talent out of his path; all poets disgust him; of the other arts he
knows, thank God, nothing. . . .
His assertion that young women strive to please in order to be sure
to get a new husband when their present one is dead—a notion
which he repeats several times—is really worthy only of the most
vulgar type of social jester and could have come only from an old,
old bachelor like himself.

December 19, 1798

To Schiller

My state just now is nothing to brag of. One should be in a great
city at such periods where the outer stimulations help one to forget
oneself. I can't accomplish the simplest mechanical things and every
intellectual effort is doomed to failure. I can see from this letter that
I can't concentrate as I usually do.

December 24, 1798

Schiller to Goethe

I'll take this week to have the copy of the play properly written out
for our theatre and reflect further on the astrological scene. . . .
Since I do not know whether a certain sum of money which I am
expecting will arrive promptly, I'll stop waiting and in the hope
that, at need, you will lend it to me, draw up the accounting now.
I do thank you for your kindness in obtaining the lodgings in Weimar for me. My brother-in-law will be able to lend me some pieces
of furniture but not beds. If you could lend us those I would have
less to transport.

1799

January 5, 1799

To Schiller

I am told to my great pleasure that you have arrived in Weimar and
I write to ask what disposition you are making of the day. If you
would like to dine with me you are most truly welcome. I'm not as
well as usual and had better not go out.

January 17, 1799

To Schiller

Since I am uncertain whether I'll see you at dinner today and since,
at the same time, the Duke has invited me to come to see him, which
I must not neglect to do, I'll accept his invitation and expect you,
my dear friend, at my house this afternoon at 4 o'clock where there
will be a gathering of the theatre people.

January 30, 1799

To Schiller

So the day is here! Tonight is that first night to which we're looking
forward. Don't forget the cap for Wallenstein; there must be some
heron feathers in the property room. And don't you want to get
another red cloak for Wallenstein? In the one he wears he doesn't
stand out sufficiently from the others.

February 3, 1799
To Schiller

I was very happy to hear that yesterday's performance was a great improvement on the first. Now we must consider what to do in order to raise the third to a still higher level. Do me the kindness of having dinner with me today. Tomorrow you are invited to dine privately with His Serenity.

March 3, 1799
To Schiller

Körner's letter seems very curious to me, as indeed everything that is strictly individual does. No man seems able to find his way either to himself or to others; he must weave his own web, from the midst of which he can be effective. Such reflections lead me back more and more to my creative work. Engaged in that one satisfies oneself and establishes a sound connection with others. . . .
I am trying to get through my business matters with all possible speed in order to gain some free time in the near future. I am in an exceedingly ill humor which is not likely to improve until I have succeeded in some significant piece of work.

March 5, 1799
Schiller to Goethe

I was often grieved this winter to see you less cheerful and courageous than usual. I wish I had had more peace of mind to be more helpful to you. Nature destined you to creative activity; anything else, if it lasts for any period, is in conflict with your character. A pause as long as has come into your activity now should not be permitted to recur. You must make a supreme effort to that end.

March 15, 1799
To Knebel

. . . Since the controversy set in concerning the age of the Homeric poems and the writing of *Hermann and Dorothea,* these matters have rarely left my mind. So I have thought out a plan toward a poem which would be a continuation of the *Iliad* and deal with the death of Achilles. Since I am able to think only insofar as I am productive this bold attempt keeps me delightfully busy.

Jena, May 12, 1799

To Christiane

Since the famous sweeping of the chimneys will not take place till Monday, the 20th, it suits very well for you to come to see me. I have had time enough this week to accomplish what is most necessary. So come on the evening of Saturday, the 18th, toward 6 o'clock. I'll send the driver to meet you. . . .
I want you to bring along the following items:

> 6 bottles of red wine 5
> a couple of small bottles of eau de Cologne
> some Cervelat sausage
> cold cuts for our supper the first evening
> a handful of wax candles

You will find everything very well arranged here and we ought to be able to be quite contented for several days and talk ourselves out. You might also bring along some of that good oil and whatever else you consider necessary for this countrified household. You might as well stay a number of days because I can work without any disturbance in the castle.
I am sending you two copies of *Hermann and Dorothea*—one for Mother and one for you. But don't let too many people handle yours. If it were to get soiled, it would not be too easy to replace it.

May 24, 1799

Elisabeth Goethe to Her Son

Dear Son, Give my dear daughter my hearty thanks for the admirable copy of *Hermann and Dorothea*. The work deserved to be beautified by the illustrations, for it is a masterpiece without equal. I carry it about with me as a cat does her young. . . . With great joy I learned that you are blessed with a carriage and horses now and can take your pleasure the more easily. . . . Since I see from the same letter that you and yours are in Jena, enjoying the spring in a garden, I am sending this letter in the care of Councillor Schiller.

May 26, 1799

To Wilhelm von Humboldt

I cannot say that I was ill during this past winter, yet I was not as well as usual. Nevertheless we put on in our theatre Schiller's *Wallenstein* trilogy which involved much labor but also much delight . . . Your critical essay concerning my *Hermann and Dorothea* has now arrived in printed form. I have re-examined it section by section and I thank you for it once again. In how far I am likely to profit by it and improve in my efforts you will judge for yourself when, some day, you visit us again and find a more extended epic work at least in progress, if not completed. I dare not indicate even its subject to you at the moment, for I do not wish to render you anxious, lest I am preparing to don a pair of Icarian wings.

June 1, 1799

To Schiller

The Duke left for Eisenach and Cassel yesterday and I am now at peace in my tranquil house. I am waiting to see what the next week will bring forth. I'll be satisfied if I can just do some preliminary work. I hope that for you the deeper springs of productivity will flow.

June 5, 1799

To Schiller

As far as I'm concerned only complete resignation saves me from an equal misery, for I seem unable even to think of any continuous effort. I spend my time puttering around and hope for better hours in July.

June 14, 1799

Schiller to Goethe

It was Coleridge who did, some years later, translate *Wallenstein,* of which he wrote: "It is the greatest of his works; it is not unlike Shakespeare's historical plays—a species by itself."

It begins to look as though my plays are going to have some luck in England. Within a week I have had two requests from London to send manuscripts. To be sure, these requests came only from publishers and translators and included no definite offers of money. But since a demand exists, some prospects may arise.

June 19, 1799

To Schiller

I don't mind telling you that any loss of time begins to seem to me more and more serious. I am making all kinds of rather odd plans for saving several months of each year entirely for poetry. I'm afraid little will come of them. It is outer circumstances which dictate our life and steal it from us at the same time. Yet a compromise must be effected, for to isolate oneself completely, as Wieland does, is not advisable either.

June 22, 1799

To Schiller

. . . When you and I take up our treatise on dilettantism, we must give it adequate breadth. . . . There will arise of course the most acrid quarrels, for we will flood all that happy valley in which the dabblers have chosen to dwell. For the chief characteristic of the dabbler is his incorrigibility and those of our time are more especially afflicted with the beastliest arrogance. They will howl that we have soaked their gardens and when the water recedes they will reconstruct everything, as ants do their hills after a rainstorm.

June 25, 1799

Schiller to Goethe

I'm afraid even these few lines will show you my wretched state. My sister and her husband are here. He is a small-town Philistine of 60, industrious, not without ability, but depressed and limited by circumstances, enfeebled moreover by fancied illness. I admit that he is not ignorant of modern languages and German etymology and certain departments of literature. Nevertheless you can imagine how few contacts for conversation exist between us and what my discom-

fort must be. The worst of it is that he represents a small and not
even contemptible class of readers and judges of literature because
in Meiningen, where he is librarian, he must be head and shoulders
above everybody else. And his narrow way of thinking, about which
nothing can be done, reduces me to despair.

July 9, 1799

To Schiller

I hate to send this note instead of coming myself. But the Duke
believes that my presence is useful to rebuilding the castle and it is
my business to respect this opinion of his, even though I don't agree
with it. There are, to be sure, many other things to take care of,
so that my time, though not well used, is at least used. . . . May the
Muse be more gracious to you. . . .

July 12, 1799

Schiller to Goethe

. . . We have been told that we are to receive a beautiful present of
silver from the reigning Duchess. Poets should always be rewarded
by presents and not paid fees or salaries. There is a deep inner kin-
ship between fortunate ideas and the gifts of fortune: both fall down
from heaven.

July 31, 1799

To Schiller

I happened to pick up *Paradise Lost* a day or two ago and it gave
rise to some rather curious reflections. In this poem, as in all modern
works of art, it is essentially the poet as an individual person who
is manifest within the work and arouses our interest. The subject
matter is abominable. . . . But it is unquestionably a fascinating
man who speaks to us—a man of character, deep feeling, keen understanding, broad knowledge, poetic and rhetorical gifts. . . . A great
influence has been exerted upon the design and development of the
poem by the strange and unique circumstance that Milton, a revolutionary whose revolution finally failed, identifies himself more closely
with the Devil than with the Angels. . . .
I must tell you that in order to get out of my noisy street I have de-

cided to move back to my old garden. There I shall await the arrival of the Duke and of Voigt who, I hope, will release me from my immediate situation.

August 3, 1799

To Schiller

I am using my old garden retreat primarily to have my lyrical poems properly arranged and copied for the volume which Unger will bring out. For an editorial job of this kind you need concentration and balance and a certain universality of mood. If I could add a couple of dozens of poems in order to fill in certain gaps and enrich certain categories which are rather meagre, the whole might be quite interesting. . . . In the afternoon I continue to read Milton. . . . I still feel that the poet is a remarkable man, interesting in every sense, capable of sublimity, and it is to be observed that his trite subject matter helps rather than hinders him in the exercise of this faculty.

August 7, 1799

To Schiller

In my solitariness in my garden I continue my poetic work sedulously . . .

1799

NATURE AND ART

Nature and Art, they seem so disunited
Yet find each other ere we are aware;
I, too, no more that old aversion share
And see the balance of attraction righted.
We need but strictest love of tasks unslighted!
And having learned in measured hours to bear
With undivided mind Art's stringent care,
Nature once more may glow in hearts delighted.

This is the final law of all creation:
Ungirdled minds will meet with sure disaster
Were they to strive to pure perfection on.

High aim demands profoundest concentration;
Self-limitation will reveal the master,
And under law alone is freedom won.

                                                    August 9, 1799

To Schiller

It's extremely kind of you to take care of August, because, since I
could not escape to Jena, my family had to get out of the way. It
can't be helped, but I can produce nothing except in absolute solitariness. The silence of this garden is most precious to me.

                                                    August 21, 1799

To Schiller

I continue to arrange and revise my shorter poems. The process
proves to me again that everything depends upon the guiding principle according to which one works. For instance, now that I acknowledge the necessity of a stricter versification, it helps and by no
means hinders me.

                                                    August 26, 1799

To Karl Friederich Zelter

> Karl Friederich Zelter, 1758-1832, composer and founder and first direc-
> tor of the once famous Berlin Academy of Singers. He was of humble
> origin, having been a bricklayer in his youth. He became one of the
> most beloved friends of Goethe's later years. His settings of many of
> Goethe's lyrics which the poet himself preferred to all others, have
> fallen into oblivion.

It is with sincere thanks that I reply to your kind letter. You tell me
in words what I have long felt from your musical compositions,
namely, that you have a vivid sympathy for my poems and, with true
affection, have made many of them your very own. The lovely thing
about so active a sympathy is that it inspires productivity. My songs
occasioned your melodies; I can truly say that your melodies have
inspired me to many a lyric. If we lived nearer to each other I am
sure that I would more frequently attain the lyric mood. I shall

look forward to all communications from you with the sincerest pleasure.

August 27, 1799

To Schiller

I come to the question of Weimar lodgings for you. The matter stands as follows: the present lessor seems to have agreed with another person to sublease from her. Such, at least, seems to be the case. The landlord, the wig-maker, is not obliged to consent to this subleasing and, upon my persuasion, is willing to lease the quarters to you. All that he desires is that you sign a lease for a couple of years, which you can well do, since you can always find someone to whom to turn it over. Now the next thing is for you to see the place and discuss the matter and come to a decision.

September 1, 1799

Schiller to Karl August

. . . Since I intend to rely for my income chiefly on the fruits of my industry and to increase rather than to diminish my efforts, I venture most humbly to request Your Serenity to give me an increase in salary and thus to ease the meeting of the added expenses accruing from my moving to Weimar and the necessity of a double establishment. . . .

September 17, 1799

To Knebel

. . . My August is growing up and very apt at many things, such as writing and languages and everything that enters through the eye, and he has a very good memory, too. My chief care is to have him cultivate his real aptitudes and to learn whatever he does learn thoroughly. Our usual education distracts children needlessly with too many subjects. We see the false tendencies thus produced in adults. I don't want to send him away to school. A few years from now I'll take him with me on some journey. He did go to Frankfurt with me and I let him travel about quite a little in our vicinity.

Garden House, September 19, 1799

From the Diaries

Schiller arrived and I decided to leave the garden and accompany
him to Jena. I have been here in the garden six weeks and busied
myself with many things: collected my lyrics, studied metrics, read
Herder's *Fragments,* studied the moon through a telescope, started
to read *Athenaeus,* helped supervise the rebuilding of the castle. . . .

Jena, October 1, 1799

Spent the evening reading *The Arabian Nights.* The story of Abu
Hassan. Reflection concerning the union in these tales of the wildest
magical exploits with the earthiest realism.

Jena, October 3, 1799

To Christiane

Since I'm staying away so long I must write you a word in my own
hand and tell you how fond I am of you and how constantly I think
of you and the dear child. I was busy enough the first two weeks, but
not at anything of great importance. Finally I took up a task which
seems to be succeeding. You must have heard me say that His Serenity would like one of the French tragedies translated. Well, I couldn't
seem to get at it. Finally I have a play that appeals to me and the
work goes well. . . . In addition I have, of course, the advantage
and pleasure of being with Schiller. . . .
I live very simply and have done a lot of walking, because I couldn't
use the horse. But now it is quite well again. The veterinarian did
a good job and I am sending him half a dozen bottles of wine. . . .
The cook is bleaching your cotton in the yard. . . .

October 16, 1799

To Schiller

I am so happy that your wife and the new-born infant are as well as
possible. May all go well with both. . . .

Herewith I send your dear wife a bottle of eau de Cologne. May it refresh her. I have wrapped the bottle in the sheets of the *Muses' Almanach* which you did not have.

October 23, 1799

To Schiller

From Frankfurt comes the news that Schlosser is dead. The French and his garden beyond the gates were the immediate causes of his death. He was out in his garden, as the French approached Frankfurt. He was delayed and found the nearest gate locked. He had to hurry a great distance to another gate. At home his rooms were overheated. Next he was summoned to the City Hall. A fever ensued which proved fatal.

October 25, 1799

Schiller to Goethe

Since the evening on which I last wrote you my situation has been most melancholy. That very night my wife got much worse and her attacks developed into a nervous fever which frightens us all. . . . I have suffered deeply, as you may imagine. . . . My wife cannot be left alone and can bear no one near her except myself and her mother. The fantasies of her delirium cut me to the heart.

Jena, December 6, 1799

To Schiller

I am doing some close study of the old English theatre. Malone's dissertation on the probable order in which Shakespeare wrote his plays, as well as a tragedy and a comedy by Ben Jonson, and two apocryphal Shakespearian pieces—these things have given me new insights and led to many reflections.

December 6, 1799

From the Records of Ludwig Tieck

Johann Ludwig Tieck, 1773-1853, poet and playwright of the most pronounced romantic tendency.

Tieck had completed his play *Genoveva* and began to show it to his friends. Now came the opportunity to read it to Goethe who had lodgings in the castle in Jena. Since the first evening did not suffice, the reading was completed on the second one. Goethe listened with sympathetic attention. He expressed himself kindly and appreciatively. Then he turned to his nine-year-old son who was present on the second evening. He stroked the boy's hair with his hand and said: "Well, my little son, what do you say to all these colors and flowers and mirrors and magic arts, concerning which our friend has read us? Isn't it all rather marvelous?" He also made some specific criticisms which were incorporated in the play later on.

December 16, 1799

From Elisabeth Goethe to Her Son

Dear Son, Today a box with Christmas gifts has gone off by the post. May everything give pleasure. I hope that the material for a dress will please my dear daughter. I have emptied all my drawers in the hope of giving you some pleasure. . . . Dear Son, After the return of Mama la Roche from Weimar it came all over me how sweet it was of you to be contented with my dwelling here. She gave a wonderful description to me and to all your friends here of your house and of your whole establishment and of the delicious banquet you gave her and of the wonderful room hung with green satin and the draperies and the big painting—oh, she took a whole day to tell me all about it—and what a day that was to me I leave you to imagine!!! O God, preserve and bless him and let it be well with him and let his days on earth be long—and that will come to pass, for the blessing of a mother builds the houses of her children. Amen. In spite of all which, I do hope that some day you will again come to pay me a visit.

December 17, 1799

Charlotte von Stein to Goethe

Do forgive me for not returning the manuscript of your translation of Voltaire's *Mohamet* before. I could not bear to part with your beautiful verses.

December 17, 1799

To Schiller

The Duke and Duchess will take tea at my house today and lend, I am sure, a favorable ear to the reading of my version of *Mohamet*. If you would like to join us on this occasion, you are cordially invited.

December 23, 1799

To Schiller

I do wish you would decide, whatever comes or goes, to come to my house at 8:30. The rooms will be warm and brightly lit; there will be friends and a cold supper and a glass of punch—all of which are things not to be despised on these long winter nights.

1800

January 1, 1800

To Schiller

It gave me a quiet pleasure to end the year with you last night. . . . Let the beginning be as was the end and the future resemble the past. I am dining with people who always make you stay late. But I will look for you at the opera.

January 2, 1800

To Jacobi

Since the days when we were in close touch, I have, I hope, trained my mind to some advantage. There was a time when my decided hatred of sentimental enthusiasm, of hypocrisy and of presumption sometimes rendered me unjust against the good in man, of which the empirical manifestation does not measure up to the ideal. Time teaches us in respect of this as of many other things and one learns that all evaluation must be tempered by forbearance.

January 9, 1800

To Schiller

I was overhasty yesterday when I invited you to the reading for to-day. It won't take place till tomorrow. If you are willing to spend this evening alone with me, you are most heartily invited. If you would like to take an hour's drive, I'll fetch you with a sleigh at noon.

February 2, 1800

To Schiller

Would you be so very kind as to send me over a bottle of that red wine which the dealer let us have? At the same time may I ask to know, whether I'll have the pleasure of seeing you this evening at my house, as I so much desire.

February 11, 1800

To D. Vanderstrass

An otherwise unknown student of medicine at Jena.

Your intention of earning the means of pursuing your studies by work in another field is praiseworthy in itself. But you will not achieve that purpose by means of the play which I herewith return to you. It will have luck neither on the stage nor in the study. A fine work of art has such an air of ease about it that many a good young man is seduced into the belief that it is equally easy to write. Nevertheless, if this unhappy attempt persuades you to the firm determination, never to try to undertake anything like this again, you will have profited by the experience, for you will save your time and strength for the development of those other abilities which nature does not seem to have denied you.

February 16, 1800

To Schiller

I am very glad that the phlebotomy agreed with you.
I am sending the English dictionary.
I'll attend to the other things you want done.

I've heard no details about the performance of your play except that the audience consisted of 422 persons.
I may drop in to see you around 6 o'clock.

March 23, 1800

To Schiller

Since I have given in and consented to be ill, which I tried to avoid as long as possible, my physician is tyrannizing over me. How I wish that you were well enough to come to see me soon!

March 24, 1800

To Schiller

Your visit yesterday was as agreeable as it was unexpected. If the outing did not disagree with you too much, it would be so pleasant if you could drop in again today.

April 5, 1800

To Schiller

Are you going to the play this evening or will you come to see me? I will be guided by your preference. But I would like you to come for dinner tomorrow. Voigt will be here and maybe Wieland, too.
I hope you are more active than I am. I can't write a sentence, let alone a stanza.

April 11, 1800

To Schiller

I'm very pleased that Cotta took the liberty he did. He wrote me a letter about *Faust,* probably at your suggestion, and for which I must thank you. Because the letter made me take out the manuscript again and begin to think about it.

April 27, 1800

Elisabeth Goethe to Her Son

Dear Son, I am sending along a summer hat in the very latest fashion. I hope it will please my dear daughter—it should give her a most festive appearance. By next post I will send a cheaper straw hat to be worn for every day as well as nankeen for a suit for August. May he wear it out in health.

Leipzig, May 4, 1800

To Schiller

After my long isolation the contrast of being here is agreeable. I expect to spend another week in Leipzig.

The Fair really offers you the world in a nutshell. One sees very clearly all the crafts of man and all the mechanical techniques that are used. In all this there is very little akin to mind or spirit. It rather reminds you of the dexterity of certain animals.

Leipzig, May 5, 1800

To Christiane

Since August can't come with your brother, let us stick to the plan of your coming here for me. . . . It will give both you and the boy much pleasure to see Leipzig in the fine season. The walks around the city are as beautiful as possible. The so-called panorama in which one gets a bird's-eye-view of the entire city of London is really remarkable and will amaze you both. . . . We won't get along without shopping; I can foresee that. . . .

I leave it to you whether you want to use our carriage or the carriage of the stableman whose horses you are hiring. But I want everything to look rather elegant, because we'll take drives. . . .

Bring only white dresses with you. Everybody wears them here. A little hat you can buy when you arrive. . . .

May 22, 1800

Lotte Schiller to Goethe

Schiller asks me to give you his regards. He would like you to come to see him at your earliest convenience. He asked me to find out, in addition, whether you knew exactly when Cotta arrives and whether you and Cotta would like to meet him in Ettersburg. In my opinion it would be better if Schiller came here, for Cotta will doubtless want to attend to other business while he is in the city. You are the best one to persuade Schiller, if you drop in to see him today or tomorrow.

June 15, 1800

To Schiller

The performance referred to was that of Schiller's tragedy *Mary Stuart*.

We have every reason to be satisfied with the performance and the play is indeed an extraordinary one. I would be so happy if you could come in to see me at 6 o'clock this evening. I am dining at Court today and will hardly get home before that hour.

Summer, 1800

Falk's Reminiscences

Occasionally Goethe dined with the Dowager Duchess. He complained that the Ducal chef served sauerkraut far too often. One day when it was served again his annoyance was so great that he got up and went into the next room where an open book lay on the table. It was a novel by Jean Paul. Goethe read for a while. Then he jumped up and said: "Oh no, that is too low! First sauerkraut and then 15 pages of Jean Paul. That's more than I can endure."

July 22, 1800

To Schiller

I have come to the instantaneous decision to leave right after dinner and go to Jena. Once and for all, there is no way for me to come to my senses in this place.

July 30, 1800

Schiller to Goethe

The cheerful tone of your letter proves to me how much better you feel in Jena. I wish you much luck. I congratulate you on the progress of your work. . . . The Court Chamberlain sent me a very welcome sum of money today, for which I owe thanks to you.

Jena, August 1, 1800

To Schiller

Yesterday I attended to a business matter and then solved a small
problem in *Faust*. If I could stay another two weeks the whole poem
would look different. Alas, I imagine that I am necessary in Weimar
and sacrifice my very dearest wish to this imagined necessity.

August 12, 1800

To Schiller

I am sending a copy of my poems for your dear wife. Don't let her
have it bound until I have talked to her about it. The wrinkles in
the paper are caused by the binder and can be prevented.

August 28, 1800

Lotte Schiller to Goethe

Since I like to say, as best I can, how happy I am, dear friend, that
you are near us on your birthday and yet have really no words to
express my happiness, I have sought for other means of communication. To one so favored by the Muses as yourself, nothing more beautiful can be said than what he himself has said. Nor is there any gift
which can convey to you the affection and the honor in which we
all hold you. And all things, even such as convey the deepest feelings, are transitory in themselves. But I know that you do believe in
our affectionate loyalty to you.

September 6, 1800

Schiller to Goethe

Cotta gives me excellent news about *Wallenstein*. Most of the 4500
copies have been sold and he is getting ready to print a new edition.
That the public was not deterred by the high price is a very good
omen for your *Faust*. It is certain that Cotta can risk an initial edition of 6 to 8000 copies of that.

September 12, 1800

To Schiller

The mention of Helena is the first extant reference to the second part of *Faust*.

After various adventures I did not succeed in reaching the tranquility of Jena until this morning. My mind began to work at once but nothing is yet accomplished. Happily I could keep in mind during the last week the ideas and situations of which I told you, so that my Helena has truly arisen. . . .

September 17, 1800

Schiller to Goethe

I am told that Cotta's *Lady's Book* is making quite a stir here. You will have seen it, as I have, and regretted the pitiful effeminate scribbling and poverty-stricken publisher's tricks of our friend. He thus puts himself on the level with the vilest rogues in the business. Did he have to head the thing with the Queen of Prussia, so that he might not avoid even the lowest level?

Jena, September 23, 1800

To Schiller

I have made some progress with my Helena. The chief elements of the plan are conceived and since these have your approval I can proceed to the execution with higher courage.
I would like to hold on to myself and not look too far into the future. But I perceive already that the right view over the whole work will be seen from this peak. . . .
If I were not afraid of bringing down the curse of wives upon me, where it already rests, I would invite you to come here. . . .

Late September, 1800

Elisabeth Goethe to Christiane

The French sons of freedom have threatened to impose another fine on our city. Our good humor was not increased thereby, especially as, barely a month ago, they blackmailed our city out of 300,000

gulden. But then came the good news from all of you and made me
very happy and I thought to myself: money comes, money goes; if
everything is well with my loved ones in Weimar I'm going to sleep
in peace. And that's what I did during all the confusion.

Jena, September 26, 1800

From the Diaries

I have succeeded in using the sublime to mediate between the beautiful and the trite. Made progress on Helena this afternoon.

October 1, 1800

Schiller to Goethe

Cotta seems to expect a word from you and is worried by your silence. He now has trouble with the piratical reprinters of *Wallenstein*. One such edition is being already sent out from Bamberg;
another man in Vienna managed to get an imperial license to print.

Jena, November 18, 1800

To Schiller

Several good motives turned up toward the Helena theme and if I
can write about a dozen letters which I owe people while I am here,
that will be something gained.

Jena, November 19, 1800

Goethe to a French Translator

If a writer may well be proud to be known among foreign nations,
it is, it seems to me, even more gratifying to be appreciated by men
who know the great models which have inspired his efforts.
You have considered *Hermann and Dorothea* worthy of translating
into French, which I value the more because you illustrated, before
you did that, your insight into our teachers, the Greeks, and your
feeling for the charms of patriarchal society both by your translated
and your original work.

November 23, 1800

Schiller to the Countess Charlotte Schimmelmann

Wife of the Danish Minister of Finance.

Certain observations in your letters lead me quite naturally to speak of my friendship with Goethe which I still, after an interval of six years, regard as the most beneficent event in my entire life. I need tell you nothing concerning the qualities of his spirit. You acknowledge his merits as a poet, though not in the same degree that I do. It is my profound conviction that no other poet comes near being his equal in depth and delicacy of feeling, in nature and truth, and at the same time in the high perfection of his art. No more gifted man has arisen in the world since Shakespeare. . . . And yet it is to be remembered that he has used a great part of his life to perform the duties of a minister of state which have been neither small nor insignificant because this Duchy is small. Yet it is not these singular merits of his spirit which bind me to him. If his human worth did not seem to me the highest among all men I have known, I would have been content to admire his genius from afar. But I am able to say that in the six years of our intimacy no slightest doubt of his integrity ever arose. He possesses the highest veracity and sense of honor and the deepest earnestness in the pursuit of what is right and good, and it is for this very reason that the gossips and the hypocrites and the wrongheaded have always been so uncomfortable in his presence. . . .

How I wish that I could justify Goethe as warmly in respect of his domestic relations as I have so confidently been able to do in respect of his literary and moral virtues. Unfortunately, through false notions of what constitutes domestic happiness and through an unhappy nervous fear of marriage, he has slid into an entanglement which oppresses him and makes him wretched in his very home and which he is too weak and too soft-hearted to shake off. This is his only vulnerable spot. It hurts no one but himself and is not unconnected with an otherwise very noble aspect of his character. I must ask your forgiveness for this lengthy account. But it concerns a friend whom I honor and love and esteem and whom I hate to see misunderstood. If you knew him as I do and had had the same opportunity of

observing him, there are few human beings whom you would find
worthier of your respect and affection.

December 11, 1800

To Schiller

As you know I intended to go to Jena tomorrow. But we are now
working on the staging of Gluck's *Iphigenie,* and if the production
is not vividly and skillfully done, it will fall flat. I wonder if you
would help with it. Perhaps you would be willing to drive over with
me to the rehearsal at 3 o'clock and get a general notion.

Jena, December 22, 1800

To Schiller

I have continued my lonely life here and taken only a single walk,
on the one clear day. . . . But I have spent long evenings in reading
and so have not wholly wasted my time.

December 30, 1800

To Schiller

If you would like to partake of our usual frugal supper in a philosophical and artistic group, you are most cordially invited.

December 31, 1800

The Recollections of Hinrich Steffans

A Norwegian by birth and professor of philosophy successively in Halle,
Breslau, and Berlin, 1773-1845. Friedrich von Schelling, 1775-1854, the
well-known philosopher was teaching at Jena during this period.

I celebrated the real beginning of the new century with my Jena
friends though the actual scene was Goethe's house in Weimar. . . .
After midnight Goethe, Schiller and Schelling withdrew into a
smaller adjoining room. I was permitted to join them. Several bottles
of champagne stood on the table and the conversation grew ever
livelier. Since my Nordic virtuosity permitted me to remain more
sober than the older gentlemen, I could not but observe the varied
effects of the wine on the two great poets. Goethe was uninhibitedly

gay and ever merrier, the while Schiller became of a deadly seriousness and expatiated in a doctrinaire fashion on intricate aesthetic
matters. . . .

This night assumed a greater import to me when I learned a little
later what serious consequences it was to have for Goethe. For almost
the first time in his life it led to a very acute illness. The thought of
approaching death which tormented him for several succeeding
years, was a result of this illness.

1801

From the Supplementary Confessions

At the beginning of 1801 I was afflicted by a cruel illness, the occasion of which was the following. . . . Late in December I had gone
to work in Jena where I had always found the right mood in the
very large rooms of the Ducal castle. This time, too, the conditions
were favorable to my work, but I let my intense absorption in it
make me overlook the adverse influence of the locality. The building
is situated at the lowest point of the town close to the mill pool; the
stairs and the stairwell are constructed of a kind of stone which
sweats moisture whenever it thaws. . . . At all events, I was seized
with a violent catarrh. . . .

At that time both older and younger physicians were interested in
a certain new treatment of English origin. A young friend of mine
was one of its adherents and knew as a matter of experience that a
balsam brew of the Peruvian bark, combined with opium and myrrh
put an instant stop to the most acute affections of the chest and
prevented their dangerous development. He advised me to try this
remedy and I was immediately relieved of cough and phlegm. Calmly
I went to Weimar with Professor Schelling, when at once the catarrh
returned with redoubled violence and I fell into a state of uncon-
sciousness. My family was in despair and the physicians helpless. My
dear Lord, the Duke, realizing my danger, took a hand in the matter
and sent a mounted messenger to summon Doctor Stark from Jena.
Several days passed before I wholly recovered consciousness. But
when the power of nature and medical assistance brought me back
to awareness of myself, I found a great swelling surrounding my right

eye which impeded its use. I was altogether in a wretched condition. But the experienced physician, skillful in all practical measures, exerted himself to the utmost, and thus both sleep and proper transpiration gradually set in once more.

January 1, 1801

Karl August to Goethe

A thousand thanks, my dear old friend, for the various good and lovely things that came from you this morning. You are yourself too aware of the great share you have had in everything that has thriven among us these twenty and odd years than that I should have to rehearse it to you and thank you for it. I know you do not doubt my gratitude nor the justice which my heart does your rare merits. Cease not to love me and keep well. . . .

January 19, 1801

Elisabeth Goethe to Christiane

Praise, thanks and adoration be to God Who can save from death and sends us help, in order that our faith in Him be renewed and we may with ever greater courage hope in Him and trust in Him alone. May He give strength to my dear and beloved son! May He restore to him all power and let him flourish as a blessing and joy to all who love and esteem him. . . . The illness must have come after the New Year, for your letters at Christmas spoke of your and his well-being. Let me thank you a thousand times for your true and loving care of him—and for the letter to me! How easily could I have learned the news in some frightful fashion from strangers!

January 20, 1801

To Charlotte von Stein

It's bad to be alone too long. One permits one's whole mind to be absorbed by certain interests. Then when one returns to the world, even to friends, one finds, of course, no trace of what had been one's entire inner preoccupation. And so it is hard to find the way back. This reflection is in answer to your friendly note. Shall we see you today? Some fine things will be played at my house.

January 29, 1801

To Schiller

Would you come over for a little supper after the rehearsal tonight, which is sure to be over by 8 o'clock? You would be so very welcome. My coachman can attend your commands in the theatre and fetch the carriage when the fifth act begins. If you want to drive to the theatre, too, please give him an order to that effect. I feel quite tolerable.

January 12, 1801

Charlotte von Stein to Fritz

I didn't know that my former friend Goethe was still so dear to me and that a serious illness, which overcame him nine days ago, would so shake me to the very core. He can't rest in bed and must be kept upright, otherwise he would smother to death. I won't send this letter until it can tell you either of his improvement or his death. Lotte Schiller and I have shed very many tears in the course of these days.

January, 1801

Charlotte von Stein to Fritz

August spent many hours with Charlotte during his father's illness.

I am so sorry for the poor boy; he is so dreadfully sad. But he is already accustomed to drown his sorrows. The other day at a party which his mother gave for people of her class, he emptied 17 glasses of champagne. I have a hard time keeping him away from wine when he is at my house.

February 1, 1801

To His Mother

This time, dear Mother, I am writing you by my own hand in order that you may be convinced that my health is quite tolerable once more. I cannot say that I had no warning of the illness, for I had not felt quite as one ought for some time before. If I had taken the cure at some watering place, as I used formerly to do, I would prob-

ably have gotten along far better. But since there were no definite
symptoms, even the most skillful physicians hardly knew what to
advise. They tried to persuade me to go to Pyrmont but inertia and
business and the desire to save money kept me from going and so
the incurring of this critical illness was left to chance. . . . As soon
as I recovered consciousness, everything began to go better. My
bodily strength is gradually returning and my mental powers seem
to be almost normal. . . .

You can easily imagine how good and solicitous and loving my little
girl proved herself on this occasion. I cannot sufficiently praise her
untiring helpfulness. . . .

I was consoled, too, by the sympathy shown me by the Duke, the
princely family, the city and the region on the occasion of my illness.
At least I may flatter myself that I am regarded with some affection
and that a measure of significance is attributed to my existence.

                                                    February 7, 1801
Elisabeth Goethe to Her Son

. . . I got your dear letter on the 6th of February and it occasioned
jubilation and a feast of prayers and thanksgiving for me. . . . Our
whole city was alarmed over your illness. So soon as the news of your
improvement was printed in the papers everybody came running to
me with copies of these papers. Each desired to be the first to bring
me the glad tidings.

                                                    February 7, 1801
To Reichardt

. . . It is told of a certain poet that he once fell down a flight of
stairs upon his head. No sooner had he picked himself up than he
repeated to himself the names of all the Chinese emperors in the
right order to make sure that his memory was not impaired. I cannot be blamed for putting myself to similar tests. Now I have had
two weeks in which to pick up the various threads which tie me to
life, to business, to science and to art. None seems broken; all the
old combinations work; even productivity seems to be lurking in a
corner. . . .

The keenest need I felt after my illness was the need of music. People about me did what they could to satisfy it. Do send me your latest compositions. I will cause them to be performed on a festal evening for myself and sundry friends.

February 11, 1801

To Schiller

. . . The best thing about a good artist is that he has nothing to lose if truth turns out to be true. So many men fight genuineness and veracity for the single reason, that they would be destroyed, if they had to admit its existence.
Faust keeps moving along. Though I do but a very little daily, yet that little preserves my sense of the whole.

February 12, 1801

To Schiller

I can't leave the house today, because the physician undertook a painful but, I hope, final operation on my eye this morning. He forbade me to risk the cold. I will therefore send the carriage for you at half past five and have you driven home after supper.

February 28, 1801

To Schiller

Do take it in good part that, as a souvenir of your recent and kind cooperation, I send you a portion of the order which my wine merchant has just delivered. I add the hope that you will try and relish the other vintages at my house.

March 18, 1801

To Schiller

Although I miss you badly I want you to stay as long as possible. I have always recently found that solitariness is such a favorable condition, that I want you to share it.
I can't say that *Faust* is at a standstill, but progress is feeble. Since all the philosophers are looking forward to this work, I had better pull myself together. . . .
By the way, I said to Meyer the other day: "Our attitude to recent

art is very like that of Julian, the Apostate, toward Christianity, only
that we see much more clearly than he. It is strange how certain ways
of thought can become general and sustain themselves for a long
time and are regarded, during that period, as constant elements in
human nature." . . .

March 20, 1801

Elisabeth Goethe to Her Son

Dear Son, My first thought upon your recovery was to give you some
pleasure and to send you a present. But I hardly knew how to manage, because in May we have to pay war taxes again. . . . But I
spread all the sails of my brain and finally found what I could do.
For the end of May I promise you 1000 gulden. I'll tell you the minute I have them. Now one thing more: I have reported you to the
War Department as having holdings in the amount of 10,000 florins
here. If you're worth more than that I must know it; the taxes have
to conform to the estimate. . . . Praise and thanks be to God that,
though I am in my seventieth year, I do not permit these annoyances to rob me of my good humor.

March 25, 1801

To Schiller

If your stay in Jena is not as fruitful as you hoped it would be, set it
down to the common fate of poetical intentions. Meanwhile one
must be thankful for the least that one receives.

March 29, 1801

To Friederich Rochlitz

Rochlitz, 1770-1842, a writer of comedies, resident in Leipzig.

I would prefer to answer your questions concerning *Wilhelm Meister* by word of mouth. Whatever be the intentions of an artist in
regard to works like that, they end by being confessions of a kind,
and this comes about in a way for which he himself finds it difficult
to account. Something of impurity clings to the form of the novel.
One must be grateful to God if one succeeds in putting enough content into such books that feeling and thinking people may be persuaded to take the trouble to extract it. The review you refer to is,

to be sure, extremely inadequate from the point of view of anyone who has given the book some thought. It is not without merit, if you regard it merely as the expression of one man's opinion and reflections. Of course, one has a right to demand more of a review, especially of one that comes so late.

Oberrössla, April 4, 1801

To Schiller

My stay here is agreeing with me, partly because I spend the whole day in the open air, partly because contact with the common things of life reduces my inner intensity and thus gives me a feeling of ease and indifference which I have not known for long.

In regard to the questions raised in your last letter, not only do I share your opinion; I go much farther. I believe that everything accomplished by genius according to its own nature is unconscious in character. The man of genius can use the greatest good sense and act from conviction after due reflection. But that is a side issue as far as he is concerned. No work of genius can be improved or freed of its faults by taking thought or by the consequence of taking thought. What genius can do is to raise itself by both reflection and action to a level upon which it at last produces faultless work. The more genius inheres in a given century, the better will the chance of the individual genius be. . . . This is my confession of faith. It makes no claims on anyone else.

Oberrössla, April 27, 1801

To Schiller

While you are enjoying all kinds of extraordinary theatrical delights, I am staying in the country fighting both legal and extra-legal battles. My only diversions are visits in the neighborhood and other realistic goings on of that kind. If I can I'm coming in on Saturday. Tell me briefly how the staging of *Nathan the Wise* is coming along and what is happening to your new drama. All I can say is that my stay here is doing me some physical good. . . .

Oberrössla, April 28, 1801

To Schiller

What I have gone through these days has little to do with the fine
arts. I have been in contact with nature in the raw in the form of a
dispute on the detestable subject of Mine and Thine. Today, at
last, I got rid of my old lessor and now there is all kinds of work and
worry because the new one can't move in for another three months.
So I don't believe that I can come in on Saturday.

May 19, 1801

Elisabeth Goethe to Her Son

Dear Son, Yesterday the power of attorney arrived. It is in proper
form and I thank you in the name of those who need it. I'm very
glad that the material I sent pleased you all and that the summer
hat suits my dear daughter. Use it all happily and in health. I am
very glad that it will be convenient for you to get the money by the
end of May. It is then that I will have it.

May, 1801

Charlotte von Stein to Fritz

Day before yesterday I was sitting with Frau von Trebra in the
former rose garden. Goethe passed us with his chambermaid at his
side. I burned with vicarious shame and hid my face behind my
parasol, pretending not to have seen them.

May, 1801

Christian Gottfried Schütz to an Unknown Correspondent

Schütz, 1747-1832, professor of rhetoric at Jena.

At a very charming and brilliant party at which Goethe was present,
an old Rhenish folksong was sung. The verses were trite and common but the melody was exquisite. Goethe was deeply touched and
promised to write a lyric of his own to be set to the old tune and,
true enough, on the very next day he sent us "The Shepherd's
Lament."

High up on yonder mountain
A thousand times I stand,
Bent on my crook and looking
Down to the valley land.

I follow my flock at its grazing
Under my sheep dog's eye,
I have been brought low and lower
And know not the how or why.

The springtime flowers their petals
On the fair meadow lift,
I pluck them without knowing
To whom to bring my gift.

Under my tree the thunder
And rainstorms pass me by;
Yon door will never open,
A dreamer still am I.

A rainbow curves its colors
Over the cottage there;
The place is empty of her
Who set out far to fare—

To lands beyond the ocean,
Perhaps to a foreign shore—
Forbear, O flock, to linger,
The shepherd's heart is sore.

Göttingen, June 11,

To Schiller

Before I leave Göttingen I must prove to you that I am still alive.
It has been very agreeable here. I have seen very interesting institu-
tions and made the acquaintance of most of the professors. Their
attitude is most kind and appreciative and I confess that I have not
for long been so well or cheerful. . . .

August, my traveling companion, who sends his fond regards to your Karl, bears some responsibility for my lack of industry. But he is very happy and is making progress and his presence causes my relations to people to be gentler and happier than they would be without him.

July 10, 1801

Elisabeth Goethe to Christiane

It did me much good to hear that my son and dear August are happy and well. May God bless the cure in Pyrmont. Dear August wrote me a long letter and my son added a few lines. . . . You did well to lease the farm at Oberrössla. Do not assume more burdens than you can bear. Your health might suffer. . . . I hope that you will follow my maternal advice.

Pyrmont, July 12, 1801

To Schiller

Since taking the cure here makes work quite impossible, I really haven't been well satisfied. Yet I should not forget the many sound and interesting conversations. . . .
The Duke has just arrived and is in the state of mind of all new arrivals: he is full of hope and amuses himself. I, on the contrary, as one who is soon to depart, find little profit here and each day more of a bore. And so I look forward to my release from here which will probably take place on the 15th.

Pyrmont, July 12, 1801

To Christiane

I must write you a few words before I leave here. I feel tolerably well and expect the cure to have favorable results. The best part of it is the exercise and the distraction. . . . Only the weather is bad and is quite horrible at this moment. August has behaved very well and given me much pleasure. You'll be surprised when you see him. The expenses have been moderate, but then I have been extremely careful. I've done a little shopping for you, but the rest can be done in Cassel, where things are just as good as here.
I'm going to Göttingen on the 15th where I expect to spend some

additional time. I will let you hear precisely when you are to meet me in Cassel. . . .

There were many chances for flirting here, but I don't seem to be so apt at it any longer.

The Duke is cheerful and gay, while I have been rather depressed recently. The weather ruined everything—the cure and the walks and all social occasions. Today there is a rainstorm and I have ordered a fire.

Göttingen, July 24, 1801

To Christiane

I've been here a week now and feel fairly well. Although Pyrmont did not cure me completely, I hope that the physicians are right in their opinion that the effects improve with time. I'm going to stay quite quietly here for a while and do some work. The university library is proving very useful. Meanwhile, since letters from here seem to make such bad time, let me tell you my plan now. I want you to arrive in Cassel on Saturday, August 15. I will arrive on the same day. You will go to the inn on King's Square. Whichever of us arrives first will order two rooms—one for you and Gus and one for me. . . . Tell no one how long I am staying. Bring along some money, say, 100 thaler. . . . I've bought you a dainty petticoat and a big shawl, both in the latest style. In Cassel you can buy yourself a hat and a frock.

From the Supplementary Confessions

I passed my time at Göttingen most agreeably and usefully. Finally, however, I perceived the danger of approaching so vast a mass of learning. While I looked up certain dissertations bound together with others, I found so much to lure me away from my specific purpose that, in view of the ease with which I am influenced and my previous knowledge of various departments, I was pulled hither and yon. . . . At all events, I returned to Weimar on August 30 in very good spirits indeed. Various matters pressed upon me at once and I forgot that I might still lack my full strength in view of the seriousness of my illness and the risk attending on the Pyrmont cure.

. . . Schiller arranged Lessing's *Nathan the Wise,* an enterprise in
which I actively collaborated. The first performance took place on
November 28. . . .

Autumn, 1801

Recollections of Henriette von Beaulieu

> Luise von Göchhausen, 1733-1807, lady-in-waiting to the Duchess Anna
> Amalia.

One forenoon when by chance only a few of her women friends and I
were having *dejeuner* at Luise Göchhausen's, Goethe turned up and
was amused by the circumstance that he was like a pasha in a harem.
. . . The conversation was very lively and the subject was what
Goethe chose to call the misery of the conditions in our society. As
the saying goes, he piled Pelion on Ossa. In the most glaring colors
he delineated the intellectual emptiness and the lack of spiritual
perception which were spreading at present and were especially
prevalent in our social life. In this respect, he believed a frightful
deterioration to have set in. While he discoursed on that matter as
didactically as a professor, he grew more and more heated until at
last he poured out the vials of his wrath on the devil of snobbishness
and false pride which had banished all simple contentment and
cheerfulness from the world and had substituted for them the most
intolerable boredom. With united energy, he said, one should launch
a battle against this evil demon.

November 27, 1801

To Schiller

Since it is about time that we see each other again, I am coming this
evening at 7 o'clock with the carriage to fetch you. I hope this suits
you. If you really want to go to the ball, the carriage is at your disposal after supper, too.

Late December, 1801

To Schiller

It grieves me that you cannot attend our little festivity. In one way
or another we'll see each other soon. May you soon wholly recover
from your indisposition!

1802

Elisabeth Goethe to Christiane

. . . I would like well enough some day to see performances at the theatre of Weimar which is so famous everywhere. But dear God!! Me and travel!! I wish I had the courage and the adventurousness of Frau von la Roche. Well, I haven't got it and so, I suppose, things will remain as they are. You just go on dancing, little woman, all you like. I am fond of merry people, and when they belong to my own family I am doubly and trebly fond of them.

Jena, January 19, 1802

To Schiller

I am always a happy man in Knebel's old room in Jena. There is no other place on earth to which I owe so many productive moments. It is amusing, but on one of the window frames I have made a note of everything of any importance that I have written in the room since November 21, 1798. I wish I had begun the list earlier. Much else would be recorded that I owe to our friendship.

January 20, 1802

Christiane to Goethe

It saddens me that my sweetheart has such a hard time with food. That's always the worst about your stay in Jena. I wish I were over there and could cook everything for you myself. When we meet again you'll have everything that is good. . . . Yesterday I was in the sleigh all alone and drove by myself. . . . I drove through all the alleys of the town and made all the corners well and was much praised. . . . If we have a good snowfall when you come back, you must let me drive you sometimes. I drove August, and next year he must himself learn how to drive. . . . I'm sending you the whole haunch of venison just as it came to me and two partridges. Make

the cook roast these; then you have enough for several meals. The
Chamberlain promises me the caviar, too.

January 28, 1802

Recollections of Anton Genast

The actors were doing their first reading of Voltaire's *Turandot*.
Goethe said to the actors who were to take four of the parts: "I want
you to observe first of all that there must be a significant shading in
the characterization of these four personages in gesture, mimicry, and
in the reading of the lines." Thereupon he himself acted out for
us the scenes involved and displayed so drastic a comic power that
the whole company broke out in uncontrolled merriment. He himself was extremely amused. "Now," he said, "try in somewhat this
manner to carry out the intentions of the author. But don't copy me.
Let each one be guided by his temperament."

Jena, February 12, 1802

To Schiller

The rearranging and cataloguing of the university library is a disagreeable rather than a difficult business. It is annoying chiefly because space is lacking for an effective distribution of what we have.
I have, however, made definite plans. The worst of it is, however,
that no one here is competent to execute a plan. . . . Do help me
work my way through these earthy tasks, so that we both may reach
the super-sensual things again.

Jena, February 19, 1802

To Schiller

My stay here is quite delightful this time. There has even been a
poetic stirring and I have written a couple of lyrics. . . .

1802

A CHANT OF NIGHT

On thy soft couch drawn nigher,
List at dream's ivory door
Unto my stringèd lyre;
Sleep on—what wouldst thou more?

Unto my stringèd lyre
The starry benisons pour
On deathless heart's desire;
Sleep on—what wouldst thou more?

The deathless heart's desire
Uplifts me to restore
From mortal mirth and mire;
Sleep on—what wouldst thou more?

From mortal mirth and mire
Thou cleavest me to soar
In chilly vastness dire;
Sleep on—what wouldst thou more?

In chilly vastness dire,
Deaf at dream's ivory door,
On thy soft couch drawn nigher
Sleep on—what wouldst thou more?

Jena, March 16, 1802

To Schiller

Since I have fled from the storms of Weimar I've been living contentedly and happily nor wholly inactive. Some lyrical trifles turned up which I do not regard as works but merely as symptoms.

Silence does not please the poet;
All he is, the world must know it
With the praise and blame thereof.
Prose is harsh for our confessions,
But we like *sub rosa* sessions
In the Muses' tranquil grove.

All my erring, all my striving
All the anguish of my living
Are like gathered flowers in prime;
Age and youth and sin and virtue,

What has healed you, what has hurt you
Charms when it is wreathed in rime.

Whatever as either truth or fable
In myriad volumes thou hast spied,
Is all but as a Tower of Babel
Unless by love 'tis unified.

Did not the eye partake of sun,
Sun would be darkness to our seeing;
No splendor could from the divine be won
Were God not part of mortal being.

March 22, 1802

Elisabeth Goethe to Christiane

. . . How true it is that Weimar is the only seat of the Muses! Its
happy denizens can form their taste properly. All they see is beautiful and excellent. Their eyes become accustomed to all fair forms.
In brief, they are enlightened in every respect, while we poor mortals
remain eternal children, for of most of my countrymen here it can
be said that their belly is their god. The money they spend on their
banquets could support the greatest painter, nay, a whole academy,
and these bacchanalia are such a bore and are as alike as one drop
of water is to another. Enough of this worthless generation! . . .

Jena, March 23, 1802

To Schiller

I suppose I shall soon decide to break off my stay here and come back
to you and Weimar. I look forward to our evenings together, especially since we have new things to communicate to each other. . . .
Our theological friends at the university here are in evil case. The
one suffers from his feet, the other from his wife. The woman is so
ill that they fear for her life, and nature will have to make long
efforts before producing again so odd a creature.

April 25, 1802

To Schiller

Herewith I am sending the money you desired, as well as the Hogarth prints.

I take occasion to ask what your plans are for today? If you fear the night air, come early and return home before sunset.

April 26, 1802

To Herder

I am sure, my dear old friend, that you will be so gracious as to introduce my son into the Christian community and to do it in a more liberal fashion than tradition prescribes. I thank you cordially in advance. I shall be glad to know that he takes this step, toward which every child looks forward with some apprehension, under your guidance and in a manner which coincides with the present stage of his education. He will shortly present himself to you, his teacher. Receive him kindly and use your best judgment and think of me.

May 3, 1802

Elisabeth Goethe to Her Son

All Frankfurt resounds with the news that you're coming here. You can imagine how happy it would make me. But since I've not heard from the person chiefly concerned, I don't believe it. . . . My only comment is that if you don't come this year—I refuse to give up all hope yet—that you will certainly not put off coming longer than until 1803. It is now five years since you've been here, and that is no joke.

Jena, May 4, 1802

To Schiller

. . . What stands in the way of putting the library in order and annoys me is a way which the people of Jena have quite reminiscent of the divine idleness of the Italians. . . .

As far as I am concerned and my inner life, many things happen. Even some lyrical impulses have found their way.

1802

SELF-DECEPTION

My lovely neighbor's curtains sway
And flutter up and down.
Doubtless she peers across the way
To see if I'm in town,

And if the sullen jealous mood
In which I turned on her
Still lingers, as I said it would,
Or ceased my heart to stir.

Alas, poor fool! Such thoughts as these
The lady would amaze.
I see it is the evening breeze
That in her curtains plays.

May 12, 1802

Schiller to Goethe

A letter which I received several days ago informs me that my mother died on the very day on which I moved into my new house. A man cannot but be grieved and deeply affected by these strange intertwinements of destiny. . . .
The money which you were so kind as to advance me is ready and I await your directions as to its disposition.

May 17, 1802

Schiller to Cotta

For publication sometime next year Goethe is preparing a sheaf of lyrics which he has written to well-known folk melodies. I've heard some of them sung. They are admirable and it may well be said that they lift the tunes to their own level. . . . The inherent value of this work and the name of Goethe and the fact that the lyrics can at once be sung, ought to assure a considerable sale. I suppose, therefore, that there will be no question concerning your paying him the 1000 Reichsthaler which he demands. I admit that a great many copies will have to be sold before you come out even.

June 13, 1802

From the Diaries

Little Gus was confirmed today.

June 14, 1802

To Herder

I felt and was grateful to feel the pleasure which it gave you to perform your task yesterday. I commend my boy to you for future guidance and enclose your fee.

Lauchstädt, June 28, 1802

To Schiller

Lauchstädt, a lesser-known watering place, which Goethe and later Christiane visited from time to time.

A key to my garden and garden house will be given you. I want you to have as good a time there as possible and enjoy the tranquility of the valley. I dare say that I'll soon go back to Weimar. The outer world brings us no particular salvation; it offers you mere fragments of what you already possess.

Lauchstädt, July 5, 1802

To Schiller

All business resembles marriage. You imagine you've done a great thing when once copulation is accomplished, and it's exactly then that hell breaks loose. The reason is that no phenomenon is isolated and everything effectual must be regarded not as an end but as a beginning. . . .

Meyer is cursing his sojourn here and yet I believe that the bathing is going to agree with him. If, instead of paying high prices in the pharmacy for bottled Pyrmont water, he had ordered himself a case of port from Bremen, he'd be a lot better off. But it is an old story that a man, however free from prejudices in every other way, succumbs to them so soon as it's a question of his physical health. But let's not brag; the same thing might happen to us.

July 6, 1802

Schiller to Goethe

I grant you that I should concentrate more upon the dramatic effectiveness of my plays. I grant you, too, that this requirement is dictated by my art, without any regard for the theatre or the public. But
I can seek to attain it only insofar as it is an artistic requirement. If
I were ever to write an effective play, I can do it only in harmony
with my art. Any factitious force, such as ordinary talents occasionally gain by the exercise of skill, I can neither aim at nor reach, even
if I would.

July 29, 1802

To Schiller

I am offered about 160 bottles of excellent port wine from Bremen
at about 10 groschen. I am inclined to order this wine, if several of
my friends will share it with me. I beg of you to let me know the
number of bottles you will take. The order includes a proportional
share in the loss in case of damage or accident.

Jena, August 17, 1802

To Schiller

Although my sojourn here has not been very productive and I don't
really know why I am here, I let you hear from me and tell you how
things look.
Today I've been here two weeks. But since it usually takes me that
long to get into the right frame of mind, I'm willing to see whether
the blessing of productivity will come. I ought to say that several
rather disagreeable incidents which affect me rather more than ordinarily have retarded me, too. The very fact that I decided to bathe
every morning was not favorable to my plans. . . .
I'm curious to know whether the Muse has been kinder to you, and
whether she will deign to visit me during the rest of my stay.

September 22, 1802

From the Diaries of Gottfried Schadow

Schadow, 1764-1850, a visiting sculptor from Berlin.

My third visit in Weimar was to Herr von Goethe. . . . He came in
with rapid strides in a long blue coat and boots. "So you're giving
us the pleasure of your visit?" he said. He asked us to sit down. He
first asked how Zelter was, from whom I had a letter. The conversation stuck at that point, although he really said very little. I wanted
to change the subject and asked him, whether he would permit me
to measure his head and make a preliminary sketch. He drew back
and said with a half-jeering laugh: "Well, now that's rather a doubtful matter! The people of Berlin are likely to draw queer inferences.
We had a phrenologist here, too." A footman now came to summon
him. He stayed away quite a while. . . . When he returned he
excused himself and, since we had arisen, the brief conversation continued while we were standing. . . .

October 13, 1802

Friedrich Schelling to A. W. Schlegel

Schlegel, 1767-1845, critic and chief author of the German translation
of Shakespeare.

Imagine the coarseness of Schadow. He had barely been bidden welcome when he asked Goethe to let his head be measured. Goethe said
it reminded him of Oberon in Wieland's poem who asked the Sultan
first off for a couple of his molars and some hairs from his beard.
Judging from the impression he made on Goethe, Schadow must
have behaved like a perfect oaf.

October 16, 1802

To Schiller

I'm sending you a memorandum about the new edition of Cellini.
Would you kindly look at it? One might send it to Cotta to begin
negotiations. If all goes well, it can be used for advertising purposes.
I'll walk back home with you after the play tonight; we might discuss
it then.

November 15, 1802
To Friedrich August Wolf
The famous classical philologist and critic of Homer, 1759-1824.

I suppose you have heard that our excellent Voss has decided in short order to buy a house in Jena and settle down there. Of course, it is a wonderful thing for us to have a man of such gifts and such seriousness among us. Your intention to come to see us should now be put into effect, seeing that you will have so close a friend of yours here. We have often talked about you with the most vivid sympathy. Professor Meyer, who has hitherto lived with me, just got married. You and your dear daughter will therefore be cordially welcome in my modest house.

November, 1802
Recollections of Ernestine Voss
The wife of the poet, 1756-1834.

When we were settled in our new house Goethe came over to Jena for several weeks and called on us frequently. Sometimes he would take Voss out driving. Our request that from time to time he should pass an evening just with us, he accepted gladly. But he was not to be persuaded to make a definite engagement, adding that the smallest bite of supper would suffice him. He was always perfectly charming to me. . . . He used to discuss August's education. Sometimes he brought the boy along. August was a pleasant, lively boy. Voss advised that he be accustomed to devoting definite hours to a specific purpose and giving an accounting of what he had grasped. Goethe accepted our offer to have August with us for an hour or longer each day with great pleasure. At first this worked very well, so long as August thought it was a game. After that he fell asleep over the book.

December 16, 1802
To Schiller
Thank you for your kind concern. A very tiny girl was born to us today. So far all is well.

December 19, 1802
To Schiller

As you may have noticed from my behavior at the opera last night, things aren't going well at home. The new guest is not likely to tarry long and the mother, composed as she usually is, suffers in body and in spirit.

December 31, 1802
Elisabeth Goethe to Her Son

Dear Son, Your last letter grieved me. Frustrated hopes hurt. Nothing helps but time which pushes the pain into the background. I have no patience with consolation, for few people can put themselves in the position of those who mourn. So expect no consolation from me, but my gratitude to God that He has kept you well and my prayer that He keep that treasure in His care.

1803

January 13, 1803
To Schiller

I was told yesterday that you had again taken up your idea of last year to invite a group to meet every Saturday after the play. I forgot to ask you about it. Tell me how far your plans have advanced. I am also told that His Serenity had a similar intention and so he would like the two plans to coalesce and not to cancel each other.

January 24, 1803
To Johann Jakob Willemer

Willemer, 1760-1838, a cultivated banker of Frankfurt.

Although I must send back the clever little play as not appropriate to our theatre, I must not neglect the duty, considering our long and friendly association, to give you the exact reasons.
On our stage here we seek, so far as possible, to avoid anything that may expose science and research to the contempt of the masses. We

do this partly in obedience to our own principles and partly because our neighbor, the University of Jena, would rightly regard the devaluation of the life work of so many of our members, as an unfriendly act. . . . So, for instance, we have carefully avoided the treatment of philosophical and literary controversies or new medical theories. . . . I am grateful to you, nevertheless, for having thought of me on this occasion.

January 27, 1803

To the Wilhelm von Humboldts

An indisposition confined me to the house early this year, though it did not prevent a tolerable existence indoors. . . . I have used the best hours of these weeks to prepare for the new edition of my translation of Cellini an appendix, the purpose of which is to bring closer to the reader the condition of that age and its art. If you read it in Rome, do so with indulgence. What I have been able to write is but an echo of the real music.

Schiller will write you himself. I haven't seen him for several days. He sticks to the house to complete a piece of work very happily begun.

February 8, 1803

To Schiller

Would you let me know as soon as possible whether you will come over tonight, as per my invitation? And whether after the concert or before? If you would like to drive in this bright weather, I'll send the sleigh for you around noon.

March 21, 1803

To the Ducal Commissary of Public Institutions

Your Honor is aware of the tranquility and seemly behavior usually shown by the audiences in our theatre and more especially by the students from Jena. . . . All the more unexpected was the manifestation which took place at the close of Schiller's *Bride of Messina.* Though it was meant to approve the poet, it was of an inappropriate extravagance. . . . I am therefore obliged to request Your Honor, by virtue of your office, to admonish our academic youth to continue its tempered expression of sympathy with our efforts. . . . We will tolerate no expression of impatience. Displeasure must be manifested by silence, approval by applause. No individual actor is to be called out nor the repetition of any aria demanded. Any incident which interferes in any way with the comfortable procedure of the performance from the beginning to the end, as it has not occurred hitherto, must also be prevented in future. . . . Your Honor's very obedient servant

J.W.v.Goethe

P.S. His Serenity specifically instructs me to request you to convey to Councillor of the Court Schütz that our Lord would have expected a better bred behavior from the Councillor's son.

March 22, 1803

To Schiller

I'm sending you Ottway's *Venice Preserved*. If you have time, do look it over. We can discuss it tonight. I want very much to see you. The damned rumpus in the theatre the other night caused me several disagreeable days. Tell me the hour at which you want the carriage to call for you.

April 4, 1803

To Marianne von Eybenberg

The Jewish wife of Heinrich XIV of the Principality of Reuss.

Several weeks ago I ought to have thanked you for your excellent chocolate which I enjoyed at every breakfast, and now comes your dear letter to remind me anew of my agreeable duty.

Let me for once praise you quite directly and say that among your many amiable qualities this one is especially to be appreciated, that you pay attention to the small whims and wishes of your friends and do not rest until you have satisfied them. Perhaps you do not yourself know how rare this quality is. People love their friends and value them and occasionally render them some tangible service and even make some sacrifice for them. But we are all, as a rule, too easygoing, too careless, too dry of heart, too falsely proud to satisfy a fleeting taste, a moody desire, a whim of some kind, forgetting that the satisfaction of such apparently curious desires affords the most agreeable enjoyment. . . .

April 5, 1803

To Lotte Schiller

You know how rarely a poet in our time hears a voice which truly understands the thing he has communicated. I was the happier to get your note which is a truly beautiful reward to me for my quiet, faithful efforts.

April 6, 1803

Charlotte von Stein to Goethe

Since there are times, dear Goethe, when your kindness is truly great, I beg you for a copy, if you can spare one, of your brilliant and interesting new play [The Natural Daughter, *a minor work*]. The reason is that I won't soon get to see it and I would like to read it to poor Fritz, who is ill. It goes without saying that the manuscript will not leave my hands.

April 21, 1803

Christiane to Meyer

This letter is extant only in edited form.

I am very much worried about the Privy Councillor. He is sometimes quite a hypochondriac and I have a lot to put up with. I am glad to bear it all because it's only morbid, but I have no one at all in whom I can confide. Don't answer this letter because nobody must tell him that he is ill. But I believe that one of these days he will be very ill. The other day when your letter came he was very much amused and he said to me: "You see, how short and insignificant the doctor's letters to you are getting to be. If you'll remember I prophesied that long ago and pretty soon you won't get any."

May 22, 1803

To Schiller

I have now arrived at a point of vantage from which I can survey all that I was and did historically and as part of the fate of someone else. The naïve inadequacy, the awkwardness, the impassioned violence, the confidence, faith, pertinacity, industry, the delay and procrastination and then again the storm and stress—all these things give an interesting aspect to the papers and documents which I am surveying. But I am mercilessly excerpting and cataloguing only what seems useful to me from my present point of view. The rest is being burned. The dross must not be spared, if the pure metal is to be obtained.

June 24, 1803

Elisabeth Goethe to Her Son

The great joy that was my portion on June 19 must not be passed over in silence. It would be a sin. . . . The King and Queen of Prussia were in Wilhelmsbad and the Queen uttered the desire to see Madame Councillor Goethe. . . . At 2 o'clock in the afternoon, therefore, a beautiful carriage drawn by four swift horses came to call for me. At 4:30 we arrived in Wilhelmsbad and I was led into a beautiful room and there the Queen appeared like the sun among stars. . . . Full of jubilation as I was, who do you think came in?? Our Duke of Weimar! God!!! What joy for me—O! How much that is dear and good did he say of you. Moved to the very heart I thanked him for his kindness to you during that last desperate illness of yours. He said—as much moved as I was—"He has done as much for me— we have been comrades and borne each other's burdens for thirty years.". . .

June 28, 1803

To Christiane

Christiane had gone to Lauchstädt in the middle of June.

It's very dear and sweet of you to write at such length. Continue to do so. It gives me much pleasure to learn all details. You can stay in Lauchstädt as long as you like. I would prefer to have you stay the whole month of July, because I have undertaken an important piece of work which will profit by my being alone, even though I long for you quite often. If I finish the job I'll come after you; that would do me good.

The household goes quite well and since the Duke is in residence I am frequently invited at the Court. Occasionally I am in Tiefurt and since I can do my riding there, I don't miss the horses. So have a good time and don't worry. August behaves very well and is glad to be with me. We often take walks together.

You will see from the enclosed letter what a great joy came to my good mother. Show the letter to no one, although you may tell people the facts.

Jena, July 5, 1803

To Schiller

> Ernst Frommann, 1765-1837, bookseller and printer in Jena with whom and whose family Goethe was on increasingly cordial terms.

I am here in order to make arrangements with Frommann about printing all this stuff which I mean to send out into the world. Frommann has all the equipment; he even has an excellent designer. So this business can be easily settled.

July 7, 1803

To Christiane

I got your letter yesterday. It gave me real pleasure. Continue to write me daily in diary form. Then someday we'll look it over and it will make us remember the rest. . . . I seem to observe that the little flirtations thrive rather vigorously. See to it that they do not do too well. . . .

◇◇◇◇◇

July 12, 1803

Don't worry about your expenses; soon enough you'll be back amid your household accounts. On Saturday the 16th the money for the sale of the farm at Oberrössla will come in. For this and other reasons I can't come to Lauchstädt. . . . If I can manage it I'll send Gus to take along with you to Dessau.

◇◇◇◇◇

July 14, 1803

Since my return from Jena the cook is making special efforts and is doing very well. . . . Councillor Schiller just arrived and brought me your letter. I am glad you are having such a good time and I'm sending you this letter by my very dear messenger, August. . . .

At your convenience send me your new shoes which, as you tell me, you have worn out dancing. Then I'll have something of yours to press against my heart.

◇◇◇◇◇

July 20, 1803

Everything went smoothly with the sale of the farm. . . . Circumstances enable me to invest the money at a quite decent rate of interest. When you come back we'll put our household in good order and pay up some old debts.

Now do me one favor and don't dance to the point of excess during these last days. End your stay there with moderation.

September 1, 1803

To Karl August

In our present situation it will be quite necessary to reconsider the university and all that goes with it from every angle and to exert both the powers of learning and the efforts of the administration. I foresee for myself three months of work, worry, annoyance and danger which will all be in vain, if the levers of gifts and grace and Ducal favor and sincere interest are not applied.

September 1, 1803

Letter to an Anxious Mother

Madame! Sometime ago a young man appeared at my house and asked for a position in our theatre. I put him to an exacting test and found him not devoid of talent. I inquired after his family and circumstances, wherefore I am impelled to make the present reply to your maternal letter of August 12.

Among us the professional actor is by no means regarded as he still is in North Germany. Participation in this art excludes him neither from good society nor from other desirable human relationships. If he is minded to withdraw from it, nothing will prevent him from assuming a respectable position in the world. His station in the profession will depend on his achievement and behavior and on whether he is able to gain the approval and respect of the public.

Taking all these things into consideration and having repeatedly interviewed your son and reflected about him, I cannot advise him not to carry out his plan. . . .

Passions, stealthy as well as stormy ones and calculated to embitter human life, arise amid people of all classes and occupations, as you have learned from the history of your own family. Happily a man can develop and cultivate his moral nature in every calling and in any class. I therefore beg of you not to withdraw from your son either your maternal affection or the financial aid which he will require until the cultivation of his talent enables him to aspire to a more lucrative position.

September 7, 1803

To F. A. Wolf

> Friedrich Wilhelm Riemer, 1774-1845, had been the tutor of Humboldt's children in Rome. He remained August's tutor until 1812, whereupon he became professor and librarian at the gymnasium in Weimar. He collaborated with Goethe in editorial and research undertakings and became co-executor of his literary remains.

Herr Riemer who accompanied one of your colleagues from Rome has decided to stay with us this winter and to assume the instruction of my son in Greek and Latin. You know how lively the boy is and you know that his knowledge of the ancient languages was nothing to brag of. This was a matter of great concern to me, but I seemed unable to do anything about it. Now I believe that it is settled and I myself hope for no little profit from association with Riemer.

October 6, 1803

To August Wilhelm Schlegel

My last letters were, so far as I remember, about nothing but *Julius Caesar.* I am sure that you shared my interest and did not blame me for my passionate preoccupation. I am having rehearsals of the play tonight and tomorrow night in order to perfect and improve the performance which will be repeated on the 8th.

I would like to tell you about a device which I am using in order to stimulate and employ the sensory perceptions of the audience. I have extended the funeral procession far beyond the obvious demands of the Shakespearian text. According to well-authenticated ancient tradition I have added brasses, lictors, banner bearers, floats which illustrate cities, fortresses, rivers, ancestral images, as well as a train of freedmen, wailing women and kindred. Thus I hope to attract the illiterate mass, to create in the half-educated a better approach to the content of the play, and to win from the understanding at least an indulgent smile.

October 26, 1803

To Charlotte Kestner

There is no way in which I can show more warmly how your remembering me and your trust in me delight me than by an immediate answer. Let me say that I have written today to Göttingen for the recommendations of your son's teachers and friends. Whatever I receive that is useful I shall send, accompanied by a letter from myself, to the magistrate in question. I shall notify you when that is accomplished and forward copies of the documents to you. I most sincerely hope that this will contribute to ease your situation which I heartily deplore. Forgive the brevity of this letter which is due to the necessity of a quick reply and continue to think of me with the affection and friendship of old.

October 29, 1803

To Schiller

I am sending you a copy of *The Merchant of Venice* so that you may kindly undertake to do the stage version and to superintend the rehearsals. As you read it through, put your mind on the casting once more and we'll discuss it. Perhaps you would like to come over tomorrow at 6 o'clock; there will be all sorts of dramatic and musical auditions.

November, 1803

Recollections of Ernestine Voss

In the period of the wine harvest Goethe once more spent some months in Jena. . . . Once he dropped in when I had just received a charming cordial letter from his niece Nicolovius. [*Cornelia's only daughter, Maria Anna Luise*]. In her own dear way the girl told anecdotes of her domestic circle which I knew so well. I had often talked about this niece. "If you read this letter," I said to him, "you see the child just as she is." He took it from my hand with a cheerful expression and began to read it. Gradually his face grew grave and before he had finished the tears ran down his cheeks. He sat for a while in silence and then exclaimed in an impassioned voice: "She is the true image of my Cornelia!"

November 23, 1803

To Charlotte Kestner

The recommendations from Göttingen have arrived and I have promptly forwarded them to the magistrate in Frankfurt. They sound very well indeed and I trust they will have the right effect. Your letter and your commission gave me great joy, my dear friend. Continue to think of me and do not fail to let me know what turn the affairs of your son take.

November 30, 1803

Schiller to Goethe

Anne Germaine de Staël-Holstein, 1766-1817, French novelist and political writer. As a liberal she protested against the excesses of the Revolution and was definitely influential in the Directoire. With Napoleon's resumption of power her political career was at an end. The novel *Delphine,* published a year before, established her European fame. Her report on Goethe and the Weimar visit was incorporated in her book *De l'Allemagne* [Concerning Germany], 1813.

It is a fact that Mme. de Staël is in Frankfurt and that we may soon expect her here. If she understands German, I don't doubt but that she will meet her match. But it would be quite a task to explain our convictions in French phraseology and to prevail against her French volubility.

December 2, 1803

Elisabeth Goethe to Her Son

My dear daughter writes me that she is getting to be somewhat corpulent and that all her clothes are getting tight on her. Well, Santa Claus is taking care of that and is sending material for two beautiful new dresses, one of taffeta, the color of Egyptian clay, and one of cotton easily washable which everyone thinks is silk—very beautiful. . . . Tell Schiller that his *Maid of Orleans* will have its first performance here on New Year's Day. I shall report on the success. You will have received the chestnuts—and therewith I commend you to God's protection.

Jena, December 13, 1803

To Schiller

If Mme. de Staël comes to Weimar, it is to be foreseen that I'll be summoned there. I have thought the matter over carefully, in order not to be taken by surprise, and I have decided to stay here. In this horrible winter weather I have just enough strength to get along at all. . . . If Mme. de Staël wants to see me, she shall be well received. . . . What I am doing here can be done in occasional quarter hours. She can command my spare time. But it is quite out of the question for me to travel in this weather, to dress up, to appear at Court and in society. . . . The preparation of the University material is an alien element to me. I splash around in it or, rather, just paddle. I lose my time and get not the least satisfaction. But since, as Polygnotus and Homer teach me more and more, our hell is really here on earth, you may call this a life, too.

Jena, December 20, 1803

To Lotte Schiller

It is the most damnable aspect of these mortal affairs that our friend, de Staël, had to arrive at a time like this. . . . Ordinarily I would gladly drive thirty miles to meet her. But this is the most depressing part of the year to me. In December I always understand so well how Henry III ordered the execution of the Duke of Guise, just because the weather got on his nerves. At this moment I envy Herder on hearing that he is about to be buried.

December 21, 1803

Schiller to Goethe

You will find Mme. de Staël precisely as you imagined her. She is all
of a piece without one alien or false or pathological trait. . . . She
represents the intellectual culture of France in its purity and places
it in a most interesting light. . . . The only trouble with her is her
quite extraordinary volubility. One has to turn oneself into one concentrated organ of hearing in order to follow her.

Jena, December 23, 1803

To Lotte Schiller

It is agreed, then, dear friend, that tomorrow, Saturday, at 1 o'clock
you and Schiller come to my house and invite Mme. de Staël to join
you there. Ask her to forgive me for not having called on her. I can't
get away from here early enough to do that.

End of December, 1803

Amalie von Imhoff to a Friend

Author, 1776-1851, of forgotten plays and novels, then resident in
Weimar.

Goethe looked forward to meeting Mme. de Staël quite as eagerly
as she did to meeting him. After the first meeting Goethe reported
to his friends: "A most interesting hour. I didn't get a chance to say
a word; she speaks well but far, far too much."—A group of ladies
in the meantime inquired of her, what impression our Apollo had
made on her. She, too, averred that she had not had a chance to speak
a syllable. "But," she sighed, "one loves to listen to a man who speaks
so well."

From the Supplementary Confessions

Mme. de Staël desires everything to be explained, seen through, precisely measured. She will not allow the existence of anything dark or
inaccessible. What her torch does not illuminate does not exist. Hence
arises her prejudice against philosophical speculation. In her opinion

it leads to mysticism and superstition and creates an atmosphere in which she dies for want of air. She has no sensibility for what we call poetry. In poetical works she recognizes only the passionate, rhetorical and general elements. Yet she will value nothing that is shoddy, only sometimes fail to value what is precious. From this it is evident that the clarity, decisiveness and vividness of her temperament have an agreeable effect. . . . Schiller's opinion coincides entirely with mine.

1804

From the Supplementary Confessions

The year opened with winter in all its severity. . . . And this time, too, I felt the ill effects of residence in the castle at Jena. . . . I returned to Weimar with a violent catarrh. It was not dangerous, but kept me in bed for several days and indoors for weeks. Therefore a part of Mme. de Staël's visit came to me historically and at second hand. Friends told me what took place at social gatherings. She and I communicated by notes, then by private interviews, later by meetings with a very few people present.

January 8, 1804

Charlotte von Stein to Goethe

I hear, dear Councillor, that you are ill, and since everything around me seems to be dying, I am filled with terror for those who are dear to me. Send me a word to tell me that you are better.

January 13, 1804

Elisabeth Goethe to Her Son

I am told that Mme. de Staël is now in Weimar. While she was here she was like a millstone around my neck. I tried to avoid her as much as I could and refused invitations to parties where she was present and breathed more freely when she had left. What did the woman want of me?? I haven't so much as written an A.B.C. book for infants and I am sure that my temperament will prevent me from any such thing in the future.

January 14, 1804

To Schiller

Since I am ill and peevish it seems impossible to me ever again to
converse with Mme. de Staël. Because it is really a sin against the
Holy Ghost to pretend ever to be in the slightest degree of her
opinion.

January 23, 1804

Böttiger's Anecdotes

Benjamin Constant, 1769-1830, well-known French philosophical writer,
accompanied Mme. de Staël on some of her German visits.

Mme. de Staël and Constant drove over to Goethe early and spent
about an hour with him. The chief subject of the conversation was
the difference between French and German poetry. The former, according to Goethe, was the poetry of reflection, the latter of situation.
The French poet delineates appearance, the German being. It was
soon apparent that Goethe was unwilling to be questioned and withdrew into himself, refusing to be pressed. . . .

January 23, 1804

Recollections of Joseph Green Cogswell

The American naturalist and bibliographer, 1786-1871.

When Benjamin Constant was first introduced to Goethe he
showered him with flattery in the true French fashion. He said that
the whole world was filled with admiration of his astonishing works
which assured the immortality of his name. Goethe fixed his great
fiery eyes on Constant and said: "I know it, I know all about it. I
know, too, that the world thinks of me as though I were a shipwright
who, on an impulse, has constructed a man-of-war high in the mountains, a thousand miles from the sea. But you will see that the water
will rise and that my ship will float and carry its builder thither
where no other human spirit has ever gone."

January 23, 1804
To Schiller

Today for the first time Mme. de Staël was in my house. The impression remains the same. With all her courtesy there is something coarse about her attitude as of a visitor among the Hyperboreans, whose sturdy old evergreens and oaks, iron and amber, may yet be turned into something both useful and ornamental. Meanwhile she compels one to take down from the wall the rusty old weapons in one's own defense.

January 26, 1804
To Schiller

Mme. de Staël was here again today. The Duke came in which made the conversation very cheerful and which prevented the discussion of a French translation of one of my poems. . . .

January 26, 1804
Heinrich Voss to a Friend

The son of the poet, 1779-1822, teacher at the Weimar Gymnasium.

Not long ago we had a wonderful evening with Goethe. . . . My father, pretending anger, said to him: "It is shameful that you publish a thing as magnificent as your collection of lyrics and keep it a secret from your friends." Goethe's eyes shone; he embraced my father. He could not sufficiently express his joy that he had written things that pleased so fine a judge. He grew ever warmer and spoke of the things he still meant to write, if gods and men were favorable. . . .
He was angry over Schlegel's completely negative view of whatever did not please him—if, indeed, one can attribute anger to Goethe which, in the strictest sense, he nurses against none. For he regards men as the products of nature. How, then, could one be "angry" at even the poisonous? . . . When it comes to action, Goethe, of course, abandons this contemplative attitude.

February 16, 1804

To Schiller

I am writing to ask whether I may have the pleasure of your company this afternoon and evening. Mme. de Staël and M. Constant will arrive at 5. I shall order a supper to be ready if the company desires to stay. I would be so happy to have you join us. Command the carriage for an hour convenient to you.

February 16, 1804

Recollections of Benjamin Constant

A very stimulating meal at Goethe's house. He is full of spirit and fire and depth and fresh ideas, but as devoid of good nature as any man I have ever known. Discussing his *Werther* he said: "The book is dangerous because in it weakness is delineated as strength. But if I write something according to my intentions, I am careless of the consequences. If there are fools with whom the reading of a book does not agree—that's not my business."

February 21, 1804

Heinrich Voss to a Friend

. . . He discoursed on the saying of Plato that the sense of wonder is the mother of both beauty and goodness. . . . He spoke at last about the susceptibility of human feeling and that, according to him, a truly living mind saw nothing but miracles in the universe and the very revelation of God.

February 27, 1804

To Zelter

My silence, my very dear friend, has been long and often I have missed you sorely. This winter has gone by almost entirely without music and I feel that thus I lose a lovely part of life's enjoyment. . . . Mme. de Staël has been honoring us with her presence since Christmas. She will soon leave for Berlin. She is a rare person and I am giving her a letter of introduction to you. Do see her soon! She is not difficult to get along with and will doubtless take great pleasure in your musical achievements, though literature, poetry, and philosophy are closer to her than the other arts.

February, 1804

Mme. de Staël's Recollections

Goethe's conversation is marvelously brilliant. It suits him well; a distinguished mind should have this gift. When he can be gotten to talk he is admirable. His eloquence is packed with thought and even his lighter chat is charming and philosophical. His imagination is absorbed by the outer world, as was that of the ancient artists. Nevertheless his intellect has all the ripeness of our age. Nothing troubles the power of his mind; even the contradictions of his character, his moodiness, his embarrassment, his reserve are but as shadows at the foot of that mountain upon whose peak his genius has its place.

Jena, March 21, 1804

To H. K. Eichstadt

Editor of the *Jena General Literary News,* to which Goethe gave editorial supervision.

Some day, as I have said before, we must have a thorough discussion about the belletristic contributions. When dilettanti sit in judgment on each other the result is a frightful mess. The nail has no head and the hammer strikes into the void. Unless I am mistaken the manuscript you are talking about is one of those quite current nowadays—empty without being bad. It is empty because it has no content; it is not bad because the author has a faint notion of the general aspect of good models. . . . It has come to the point where these mediocre productions give more trouble than works that are positively either good or bad.

March 28, 1804

To Charlotte von Stein

Would you mind calling on me tomorrow morning at 11? You would give me such pleasure. I shall receive you in the front room and beg you to have the carriage stop at the street entrance. The road through the garden is impossible since the last snowfall. If you want to bring one of your friends, she will be welcome.

March, 1804

From the Diaries of Henry Crabb Robinson

During my occasional visits to Goethe I saw the companion of his table, the mother of his children and future wife. She had an agreeable countenance and a hearty cordial tone. Her manners were unceremonious and free. When she was young, queer stories were told of her undignified ways and the freedom of her intercourse with him. She had survived all eccentricities of that kind now. . . . The sight of Goethe is enough to correct the childish misconceptions we form of a poet and a man of genius, as if they were wonders and shows merely to be stared at. In Goethe I beheld a man of terrific dignity; a penetrating and insupportable eye; a somewhat aquiline nose and most expressive lips; a firm step ennobling an otherwise too corpulent body; a free and enkindled air and an ease in his gestures, all of which combined the gentleman with the great man.

April 9, 1804

Heinrich Voss to a Friend

. . . Never is he more agreeable or amiable than in the evening in his own room, when he has taken off his garments and either stands with his back against the tile oven or sits on the sofa. . . . Whether it is the calm, the silence of the evening or the feeling of relief after the difficult work of the day, at all events he is most cheerful and talkative, most frank and hearty at such times. Oh yes, Goethe can be cordiality itself and at such times his commanding glance loses all its terror.

May 2, 1804

Heinrich Voss to a Friend

I was at Goethe's house when my doctoral diploma had been made out. It had been sent to me from Jena in care of Goethe. He said nothing about it. But he sent August to the park to gather laurel leaves. So while we were eating I was aware of nothing. After the meal Goethe said to the Vulpius: "My child, it seems to me that Voss still looks hungry. What kind of hospitality is it not to give

one's friends enough to eat?" In the same gay tone I assured him that
I had had all I wanted. He still insisted that August must go out
and fetch the dessert. August came back with a platter which he put
on my head. . . . The diploma was on it. Fancy my astonishment!
I looked at Goethe and knew not what to say. Now he and August
and the Vulpius congratulated me. . . . "It is advisable," said he
to the Vulpius, "that we drink the health of the new doctor." And
so he sent her to the cellar to bring up champagne.

July 17, 1804

To Christiane

I haven't been so well for a long time as I have been these last few
days. I am even able to rewrite *Götz*. I am therefore doubly glad
that you are having a good time in Lauchstädt. Stay as long as you
like and have the cashier give you what money you need. . . .

⬦⬦⬦⬦⬦

July 24, 1804

Remember me to the members of our theatrical troupe in Lauchstädt. Explain to them that the apparently liberal and elegant ene-
mies achieve their purpose only if one permits them to cause one
irritation. Of course, those who envy us are put out when the Queen
Mother of Prussia says everywhere and repeats it that she never saw
as fine a production in Berlin as our company's performance of
Wilhelm Tell in Lauchstädt. So the resultant bitterness and gall are
spewed forth in the newspapers. . . .

⬦⬦⬦⬦⬦

July 28, 1804

The carriage has returned and August is beside himself with delight
now that he knows why it came. It will take him and Riemer to you
and I wish you all much pleasure. I am glad that everything is to
your liking and I am looking forward to your return after dinner
on your birthday, August 6. A bottle of champagne will be in readi-
ness. . . .

July 30, 1804

To Wilhelm von Humboldt

. . . Schiller's *Wilhelm Tell* has been finished and has been played.
It is an extraordinary creation, in which his dramatic art puts forth
new branches. It is but just that it is creating a sensation. . . .
I am deeply obliged to you for the communication of your translation of the Pindaric Ode. Riemer and I passed an agreeable hour
discussing it. . . .

August 1, 1804

To Christiane

I am so glad you are all coming back on Monday. I wish the day
were today. When we're together we don't realize how well off we
are, because we are accustomed to it. . . . All goes well in the household and I am very comfortable. . . . It grieves me to tell you that
Schiller has been very ill, although he seems out of danger now. His
wife has given birth to a daughter.

August 3, 1804

Schiller to Goethe

I had a very serious attack, which might easily have been dangerous.
The worst seems to be averted, if only the unbearable heat will permit me to recover my strength.

August 5, 1804

To Schiller

Nothing could have made me happier than to see your hand once
more. I did not learn of your illness at once. It made me quarrel
with fate and angered me. You know how grief manifests itself in
me. . . . I am sending you a letter from Zelter to both of us. What
a powerful and forthright person he is; he should have been born in
a rougher and severer age. . . .

September 15, 1804

To H. K. Eichstadt

. . . When I come to examine with some strictness either my own or
someone else's career in both life and art, I find that tendencies,

correctly regarded as false, may represent to the individual an indispensable détour toward his true goal. Every retreat from error has a powerful influence, both specific and general, upon a man's development, so that it is quite understandable when those who search the heart prefer a repentant sinner to 99 who are righteous.

October 11, 1804

Elisabeth Goethe to Her Son

Dear Son, A few days ago I read a work of yours which I could not sufficiently admire and which gave me intense pleasure—the life of that great artist and even greater person, Benvenuto Cellini. . . . The chestnuts which I'm going to send will, I hope, be excellent this time. For, God be praised, the wine harvest is an excellent one this year—and as the wine is, so are the chestnuts. . . . I am told that the Emperor Napoleon was in Mainz. It concerns me little, though so many Frankfurters went to look at him. . . .

October 29, 1804

Heinrich Voss to a Friend

The last week I was constantly with him, nearly every noon and every evening and the time was passed in conversation and in reading Greek. It is a marvelous thing to read with Goethe; on such occasions the treasures of his soul come forth. . . . We have read a good deal of Sophocles together and Sophocles, illuminated by Goethe's mind, becomes a school of all that is beautiful and magnificent.

November 5, 1804

To Schiller

I don't want to disturb you but I would like to know how all things go with you. Do send me a word to tell me whether we can meet tomorrow.

November 30, 1804

Elisabeth Goethe to Her Son

. . . There is nothing else my heart desires, except that when you
come upon something really beautiful to read, you will think of me.
On New Year's Day Schiller's *Tell* will be performed in our theatre.
So think of me that evening at 6 o'clock. The people who sit near
and about me had better not so much as blow their noses. They can
do that at home.

December 24, 1804

To Schiller

How gladly I would have come to see you today to tell you that my
work goes well, but I am in no condition to risk going out into the
winter air. I trust that you are serene and active.

1805

January 1, 1805

To Schiller

With my best wishes for the New Year I am sending you a package
of plays to be read. Use your good humor in the task and make a
brief notation concerning each manuscript. In the end that is instructive.

January 9, 1805

To Schiller

Do send me, my dearest friend, a word about yourself and the progress of your work. My attempts to dwell in the goodly world of the
imagination have not been too successful. For at least some days I
am again confined to the house, so that I would welcome some happy
news from the tower on which you keep watch.

January 14, 1805

To Schiller

I hope you're well and mindful of me. The minute I can venture out of the house I'll spend an evening with you. Boredom has driven me to miscellaneous reading, among other things, the *Amadis de Gaul*. What a disgrace to grow to be my age and never to have known this excellent work except from those who wrote parodies of it.

January 17, 1805

To Schiller

Whether, according to the older theory, the hurtful humors wander about in the body, or whether, according to more recent notions, our weaker parts are first afflicted, it suffices to say that I ail now here and now there. From the bowels the discomfort has gone to the diaphragm, thence to the chest and up to the throat and finally to the eye, where I hate it worst. . . .
Since I won't be able to go out soon, maybe you'll come over for a little while, say, around noon. I'll send the carriage for you.

Middle of January, 1805

To Charlotte von Stein

Let me thank you for the magnificent fish; it will be a sort of Lenten tidbit to me tomorrow. I was recovering when I caught a new cold in my throat on Thursday night last which doesn't get better and which will prevent me from seeing you and your friends this Thursday.

January 23, 1805

To H. K. Eichstadt

. . . It is but just that, in general, we should know better what is profitable to the public, than it can know itself. The inhabitants of a city have a right to demand that the wells keep running and that the water suffices their needs. But only the engineer may choose the source from which the water is to be brought.

February 12, 1805

Elisabeth Goethe to Christiane

I am so grateful to dear August that he wrote me about my son's indisposition for, as is usual, rumor exaggerates everything. I hope that the illness will soon pass and I know how grateful I will be to God for my son's recovery. . . . I do not need to commend him to your care. I know that you will do everything that is humanly possible.

February 22, 1805

Schiller to Goethe

I am so glad to see once more a few lines in your handwriting. It restores my faith that better times may return, of which I have sometimes despaired. The two severe bouts of illness which I suffered within the last seven months have shaken me to the marrow, and it will not be easy to recover from them.

From the Supplementary Confessions

In the early months of 1805 both Schiller and I were interrupted in our important work by illness, so that Schiller continued the translation of Racine's *Phèdre* and I that of Diderot's *The Nephew of Rameau*. We had no strength for productions of our own.

Late February, 1805

Heinrich Voss to a Friend

On that evening, earlier this month, Doctor Stark came from Jena—it was a Friday evening—and declared that if Goethe lived until Sunday, hope would revive. But that very night he seemed to pass the crisis of his illness. The convulsions eased and the fever decreased. . . . At 11 o'clock he sent for me. . . . I was deeply moved as I approached his bedside. . . . He gave me his hand and said: "My dear child, I am not leaving you yet. You mustn't cry." . . .
Two days after that night he got up for the first time and ate a boiled egg. Soon, too, he asked to be read to again. It was difficult

to satisfy him. He wanted amusing things, such as no one writes nowadays. I brought over Luther's works and read to him. He stood it for an hour. Then he began to curse and swear and revile the accursed and spooky imagination of the Reformer who peopled the whole visible world with the devil and personified it as the devil himself. . . . Next day Goethe insisted that the books by Luther be taken out of his house. He began to read the short stories of Cervantes with much delight.

February 25, 1805

To F. A. Wolf

Although I can't say that I have my usual strength back, I am happy enough to be able to write you a provisional word after this last illness. I got your dear letter which refreshed me greatly when improvement had already set in. The prospect of seeing you and your dear daughter here around Pentecost will certainly hasten my complete recovery.

March 5, 1805

Elisabeth Goethe to Her Son

. . . I take every letter of yours and spread it out before me and give thanks to God. I learned that of King Hezekiah—see Isaiah, Chapter 37, Verse 14, and it has sustained me these thirty years. . . .

April 9, 1805

To Schiller

When Cotta arrives there might well take place a discussion about a collected edition of my works. Under these circumstances I find it necessary to give you all proper information about my old agreements with Göschen. I am grateful to your friendship and insight for relieving me from re-examining those rather unpleasant documents. Let me call your attention to the circumstance that Göschen issued an edition in four volumes with the deliberately falsified dates of 1787 and 1791. We never agreed on any such thing.

April 9, 1805

Elisabeth Goethe to Her Son

Dear Son, Last night around 9 o'clock when I got home it was a
lovely vision that met me. I recognized August at once, though he
has grown so tall and good-looking. . . . He sleeps in the room
next to mine and I hope he will be happy with me. We'll manage
to entertain him, because he seems to share his grandmother's love
of the theatre. So I've subscribed for 18 performances to be given
during the Fair.

Late April, 1805

To Schiller

It filled me with sorrow that you were not present at our little festivity. One way or another we must see each other soon. May you
soon recover entirely!

May 2, 1805

Elisabeth Goethe to Her Son

I, the undersigned, beg to bear witness in this letter that the young
gentleman, named Julius August von Goethe, has behaved himself
admirably during his stay here, so that it would appear as though
he had inherited the right ring mentioned in the parable in Lessing's *Nathan the Wise* and has thus the ability to make himself
pleasing before God and man. That this is true of the above-men-
tioned Augustus von Goethe is herewith confirmed by his loving
grandmother

E. Goethe

From the Supplementary Confessions

Two frightful accidents, violent conflagrations, which occurred in
close succession and which each time threatened my house, caused
my ill health to recur. Schiller, too, was tied down by illness. Our
personal meetings were interrupted; we exchanged brief notes. . . .
At last on an early day of May I ventured out of the house and met

him as he was about to go to the theatre. I did not want to dissuade him, but since I did not feel well enough to accompany him, we parted from each other at the door of his house, destined never to see each other again. My condition both of body and of mind was such that no one dared to bring me the news of his passing. He had died on the 9th of May. . . .

Spring, 1805

Reminiscences of Charlotte von Stein

Goethe has completely recovered and comes to see me often. The loss of Schiller remains irreparable. The other day he spoke so beautifully and originally about man, both as a physical and a spiritual being, that it's a pity I could not write it down.

June 1, 1805

To Zelter

Since I last wrote you I have seen few good days. I thought that I was losing my life and instead lost a friend who was the very half of my existence. I should, in point of fact, seek some new way of life. But at my age no other paths are open. And so I try to live from day to day and perform each duty as it arises without reflecting on the consequences. . . . Wolf of Halle is visiting here at present. I wish I could indulge the hope of seeing you this year. Perhaps you could meet me in Lauchstädt toward the end of July.

June 1, 1805

To Cotta

In answer to your question, dear Herr Cotta, whether the German theatre should not institute some memorial to our Schiller, the only thing I can answer at this moment is that many similar questions have been addressed to me. Now it is my conviction that when art deals with grief, it is to renew grief *only* in order to soften it and to transmute it into a high feeling of consolation. Hence I should be inclined to represent in art rather that which remains to us than that which we have lost. I have a plan which I hope to execute in the near future, but I cannot set a term for its completion. If I suc-

ceed in working out something not unworthy of the cause, I shall be
happy to let other theatres have it and to transmit to you both the
manuscript and the score.

June 12, 1805

To Karoline von Wolzogen

I haven't yet been able to gather the courage to come and see you.
Just as a man, after a severe illness, dislikes looking at himself in a
mirror, so one naturally shuns those with whom one has shared a
desperate loss. Let me therefore convey my greetings to you and your
sister in this manner and let me hear a word from you.

June 19, 1805

To Zelter

I am enclosing the wretched rag from Frankfurt. This is what they
write in the papers: He died poor; he left four children behind him,
and thus the dear public is invited to the obsequies. . . . It is a
man's friends who have a right to indulge a deep feeling of loss.
These Frankfurt people who usually value nothing but money,
would have done better to express their sympathy more realistically.
Between ourselves, they never bought the rights of a manuscript from
our great friend who was a hard worker, but always waited until
they could buy one of his plays in printed form for 12 groschen.

Late Summer, 1805

Heinrich Voss to a Friend

During Schiller's last illness Goethe was frightfully depressed. I came
upon him once in his garden while he was weeping. Only single
tears gleamed in his eyes. His spirit wept. . . . When Schiller had
died no one knew how to convey the fact to Goethe. Meyer was in
the house and he was called out and told the news. He didn't have
the courage to go back in. He went home without saying farewell.
Goethe began to feel that he was being avoided; he sensed the confusion and finally said: "Schiller must be very ill." He withdrew
and was heard to weep during the night. In the morning he said to

the Vulpius: "Schiller must have been very ill yesterday?" The emphasis with which he spoke made her lose her self-control. She sobbed aloud. "Is he dead?" Goethe asked with firmness. "You have said it," she replied. "He is dead!" Goethe repeated and hid his face in his hands.

Summer, 1805

Riemer to Frommann

He gave, at the time, no evidence of the impression that Schiller's death had made upon him. He permitted no one to mention it all day long. Finally he himself began to discuss the loss which our literature had sustained and of all that Schiller had been planning to do and to achieve.

FROM THE EPILOGUE TO SCHILLER'S THE SONG OF THE BELL

A pageant based upon Schiller's *The Song of The Bell* was performed in Lauchstädt in connection with the marriage of the Hereditary Prince Karl Friedrich of Weimar to the Grand Duchess Maria Paulovna of Russia. The epilogue from which the best known stanza is here quoted was written by Goethe for this occasion.

(August)

> For he was ours—ours! May this word of pride
> Outsoar the sorrow in our hearts prevailing.
> Safe was the stead we gave him to abide
> After the stormy struggles unavailing.
> And now his spirit with heroic stride
> Conquered the eternal world of truth unfailing,
> And left behind in distance ever vaster,
> The mean and trivial, mankind's common master.

August 6, 1805

To His Mother

Let me thank you, dear Mother, for all the kindness you showed to our August. I trust that his presence gave you half the joy which his stories about you give us. . . . His first venture out into the world has succeeded so well that I look forward hopefully to his future. His early youth has been so happy that I desire him to mature in equal cheerfulness and gladness. His description of your continuing well-being makes us very happy; we never tire of hearing him repeat it.

Lauchstädt, August 12, 1805

To Charlotte von Stein

Zelter came to stay with me for several days which was an immense pleasure. I recapture some faith in life when I see a man like him, so able and so honest, and compare him to the many who sway like reeds in the wind.

I am planning a little journey with Professor Wolf of Halle and August to the old university town of Helmstadt to visit that strange old antiquary and collector, Doctor Beyreis. He is so aged that one must hurry if one wants still to see him and his collections. . . . I am curious to see all that with my own eyes.

Lauchstädt, August 28, 1805

To Karl August

Your honored letter greeted me in Halle on my way home. . . . At Helmstadt we stayed for several days with that old Merlin, Doctor Beyreis. He is 75 and very lively; he is still intensely interested in his collections which surround him like a baroque magic circle. . . . He has been collecting so long that there are necessarily precious things among his possessions. Among his paintings is a self-portrait of Albrecht Dürer. . . . Among his coins are marvelous Greek things, especially in silver. He has an almost complete series of the gold coins of the Roman emperors, and many modern objects in silver and gold, some of them rare and curious. . . .

On the way to Halberstadt we visited the Councillor von Hagen on his estate. Your Serenity has probably heard of him and I must say that, despite the excellent food and wine, he lived up to his nickname of "the mad Hagen."

August, 1805

Reminiscences of Friedrich Weitze

Weitze, 1786-1841, was at this time the tutor of the children of the "mad" Karl Ernst von Hagen, 1749-1810, on the latter's estate of Nienburg where Goethe was entertained.

Herr von Hagen ventured to argue with Goethe. As a thoroughgoing Kantian he asserted that the highest object of artistic representation would be a person who completely fulfilled the conditions of the categorical imperative, for such an one, being morally perfect, exemplified true greatness which must be a moral greatness. Goethe contradicted this argument. "Complete moral greatness," he said, "exists in no human individual. It is a concept and not a fact of experience. Therefore the delineation of such a character lies outside of the realm of beauty which always craves a sensuous embodiment. . . . The Kantian imperative automatically and autocratically establishes as its premise a human being in whom the passions can scarcely arise and certainly not prevail. Now it is a common observation that man is in the power of invisible and irresistible forces which direct his course; his inclinations and his actions exert their arbitrary rule in a realm that transcends all law. Hence everything, even that which is morally quite abnormal, has its own aspect of greatness." . . .

Late that night the company assembled at the table again, more for the sake of conversation than of refreshments. The host brought out a bottle saved for very rare guests. The bottle, he added, was one year older than Goethe and himself who had both been born in 1749.

Lauchstädt, September 5, 1805

To F. A. Wolf

It has happened to me before that when I linger abroad, I am finally summoned home in great haste. My little housekeeper has arrived here with messages and commissions which make it necessary for me to be home by tomorrow evening. . . . The many kindnesses you have shown me on our journey I shall not easily forget, and I shall always be grateful to you for the patience you showed toward one still ill and recovering with difficulty.

October 10, 1805

Elisabeth Goethe to Her Son

. . . You will have seen by the papers that wars and rumors of war
abound here. We're so used to those things that cannons and muni-
tion trucks no longer frighten us. A good twenty years ago Mephistopheles sang in your *Doctor Faust:* "The dear old Holy Roman
Realm, how does it hold together?" Now the question is timely indeed. The Elector Princes and the other Princes—they keep running hither and yon—and nobody knows to whom anybody is to
stick. It will all come out all right; our dear Father above the stars
will see to it that people do not outgrow their clothes. He'll put
everything in order again.

November 25, 1805

To Cotta

The specimen of type which you sent me is readable and not disagreeable, but neither as modern nor as amusing as we are accustomed to in this part of the country. I leave it to your judgment
what you can do for the elegance of the book in respect of a good
face and similar matters. I am much more concerned over accuracy.
Even on this specimen page there were printer's errors. . . .
I don't think we had better have either woodcuts or anything else of
that kind for *Faust.* It is exceedingly doubtful whether anything can
be done which will be appropriate to either the sense or the music
of the poem. Copper plates and poetry usually parody each other. I
think we'll let the wizard stand on his own feet.
While the most curious things happen on the banks of the Danube,
our Thuringia is beginning to be overrun by soldiery. The incalculable element in this political situation leaves one suspended between fear and hope. The best one can do is to get through the moments as they come. Give me your opinion one of these days. I have
great faith in it. Best regards.

December 21, 1805

To Voigt

One should always take good care of one's dependents, and especially at this bitter time of the year. And so I'm asking Your Excel-

lency if it would not be a nice thing to permit our library attendant to collect New Year's gifts among the persons who use the library? Since begging is so general this instance might fairly be added. If it is necessary a notice might be sent to police headquarters and inserted in the official bulletin.

Book Six

SECOND SUMMER

1806-1823

WEIMAR
1806-1823

1806

Henriette Knebel to Her Brother

I would like to tell you about Goethe's recent lecture. . . . His subject was the relationship which man sustains to himself and also to the things in the world without. The discourse was so rich and ripe and gentle; I never heard anyone speak like that. I wish I could have recorded what he said, for it seems to me that this utterance alone would justify the fame of so rare a person.

January, 1806

Recollections of Charlotte von Stein

Last week his sister-in-law died (that is, the youngest sister of his demoiselle), and it happened while we were all at his house. But Goethe insists that all deaths in his circle be kept from him until he discovers them for himself. Yet he is said to have shed tears. Poor Goethe, who should have been surrounded only by noble natures! Yet there is that other aspect in himself.

March 4, 1806

To Charlotte

On Thursday and Friday I really suffered and I haven't pulled myself together yet. And so I don't dare try to welcome my honored company tomorrow. Do pardon me and give me your sympathy.

March 9, 1806

To Achim von Arnim

Arnim, 1781-1831, romantic poet and a literary scholar who had just,
in collaboration with the poet Clemens Brentano, 1778-1842, issued the
famous collection of German folk songs, *The Boys' Magic Horn.* Goethe
at once reviewed the volume enthusiastically and in great detail. Arnim
married Bettina Brentano, daughter of the friend of Goethe's youth.

It is told of the secretary of the Royal Society at London, that the
only way he could keep up with his enormous correspondence was,
never to open a letter except with a pen and a sheet of blank stationery already on his desk.

Had I followed that excellent example I would, in my humbler station, have answered many an excellent correspondent whom I left
without reply because I delayed. For certainly the first reading of
any letter arouses the impulse to reply. And so I will thank you at
once for your delightful letter and your charming gift. *The Magic
Horn* is so vivid and permanent a source of joy to us that it is fair
to bear witness to that fact. This is the more true, as our period is
not so rich that either ignorance or prejudice should make us forego
so pure a delight, so easily and plenteously obtainable.

March 9, 1806

Charlotte von Stein to Goethe

. . . I have a request to make of you and I hope it will find you in
good humor. An old friend talked me into giving him some drawings
of yours. Suddenly he sends them back magnificently framed. Since
it would make him so happy, give me some idea of the origin and
date of these drawings. You once sent them to me from Italy. . . .
I wrote this yesterday and now I hear that you are ill again. So I
send it today and beg for a word to tell me how you are.

March 12, 1806

To Zelter

I have recently been much tempted to visit Berlin and yourself. But
many things keep me so closely confined here that I hardly see any

opportunity of leaving. But since I do feel keenly the desire to be in more direct contact with you and to have a clearer idea of your environment, it occurred to me to send my son to visit you. . . . Although he is neither flighty nor immature I would not have him quite on his own in the metropolitan tumult. The question arises, therefore, whether you could find him lodgings in your immediate neighborhood.

◇◇◇◇◇

March 22, 1806

I am obliged to resign myself to an obstacle which makes it impossible for my August to be with you during Easter week. But I thank you from the heart for your willingness to receive him and to supervise him. . . . Your suggestion that I come to fetch him home is quite a good one. But I am afraid nothing will come of it. My physicians insist once and for all that I go to Karlsbad for the cure.

◇◇◇◇◇

March 26, 1806

Zelter's second wife had just died quite unexpectedly.

Scarcely had I written to tell you of the delay in August's departure when I received the tragic news which quite upsets me. . . . Just at the moment when I hoped that my boy would bring me back a living image of yourself and of your life, as he did last year of my mother, just at that moment you suffer this dreadful loss which my imagination thoroughly shares. . . . I can apply the example to my own situation and realize what so frightful a loss would mean to me.

April, 1806

Recollections of Adam Oehlenschläger

Oehlenschläger, 1779-1850, one of the most distinguished of Danish poets.

Goethe received me in a quite paternal fashion. I dined with him often and he made me read him extemporary translations of some of my poems. . . . The *Lay of the Nibelungen* had just been pub-

lished and Goethe read from it to us. Many words in the Middle
High German texts were cognate to Old Norse, and hence to Danish,
so that I could interpret details which were not clear to the others.
This seemed to amuse Goethe. "Just look," he cried, "there the
damned Dane comes in again." . . . Once at dinner he defended
so passionately and with so much respect and force the rights and
the honor of the plain people against the jeers of a cold-hearted
courtier who was present that, when the man was gone and I took
my leave, I could not refrain from embracing him. "Yes, yes, my
dear Dane," said Goethe, "you have a kind and sturdy attitude to
the world."
When I left Weimar I wrote a Danish translation of the "Erlking"
into young Goethe's autograph book, and added some German
verses of my own. Goethe read the verses. With a benign look in his
eyes and his hand on my shoulder he said: "Yes, you are indeed a
poet."

Karlsbad, July 3, 1806

To Christiane

I'll try to send you news directly to Lauchstädt. . . . The roads on
the way here were quite frightful from time to time and it also
rained quite hard. At last we're here and agreeably lodged and
well. . . .
The scenery is beautiful and the little town much improved since
I last saw it. Extremely pleasant promenades have been laid out.
. . . The food, too, is better than it used to be. But hard money is
exchanged at a high rate, because banknotes are losing in value.

◇◇◇◇◇

Karlsbad, July 28, 1806

I have felt very well and I only wish that I had arranged to stay here
longer, say, two more weeks without drinking the waters or taking
the baths but just to watch my state of health and yet be near the
springs, if need for them arose. . . .
I seem to observe that exercise is perhaps the most important thing
for me. If I could continue that in one way or another for another
eight weeks, all would be well. I'm very glad that you're gay and

merry. Life here is more stiff and formal than ever, but I have nothing to complain of. . . .

I haven't done much work; taking the cure and social distractions scarcely permit concentration. . . . Stay in Lauchstädt until I write you from Jena.

Jena, August 8, 1806

To the Ducal Police Commission

The Ducal Commission at Jena has deserved so well of the public in the matter of regulating the conditions of service, that it will not take it amiss if I turn to it in a matter of this kind, compelled to do so by my stay in Jena and the situation in which I find myself.

My serving man, N. N. Gensler, who has been with me for some time and is under contract to me for a further period, has carried out his duties tolerably well. On the other hand, from the moment I engaged him on, his behavior toward my family and the members of my household has been coarse, stubborn, and ill-tempered in the extreme, even in my very presence. Reproofs and threats, though of some momentary effect, have been, upon the whole, in vain. I have suffered many annoyances and only habit and the hope of improvement persuaded me to keep him in my service.

On my journey to Karlsbad, however, he yielded to his ungovernable temper so violently as to become positively insulting to my traveling companion. On the return journey he took out his rage and malice on my coachman to such an extent that vulgar quarrels took place on the box which, despite my commands, ended in a fist fight. . . . Since it was quite clear that irritation and anger would rob me of the beneficent effects of my cure and since it came to a point at which I was tempted to unseemly physical measures of self-defense, nothing was left me but to cause the fellow to be taken into military custody on my arrival in Jena and to declare that I would refuse to have him in my service from this time on. . . . I wish to request your Commission to take cognizance of the situation and to order someone to call for and receive the belongings of the aforesaid Gensler. I add the assumption that an employer is not obligated to indemnify a person so useless and dangerous for the remaining period of employment foreseen in the contract.

August 10, 1806

Recollections of Heinrich Luden

Luden, 1780-1847, was professor of history at the University of Jena.

It was at dinner at Knebel's. We sat about a round table. At first the conversation was general and miscellaneous. But after a little while Goethe decided to entertain the company. And he did it marvelously. He told us anecdotes and adventures, especially concerning his last stay in Karlsbad. He characterized people with extreme vividness. . . . Several of these anecdotes which Goethe told were particularly memorable. . . . Let me record one of them in Goethe's own words: "Walking up and down on the promenade according to my fashion, I had on several occasions passed an old gentleman of 78 or 80 who used the same promenade, supporting himself on his gold-headed cane. I was told that he was a retired Austrian general, of a very ancient and distinguished house. . . . Once I stepped aside a little on the promenade in order to have a better view of something, I no longer remember what. The old gentleman approached me in friendly fashion and greeted me. I returned his greeting. He addressed me as follows: 'Your name is Herr Goethe, isn't it?'—'Quite right.'—'And you're from Weimar?'—'Yes, I am.'—'And you have written books, haven't you?'—'Oh, yes.'—'And written verses?'— 'That, too.'—'They say it's a fine occupation.'—'H'm.'—'Have you written a great deal?'—'Oh, quite a little.'—'Is it hard to make up verses?'—'So-so!'—'I suppose it depends on your state of mind, whether you have eaten and drunk well, eh?'—'It may be so.'— 'Well, look, in that case you ought not to be stuck in Weimar; you ought to come to Vienna.'—'I have thought of it.'—'Because, look you, it's fine in Vienna; we eat and drink well.'—'H'm.'—'And we think a whole lot of people who can make up verses.'—'Yes?'—'Oh yes. People of that kind, if they behave themselves, you understand, and have good manners, are received in the best and most distinguished houses.'—'Really?'—'You come and let me know when you're coming. I have friends and kinsmen and influence. You write on a slip of paper: Goethe from Weimar, met him in Karlsbad. I need that to remind me because, look you, I've got lots of things to keep in my mind.'—'I shall do so.'—'But tell me, what have you written?'—'All kinds of things, from Adam to Napoleon.'—'They tell me you're famous.'—'Perhaps, somewhat.'—'What a pity that I never read anything of yours and never heard of you before. Have new and improved editions of your writings been published?'—'Oh yes, that, too.'—'But there will be later ones?'—'I hope so.'—'Well, look you, in that case I won't buy your works. I buy nothing but editions that have the final revision of the author; because otherwise I have only the annoyance of either owning an imperfect book or of having to buy the same book twice. But I want to be sure and so I never buy the works of an author until after he is dead. That is my principle and I am in no position to make an exception in your case.' "

August, 1806

Knebel to Luden

Goethe said: "A man must make his public appearance when he is young and continue to do so. The beastly public thinks, he who gives much must have much to give and he who brings many gifts must be rich. And when thus one has found a group of admirers, it will not be long before some of them are devoted to you unconditionally and will accept as excellent whatever bears your name."
Goethe condemns smoking and snuff-taking. He says that smoking makes people stupid, incapable of thought or creativity. It is for idlers and for those who are bored. . . . He couples beer-drinking with smoking. The overheated gums need to be cooled. . . . If this thing goes on, he says, as it seems to do, you will see within two or three generations what these beer bellies and walking chimneys will have made of the country. . . . "And look at what these horrors cost! At this moment 25 million thaler go up in tobacco smoke in Germany alone; the sum can rise to 40 or 50 or 60 millions. And none who is hungry is fed and none who is naked is clothed."

Weimar, October 14, 1806

From the Diaries

On December 2, 1805, Napoleon had definitively defeated the Austrians at Austerlitz. He now turned against Prussia and her confederates, of which the Duchy of Sachsen-Weimar was one. Goethe, after his return from Karlsbad, had retired to Jena to work. The arrival of Prussian soldiery and the attendant agitation drove him back to Weimar on October 6. Early on the 14th a cannonade was heard. At first rumor reported a Prussian victory. By afternoon the Prussians, retreating through the town, proved that Napoleon had won the Battle of Jena, too. Late in the afternoon a young French officer appeared at Goethe's house. It was Wilhelm von Türckheim, Lili's son. By evening 40,000 French troops occupied the town. Sixteen Alsatian cavalry men came to occupy the servants' quarters in the house. Late at night other French troops threatened to break into the house. Riemer admitted and fed them. Goethe in his long white dressing gown came down to calm them. A little later, heated by wine, they stormed up the stairs to Goethe's room. Christiane fought them off at the head of the stairs and persuaded them to retire.

Heavy firing from Jena. Rout of the Prussians. By 5 o'clock in the afternoon cannon balls crashed through roofs here. At 5:30 the French entered the town. By 7 o'clock there were fires and plundering. A dreadful night. Preservation of our house by both courage and good luck.

October 14, 1806

Recollections of Riemer

When the French soldiers had penetrated into his house I went up to Goethe and asked him to come down and show himself to the people who might be warded off by the weight of his personality. He did so with every appearance of calm. . . . In his voluminous white dressing gown which, jestingly, we called his prophet's cloak, he came down the stairs. . . . His dignified and majestic figure and spiritual distinction did seem to inspire respect. They were suddenly courteous Frenchmen. They filled their glasses and asked him to clink glasses with them.

Weimar, October 15 and 16, 1806

From the Diaries

Goethe had to accept heavy billeting, though only of high-ranking officers. At one time there were as many as 28 additional beds occupied in his house.

At Court in the matter of the arrival of the Emperor. Then back home. Employed arranging for safety of house and family. Dined with the French Marshal. Many acquaintances. Active sympathy of a number of French officers.

October 16, 1806

To Meyer

Tell me what you need and what I can send you, coat, waistcoat, linen—I'll send them at once. Maybe you are in need of food, too?

October, 1806

Heinrich Voss to His Friends

It was very moving to see Goethe on the second night after the battle. We gathered about him. He thanked the Vulpius for her faithfulness during these tumultuous days and said: "God willing, we shall be man and wife."

◇◇◇◇◇

October, 1806

In those two days I saw him shed tears. "Who," he cried, "will take from me the burden of my house and possessions, so that I may fare forth into the world?"

October 17, 1806

To the President of the Consistory and Court Preacher at Weimar

During these days and nights an old purpose of mine came to maturity. I desire to give full civic recognition to my little friend who has deserved so well of me and has been my companion through these hours of trial.

Kindly tell me, Reverend Sir and Father, how it can be managed that the ceremony be performed so soon as possible, let us say, on Sunday. What preliminary steps are necessary? Could you not perform the ceremony yourself which I desire to be performed in the vestry of the church? Kindly reply by the messenger I send.

October 19, 1806

Voigt to Goethe

The minute I received Your Excellency's note yesterday, I took the necessary measures and communicated the results to the Consistory. It goes without saying that a special dispensation, as well as all other formalities, will be eliminated. May I express the wish that the regularization of your domestic situation will contribute to the tranquility of your life, which your faithful companion will now share and help to prolong?

From the Records of the Court and Garrison Church in Weimar

On the twentieth Sunday after Trinity, that is to say, on October 19, 1806, there were quietly given in marriage to each other by the Chairman of the Ecclesiastical Consistory (August von Goethe and Dr. Friedrich Wilhelm Riemer being witnesses), His Excellency Herr Johann Wolfgang von Goethe, Ducal Saxon Privy Councillor of this city, to Demoiselle Johanna Christiane Sophia Vulpius, the oldest surviving daughter of the late Johann Friedrich Vulpius, Ducal Saxon Secretarial Scrivener.

Weimar, October 19, 1806

From the Diaries

Married today.

October 20, 1806

Recollections of the Revenue Inspector

His daily familiars and business associates were not a little astonished when he introduced his lady to them with the following words: "She has always been my wife."

October 20, 1806

To Nikolaus Meyer

A Bremen physician who had passed the winter of 1799-1800 in Weimar.

In order to brighten these dark days by a festive event, my little friend and I quite formally entered the holy state of matrimony yesterday. With which announcement I beg of you to send us from Bremen a quantity of butter and other easily transportable victuals. In calmer hours I shall reply at length to your agreeable letter.

•   October 27, 1806

Elisabeth Goethe to Her Son

I send my blessing and best wishes for your well-being in your new station. You have acted as I would have had you do. May God preserve you both. I send you once more my blessing in fullest measure, which is all I can send you in this crazy and miserable time.

October 31, 1806

To Schelling

I hasten to thank you for your kind and sincere sympathy and to give you good news of myself and all that immediately concerns me. . . . We have easily gotten over the expense in mental and physical force, in money and supplies, because so much, especially all that was most precious, has been saved. My health was scarcely shaken. . . . The laboratories and libraries in Jena and Weimar under my immediate supervision have hardly suffered. Everybody is trying to recover. Lectures at the university are being resumed on November 3.

Early November, 1806

Johanna Frommann to Goethe

> The wife, 1765-1831, of the Jena bookseller and foster mother of the orphan Wilhelmine Herzlieb, 1789-1865, whom Goethe had loved almost from her childhood on and who became the original of the character of Ottilie in *The Elective Affinities*.

Oh, it is wonderful to be relieved of our anxiety for you. We do thank God! How our hearts bled when we thought of the possibility of any danger to your health, your manuscripts, your works of art. When the good news of you arrived last night, Minnie and I were happy beyond all description.

November 14, 1806

Johanna Schopenhauer to Her Son

> The mother of the philosopher Arthur Schopenhauer, 1770-1838. Shortly
> before the Battle of Jena she had taken up her residence in Weimar,
> where she was to write most of her extremely popular novels. Her
> Thursday evening receptions were useful to Goethe for introducing
> Christiane to Weimar society, from which she had hitherto been ex-
> cluded.

I dined at Goethe's house on Monday. Meyer was there and Knebel
and his wife and a few visitors. I can't see enough of Goethe. Everything about him is extraordinary; he is infinitely amiable, too. But
this time I saw him angry. His son, a clumsy sort of creature, though
he bears a certain resemblance to his father, broke a glass with a
great crash. Goethe, who was just telling a story, was so startled that
he cried out. He looked at August just once, but that look was of
such severity that I was surprised not to see the boy fall under the
table.

November 28, 1806

Johanna Schopenhauer to Her Son

Goethe comes to my house often and seems to be comfortable there.
. . . At first he is always a little silent and rather embarrassed in a
way, until he has looked the company over and knows exactly who
is there. He is in the habit of sitting down next to me with his chair
pulled back a little, so that he can lean against the back of my chair.
Then I begin by talking to him alone and he grows lively and amiable beyond description. . . . He has a fine figure and holds himself
very straight. He is very carefully dressed, always in black or the
darkest blue. His hair is tastefully arranged and powdered as be-
seems his age.

Early December, 1806

Johanna Schopenhauer to Her Son

I bade Christiane welcome, as though I had never known who she
had been. I saw at once how this gesture delighted him. There were
several ladies present who were at first stiff and formal. Later they

followed my example. Goethe stayed nearly two hours and was more talkative and friendly than these people remembered to have seen him for years. He has as yet introduced her to no other house. He trusted that I as a stranger and one accustomed to great cities would take the matter of his wife as it must be taken. She was, indeed, very embarrassed. I did my best to help her along.

December 9, 1806

To Cotta

Your kind offer of a pecuniary advance touches me all the more, since I confess that in our worst moments here I had indeed remembered your friendly attitude and placed some hope in you, if need were to arise. At present I and my family are faring not too badly. I think we can hold out for some time yet although, under these circumstances, you can imagine how billeting and taxes and requisitions and charitable gifts have pretty thoroughly emptied cellar and cupboard and purse. . . .

December 12, 1806

Elisabeth Goethe to Her Son

We still have some billeting, too, but not enough to be a trouble. He who has crossed the ocean does not fear to ford a river. I thank your dear little wife for her sweet letter. Her lovely and heroic and housewifely behavior was a joy to me. O God, preserve her fine courage. A merry heart is a daily benefit, we read in the Wisdom of Solomon.

December 24, 1806

To Cotta

Cotta's *Allgemeine Zeitung,* or *General News,* had printed an ugly satiric article on Goethe's marriage and on the plundering of the house of Christiane's brother.

I am not sufficiently distinguished to rate a newspaper article concerning my domestic affairs. If, however, a subject like that is to be mentioned, I believe that I have deserved well enough of our country to have whatever steps I take approached in a serious spirit. I have lived a serious life and I still do so. I have been silent hitherto because I do not take such things hard. . . . Nevertheless if the editor of a political newspaper forgets himself so far as to introduce private matters of this character, which are reprinted by other papers which, though too decent to originate such gossip, do not hesitate to spread further what has already appeared in print—if this is to be so, then, in my opinion, Germany is much more deeply menaced by an inner rottenness than by that foreign power, of which, at least, one can recognize the intention and the ability.

December 25, 1806

To Karl August

> Karl August was in Berlin where, to his own dismay but with the consent of the King of Prussia, he severed his alliance with Prussia which Napoleon demanded as the price of the preservation of his duchy and of his throne. During these very days the Duke's mistress, Karoline Jagemann, who had been a member of the Weimar Theatre since 1797, had given birth to a boy.

I imagine that after so many evil things Your Serenity is eager enough to hear some joyful news. But it is only today that the little knight consented to start his progress in the world. He seems well and sound. I'm sure he will be brave, seeing that, together with his mother, he passed safely through these times of terror. . . . When we consider here what has been lost, we yet have reason to rejoice over what has been preserved. The library was saved as by a miracle. . . . Nor must I forget to say that the collection of coins was taken out of town. It can now be brought back. . . . I haven't yet been able to bring myself to go to Jena, just as I have torn up many letters to you which had already been begun. The revolution in our affairs is so close to us that whatever one says seems inadequate or inappropriate. . . . Let me think of some other pleasant circumstance to communicate. . . . It is this, that the park suffered almost no harm. The center from which the paths diverge is almost untouched. No trees were cut down. It will take no more than two weeks to restore everything with, perhaps, more agreeable plantations.

While I was jotting down these various items I learn that we are not to see you as soon as we had hoped, but that you are instead faring farther. This fact embarrasses me somewhat, because I had meant to speak of a certain matter to you later and here and after you had renewed your insight into our local conditions.

But now you must forgive me for speaking of our situation and of myself. No one is making any progress these days; it is usually the reverse. I, too, have suffered losses on all sides. It goes without saying that my mother's fortune in Frankfurt has decreased. It was equally inevitable that I, having escaped the plundering, had to establish an equilibrium between myself and others by gifts and contributions. This would not depress me, were it not for my dear family, of whom I must think in the case that one fine day death may knock at my door.

Now it is out! As a reliance for those for whom I am responsible I have, at the moment, nothing to point to but my house. I owe it to your thoughtfulness and kindness, but its possession has never been legally confirmed. At the time in question there were very valid hesitations against deeding the property to me. Time has obliterated these. Everyone considers me the owner and in happier—it now seems to me in opulent—times, I have invested almost more than I could afford in the property. And I have done so less to increase the luxury of my environment than to further and increase the influence of art and science. But for that very reason I have suffered the more from the harsh burdens of war. A word from you to Privy Councillor Voigt will suffice to settle the matter instantly and privately. It was brought to my attention in connection with the war taxes which I offered to pay. This then is my request: that you confirm your gift to me. I shall be doubly and trebly in your debt.

Weimar, December 27, 1806

From the Diaries

The proclamation of peace was issued in the theatre. An evening of music followed.

1807

January 7, 1807

K. L. Fernow to Böttiger

Fernow, 1763-1808, librarian to the Duchess Anna Amalia.

I happened to discuss the state of the German press with Goethe. You know how strongly he has always felt about the vulgar pursuit of mere news. . . . He added that in this period of crisis it was really treason to continue that old frivolity and to treat without respect places and men which as the seats and furtherers of culture deserve public courtesy. The enemy was less likely to treat us honorably if we did not treat each other so and were in haste to uncover our wounds to the public eye. And, above all, Weimar and those in Weimar who had contributed to the respect with which the French regard our literature, should now be treated with special consideration, the more so as the Emperor Napoleon's attention had been called to that city.

Early January, 1807

Recollections of Riemer

Goethe said: "No activity should be professional. I loathe that. I want to do everything that I can do in the free spirit of play, as it comes to me and so long as the delight lasts. In my youth I did this unconsciously; now I will continue to do so consciously for the rest of my life. To be useful, to provide uses—that is your business. You can make use of me, but I cannot consider the question of sale or demand. What I can do—you can use it whenever you like and whenever you need it. But I will not consent to be an instrument, and every profession is an instrument or, if you want a more distinguished expression, an organ."

January, 1807

Johanna Schopenhauer to Her Son

Goethe is an indescribable being. . . . On New Year's Day he sat for a long time in the farthest of my three rooms with Adele [*her daughter, 1796-1849*] and her friend, a pretty frank girl of 16. We noticed from afar how lively was the conversation of those three. After a while they went out and didn't come back for a long time. Goethe had gone with the children into Adele's room and had looked at all of her treasures, one by one, and had made every doll perform a dance. Now he came back with the happy children and with an expression of countenance so dear and gentle as no one can imagine who did not see it.

Berlin, January 12, 1807

Karl August to Goethe

. . . I am most happy to learn that you are serene, active and of good courage and that you have set your house in order. May you long enjoy your agreeable situation! I have ordered Voigt to see to it that your house be in fact your own. I am grateful to you for the kindness you showed to the fruit of my fertility; I am looking forward with joy to finding mother and child in good health. It augurs well for the future that a boy saw the light of day. I am almost sure now that I can get home by the end of the month. . . .

February 25, 1807

To Knebel

If it were possible to foresee things in this world, it would have been necessary to foresee that the highest phenomenon possible in history would arise upon the peak of the, one might say, overcultivated French nation. It is only natural to deny the monstrous so long as possible, and to refuse to have the right insight into the details which compose it. When you hear people give a naïve description of this Emperor and of his environment, you are bound to admit that nothing like it has ever been nor will be again.

March 23, 1807

Johanna Schopenhauer to Her Son

It is indeed a high delight to hear Goethe read. He enchants us all with his indescribable power and fire and plastic mimicry, although he doesn't really read well. He is far too tumultuous and declamatory. . . . Also he impersonates every part that pleases him, so far as is possible in a seated posture. Moreover, he will read twice and thrice any passage that stirs him deeply and comment upon it at great length, and his comments are finer than the text he is reading. In brief, he is unique, and woe to any who would seek to imitate him.

March 24, 1807
Recollections of Riemer

Goethe said: "The transference of things to a higher and intenser stage can be effected in aesthetic and moral matters, too. Love, as it manifests itself in modern times, is an enhanced and intensified phenomenon. It is no longer the expression of a simple natural need; it has been transformed and condensed and uplifted. Yet it were foolish to condemn this instinct when the simpler forms still show themselves."

March 30, 1807
To Christiane

Christiane had left on March 23 to visit Goethe's mother in Frankfurt.

I must say I am glad that the dear good mother still thinks me a genius in my work and ways. It is more than ever necessary to be one in order to cope reasonably with life and to enjoy it.
That my dear wife arrived safely calmed me. The letter announcing the arrival came at the precise hour expected and convinces me, as I foresaw, that the meeting would be an altogether happy one.

April 17, 1807
Elisabeth Goethe to Her Son

Christiane had returned home on April 12.

Dear Son, Your letter telling me of the happy arrival of my dear daughter has made gay my heart and my countenance. Yes, we were very merry and very happy! You may well thank God, for such a dear and fine and unspoiled creature is seldom met. I am very calm about you now that I know her so well and it pleased me inexpressibly that all my acquaintances became fond of her at once.

Weimar, April 18, 1807
From the Diaries

The Dowager Duchess died today.

May 2, 1807

Elisabeth Goethe to Her Son

Dear Son, The death of our dear Duchess moved me deeply and the lovely souvenirs I have of her are now doubly precious to me. As is not uncommon in human life, she and I lost touch in recent years, but the friendly memories of that older period have never been extinguished in my mind.

May 7, 1807

To Zelter

. . . When a piece of work gets stuck one never knows whether the fault is ours or that of the subject. Usually one takes a dislike to something which one cannot complete with the feeling that it resists us, so that we cannot master it. I must say that during the recent reissuing of my works, I felt very keenly how alien some of these writings had become to me. I could scarcely force myself to take an interest in them. That went so far that without friendly and continuous assistance I could not have done the editorial job. Now most of the work is behind us and the material will be in Cotta's hands in a few days. Whatever my future fate, this much has been rescued. I look forward to the fun which the continuation of *Faust* will cause you. There are things in it that will interest you from the musical angle, too.

May 16, 1807

Elisabeth Goethe to Christiane

. . . So the Brentano girl did get her wish and saw Goethe. If she hadn't, I am convinced she would have gone out of her mind. I never saw such a thing all my life. She threatened to dress up as a boy and run to Weimar on foot. Last winter I was really frightened about the girl. Well, thank goodness, she got her will in a decent way. She isn't back yet. So far as I know, she's still in Cassel. So soon as she turns up I'll tell you all about her. . . . Yes, dear daughter, the accursed catarrh and head cold prevented my showing you my brilliant talent for telling fairy tales. Writing books? No, I can't do that. But in recounting what others have written—in that art, let someone try to surpass me!!!

This long and carefully composed letter (I am using the second fresh pen) ought to make several things clear: firstly, that my physician has actually cured me or, rather, patched up grandmother again; secondly, that I have been obliged to take to tobacco again— you may observe that from the fluidity of my style. Without a pinch of snuff my letters were like straw—like bills of lading. But now, it goes as though oiled! The comparison is not a pretty one, but none other occurs to me.

P.S. Spelling and well-formed script are not among my talents. You must forgive me. 'Twas the fault of my school teacher.

Late May, 1807

Recollections of Heinrich Luden

Sometime after the Battle of Jena I made inquiries as to how Goethe had fared during those unhappy days. All informants agreed that he, too, had borne his burden and shared in the general woe. . . . Sometime still later I met Goethe at Knebel's house. It was the first time that he had returned to Jena. His expression was severe and his attitude showed that he felt the weight of the times. Goethe turned to me and said: "I am told that you suffered severely." I summed up my fate briefly. . . . Later I took occasion to ask Goethe how he had fared in those days of humiliation and misfortune. He answered in the following words: "I must not complain. I was like a man who from the height of a cliff surveys the raging sea. Though he cannot succor the shipwrecked, neither can he be reached by the tumultuous waters. Thus I stood and let the wild alarm storm past." I cannot deny that at these words spoken with a measure of ease and complacency, a chill crept into my breast.

Late May, 1807

Recollections of Riemer

At noon we were in Jena. Dinner at Major von Knebel's. After dinner we were at the Frommanns. Goethe profoundly irritated by political events and by the barking of dogs. We took a walk through the city. He joked about an old book of proverbs and sayings. Spoke of the serious ones, too. The author defines God as an inexpressible sigh which arises from the depth of the soul. Goethe quoted still another: *Nihil contra Deum, nisi Deus ipse.* (*Apothegmata* by Zinkgraf. Strassburg, 1626.)

Karlsbad, June 1, 1807

Christine Reinhard to Her Mother

During his stay in Karlsbad this year, Goethe formed a friendship with Count Karl Friedrich von Reinhard, 1761-1837, a professional diplomat now in the French service, and his wife Christine.

You will never suspect, dear Mother, with whom we are associating in Karlsbad at present. . . . Day before yesterday we were chatting in my drawing room and people were asking whether Germany and the German language were destined wholly to disappear. "No," said someone. "I don't believe it. The Germans, like the Jews, will permit themselves to be oppressed, but no more than the Jews will they permit themselves to be exterminated. They will not be discouraged and they will remain strongly united, even if it were to happen that they have no country any more." Guess who it was that spoke thus! It was Goethe.

Karlsbad, June 2, 1807

To Christiane

Since the mail leaves tomorrow I'm getting ready this letter to tell you that I feel incomparably better than I did when I left home. . . . I get up at 5 o'clock in the morning to drink the waters. Breakfast comes between 8 and 9. Then I rest a little, dress for the day, dictate for a while, take another walk and then eat dinner. After that I spend some time drawing in my room. Late afternoon I go on the promenade and thereafter the time is spent in various ways. The food is tolerable and so is the wine; neither is tempting to the point of indulgence. Tomorrow the first week is up and therefore it is pay day. I have kept all accounts very accurately. Today I exchanged money and got 103 paper gulden for 50 in currency. A week from now I'll let you know the exact expenses.

Karlsbad, June 11, 1807

Christine Reinhard to Her Mother

Dear Mother, I meant to write you yesterday, but Goethe came to us
for tea. He gave us a regular hour of instruction concerning his new
theory of colors. His point of view and his method of exposition are
highly interesting. But the moment one withdraws oneself from the
influence of his genius, one is bound to remember that authoritative
scientists reject these theories of his completely. Karl is, of course,
better able to follow this dazzling mind than I am. . . .
The poet brought us his autograph book and asked us to write in
it. But I rather feared to do so, because he has his own theories about
handwriting which, in his opinion, reveals the character of the
writer. He has made a profound study of Napoleon's handwriting.

Karlsbad, June 24, 1807

Christine Reinhard to Her Mother

My husband ran into Goethe and told him that the battle of Fried-
land, which was foreseen, has now been fought. *"Il y en aura bien
d'autres,"* said Goethe, using French for the first time. After the
concert Goethe deliberately came over to us and as deliberately
walked with us on the promenade. This manifestation caused wide
comment.

Karlsbad, June 28, 1807

From the Diaries

Dined with the Duke. One of his gentlemen brought a newspaper to
the table. He didn't think it very interesting but read us an excerpt
from a news story sent in from Constantinople: "Upon thorough
examination the new Sultan Mustapha found all the members of
his predecessor Selim's harem to be virgins."

Karlsbad, July 1, 1807

To Christiane

. . . According to doctor's orders I have to be idle a good many hours a day. So I sneak around in shops and buy all sorts of little things, of which a package is going off to you. If you do go to Lauchstädt, be comfortable and at ease. Hire pleasant lodgings and don't be nervous about the expense. I'll manage to get hold of the money. I have done some work here and will do some more pretty soon.

Karlsbad, July 5, 1807

Christine Reinhard to Her Mother

Goethe asked us to visit him in Weimar on our way back. On this occasion he said to Karl: "I'd like to have you make the acquaintance of my wife. I owe you a delineation of her, which I don't want to go into before your wife. First of all I'll tell you that my wife has not read a line of all my works. The realm of the spirit does not exist as far as she is concerned. But she's a wonderful housekeeper. She releases me from all domestic cares and that activity is her life and her domain. Also she loves to dress up and she loves society and she loves the theatre. So she is not lacking in a certain kind of culture which she has gained from living with me and from the theatre. It's unbelievable how instructive the theatre is if you visit it every night for ten years."

Karlsbad, July 10, 1807

Christine Reinhard to Her Mother

. . . Karl confessed to Goethe that it was difficult to follow the flight of his mind and that one was often dazzled by the correctness and boldness of his observations. This homage seemed not to astonish the poet. He replied that it was, indeed, necessary to be accustomed to his language, in order to understand him. For this reason he had long given up miscellaneous conversation and discoursed only when he found people on his own level, such as Karl and such as Schiller had been. He then pronounced a panegyric on Schiller without a single implicit reservation or comparison or rivalry.

Karlsbad, July, 1807

Karl Reinhard's Diaries

We were talking about the ancients. He said: "When you consider what the Greeks achieved, what knowledge flourished among them, and how that whole civilization was destroyed—when, next, you look about in this world today and consider what may befall us, one is tempted to do nothing at all. Yet we must not lose courage. I have always had an inner drive and worked hard." . . .

He said: "I am not sorry that my son has not the least talent for poetry." . . . "The differences between us hurt Schiller. As a matter of considerateness and delicacy we ceased disputing. But the matter was close to his heart and so there suddenly appeared in *The Hours* his essay on ancient and modern, on sentimental and naïve poetry. Since I was quite aware of my one-sidedness—even as every human being is and must be—the essay delighted me and I recognized the fact that I, too, by virtue of the very age and of my own development, belonged among the modern poets."

Karlsbad, July 27, 1807

To Zelter

I have made a variety of interesting acquaintances here. Among them the resident French Minister Reinhard who used to be in Jassy and of whose fate and career you may have heard. Beyond that I am rather isolated. You hear nothing but Jeremiads in society and, though they have been inspired by great evils, yet the phrases sound hollow. . . . When people complain of their lost investments or their ruined careers, it would be inhuman not to feel for them. But when they talk as though the world in its entirety had suffered the slightest loss on that account, I cannot possibly agree.

Karlsbad, July 28, 1807

From the Diaries

In France there is a family by the name of Moncul. A beautiful woman who bore this name wrote to a friend, inviting him to her chateau: *"Moncul n'est qu'un trou, mais les environs en sont char-mants."*

Karlsbad, July 29, 1807

To Christiane

Christiane had gone to Lauchstädt where the Weimar Court Theatre company was then playing.

Since we are enjoying peace before we had a right to hope for it, let us enjoy the coming winter quietly and modestly but cosily. Make all arrangements to take up our former hospitality again. I am providing excellent porcelain for our dinner table and tea table. I am also bringing along a silver tea urn and cream pitcher which were a bargain and acquired by accident. Just before he left, the Duke made me a present of a massive bronze mantel decoration which had been meant for someone else. . . . By adding a little money I was able to exchange it against the porcelain which will give you pleasure. I have also had a necklace made for you. It's very lovely. If I get a chance to send it, it will reach you on your birthday.

Karlsbad, August 23, 1807

To Christiane

August has arrived safely and has a good time admiring the strange cliffs and the warm springs. . . . You'll have to join me here for at least a while next year, so that you know what we're talking about, because Karlsbad and its like cannot be described. . . . It's quite empty now, by the way; they don't even light the great candelabra in the public halls and all social amusements have ceased. . . . I have ordered the coachman to return here on September 5, so that we can leave for Jena on the 7th and arrive there within three or four days. From there I'll let you know further.

Karlsbad, August 24, 1807

Recollections of F. Schubart

On a beautiful day this summer the great poet sat in the open at a table surrounded by rustic benches with his friends. Deep in inter-

esting conversation the friends who sat with their faces forward saw
Goethe's son come down a declivity. The young man, who was a
student at Heidelberg at that time, had undertaken a walking tour
to Karlsbad to surprise his father. As he approached he motioned to
his father's friends not to betray his presence. Softly he approached
and suddenly, according to the common jest, he put out his arms
and placed his hands over his father's eyes. When Goethe loosened
himself from this grasp and turned around and unexpectedly beheld
his son, the joyous paternal feeling overcame him so powerfully that
his friends were shaken to the core. The manifestations of this
revered man's power and depth of emotion were such that the onlookers were frightened and prayed for the tranquilizing of his
spirit.

Karlsbad, August 28, 1807
To Karl Friedrich von Reinhard

. . . I would have wished you to read *Tasso* in Leipzig, just as you
did. That play is a result of many attempts and exertions on my
part; and since the art of the drama is truly written in water, it comforts me that the lineaments of this play have graven themselves
upon your perceptive mind and sympathetic heart.
Meanwhile the beautiful box of books which you so kindly sent me
has proved in the good sense a casket of Pandora to me. The works
of La Fontaine as well as the older and newer novels entertained
and stimulated me. The writer I found most astonishing is Mon-
tesquieu. The entire history of our age is literally set down in his
work, even as physicians find in Hippocrates the very diseases of
which their patients die today. . . .
I close with a reflection aroused by a passage in your letter. The evil
will bent upon destroying the reputation of an eminent man often
produces the contrary effect. It calls the world's attention to the
personality in question, and since the world, though not just, is at
least indifferent, it does not mind gradually becoming aware of the
excellent qualities of one who has been exhibited to it under the
darkest aspect. . . .

Karlsbad, August 28, 1807

To Adam Heinrich Müller

A. H. Müller von Nittendorf, 1779-1829, political pamphleteer.

. . . The world does its best to make us indifferent to praise and blame; but this does not succeed, so that whenever we hear favorable judgments of ourselves and such as coincide with our convictions, we are only too pleased to exchange resignation for relish. . . .

Karlsbad, August 30, 1807

To Zelter

. . . There is really something Promethean about your way of being, which I cannot but regard with astonishment and reverence. While you bear the scarcely bearable composedly and tranquilly and make plans for happy, creative future activity, I seem to take on the aspect of one who has already crossed Cocytus and has at least tasted of the Lethean flood. However, insofar I still feel myself to be a dweller on this earth I, too, have done my share, have gathered experience and learned and read and noted down and transformed creatively the little that I could. . . .

On the return journey from Karlsbad
September 7, 1807

From the Diaries

The crucial thing is that a man be constantly reminded of the three necessary demands of the human spirit: God, immortality, virtue, and that these be guaranteed him as far as possible.

September 15, 1807

To Zelter

You are a splendid friend! On my arrival home I found your compositions. Already we are founding a small choral society. Gradually we will draw into it the singers from our theatre and people from the city and see how far we get. We can use the auditorium of the theatre. . . . I shall say nothing of my various preoccupations, but

I hope soon to be able to communicate to you some results of my
industry.

October 7, 1807

To Cotta

I will gladly continue to send you for your papers whatever we have
here or produce of an aesthetic character. . . . But I want to repeat
my emphatic request that you refuse to print any political news
which does not come directly from myself. This little country has
never been politically important. What importance we possess consists in a patronage of art and science disproportionate to our
power. In every other respect we are less today than we ever were. So
long as the political situation of Germany is not decisively clarified,
all its component parts, especially the smaller states, can have no
better luck than to be ignored. . . .

October 8, 1807

Elisabeth Goethe to Her Son

. . . The Fair this year was rich—in professors!!! Since a great part
of your fame and repute falls like a cloak upon me, and since people
imagine that I have contributed to your great talent—well, so they
come gawp at me and I, I do not hide my light under a bushel but
set it on a candlestick and tell the people that I did not make the
slightest contribution to your greatness as a man and a poet (for
who would accept undeserved praise?), but I do know very well to
whom praise and thanks are due, seeing that in the germ in a
mother's womb all that is you already existed without any help
from me.

October 27, 1807

Elisabeth Goethe to Her Son

. . . I rejoice in life while still my candle shines; I seek not the
thorns, but grasp after the little joys. If the doors are low, I bend;
if I can remove a stone from the road, I do so; if it is too heavy I
walk around it, and so I find some daily small delight, the while the
stone of the corner, my faith in God, makes my heart glad and
brightens my countenance.

November 10, 1807

Recollections of Charlotte von Stein

I was with the Duchess yesterday. Goethe has written new scenes for *Faust* and read them to us. In about six weeks the printing will begin.

Jena, November 19, 1807

To Charlotte von Stein

Out of the depth of this solitariness and stillness I must tell you how I fare. . . . My work moves ahead gently. You will take pleasure in certain things, dear friend, which I am preparing. Other things I am writing and having printed in a spirit of hope. The present hour seldom produces the mood for its own treatment. The co-existent seems destined to conflict. . . . Although the calm here corresponds to my desires and purposes, yet sometimes I wish I were in Weimar. Especially the evenings seem unending here.

November 20, 1807

Bettina Brentano to Goethe

Dear Goethe, Attribute my curious ideas to the curious place in which I am. I am in the church of the Carmelites, in a hidden corner behind a great pillar. I go there every day at noon and see the autumnal sun shine through the windows and throw the shadows of the vine leaves on the flagstones and on the white wall and watch the wind stir them and cause them to fall, one by one. Here I find a great aloneness, and the people that come here at this unwonted hour are surely those whose dead are buried here. Here near the great door is the sarcophagus where my father and mother and seven brothers and sisters lie buried. . . .
I still remember my mother and her great beauty; it was both delicate and lofty and her face was not like the faces of others. It was you who said that she was created to be the playmate of angels. Your mother told me how, the last time you saw her, you beat your hands together at her beauty. That was a year before she died. . . .

December 14, 1807

To Lili (Schönemann) von Türckheim

Your dear letter, my honored friend, came too late. Your son forwarded it to me from Dresden. He was with me, and I knew not who
he was. I confused the two families of the same name and held him to
be one of the others. . . .
But you will permit me to say how infinitely happy it made me to
receive, after so long a time, a few lines written by that dear hand
which I kiss a thousand times in memory of days which I count
among the happiest of my life. . . .

Jena, December 16, 1807

To F. A. Wolf

Zacharias Werner, 1768-1823, playwright of the first romantic generation; author of the "Fate Tragedies," *The Twenty-Fourth of February,
The Sons of the Valley.* From the latter derived his nickname.

Werner, the son of the valley, has been here these two weeks. His
personality serves to introduce one to his writing. His reading of
them and explanations and commentaries smooth out a good deal in
them which, black on white, was repellent. His is a strange nature
and a graceful talent. . . . He's going back to Weimar with me
within the next few days.

December 18, 1807

Charlotte von Stein to Fritz von Stein

Goethe seems fond of Zacharias Werner. The other day they were
together at the Knebels in Jena. Frau Knebel was serving tea and
their little boy was playing with his building blocks and Werner was
declaiming at the top of his form. Suddenly the little boy pipes up:
"That man is a crazy man!" Knebel jumped up: "Hold your tongue,
rascal!" Frau Knebel was very much embarrassed. Goethe roared
with laughter. "You leave that child alone," he said, "the boy has at
least one-half of the world on his side."

December 20, 1807

Knebel to His Sister

Goethe returns to Weimar tomorrow. Last night he read us some extremely charming sonnets which he wrote during his stay here.

1807

EPOCH

By flaming script Petrarca's breast was riven.
The letters spelt of all the days one day,
Good Friday. Thus to me in equal way
Shines Advent time of eighteen hundred seven.
I nursed anew a love in past years given,
Who early in my heart had come to stay,
Whom later prudence taught to put away,
But toward whom again my soul was driven.

Petrarca's love, the lofty, infinite
Was unrewarded, bleak and melancholy,
A heartache, a perpetual Good Friday;
To me shall beckon ever brightly lit,
Sweet amid jubilant palms in rapture holy,
My lady's Advent, May's eternal high day.

1807

FRIENDLY MEETING

Swathed in a wide cloak to the very chin,
I took the mountain path, the rough and bold,
Down to the meadows with their wintry mould,
Ready for flight, disquieted within.
Suddenly a new day seemed to begin:
There came a girl, exquisite to behold,
To lovely ladies praised by poets old,
And apt to still my yearning, close akin.

I turned aside, determined not to move her,
And closer in my cloak sought to enfold me,
Defiantly in my own warmth to stay;
Yet followed her. She stood. Then all was over!
The heavy mantle could no longer hold me,
I tossed it far and—in my arms she lay.

1807

THE GIRL WRITES AGAIN TO HER LOVER

Why I once more above this paper bend
You must not ask with such exacting care!
For I have naught to say but that 'twill fare
Until it reaches your dear hands, sweet friend.
Because I cannot come this that I send
My undivided heart to you shall bear
With ecstasy, with longing, with despair,
With all that no beginning has nor end.

Nor of today would I to you confide
The dreams, thoughts, yearnings that are but a token
Of my true heart turning to yours to greet it!
Thus seeing you I once stood by your side
And spoke no word. What word could I have spoken,
Since all my soul was in itself completed?

1808

January 11, 1808

To Jacobi

For the past few months I have had no communication with the
outside world. I have been fathoms deep in work and have associated
with my friends here or those who visit us. Especially Werner, the
son of the valley, whom you know, too, has entertained and stirred
us by his character and his works. It seems odd enough to an old
pagan like myself to see him plant the cross, as it were, on my own

territory and to hear him preach the power of the blood of Christ, without being entirely revolted. Well, we owe that to the high vantage place to which philosophy has raised us. We have learned to appreciate the ideal, in however curious a form it may manifest itself.

January, 1808

Recollections of Riemer

Goethe said: "The general interest in art and poetry now so widespread in Germany neither avails the arts nor will it contribute to the appearance of a single original masterpiece. The genius of mankind itself is productive in all ages and out of its plastic substance has made in the course of the ages Homer, Aeschylus, Sophocles, Dante, Ariosto, Calderon and Shakespeare. (Perhaps this age can show Goethe and Schiller.) The important difference is that in our time mediocrity and the secondary figures have their chance by virtue of artistic traits which are matters of technique. Thus the valley shines bright, whereas in other ages only the mountain peaks received the sun."

February 1, 1808

To Heinrich von Kleist

The dramatist and writer of novelettes, 1777-1811, whose fame has grown with every decade since his death.

I cannot say that your play appeals to me. It is so strange in kind and moves in regions so alien that it would take time for me to establish true contact with either. You must also permit me to say (for if one is not to be frank, one might better be silent), that it grieves and depresses me to see young men of spirit and of talent waiting for some theatre of the future. A Jew who waits for the Messiah, a Christian who waits for the New Jerusalem and a Portuguese who waits for Don Sebastian to return do not cause me keener annoyance. At the foot of the rudest scaffolding I would say to a true theatrical genius: *hic Rhodus, hic salta!* I would venture to go to any Fair, to lay boards across barrels, to take one of Calderon's plays and, *mutatis mutandis*, to entertain and delight both the educated and the uneducated crowd. Forgive me my forthrightness; it bears witness to my sincere good will.

March 7, 1808

To Jacobi

I have recently come to entertain the highest respect for Roger Bacon, while his namesake, the Chancellor, seems to me like a Hercules who cleans a stable of dialectic dung only to cause it to be filled with empirical refuse. . . .

Among the ancients, during their best period, the sacred arose from the sensuous perception of beauty. The Olympian image did serve to complete the notion of Zeus. The modern man takes moral beauty as his foundation and, if you like, opposes sensual beauty to it, and I don't at all blame you, if you can't bear the hitching up and copulation of the sacred with the beautiful or, rather, with the agreeable and the charming. For from this process arises, as Werner's performances prove, a lecherous mess, fit for balls and bawdy houses, which is likely to get worse.

March 7, 1808

Bettina Brentano to Goethe

Here in Frankfurt it is wet, cold, accursed, horrible. No good Christian would stay here, the winter would be unbearable, were it not for your mother. . . . But I have a rival at her house now, a squirrel which a handsome French soldier left behind him. The squirrel can do as he pleases; your mother calls him Johnny, and Johnny is quite free to gnaw the tables and chairs; he even ventured to sit down on her very best cap and nibble at its flowers and feathers. . . .

March 28, 1808

Elisabeth Goethe to August

> On his way to resume his studies at Heidelberg, August visited his grandmother.

Dear August, I write you by the earliest post, in order that you may know how things will be. You are not to lodge with strangers; your little room is ready. . . . You don't inconvenience me at all. Your father stayed in that room, so did your mother, so did you two years ago. . . . Your grandmother is in an *allegro* mood this winter,

though she has to wrap herself up in cotton wool against her mortal
enemy, the northeast wind, and has not been to the play for months.
But she does visit friends wrapped to the nose in furs and if this
continues you'll find me healthier than your dear mother did a year
ago.

Weimar, March 29, 1808

From the Diaries

August relieved of his worry over the tapeworm. Dined alone. You
cannot destroy Germans because, like the Jews, each one is an individual.

April 3, 1808

To Bettina Brentano

> Israel Jacobson had founded in 1801 a school for Jewish children in the
> town of Seesen which was to serve the cultural Germanization of Jews.
> The Christians of the town soon asked to have their children admitted
> to the school which increased in reputation. In 1926 it was incorporated
> in the educational system of the Weimar Republic; in 1928 it had 6000
> students.

I have received the documents you sent me concerning the philanthropic efforts of both Christians and Jews, and I thank you for them,
my dear little friend. It is a curious fact, that at this time, when so
many people are killed in battle, the rest are to be charmingly and
becomingly arrayed. Do continue from time to time to inform me
concerning these beneficent efforts in which you are interested. The
savior of the Jews from Brunswick [*Jacobson*] is to be praised for
regarding his people from an ideal angle, but the Prince Bishop is
not wholly to be blamed for regarding this people as it is and may remain for some time to come. Send me a description of the Frankfurt
gentleman who is concerned for the improvement of the condition of
the Jews. If the man's actions are as sensible as his writings, much
good is bound to result.
As for me, I commend to your philanthropic and pedagogical efforts
the bearer of this missive, a black-eyed, brown-haired youth. See to
it that the city of his fathers becomes a paternal city to him.

Jena, April 27, 1808

To Johanna Frommann

You will agree that poets are generally forgiven when they make un-
due use of their privilege of expressing their feelings toward a friend,
toward a beloved. Dark passages can be explained face to face. . . .
In this spirit I would recall the beautiful days spent together. An
opportunity to renew them may be found all the sooner, seeing that
Minnie's domestic genius prevails more and more. . . . Let us not
on that account cease to rejoice in the former occasions which remain our very own. If the messenger, by whom this reaches you,
brings me a significant word, I shall come over, however late.

On the way to Karlsbad, May 13, 1808

From the Diaries

Reflected on the way on the perverse erotic tendencies of certain
among our friends—on matters of aesthetics and poetry—on the
merits and prejudices of Voss and Schlegel—on the second part of
the drama of *Faust* and of the matters that will be treated in it.

Karlsbad, May 16, 1808

To Charlotte von Stein

A word from afar! Spring is just beginning here. I am very well and
I am sending you one pound of pins. It costs 2 Rhenish thaler
and 12 groschen. Not that I mean to charge you this trifle. But other
people might want to order the same commodity and brass wire is
very dear. Metal is no longer made into wire; it is needed for cannons.

Karlsbad, May 29, 1808

To Christiane

I was glad to get a letter from you so soon. It was the first I received.
Now, I suppose, you have the things I sent back by the coachman. I
hope the mineral waters will agree with you. . . .

This place is still quite empty. Except for the natives I have seen no one. But I spend many hours a day under the open sky, sometimes with Riemer, sometimes alone and so enjoy myself.

June 3, 1808

Elisabeth Goethe to Her Son

Dear Son, Your letter of May 9 gave me new life and joy. Yes, yes, thou shalt yet plant vines upon the mountains of Samaria.—We shall plant and shout! (Jeremiah 31, 5.) Whenever I hear good things concerning you the prophecies guarded in my heart rise up. God! He sustains our faith eternally. Hallelujah!!! God! This time too He will bless Karlsbad and the cure and continue to let me receive good news of you. . . . The first volume of your works does not leave my side. Were I to make a list of all therein that gives me heavenly delight, I would have to copy the entire volume. . . . Wherever one opens the book, the eye falls upon a masterpiece. . . .

Karlsbad, June 3, 1808

To August

The secretary of the post office handed me your letter of May 23 as I was on my way to drink the waters. . . .
We are living here in our accustomed manner quietly and industriously. We are practicing greater moderation in all things than we did last year, especially in the matter of wine. And so I am very happy to see from your letter that you too are being careful not to yield to the habit of drinking wine which is more harmful than is commonly thought to the leading of a thoughtful, cheerful, active life. I commend you, too, that you are taking only a few courses and . . . I am equally pleased that the subject matter of these courses is chiefly historical. . . .
It does give me pleasure to see that your own nature will cause you to adhere to this course of study, that I need not fear that you will become involved in those philosophical and religious eccentricities which, at this time, are addling so many good brains among us, and yet, in the end, result in nothing but an abstruse self-display. . . .

Karlsbad, June 15, 1808

To Christiane

I dare say you are not likely to object to the quiet life I lead among
my old flirtations here. At all events, you are bound to indemnify
yourself, of which I request a truthful account. It would be agreeable
if we decided to take a trip together this coming autumn.
I get a lot of pleasure out of August's letters. It's not so easy to be
alone in the world and to pay cash for everything, when at home
there are so many supports and excuses. But let him get along a little while longer; let him learn the value of money. Then, on some
extraordinary occasion, we can come to his help.
Which reminds me that you and I, when we meet again, had better
consider and plan anew our budgetary accounts which have been in
a state of disorder since October 14.

Karlsbad, June 22, 1808

To Reinhard

Schlegel's review of the early volumes of my works is the only thing
of his that I have read for a long time. It gave me a great deal of
pleasure. For, though I myself know best where the shoe pinches me,
yet it is always interesting to discourse about one's self with a man of
understanding and insight. An acute stranger, entering a house, will
often observe details which the master of the house overlooks or
ignores through habit or good nature . . . I was well pleased to hear
that the dedicatory stanzas to *Faust* have been found impressive.
For the sake of truth and to record my inner processes which, unless
I err, are often misunderstood, I must add that these stanzas were
written many years ago. They did not arise from the tribulations of
this time with which I am wont to come to terms in a much gayer
way. I have not failed to observe in the course of my life that the
public hardly ever grasps the true character of a poem and never
that of a poet. I came to this conclusion so early that I have come to
be amused by a degree of mystification.

Karlsbad, June, 1808

Recollections of Riemer

Goethe has been very well during our whole stay here. He is very productive. The *Masque of Pandora* is about half done. Other poetical works have been added, too. In due time they will see the light, first of all they will be read by the candlelight of the social hour of tea.

1808

SONG OF EPIMETHEUS

(From the Masque Pandora)

He who is doomed from the fair to be fleeing,
Let him depart with glances aside!
Deep in his heart are the flames of that seeing,
Drawn irresistibly back to abide.

Ask not thyself in the face of the sweetest:
Goeth she? Do I go? Grinding the pain
Prone upon earth in the breast that thou beatest,
Holding the heart that is broken in twain.

Weepest thou? Gazest through tears that are burning,
Tears that estrange her as though she were far:
Stay! 'Tis still possible! Infinite yearning
Makes to relent the implacable star.

Grasp her again! Feel of twoness the wonder,
Both in the losing and being possessed!
Until a bolt from heaven cleave you asunder,
Closer and closer the bosoms are pressed.

He who is doomed from the fair to be fleeing,
Let him depart with glances aside!
Deep in his heart are the flames of that seeing,
Drawn irresistibly back to abide.

July 1, 1808

Elisabeth Goethe to Her Son

Dear Son, The rest of your works arrived on June 29. All the volumes
have gone to the binder's and will be bound in half calf as hand-
somely as is befitting such masterpieces. Your dear little letter of
June 22 was a consoling and lovely and wondrous thing to me. May
God further bless your cure and let all the old ills fade, and praise
and thanks to Him shall not fail the while I breathe. . . . In this
season Frankfurt is thronged with tourists. 'Tis like a migration of
peoples. They come from as far away as Norway, and all are astonished by the beauty of the town, especially the environs. The old
walls have been torn down and the old gates leveled and the whole
city turned into a park. You think you're in fairyland and forget how
it used to look. Our elderly bigwigs would not have accomplished
this until doomsday. Let the sun but shine forth and the people
crowd beyond where the gates used to stand—Christians and Jews
together in the best possible order, which makes it the most moving
sight that eyes can see. And all this was done without expense to
any. . . .

Karlsbad, July 2, 1808

To Charlotte von Stein

I can quite imagine Mme. de Staël back in Weimar. Here they tell
me about her visit to Vienna. It's always the same thing. She carries
on in her own way, regardless of others. She arouses astonishment,
if not admiration; she displeases the women and leaves an ill reputation behind her which, however, does her no harm, for when she
returns, the whole business starts over again. . . .
Since the opportunity to send a package presents itself, I am sending
you the Pandora piece up to a certain point. . . .

Karlsbad, July 2, 1808

To Christiane

What will you say when I tell you that Riemer has found a charming affinity? She even has a carriage and horses and takes him driving.
I suppose I shall hear an account of your flirtations later on.

You mustn't let it trouble you that women spoke maliciously of you
to Mme. de Staël. That's the way the world is. Everyone grudges his
neighbor the latter's advantages, whatever they may be, and since he
cannot rob him of them, he minimizes them or denies them or reports the contrary. You just enjoy what fate has given you. You have
earned it. Try to preserve it! . . . I have been able to send you an
oilcloth bag by way of Leipzig. You will probably have received it by
now. Its contents are of no great value being, however, a couple of
smoked tongues of the very finest kind.

Karlsbad, August 7, 1808

To Christiane

If you can't recover your good humor, just remember the frightful
evils we have passed through and how much better off we are than
millions of our fellow men. Think of the melancholy case of the excellent Fritz von Stein, who just lost his young and handsome wife,
the only daughter of very wealthy parents. . . .
As far as I'm concerned, I am in no mood to leave here yet. I will
not easily work as well elsewhere, as I am doing here. I am not
needed in Weimar. In fact, the Duke wrote me most charmingly from
Teplitz that he wanted me to have as good a time as possible. . . .
I have been seduced into making some purchases. But you won't
blame me when I tell you that these purchases include a very beautiful fitted toilet case for you. I would have liked to send it on, but it is
too fragile for the rough way that packages are treated by the post.

Karlsbad, August 16, 1808

To Charlotte von Stein

The end of your letter, dearest friend, was, indeed, a painful contrast
to its agreeable beginning. With heartfelt regret I hear of the tragedy
of our dear Fritz. . . .
Let me thank you for your kind reception of *Pandora*. I was glad to
note that you marked certain passages. The whole is bound to affect
readers with a sense of mystery. They feel the nature of the whole,
without being able to explain it at all clearly, but their pleasure or
displeasure, their sympathy or disinclination will proceed from this
source. The passage, however, which a reader chooses for himself, is

the passage which has a personal meaning for him. Consequently the artist who, to be sure, must be primarily concerned for the form and meaning of the whole, is yet not displeased when specific passages are received with ease and pleasure.

Karlsbad, August 17, 1808

To August

As Michaelmas approaches, do write me your own view of your studies during the past semester; in what part of them you believe to have made progress, what you intend to take up during the coming winter. At the same time give me an accounting of your finances and an idea of your budget for the coming six months. I suppose I shall have to give you an extra allowance for travel and other unusual expenditures. . . .
Our Duke is in Teplitz and, I am told, very well. Werner is here. Of the great mass of visitors only your friends, the Poles and Jews, are left. Your mother was not so well pleased with Lauchstädt this year. It was probably too quiet for her taste. . . .
She probably returned to Weimar several days ago. Write her soon, unless you have already done so, and don't scribble so illegibly. The day is long enough. If you take one-third more time to write a letter, your correspondent will read it with pleasure, instead of having to take the trouble to practice the art of deciphering.

Karlsbad, August 28, 1808

Recollections of Riemer

Goethe's birthday. We talked about the modern novel, especially his own. He said: that his idea in his new novel *The Elective Affinities* was to show forth social relationships and the conflicts between them in symbolic concentration.
In the evening he spoke of the ancient and romantic concepts of tragedy. The antique notion is that of man under the tragic aspect. The romantic has neither nature nor spontaneity; it is made, sought after, unduly heightened, exaggerated, bizarre to the point of grimace and caricature. The antique is sober, modest, restrained; the modern quite unbridled and intoxicated. . . . The antique is plas-

tic, veracious, real; the romantic as delusive as the images in a magic lantern. . . .

All mortal poetry is still too characteristic to be pure in its objectivity, that is, too individualistic, not general enough. . . . We are entering a period of a heightened Hellenism. . . .

September 19, 1808

To Jakob Stock

> When Goethe returned home on September 17 he was met by a message that his mother had died four days before. Jakob Stock, magistrate and senator in Frankfurt, was one of his mother's closest friends.

Only the assurance that our beloved mother was surrounded by admirable and sympathetic friends sustained us in these recent times during which, considering our mortal fate, her great age made us fear her approaching end. Accept, then, our sincerest thanks for taking our place and for continuing your affectionate solicitude for her to the very close of her life. Transfer your kindness to us and have the goodness to guide us in the arrangements that must now ensue. So soon as we learn that the proper moment has arrived, my wife will set out and be glad, despite the sadness of the occasion, to renew her acquaintance with such worthy friends.

Bettina Brentano's Account of Elisabeth Goethe

Far as you dwelt from her and for so long, yet no one ever understood you better than did she. While scholars and philosophers and critics analyzed your works, she was a living example of how they were to be read. She often quoted passages from your books, so appositely, with tone and mien so noble that their vivid colors were reflected in my vision of the world, too, and all else receded into darkness. The song: "So let me stay bright, let me stay light" was her favorite and she often recited it. Each syllable had a majestic sound on her lips. Indeed, all musical settings seemed trivial compared to her recitation. Never did music seem so shabby to me as that used for your poems, after I had heard them from her lips. She interpreted this poem, saying that it alone proved how deep the

spirit of religion was in you, for in it you had described the only state
in which the soul can return to its Maker—without prejudices, without a sense of selfish deserts, out of pure yearning back to its creative source. . . . She said of this poem that it was the spirit of truth
and called it her confession of faith. . . .

She loved your son profoundly. The last time he was with her she
questioned him, whether he had the right love for his father. . . .
She talked to him for hours about you. . . . The day he left she was
very lively and told me many details of his amiability. . . . When,
leaving the house, he came to St. Catherine's Gate, the last point at
which she could see him from her window he waved his handkerchief. This moved her deeply. When, next day, her hairdresser came
and told her that he had met the young gentleman the day before,
who had commissioned him to give Mme. Councillor his love the
next morning, she was very happy and attributed this greeting to
August's loving heart.

October 2, 1808

Friedrich von Müller's Recollections of Wartime

> Friedrich Müller, 1779-1849, a member of the Weimar Judiciary, ren-
> dered vital service to the Duchy on the occasion of the meeting of
> princes in Erfurt in October, 1808. The assembly included in addition
> to Napoleon and the Czar, four kings and forty-three reigning princes.
> Karl August invited Goethe to attend. Müller remained a lifelong friend
> of Goethe. He was appointed Chancellor of the Duchy in 1815. Talley-
> rand, 1754-1838, was Napoleon's Minister of Foreign Affairs; Maret,
> 1763-1839, an associate of the same Ministry, Daru, 1767-1829, General
> of the French army, Berthier, 1753-1815, a Marshal of France, and
> Savary, Duke of Rovigo, 1744-1833, another General in the French army.

It was at Frau von der Recke's house that Goethe met the Minister
Maret and made a tremendous impression on him. Maret told the
Emperor about him, whereupon Napoleon invited Goethe to come
to see him promptly on October 2. The audience lasted almost an
hour. I conducted Goethe to the anteroom and there awaited his
return. Only Talleyrand, Berthier and Savary were present as the
audience began. Soon after Goethe entered the imperial study, General Daru went in, too.

The Emperor sat at a great round table eating his luncheon. At his
right stood Talleyrand and at his left Daru with whom, while he

was eating, he discussed the question of the Prussian indemnities.
He beckoned Goethe to approach and scrutinized him carefully and
asked him how old he was. When he was told that Goethe was in his
sixtieth year, he expressed his surprise at his vital appearance and
went on at once to the question of Goethe's tragedies. Daru took
occasion to expatiate on these and on Goethe's other works, empha-
sizing, too, that Goethe had translated the *Mohamet* of Voltaire.
"That's not a good play," said the Emperor. He assured Goethe that
he had read *Werther* seven times. To prove this fact he engaged in
a penetrating analysis of the book and asserted that in certain passages there was a confusion between the motives of wounded ambition and those of passionate love. He said that this was not according
to nature and weakens the reader's impression of the overwhelming
influence of love upon the protagonist. "Why did you do that?" he
asked. Goethe admitted Napoleon's reasoning to have been correct
and acute. On that occasion, however, he answered that no one had
hitherto made that criticism, correct as it was. . . . Coming back to
the question of the drama, Napoleon made some significant observations which proved that he followed dramatic literature with close
attention. . . . He spoke next of the so-called "Fate" tragedies now
current. He disapproved of them, saying that they belonged to a
darker age. "Why talk about fate? Politics are fate!" . . .
Suddenly Napoleon arose and approached Goethe and inquired in a
gentler voice after the poet's family and his relations with the various
members of the Ducal house. . . . But soon he came back to the
question of tragedy. He said: "Tragedy should be the school of kings
and nations; it is the highest product of the poet. You, for instance,
ought to write a tragedy on the death of Caesar in a manner worthy
of the subject, more nobly than did Voltaire. That could be the highest achievement of your life. . . . You should come to Paris! I definitely want you to do so. There you have a great vision of the world;
there you will find the richest material for your creative work."
Each time when he had finished what he had to say, he added:
"Qu'en dit Monsieur Goet'?"
As Goethe was withdrawing, the Emperor was heard to say emphatically to Berthier and Daru: *"Voilà un homme!"*

Erfurt, October 4, 1808

To Christiane

> With her friend, Karoline Ulrichs, who later married Riemer, Christiane
> had gone to Frankfurt in order to settle the Goethe estate there.

Before I leave Erfurt I must say to you that I am glad you made me
go. I didn't manage to see the play; afterwards, however, everything
turned out very well indeed. I had an audience with the Emperor
who conversed with me graciously and at length. Now there will be
festivities in Weimar; I wish you could be present. Sometimes I'm
annoyed that you insisted on taking this trip. Then again I think: it
will come out all right, as so much has recently done. . . .

October 12, 1808

To Christiane

Be prudent and gentle in everything you do, so that you may gain
and keep friends. When the division of effects is made, write me. Let
nothing be sold. It might be a good idea to rent a modest lodging
not far from the playhouse and to furnish it. One has to think of
all kinds of things. It would be a pleasant place for you for some part
of the year, and we could even be together there. Because in the end,
we'll both get tired of Karlsbad and Lauchstädt.

October 16, 1808

To Christiane

At last, my dear child, I am able to send you the power of attorney.
You will find me described in that document as a Knight of the
Order of St. Anne. The Emperor also conferred on me the Cross of
the Legion of Honor. So when you come back you will find me all be-
starred and be-ribboned. I hope you will keep on loving me. The
incident showed me how many friends I have, because so many people showed their pleasure. The pretty girls at Court were most charming and told me how becoming the decorations were and there was
no end of flirtations.

October 16, 1808

Recollections of Karoline Sartorius

The wife, ?-1830, of Georg Sartorius, 1765-1828, professor of history
at Göttingen.

Goethe had saved up his loveliest gifts, his poems, for our last evening together. He appeared at the supper table with a handful of
papers. He put them down beside his plate in brilliant good humor.
After supper he began to read to us and also to recite poems by heart.
It lasted till 1 o'clock at night, and he surpassed himself. . . . He
recited to us certain sonnets, none of which has yet been printed.
They were all beautiful, but it seemed to me that those were most
beautiful in which he let the girl speak. Nothing exists comparable to
the delicacy of these, as perhaps there has never been a poet with so
deep an insight into the soul of woman.

November 7, 1808

To August

. . . I heard with great pleasure that you left Frankfurt reasonably
recovered from your illness, because the news of your indisposition
worried me greatly. I hope that nothing will prevent you from carry-
ing out your good resolutions during the coming winter. . . .
When you have registered for your courses, write and tell me what
they are and how you get along in them. I thoroughly approve of
what you have already told me. . . .
It is quite quiet here now, yet not truly tranquil. There are always
visitors and the theatre never ceases to play me tricks. Tell your
mother that I am reserving a number of things until her return, especially the arrangements for the meeting of the choral society in our
house. These are matters that need to be discussed. . . .

November 25, 1808

To Knebel

My wife is back from Frankfurt, where she was kind enough to ad-
just smoothly and generously the matters of inheritance that arose on
the death of my good mother. She sends her greetings to you and

yours and hopes to be your hostess here from time to time, for she
will hardly be able to get to Jena this winter. . . .
Frau Schopenhauer's Thursday and Sunday receptions are both interesting, each in its way. . . .

December 5, 1808

To August

Since your dear mother saw you in Frankfurt and afterwards visited
you in Heidelberg, I almost feel as though you and I had met. . . .
I am glad to hear of your industry and I think you do well to request
semiannual reports from your teachers. It amounts to a tacit but
praiseworthy guarantee that you will continue in your present
course. . . .
Mother and Karoline have told me much that is agreeable about the
neatness of your room, about your birds, about the woman who
waits on you and other such matters. . . . Mother tells me, too, that
you're embarrassed by the redness of your cheeks, especially as there
are people who assert that a high color is not necessarily a sign of
sound health. I hope that you have a better understanding of this
favor which nature has granted you and that you will continue to
live in such a manner as not to forfeit it.

December 5, 1808

To J. J. Willemer

I can quite understand that, despite the goods that fortune has
showered upon you, you are sometimes in a painful situation. . . .
Those people are usually best off who demand nothing but what the
world and nature give them; they have an advantage over those
others who demand of themselves and their fellows a higher culture
and in whom has been implanted the foretaste of nobler delights.

Late December, 1808

Recollections of O. L. B. Wolff

Writer, and improvisatore, ?-1851.

In her speech and her whole character Christiane was thoroughly
Thuringian and remained so to the end. To take care of the father

of her children and to make him physically as comfortable as possible was the chief purpose of her life which she pursued most zealously. In all other matters she resisted all attempts to change her and retained her original ways and manners. "Is it credible," Goethe once said to friends with a sort of antique serenity, "that this creature has lived with me for twenty years? But that's just what I like about her, that she has given up no part of her character and remains as she was."

Late December, 1808

Recollections of F. von Müller

With Goethe from 5 to 7:30. He said: I am studying the older French literature quite thoroughly again in order to be able to communicate seriously with the French. What infinite cultural values they experienced at a time when we Germans were still rude oafs. Germany is nothing, but every individual German has high value, and yet they imagine the contrary to be true. The Germans should be scattered and resettled all over the world like the Jews in order to develop for the weal of all nations the great mass of goodness that lies in them.

1809

January 27, 1809

To Marie Anna Louise Nicolovius

Your friendly letter, my dear niece, has lain here for long unanswered. I am a very poor correspondent and between us there exists the further difficulty that we have never seen each other or, at least, not for very long, and one's personality is the foundation of human relationships. To be sure, I have heard much that is dear and good of you; if ever we were to meet, you might find that you could get along with your uncle, too. Let me thank you meanwhile for the description of your dear family, whose diminution I sincerely regret. Our good mother left us far, far too early, yet may we be comforted by the serenity of her age and by her fortitude and independence under the pressures of this period. I thank you and your dear husband for desiring to establish a new bond at a time when old ones are dissolved.

February 28, 1809

Recollections of J. D. Falk

"The sciences," he said to me on February 28, 1809, "have become far
too highly stratified. The professors in our universities forcibly
stretch the individual disciplines according to semiannual groups of
lectures. True inventions are few, especially when one makes up a
list extending through a couple of centuries. Most of what is taught
is but a repetition of what some famous predecessor has professed.
There is next to no independent knowledge. The young men are
herded into rooms and lecture halls and, in the poverty of concrete
subject matter are fed with quotations and words." . . .
"The custom is prevalent among us to let the sciences go to seed as a
mere means of earning a man's bread or else to have them formally
pulled to pieces from the professorial chairs, so that we have no
choice but between a shallow popularization on the one hand and an
incomprehensible mess of transcendental jargon on the other. The
only subject which has recently been excellently cultivated in my
special sense is that of electricity." . . .

April 28, 1809

To Charlotte von Stein

I am forwarding to you, my dear friend, a letter from August which
will entertain you. Do show it to Frau von Schiller. Tomorrow I
mean to find out again how things look in Jena.

May 19, 1809

To Riemer

I look upon the incident of yesterday as not altogether futile. The
evil temper to which you yield from time to time was bound, sooner
or later, to lead to such a scene. I confess to you that you put my patience to an extreme test. Yet now, that the evil did reach a breaking
point and that this unhappy experience teaches you how far we may
be led, I am willing to resume my calm and try to let us continue together. However, I must impose upon you the duty of self-control
and also ask you to think of establishing yourself independently, that
is, to look about for such an office as you can honorably fill, were it
only to develop within yourself the conviction, that every situation in

life demands a definite activity on our part, and that our work and usefulness depend on our meeting the needs of others in a regular and responsible fashion.

May 24, 1809

Recollections of Friedrich Kohlrausch

A private tutor in noble families, 1780-1867.

. . . This was the first period of fighting between the French and the Austrians in the Danube Valley, and we young people were enthusiastic over the uprising of the Austrian people. . . . We reported the victories that had been won. "Yes, yes," said Goethe, shaking his head, "the fire is lit among our Germans for once; now we shall see how long the store of wood will hold out. Look, if you are at a show where a magician performs his tricks and announces that he is going to put your watch in a mortar and crush it with his pestle and yet give it back to you in perfect condition, I'll wager that he will perform the trick successfully. And just so I have been betting on Napoleon up to now; he knows this business better than the others."

Jena, May 30, 1809

To Charlotte von Stein

I hear from Knebel, dearest friend, that we'll see you here on Thursday. Nevertheless I don't want the messenger to leave today without a long overdue word to you. There is, alas, not much to be said about me. I make no great demands on the physical side of existence, but if I can't even be creatively active when I go out into the wilderness, a certain impatience in me would seem pardonable. Yet, as of old, I have prevailed by sheer patience and have within the last few days made some progress on *The Elective Affinities.* I was, of course, encouraged by the reception of the first half. . . .

Jena, May 30, 1809

To Christiane

Do your very best to let nothing annoy me during the coming week. I am at work on *The Elective Affinities* in a way I have not been able to be for a year. If I were to be disturbed now, everything would be lost of what I see straight before me and can achieve in a short time. Let me repeat, my child, let nothing even approach me for a week. All our affairs are in order. As a reward we will think of you and send you, from time to time, a fish or a good piece of venison, that you may enjoy it in peace and let nothing trouble you.

Jena, June 1, 1809

To Zelter

Since it is not advisable to go to Karlsbad yet, I withdrew to Jena where I am trying to finish a novel which I conceived and started last year in the Bohemian mountains. I shall probably be able to publish it later this very year. I am the more eager to do so because it will be a means of communication between me and my friends abroad. I hope that you will find all my old characteristics in it. I have put a great deal into it and also hidden certain things in it. May the not too obscure secret delight you, too.

Jena, June 6, 1809

To Charlotte von Stein

The shawl you sent me, for which I thank you most warmly, is so admirable that I scarcely dare draw it over my shoulders. It should be preserved as a model of its kind.

It was so kind of you to come and see us the other day and cheer our loneliness. I can't say that being solitary made me happy this time. For in spite of the fair weather and the green plains and hills and the blossoming gardens and many other good ingredients of life, everything about me in Jena lies so in ruins compared to other days and, ere one is aware, one stumbles over one of those mounds under which some fragment of one's past lies buried.

But perhaps it is by reason of these very circumstances that I am the more dependent on myself and that my work progresses well. I have conquered the chief difficulty and if I look neither to the right nor to the left for another two weeks, this curious undertaking will be safe.

August 1, 1809

To the Court Theatre Commission

Our Commission, as is but fair, refuses to interfere in any matter beyond what pertains to the theatre. But when a man gives his wife a couple of black eyes on the very evening on which she is cast to play the juvenile lead, the matter becomes the business of the theatre in a very high degree. We should therefore take this occasion to give notice that any actor who beats his wife will be turned over by this Commission to police headquarters.

August 11, 1809

To the Secretary of the Court Theatre Commission

The enclosed letter of Demoiselle E. is to be handed over to the Ducal authorities and Herr R. is to be cross-examined concerning the charge made in this letter. This fellow who continues to think he is a comedian and does not seem to grasp what it is to be a member of the Court Theatre of Weimar, should now be taken by the scruff of the neck and transferred to the guard house. For as things stand today his wife has her beatings and Demoiselle E. had to take his insults and the Ducal Commission might as well not exist.

If a kind fate reassembles us next fall, no misbehavior of this kind, God willing, will go unpunished. It often seems to me to be true of our theatre as well as of our university, that the world acts as though it were made for the ruffians and the insolent, while the well-behaved and sensible people have to beg to be kept, for God's sake, in their little jobs.

Jena, September 20, 1809

To Christiane

I need at least another week to get straightened out with what I plan to do. Not only must everything that concerns the printing of the novel be cleared up, but I must also catch up with letters long overdue, as well as with other things. If you and August have a good time together, remember that I shall spend the next few days in an effort to be with you soon without interruption. Meanwhile I beg of you emphatically to keep all visitors away from me; there is no piece of business that cannot be settled in writing.

I want August to keep calm, even though the lack of his wardrobe annoys him. As soon as he can go out at all and before he goes anywhere else, he is to pay a visit to the Councillor Voigt and to make a good impression on him not by words but by excellent behavior.

Jena, September 26, 1809

To Voigt

I am told that my August has arrived at home. He came on foot from Würzburg with just a small knapsack. It's a nice way these young people have. He is now waiting for his wardrobe to arrive; so soon as he can show himself, he'll pay you a visit. Be so kind as to subject him to the very briefest examination.

It's a curious thing to have one's son engage in a profession which is really not the father's at all. Yet it may have its advantages. On the one hand it may seem to tend to separation; on the other hand, a bond is bound to supervene because, in the last analysis, all sane and sensible things coincide.

Jena, October 1, 1809

To Zacharias Werner

. . . The novel has now been printed and I herewith commend it to your friendly attention. . . . You know me well enough to know that we can always pursue a stretch of life's road together pleasantly, wherever our paths may cross; only be careful not to make traps of the crown of thorns and strew them at my feet. Let me pursue in quietness that path which I have made and swept clean for myself, and accompany me along it when the opportunity presents itself. . . .

Jena, October 5, 1809

To Alexander von Humboldt

The brother of Wilhelm, 1769-1859, naturalist, traveler, and stylist, author of *Cosmos*.

The letters of Professor Voigt in which he tells me of your generous reception of him and of his happiness at finding himself among the treasures of Paris, renew my desire to share that experience. But since that desire is not likely to be fulfilled, let me at least send something of mine to you, that is to say, a little novel that has just been completed. I know that you will give it a friendly reception, seeing that in it your name is pronounced by lovely lips. What you have achieved so far transcends mere prose that an imaginative work may well dare during your own lifetime to reckon you among its heroes.

October 21, 1809

To Knebel

My August is looking forward with great eagerness to Jena. Permit him to be your guest from time to time. I trust that he will prove no unpleasant companion this winter.

I am not sending you the second part of my novel. You may scold me even more violently than you did over the first part. If it should fall into your hands in spite of me, I at least will be innocent. We poor authors are great sufferers, and it is an old story that our presentation copies are usually the ones that bring most trouble upon us. . . .

November 3, 1809

To Bettina Brentano

There is no point, dear Bettina, in trying to compete with you. You surpass all your friends in word and deed, in kindness and gifts, in love and entertainment. All one can do is to accept your bounty and to send you in return as much love as possible, even though that love be silent. Your recent letters have been truly delightful. They remind me of a period in which I was perhaps even madder than you are now but certainly happier and better than I have since become.

November 4, 1809

Recollections of Oehlenschläger

On this visit Goethe received me courteously, but so coldly as though I were a complete stranger. . . . I tried to suppress my grief and I did hope that, if I could read my drama *Correggio* to him, the old kindliness would come again. But nothing came of it! When I sent word by Riemer, that I had written a new tragedy and would like to read it to him, he sent me the reply that I was to give him the manuscript and he would gladly read it.—I said: "He can't read it himself; I have nothing but a badly written first draft full of changes and corrections." Nevertheless I gave Riemer the manuscript. He brought it back and said, of course Goethe couldn't read it. I'd better have it printed; then he would read it. That hurt me but I tried to control myself and be cheerful. Twice Goethe invited me very courteously to dine at his house. Since I could not be simple and cordial, I was bold and ironic. Among other things I recited some epigrams on well-known authors, quite unfit to print. Goethe said quite comfortably: "You shouldn't do such things. He who can produce good wine should not brew vinegar." "Didn't you brew vinegar enough?" I asked. To which he answered: "Why the devil should you think it right just because I did it?"

December 10, 1809

Riemer's Diaries

Among the other criticisms which the Philistine reviewers addressed to *The Elective Affinities* was this, that the book did not make visible the conflict between duty and inclination. Goethe's comment to me was the following: "The conflict takes place behind the scenes, but it is made clear that it must have taken place. The characters behave like civilized people; despite their inner conflict they observe an outer decorum. A moral struggle is never a fit object of aesthetic representation. For either morality triumphs or is defeated. In the first case, there is no reason to represent it; in the contrary case it is shameful to be the direct witness. . . . In all such delineations the sensual triumphs; but its triumph is avenged by fate, that is, by the moral principle which rescues its own freedom by death. Thus Werther had to shoot himself after the senses had become his master. Thus Ottilie and Eduard had to perish after they had given free rein to their inclination. Therein consists the triumph of the moral principle.

December 13, 1809

Wilhelm Grimm to His Brother Jakob

Wilhelm, 1786-1859, and Jakob, 1784-1863, the philologists and folklorists, universally known by their fairy tales.

I was kept waiting for some time. Then he entered all in black with the stars of his two decorations on and his hair lightly powdered. I had seen his picture again and again, and yet I was amazed at the nobility, perfection, simplicity and kindness of his countenance. He bade me sit down and conversed in a most friendly way. . . . He spoke of the *Lay of the Nibelungen,* of Old Norse poetry which seemed to him bizarre and rigid and unpalatable, of Oehlenschlager and of certain older novels that he had been reading. I stayed almost an hour. He was so kind and cordial that I almost forgot his greatness. But whenever he was silent and after I had left, I reflected again on his goodness of heart and his lack of arrogance in talking so freely with so humble a person as myself.

December 14, 1809

Wilhelm Grimm to His Brother Jakob

Next day I was invited for dinner. There were present his wife, who is a very common-looking person, a pretty young girl whose name I didn't catch but whom, it seems to me, he introduced as his niece, and Riemer. The meal was extremely luxurious: paté de foie gras, roast hare and similar dishes. He was even friendlier than on the day before and talked a great deal and constantly invited me to drink more wine by pointing to the bottle and growling softly, which is quite a habit that he has. It was excellent red wine; he did full justice to it and his wife even more. . . . The meal lasted from 1 o'clock until 3:30. Then he arose and bowed, whereupon Riemer and I left.

December, 1809

Recollections of Varnhagen von Ense

Miscellaneous writer and husband of Rahel Levin, 1785-1858.

Goethe said: "They call me a pagan! Didn't I have Gretchen executed and Ottilie starve herself to death? Isn't that Christian enough for them? Do they want anything more Christian?"

Late December

Recollections of Heinrich Laube

One of the founders of the Young Germany literary movement. He knew several of Goethe's contemporaries in their old age. 1806-1884.

A woman friend of mine said to Goethe at that time: "I cannot approve of *The Elective Affinities,* Herr von Goethe; it really is an immoral book!" According to her report Goethe was silent for a while and had then said with great earnestness: "I'm sorry you feel that way. It is my best book, and don't think that this is the mere whim of an aging man. I grant you that one loves most deeply the child of one's last marriage, the product of one's late power of generation. But you wrong both me and the book. The principle illustrated in the book is true and it is not immoral. But you must regard it from a broader point of view and understand that the conventional moral norms can turn into sheer immorality when applied to situations of this character."

December 30, 1809

To Charlotte von Stein

Since I am still confined to the house, though not to my room, I would close the year with something truly agreeable. And so, dear friend, do come tomorrow to our little session of music. Much that is lovely will be played.

December 31, 1809

To Reinhard

I really sent out *The Elective Affinities* as a circular to my friends. . . . If the general public reads the little book, too, well and good. I know to whom I addressed it and who will understand it. . . .
The public, especially the German public, is a silly caricature of the *demos* of the ancients. It really imagines itself to be a sort of court or senate and to be able to eliminate from both life and literature whatever does not please it. Against this there is no means but silent persistence. . . . When the crying and striving comes to an end in the course of the years, it will be seen that the contents of the little book will have become an unchangeable fact in the life of the imagination. . . . For what has been created takes its place as equal to what has happened.

From the Supplementary Confessions

During this year certain efforts pointed to the future. These were the preliminary preparations toward an autobiography [*Poetry and Truth*]. Great care and circumspection were necessary in making the strange plan of reconstituting the far-off days of youth. Yet finally the plan was determined upon and the decision made to be as sincere toward oneself and others, and to stick as closely to the truth, as recollection would permit.

1810

February 21, 1810

To Reinhard

I look about for something to send you and venture to add to the first part of my *Theory of Colors,* the second part. . . . When I look into these pages, it sometimes seems to me that I am getting older and . . . say what may be the right thing at the wrong time, which always seems silly to common-sense. I am glad that you accept the character of Ottilie, which is so dear to me, in so genuine and understanding a spirit, and that you are altogether fair to Eduard. He seems to me an entirely precious person, because he loves *absolutely.* . . .

Jena, March 30, 1810

To Christiane

August is rejoining you. I take pleasure in him in more ways than one, and yet there is something rather curious about the whole business. After some reflection it is clear that his stay in Heidelberg was much more satisfactory to me than his stay in Jena. About this business here there is something that I can only call higgledy-piggledy. I don't want to spoil his summer and you don't have to let on that I said so. But if this business continues, he'll have to go somewhere else next semester, whether it be Göttingen or another place. There's lots of time to discuss all this. But I tell you about it now, because I don't want to keep it from you any longer.

Jena, April 10, 1810
To the Court Theatre Commission

On the 9th of May, the anniversary of Schiller's death, which happens to fall on a Wednesday, I want a memorial evening. Scenes from *Wallenstein, The Maid of Orleans, The Bride of Messina, Mary Stuart* and *Wilhelm Tell* are to be presented. The *finale* is to be the masque of the *Song of the Bell.* My epilogue to that poem, augmented by several stanzas, is then to be recited. I would like to receive from Herr Genast his ideas and further proposals toward this plan. . . .

Jena, April 27, 1810
To Lotte Schiller

My dear and understanding friend, Inner obstacles have to be overcome to speak out after so long a silence. But your kind words demand it of me and I can no longer preserve that silence. In recent times we have been confined to painful efforts and have done what had to be done. But there was no joy in it except that it didn't have to be done over. Thus beautiful days, even very beautiful ones, dragged on without inner satisfaction or the hope of an outer one. . . . So forgive me for being rather brief. I'll be kept busy here for still a few weeks. Then I shall hasten to get to Karlsbad at the earliest moment. . . . Meanwhile I must see my family in Weimar, for I find it necessary to get rid of certain hypochondriacal influences. Fancy, for instance, that for some time past the greatest pleasure I have had is to write poems which are so obscene that I cannot even read them out loud! That is, you must admit, a pathological condition, which one should get rid of as soon as possible. Farewell. Think of me and forgive me.

Jena, April 17, 1810
To Christiane

Our business here is getting along quite well. What drives me to distraction is the food. I don't exaggerate when I tell you that for the past four or five days I have lived exclusively on cervelat sausage, bread and red wine. And I don't see any way out of this business, although it's going to end by upsetting my health. I would have come over, but business makes that impossible. Therefore I request you most insistently to send me something good, some roast, by every messenger—a leg of lamb, a capon, even a turkey, *let it cost what it may,* so that we have something for breakfast, for supper, even for dinner, when that is too bad. Something, above all, that has nothing to do with pig. I can't tell you how annoyed and angry I have been this whole time. The expense has been excessive and unseemly and I have had either to go hungry or to eat things that are obviously harmful.

Jena, April 29, 1810

Recollections of Riemer

Walking in the park with Goethe we met Frau Frommann and Minnie. There were women in the gardens picking flowers. Goethe said that they looked and acted like sentimental she-goats.

Jena, May 14, 1810

To Reinhard

The portfolio spoken of contained drawings toward the plan of restoring and completing the Cathedral of Cologne. They were sent by Sulpiz Boisserée of Cologne, 1783-1851, a wealthy historian and collector of mediaeval art.

The portfolio of drawings was given me in Jena. It gave me much pleasure. Let me add a brief comment. . . .
The efforts of this young man which gave rise to the drawings in question are most praiseworthy. He has done a thorough piece of work and the plan for the restoration of the Cathedral is one of the most fascinating things I have seen in years. The outline in perspective gives one a clear idea of the fantastic character of so vast an undertaking and makes one seem to see the legend of the Tower of Babel become a reality on the banks of the Rhine. . . . I do not at all blame these young people for steeping themselves into that period of the Middle Ages. Indeed, I recognize the phenomenon as inevitable and abstain from any pragmatic observation or historical prophecy.

Jena, May 15, 1810

To Lotte Schiller

Your very sweet letter came at an early morning hour and refreshed me. . . . I dare hardly hope to see you in the immediate future. . . . If you want to do me a kindness during my approaching absence, do be agreeable to my family which I am forced to leave longer than is quite fair. See to it that my wife has the privilege of making the acquaintance of Frau von Humboldt and give my kind regards to that dear friend whom, alas, I will not be able to see in my passage through Weimar. All my warmest greetings to Frau von Wolzogen! Preparing to leave here, I am working for all my friends. The day will soon come when you will have to go a-wandering with the same old Wilhelm Meister and meet in his company many earthly and heavenly saints. . . . Since I don't know if I'll get to see Cotta, I'm enclosing a note to him.

Jena, May 16, 1810

To Charlotte von Stein

This summer or, rather, when I set out on my wanderings, I will busy myself with those of Wilhelm Meister. On his way he will probably run into some charming girls, whom I am bringing up in secret. My immediate favorite, whom I recommend to you, is the nut-brown maid. . . .
I shall not be wholly silent from Karlsbad. Let me hear from you, too. . . . If you want to do me a real kindness, be good in my absence to my family, which I am once again abandoning for longer than is fair.

Early June, 1810

From the Diaries

A man who writes his confessions is in great danger of becoming a pitiable object, since it is one's tendency to confess only to one's morbidness and sinfulness, and never to one's virtue.

June 19, 1810

Christiane to Goethe

Dear, kind Privy Councillor, Your dear letter written in your own hand and your beautiful shawl made me very happy, because I have never had such a lovely beautiful shawl all my life. The little kerchief is wonderful, too. When we were unpacking my friend and I screamed so loud with joy that August had to ask us to be quiet, so that he could write the receipt for the postman. . . .

Yesterday we took August and my brother to the shooting pavilion and ate there. After dinner the whole Court turned up, except Her Highness, the Duchess, who went back to Jena right after dinner because the little Princess is still ill.

Karlsbad, June 27, 1810

To a Ducal Chamberlain

Your Honor has pleased me sincerely by the information imparted. If the orchestral director in question continues as at present he will be a source of profit and delight to both the Court, the public and to art itself. . . . The use of the waters has been very serviceable to me again and cured me of those convulsive evils, from which I suffered in Jena without saying much about them. I hope that our good Prince will soon arrive in Teplitz and find the benefit he seeks.

The presence of the Empress here [*Maria Ludovica of Austria*] has created quite a stir among us, although she embarrasses no one and is most agreeable and cordial. . . .

At the moment I prefer the novel above all forms of writing. Everything that is disadvantageous to the playwright benefits the novelist.

From the Supplementary Confessions

My stay in Karlsbad this year assumed a character all its own. My passion for nature and for drawing after nature left me completely. Nothing of this kind seemed to succeed. I was equally weary of the geological studies which I had formerly pursued among these familiar hills. In the company of friends of both sexes bent upon enjoyment I yielded to the distractions which stole away the days.

Karlsbad, July 3, 1810

To *Christiane*

Since the departure of the Empress, I have restricted my social life.
And anyhow the people who came here for the early season and most
of my acquaintances are gone. Of course, among so many people an
old acquaintance is bound now and then to turn up and something
interesting happens from time to time. No chance at flirtation at all.
The presence of the Empress will have been to my advantage. It has
been confided to me that she wants to confer some distinction upon
me. . . . Don't tell anybody anything. We'll wait and see. . . . You
did not acknowledge the receipt of the dried truffles and mushrooms
which were sent to you packed in a flat box.

Karlsbad, July 19, 1810

To *Georg Sartorius*

I have been lucky here in Karlsbad. For eight weeks I have heard
nothing about German literature or any branch of knowledge or of
science, nor seen a newspaper nor a play. And so I feel as though I
have been living in a golden age, in a paradise without prejudice or
sin. . . . Zelter is here and perhaps his presence will contribute to
an old desire of mine, namely, to gain some insight into the theory
of music from my point of view. . . .

Karlsbad, July 22, 1810

To *Reinhard*

It is beyond question that it is difficult for any individual to hide
himself completely behind the mask of a book that he has written.
On the contrary, the author is perhaps more recognizable from his
work than from his living person, since each one of us cuts the
world to the measure of his soul. . . .
As I see it, you cannot write history from a moral point of view.
Where the moral yardstick fits, it is very well; where it is inadequate,
the work must be so, too, and the intention of the historian is
obscure. . . . In Vienna appeared in pamphlet form a thing called
Pandora. It is but the fragment of a drama, strange in content and
odd in form. I commend it to your attention. . . .

Karlsbad, August 1, 1810

To Christiane

I don't doubt but what you're meeting old and new flirts. I wish you luck. Make as many friends as possible. This place is continuously curious and confused and sometimes ends by irritating me. . . . You know my way of gradually accomplishing something. Even if nothing is actually written on a given day, yet something is being prepared and then suddenly the right moment sets in. I have many projects that preoccupy me.

At last I have a fairly sensible letter from August. He seems also to pursue his own path and gradually to learn a little something. . . . I've bought some little things for him and am sending them on to him at a convenient moment. Beyond that I have done no shopping. The rise and fall of the value of paper money and the simultaneous rise in prices are so confusing that you never know whether anything is cheap or dear. I did buy some additional pins and needles. I haven't yet seen a better-looking shawl than the one I sent you.

Teplitz, August 11, 1810

To Christiane

I must tell you an adventure I had. I had just moved into my new quarters and was quietly sitting in my room. Suddenly the door opens and a young woman bursts in. I thought that one of my fellow lodgers had made a mistake. But it was Bettina who threw her arms around me and is just the same as when we knew her. She is on her way with friends to Berlin and at the moment is passing through here to go to Prague. She's leaving tomorrow. She told me infinite stories of old and new adventures. But I dare say that in the end she will marry Arnim. I've already taken a few baths and they agree with me. The Duke's condition varies. Zelter is always the same. His companionship makes me very happy.

Teplitz, August 22, 1810

A Prussian General to the Wife of a Poet

I see Goethe daily at the lodgings of the Duke and I can't tell you how strangely he pleases me. I have never met a human being who seemed to benefit my very soul so deeply. I cannot look at him without a smile of pleasure! There is no one to whom I would rather speak and there is no one before whom I feel so humble and at the same time tempted to cheekiness now and then. For out of one of his eyes looks an angel and out of the other a devil, and his speech is a profound irony upon all mortal things. . . . It is amusing to see how the old master treats people who try to get to him on account of his fame and to persuade him to make common cause with their onesidedness. Thus one day the lexicographer J. H. Campe accosted him and said a lot of handsome things to him in elaborate sentences devoid of words of foreign derivation. In reply Goethe addressed to the purist the simple question: "How do you like the esprit of this place?" Could anyone have been more subtly malicious? . . . Goethe speaks softly and restrainedly but with incredible assurance and a brilliancy of glance which contrasts oddly enough with his tranquil and measured words.

Teplitz, August 30, 1810

To Knebel

I can give you a good report of myself. The waters of Teplitz seem to do me good. I assure you it was necessary. I came away from Karlsbad jangled and depressed. The wretched weather there during two whole weeks contributed not a little to spoil the place for me, much as I love it. . . . I have made a very interesting acquaintance here in the person of the King of Holland. We live in the same house. . . . I have been with him a number of times. He is very friendly and very confiding. . . .

Summer, 1810

Recollections of Falk

We talked about Kleist again. What Goethe finds fault with is the Nordic sharpness and excess of this hypochondriac. It seems to him impossible for a mature understanding to enter with pleasure into the violent motivations which Kleist employs. . . . And ever again he returned to the serenity, the charm, the significant gaiety in contemplation used by the authors of the Italian *novelle* which were his great delight during this dark political period. In connection with that he reminded us of the circumstance that precisely the blithest of these tales arose in that dark hour when the plague swept over the city in which they were written.

September, 1810

Recollections of an Austrian Nobleman

Goethe was quite simply dressed. He wore boots and a round hat and displayed his decorations. His black hair is beginning to turn gray. He has a high, somewhat receding, forehead, like Homer and all the great poets. His head, rather narrow than broad, is slightly pointed at the top. His ever moving eyes are black and handsome. His countenance is longish and furrowed, the nose is that of an eagle. His ways and words are manly, serious, almost dry. He speaks of quite ordinary things in a quite ordinary way and does so intentionally.

October 8, 1810

To Karl August

Your Serenity will forgive me for a most humble request, the gracious granting of which would fill me with a deep sense of gratitude, the refusal of which I would accept in a spirit of cheerful devotion. The matter concerns my son August who is about to attain his twenty-first year and for whom I would beg of you the office of an Assessor of the Ducal Chamber. . . .
I confess to you that what may seem to you a premature request is due to the painful position in which my son finds himself in Jena. You are aware of the existence among the students of those various associations which, be they regional or secret societies or clubs for the instituting of dances and drinking bouts, all exist in a constant state of mutual quarrelsomeness which leads to actual outbreaks of violence. We discipline them but cannot get rid of them. Without hiding it from me my son experienced all this business in Heidelberg. In consideration of my position and his own, he has abstained from any such involvement in Jena. Hence he is completely isolated and

is considered an enemy by all the parties. However prudent his behavior may be, his situation is bound to be uncomfortable and
dangerous. . . .
It is for this reason that I beg Your Serenity to grant him this favor
so early. So soon as he is no longer a student, all these temptations
are removed. He can spend his evenings in the company of professors,
Ducal functionaries, merchants and other initiates of the seriousness
of life. . . .

October 25, 1810

To Bettina Brentano

. . . Instead of telling you how I fare, of which nothing worth while
is to be said, I'm going to ask you to do me a very real favor. Since
you are fond of writing to me and since I shall always be glad to hear
from you, we might turn this fact to very good account. I might as
well tell you that I am about to write my Confessions. I don't know
yet whether the result will be a novel or a history. In either case I
need your assistance. My good mother is no longer with us, nor are
many others who could help me to recall that past, so much of which
I have forgotten. Now you did live quite a long time with my dear
mother. You heard from her time and again her favorite stories and
anecdotes and you cherish them, I know, in a fresh and vivid
memory. So please sit down at once and record whatever concerns me
and my family. You will infinitely delight and oblige me. Love me
till we meet again! . . .

October 26, 1810

Recollections of Lotte Schiller

There was a great ball tonight. The master turned up with his son,
who has just been made an assessor of the Ducal Chamber, and a
most amusing situation occurred. His carriage was announced before
the supper and I accepted his invitation to be driven home. When we
got to the head of the stairs he asked me to forgive him for walking
so slowly; since noon he had been in perfect torment from his new
shoes which had been made for him by a shoemaker in Dresden.
Wasn't it hilarious that he should have picked just me to drive home
who was suffering the same way from my new shoes from Paris. We
fairly howled.

November 6, 1810

To F. C. Perthes

Founder of the publishing firm in Gotha which, in the nineteenth century, issued the Almanach de Gotha, 1749-1816.

I acknowledge with thanks the four specimen copies of the periodical you have founded. Regretfully I must decline to participate in so well-intentioned a venture. My great concern must be to concentrate my efforts in order to be equal to my obligations. Moreover, the age is of such a character that I always prefer to let a long span of time elapse before speaking to or of what is contemporary. For this reason I want you to forgive me for declining your invitation. I shall be glad to learn that your undertaking succeeds.

October 12, 1810

Karl August to Goethe

I am issuing a decree to create your son an assessor of the Ducal Chamber; this is likely to shield him from all temptations. I am always delighted when I can do something to increase the steady comforts of your life. For this purpose I dispatched to you several days ago two Polish stallions with directions for their care and feeding. They will serve your carriage. I have caused one of them to be gelded, in order that he may be more subdued in his behavior. So soon as he has recovered from his loss, he will join his comrade, a gentle animal, despite his testicles, and both will arrive to serve you.

November 8, 1810

Bettina Brentano to Goethe

You always have some reason to write me, but I don't care for your reasons nor consider anything in your letter except those last words of yours: "Love me till we meet again!" That one lovely phrase overwhelmed me and held me captured in a thousand sweet thoughts from last night until tonight. From this you may infer that your letter came about 24 hours ago and brought a current of fresh air into my room. . . . What you desire of me is so precious that I consider it worthy of being given even to you, and so I'm going to

place in your keeping what I received during two stirring years of
my life. It is little, when you compare it to much; it is infinite because it is unique.

November 14, 1810

To Bettina Brentano

At this moment I have just enough concentration and quiet about
me to tell you to go on writing with so much love and charm. Hasten
now to have me baptized! Adieu!

November 23, 1810

To Charlotte von Stein

Every morning, dear friend, I have been meaning to come to see you,
to show you manuscripts, to talk things over with you. Now it seems
that I have got to go to Jena and not come back till Monday. Meanwhile I send you some old sketches which I hope will please you
and make you think of me.

From the Supplementary Confessions

In regard to the rights of authors I would record, that it seemed
strange to me when the Ministry of the French Occupation of the
Rhineland asked me whether I would give my consent to a reprint
of *The Elective Affinities* by a publisher of Cologne. I expressed my
personal appreciation but referred the matter to my regular publisher. Even at that time, then, the concept of spiritual property and
of an equal right in this matter of higher people and humbler was
much more deeply grounded among the French than it was to be
among the Germans for some time thereafter.

1811

January 22, 1811

To Reinhard

I am so very glad that your reading of my *Pandora* makes you want to
communicate with me once again. It reminds me of a flattering re-

proach which a friend of my youth once addressed to me. He said: "What you live is better than what you write." How glad I would be if that were still true. . . .

Since these winter days are more favorable to reflection than production I have been reading a comparative history of all philosophical systems . . . The reading of this work has convinced me anew that men's philosophies are grounded in their innate differences and that therefore a thoroughgoing uniformity of conviction is impossible. A man has done enough if he knows on what ground he stands and on what particular place on this ground. Once he knows that, he can afford to be calm as far as he is concerned, as well as fair toward others.

February 4, 1811

To Georg Sartorius

Our theatre has had a real triumph. We put on Schlegel's translation of Calderon's *The Steadfast Prince*. Everyone was enthusiastic. Everyone assures us that the thing was successful beyond all expectation, especially in view of the fact that almost no one believed that this thing would be effective. . . . What we did was to take a piece written 200 years ago in a different climate, for a people of an utterly different tradition, and re-create it with a freshness as of pancakes just off the griddle. All classes of people gave us their sufferances, and I am so delighted because the considerable work and care which I have given for a couple of years to the revival of this excellent work, have been richly rewarded.

February 28, 1811

To Zelter

I don't in the least blame you for declining to compose music for *Faust*. My suggestion was as frivolous as the notion itself of staging the poem. Let the matter rest yet another year. . . .

Since I have space left, let me tell you about a very agreeable incident. The Empress of Austria presented me with a beautiful golden casket with a wreath of diamonds surrounding her name. . . .

March, 1811

To the Ducal Police Commission

According to the recently renewed police regulation it is the duty of masters to give servants not general and neutral letters of attestation, but conscientiously to explain both their merits and their faults. Accordingly, upon her departure from my service, I handed to Charlotte Hoyer, who had been a cook in my household, a document, of which copy herewith, characterizing her as one of the most fiendishly malicious and incorrigible persons in my entire experience.

The aforesaid woman did her best to confirm the fact of her malice and evil temper by taking the paper, which also bore the attestation of her former employers, tearing it into bits and strewing it about the house. . . . I thought it well to apprise the Commission of these facts . . . especially since it was the intention of the aforesaid Hoyer to enter the service of the Ducal actor Wolff of this place.

Enclosure:

Charlotte Hoyer was a servant in my house for two years. As a cook she can pass; at times she is obedient, courteous, even ingratiating. But the uncertainty of her temper finally made her presence in the house unendurable. As a rule, she does only as she pleases and cooks what she pleases. She is recalcitrant, insolently familiar and rude and seeks to wear out her employers in every way she can. Restless and full of malice, she incites her fellow servants to enmity and renders their lives miserable, if they do not side with her. To other allied vices must be added this one, that she listens at every door. In accordance with the new police regulation these facts are herewithin unreservedly set down.

March 20, 1811

Charlotte von Stein to Goethe

This little note, dear Councillor, is not to be sent to you till morning. But I couldn't resist the impulse of writing it tonight. I have just come from seeing *Tasso* performed. The oftener I see the play, the more divine it seems to me, and I think that was the impression of everyone. I would have run over this very evening to tell you so, had I not feared to break in upon your repose. . . . I'm sending you something for your breakfast.

April 21, 1811

Charlotte von Stein to Goethe

The Duchess begs me to ask you, dear Councillor, whether you would be willing to continue to delight us with your reading tomorrow evening at 6. But she does need to have an answer this evening.

April 30, 1811

To Charlotte von Stein

Announcing my arrival, my dear friend, I would like to know whether Her Serenity would like me to read this evening? I am free at the usual hour.

May 8, 1811

To Reinhard

. . . A very interesting young man is with me, Sulpiz Boisserée, whose acquaintance I owe to you. He pleases me very well and we get along with each other. . . .
Anyhow, if one doesn't wish to become wholly alienated from the world, one must let the young people prevail in their own way and keep an eye on at least a few, in order to know what the rest are doing. Boisserée brought me half a dozen pen and ink sketches by a young man named Cornelius who used to live in Düsseldorf and now lives in Frankfurt. I have seen his things in several exhibitions; they certainly arouse one's amazement. He has done scenes drawn from my *Faust*.

May 8, 1811

To Peter Cornelius

An important painter of murals of the Romantic School, 1783-1867.

Your drawings which were brought me by Herr Boisserée illustrated in a most agreeable fashion the progress you have made, since last I saw any specimens of your work. . . . First of all I would advise you to study most closely certain stone-cuts in the book of devotion in Munich probably known to you, because, in my opinion, Albrecht Dürer nowhere else proved himself so free, so brilliant, so great and

noble as in these extemporary works. Let me at the same time recommend to you Dürer's Italian contemporaries. . . .

Herr Boisserée's taste for reconstituting and making vivid to our
eyes the architectural monuments of that venerable period coincides
so admirably with your trends that I am truly delighted to see in
my house and to possess the efforts of that meritorious young man at
the same time with your own.

Early May, 1811

Boisserée to His Brother Melchior

The old gentleman kept me waiting a while. Then he came in with
his powdered hair and the stars of his decorations on his coat. His
reception of me was stiff and condescending. I conveyed the regards
of many friends. "Very nice," said he. We began at once to speak of
the drawings, the difficulties of having copperplates made, the house
of Cotta and other external matters. "Yes, yes, fine! H'm, h'm." Then
we spoke of my undertaking, of the fate of our older art and of its
history. I had determined to match his distinction in kind; so I spoke
as briefly as possible of the sublime beauty and excellence of what
the Cathedral contained and pointed to the fact that he could convince himself of all that from the drawings I had given him. All
through he had the expression of an ogre.

He didn't begin to thaw out until we talked of the mediaeval painters. He smiled when I praised the art of the modern Greeks; he asked
after van Eyck, admitted that he had seen nothing of his works and
also sought information about the painters between him and Dürer
and Dürer's Dutch contemporaries. . . . Finally we spoke of Reinhard and of his connection with the government and of Mother
Reinhard, so that all essential points were touched. That made him
a bit friendlier; he even smiled once or twice and asked me to dine
with him tomorrow. . . . Another visitor came in at that moment.
Goethe gave me one finger or, at most, two, I don't quite remember
which, but I'm sure I'll manage to get the whole hand by and by.
As I withdrew through the antechamber, I met a small, lean, little
gentleman all in black and in silk stockings with a curved back going
in to him.

◇◇◇◇◇

I'm getting along famously with the old gentleman. The first day I got one finger; the next day I had the whole arm. Day before yesterday, when I entered, he had the drawings of Cornelius in front of him. "Just look at that, Meyer!" he said to Meyer who had just come in, "those old times are brought back to life here!" That morose old fox growled (just the way Tieck imitates him exactly), but he had to approve of the workmanship, though he couldn't quite choke down an observation about the assumed mistakes in the drawing of that period. . . .

At dinner the conversation touched many points. . . . As the consumption of food and drink proceeded, he thawed out more and more. After dinner an orchestral director from Vienna played a few things on the piano. He was the polite little man whom I had run into in the antechamber. Goethe observed my attention fixed on certain symbolical and allegorical pictures which hung in the music room. He grabbed my arm and said: "Don't you know those? Look, that stuff can drive you crazy; it is beautiful and quite mad at the same time!" "Yes," I replied, "it's like the music of Beethoven which your friend there is playing; in brief, a whole age is in it." "To be sure," he said, "it is an age that seeks to embrace everything and therefore loses itself in elemental chaos, yet not without producing infinite beauty in detail."

Wednesday morning I found him in his garden. He told me that he had written to Cornelius and commended the study of Dürer's drawings to him. I had told him the day before—it was afternoon in his garden—what joy he had aroused by finally doing justice to Dürer and how wonderful it was to see this fresh and youthful flexibility at his time of life. . . . In the afternoon, after dinner, we were alone and he spoke very warmly and weightily of my work. I was uplifted by the feeling of having caused a great and noble matter to be taken to heart by a very brilliant man, despite his prejudices. . . . And so I spoke of what was so close to my heart out of the depth of my mood.

I don't know what words I used; they must have communicated my feeling. For the old gentleman was moved and pressed my hand. . . .

Karlsbad, June 25, 1811

To Ludwig van Beethoven

(1770-1827)

Your friendly letter, Honored Sir, was received by me with very great pleasure from the hands of our friend. I thank you from the heart for the sentiments you express and I can assure you that I reciprocate them sincerely. For I have never heard any of your works performed by skillful executants and lovers of your art, without desiring some day to admire your own interpretation of them and to delight in your extraordinary talent. Our dear Bettina Brentano deserves all the kindness you have shown her. She speaks of you with rapture and heartfelt affection and reckons the hours she passed with you as among the happiest of her life.

The Overture to Egmont which you sent me I shall probably find when I reach home. I thank you in anticipation. I have already heard it highly praised by many and intend to have it performed this winter in our theatre to accompany the play for which it was written. Thus not only I, but your numerous admirers in our part of the country, will have the privilege of a distinguished pleasure. I hope, above all, that our friend was correct when he gave us the hope that you would visit Weimar on the journey which you plan. I trust that it will be at a time when the Court is in residence and the public of music lovers assembled. I am sure that you would find a reception altogether worthy of your merits and sentiments. No one will take a higher interest in this matter than myself who, with all good wishes for your welfare, commend myself to your kindly recollection and sincerely thank you for all the benefits which have already accrued to me through your efforts.

Karlsbad, June 26, 1811

To Zelter

Before I leave Karlsbad, which must be earlier than usual this year, and set out on my way home, I want to thank you so warmly, my dear friend, for your letter of May 25. I had heard little or nothing

of our good Wolffs and I was all the more pleased by the news that
this talented couple is faring well in Berlin. To a certain extent that
was to be foreseen. But on the stage talent is not all that counts; so
many accidents play their part. . . . I appreciated it so much that
you interested yourself so loyally and kindly in these two good
people. . . .
Karlsbad is quite lively just now. Its physiognomy was new to me.
You see, my wife was here and she brought our carriage with her, so
that I was able to get around and be in the open more and take a
new delight in the scenery. . . .

August 4, 1811

To Körner

I left Karlsbad with a heavy heart, seeing that your approaching arrival was announced. But I had rented my quarters for a definte
period; the final date had arrived and I had to give place to others.
What made me really happy was Frau Schiller's showing me your
biographical essay. You solved a difficult problem well. The whole
course of our dear friend's life develops smoothly and pleasantly, and
it is a most happy touch that you were able to tell the story so largely
in his own words. The high serenity and freedom with which he
delineates his situation from time to time is really refreshing and
exciting; neither his closest friends nor those who observed him
most sedulously could have described him with so much propriety
as he does himself. . . .
My wife reckons it among the most outstanding and happy events
of this summer that she made the acquaintance of yourself and of
your dear family. . . .

August 26, 1811

Recollections of Varnhagen von Ense

Bettina had been reading the letters of Goethe to Frau von Stein
and she said it was perfectly clear that he was tired of her long before
he went to Italy and that the other love affairs had not been right
at all. She told us how Goethe had taken her in Weimar one time to
a merry gathering of common people, at which an itinerant woman
singer had come into the hall and sung a rather vulgar song. The

refrain was: "Oh women, women, women!" Goethe had nodded his
approval, but she herself had exclaimed: "That is horrid!" He had
turned on her with angry words: "You're never pleased with anything!" Tears had come into her eyes. He sat next to her still angry
and this was more than she could bear. As though unintentionally
she dropped a piece of bread on the floor, knowing that he would
stoop to pick it up; as he did so, she made the same gesture and
under the table kissed his hand. Thus they were reconciled.

August 27, 1811

To Fritsch

A year ago you had the kindness to eliminate the intense discomfort
caused me by the bowling alleys in my neighborhood. I could not
better express my sense of that kindness than by coming back earlier
in order to enjoy my quiet and secret garden in the shadow of your
sheltering wings. Unhappily I must denounce to you a new bowling
alley erected on the same spot as the old. It seems to be only an ama-
teur affair, but though the noise is not so intense, it is equally revolting. There is this further misery connected with it that, when
customers are lacking, the boys and children of the neighborhood
have their fun with it. There is not an hour of quiet all day long.
Even without that, I am surrounded in this suburb by craftsmen of
all kinds. I am hedged in between blacksmiths and nailsmiths, between carpenters and cabinetmakers and my most disagreeable
neighbor is a linen weaver. Now, one is willing to put up with these
necessary things; the pursuit of these crafts cannot be silenced. But
when during the evenings and on Sundays and holidays idlers cause
more tumult than do all these busy people in their hours of work,
one can be forgiven for losing patience, especially since the lovers of
these useless exercises have recently been furnished with ample con-
veniences beyond the city limits.

September 7, 1811

To Schelling from His Betrothed

The old gentleman wasn't with us so long this year and he was
pretty morose, I am told. To us personally he didn't show this aspect,
but turned his sunnier side to us. He said to me over and over again:

"Your presence, dear child, makes me feel twenty years younger."
Of course that was music to my ears.

September 28, 1811

To Wolf

Since I am unwilling to miss an opportunity of breaking a long silence, I would not deny a young man on his way to Berlin a letter
of recommendation to you. His name is Arthur Schopenhauer. His
mother is Mme. Councillor Schopenhauer who has been a resident
among us for several years. The young man studied in Göttingen
for a period, and I am told by others, knowing little myself, that he
took his studies seriously. . . . How far advanced he is and in what
branch of knowledge, you will easily be able to judge if, for my sake,
you give him a moment and, if he is worthy of it, permit him to see
you again. I would have been able to give you more details, had he
visited Weimar on his journey, as his mother led me to believe that
he would do. It was on that condition that I promised Mme. Schopenhauer to write this letter.

September 28, 1811

To Charlotte von Stein

If I were to offer myself, my dear friend, instead of the delightful
fruit, you will certainly grant me some respite. Meanwhile I want
you to be very discreet about what I'm sending you. [*Added in Charlotte's hand: The manuscript of* Poetry and Truth.]

October 10, 1811

Charlotte von Stein to Goethe

I'm going to Kochberg for a week tomorrow and I hope that the
fruit I send you is as excellent as it looks. May I remind you of your
promise to send me the later parts of the fairy tale of your life. If it
cannot be now, perhaps you will do so when I return, and meanwhile do not forget your faithful neighbor.

October 22, 1811

Achim von Arnim to Wilhelm Grimm

I executed your commission and gave Goethe your specimens of a translation of the Edda. I asked him for his opinion and, as usual, got no reply. You know that at Michaelmas the first two volumes of his autobiography will be published. It appears that this going over his youth in memory has suddenly made him intentionally old. Whereas formerly he used to try so definitely to grasp everything, he now acts as though he wanted to have nothing to do with the world in which we live. He goes to ridiculous lengths. Whatever I mention that is new in art, his reply is always the same: "Yes, those are all very charming amusements, but they don't concern me any longer."

December 17, 1811

To Barthold Georg Niebuhr

Founder of the modern historiography of Rome, 1776-1831.

I had written you a note which I took with me from Jena to Weimar, where I found your admirable work and began to read it at once. Now that I have finished reading it and intend to reread it immediately, which is most necessary to understand it truly and to make use of it, I would send you not only a general and emotional but a specific and well-motivated word of gratitude. But before I succeeded in doing that a good while would pass and, despite the best will in the world, this letter would be still further delayed. So let me at least say that I felt transported back to my own days in Rome when on an hundred occasions I became aware of the necessity of such research as you have made, but was equally aware at every step of my own inadequacy and of that of others. I have fixed my attention on the matters you treat of for so long a period, that your work is to me the desired and sudden solution of many riddles.

What becomes vivid through your work is the pre-Roman condition of Italy and the succession of the various peoples stratified, as it were, above each other. Infinitely precious is your sharp separation of legend and history, since neither is destroyed but each confirmed in its worth and dignity, even as it is infinitely fascinating to see

how these two elements coalesce and influence each other recipro-
cally. It would be marvelous to see all similar historical phenomena
treated in the same fashion.

December, 1811

Recollections of Luise Seidler

> Daughter of a university official in Jena and painter, 1786-1866. She
> made a portrait of Goethe at this time.

I succeeded in getting him interested in a widow in poor health
whose husband, a bankrupt merchant, had fled to America with the
remnant of his wife's fortune. . . . Goethe at once commissioned
me to cause the woman to send a number of her embroidered pieces
to Weimar. He arranged an afternoon at his house and invited the
leaders of society. The embroidered pieces were displayed with their
prices. Goethe himself told the story and asked those present to share
in this good deed. The profit was considerable.

December, 1811

Recollections of Riemer

He was fond of dragging out a certain kind of conversation unduly,
to repeat a given observation or to return to it, whenever he noticed
that somebody in the company was bored who had no right to play
the part of the knowing one or of one who grasps difficult matters
instantly. He used the same or a similar maneuver when he was not
in the mood to embark upon a given discussion or when he wanted
to get rid of the importunate. Bettina had an experience of that in
the winter of this year. She came every evening and wanted to talk
about her passion for him and similar matters. He interrupted her
to call her attention to the comet which was brilliantly visible that
year in the nocturnal sky. He fetched one telescope and then another
and discoursed at great length on this phenomenon of nature.

December 24, 1811

Charlotte von Stein to Goethe

It seems to me, dearest Councillor, that you are entitled from of old
to a Christmas present of a wax taper from me. My own burns hum-

bly enough, seeing that I can give you nothing more thoughtfully chosen and worthy of you. Yet it is a little flame that burns on the altar I have erected to you.

1812

January 30, 1812

To Friedrich Rochlitz

Miscellaneous writer and music critic in Leipzig, 1769-1842.

I have had to exercise great patience these last 20 years. It took several of my later works more than a decade before they gradually succeeded in appealing to a considerable public. Thus *Tasso* was not performed in Berlin until 20 years after it had been written. Patience of this order can be expected only of one who has early embraced that *dédain du succès* which Mme. de Staël claims to have observed in me. She was right, if she meant the instantaneous and explosive kind of success. I am not in the least indifferent to true success; rather has my faith in it been the guiding star of all my efforts. To attain success of this kind somewhat earlier and more completely, grows ever more desirable as the years lengthen and the hours diminish in which one can indulge indifference toward the moment and hope for the future.

February 5, 1812

Lotte Schiller to the Hereditary Princess of Mecklenburg-Schwerin

Princess Karoline, 1786-1816, was the daughter of Karl August.

For two weeks I lived on very stiff and formal terms with our Master and loved him, as one loves nature, unable to understand how it will ever return our glances. . . . Our friend Charlotte Stein hit upon the idea to show me all the papers which you, too, would like to see or have seen. Thus I gained a new insight into this marvelous human being and also deplored Charlotte's fate while living with her in that past; and it seemed to me as though my heart clung to hers and I vowed never to leave her and to follow her with my love to her grave. From the reading of these documents I happened to go to a party.

Goethe was there. Suddenly he began to speak of the past, of the very matters that I had just been reading. . . . I was inexpressibly amazed. I had just told him how charmingly Henriette Knebel had written about him. As I was going to fetch my coat, he followed me and took my hand and thanked me once more for what I had told him. He said it pleased him so much to talk to someone who understands his language, as I do, who have known him so long, so that we never can be strangers or far removed from each other. He added: "Do you know how long it is that we have known of each other? You were still beyond the hills, beyond Kochberg." . . . Tears came into my eyes and I felt at this moment that I, too, would never lose him.

February 13, 1812

To Reinhard

First of all my cordial thanks for your sympathetic reception of my autobiographical attempt. I may say that I expected it. For in recalling the times and circumstances which memory brought back to me and in organizing the matter, I thought of my absent friends as though they were here with me. I addressed them directly and so hoped from the beginning that they would receive well what I had written. . . .

Let me thank you too for sending me the fragments of the forthcoming work of Mme. de Staël. . . . Since I think that I know myself fairly well, I find various quite good perceptions in what she says. They are the more useful to me since she said all those things, only in a rather more drastic and lively fashion, to my face. . . .

I am spending a good deal of time this winter in arranging in more concentrated form *Romeo and Juliet* by eliminating from this magnificent subject various alien elements. . . . We gave the first performance on January 30, the birthday of the Duchess. . . . This task was infinitely instructive to me. Never did I gain so deep an insight into the genius of Shakespeare; yet, like all ultimate phenomena, that genius remains unfathomable. . . .

From the enclosed list you see that my collection of specimens of handwriting continues to grow. In fact, I have a couple of hundred additional specimens. In view of your many connections, perhaps you might help me obtain some specimens of the handwriting of

older and younger Frenchmen of note. It would make me very
happy.

April 8, 1812

To Knebel

. . . A man who does not grasp the fact nor rises to the vision that
spirit and matter, soul and body, thought and extension or, as a recent Frenchman brilliantly said, will and movement are the necessary twin ingredients of the universe, and will forever be, and that
these two have equal rights and may therefore be considered in their
togetherness as the representatives of God—he who has not grasped
that might as well employ his days with the idle rumors of the
world. . . .
Now on what concerns goodness of heart and excellence of character,
let me say just this: in reality we act well only insofar as we are
acquainted with ourselves. A darkness within does not easily permit
us to do what is good; it is quite as though the good were not so.
But vanity tempts us into wrong, indeed, if it is absolute, into positive evil. Yet one cannot precisely say that a man guilty of evil
actions is necessarily evil in his nature.

1812

EPIGRAMS

Low smouldered my poetic mood
So long as virtue I pursued;
High the tongues of flame were fed
When I from threatening evil fled.

◇◇◇◇◇

Let luck be ever good,
The oaf's no richer!
Skies may rain food—
He lacks a pitcher.

◇◇◇◇◇

If once—yes, once—thou wert to deceive me,
And I learn it—I'll try not to let it grieve me,

But if thou confess it to my face,
Forevermore I'll resent the disgrace.

◇◇◇◇◇

The righteous things that I have done
Are vanished and not thought upon;
The blundering wrongs incurred by chance
Like ghosts before my vision dance.

April 23, 1812

To Körner

Körner's son, Theodor, 1791-1813, playwright and martial poet. He fell
in a skirmish in Mecklenburg during the wars against Napoleon.

After all the good and charming things that have come to me from
you, your last missive gave me a very special pleasure. The two plays
of your dear son show a very decided talent. Out of the happy fullness of his youth he produces very agreeable things with ease and
freedom. At the present moment these plays are most desirable addi-
tions to our repertory. After successfully presenting Calderon's magnificent *Life, A Dream,* we were in danger of being stranded on the
sandbanks of contemporary dramatic literature. Your friendly helpfulness will keep us afloat during the spring.

Karlsbad, May 19, 1812

To Zelter

. . . I have at the moment no faith in writing a book for an opera
on the Samson theme. The antique legend has something monstrous
in it. This brutal passion of a gigantic, God-inspired hero for the
damnedest bitch that ever was, this raging lust which always takes
him back to her, though the experience of repeated treachery instructs him of his danger, this lechery which seems to be rendered
more acute by the very danger it involves and, finally, the mighty
notion that one must conceive of the immeasurable predominance
of this female creature who is able to enthrall this bull in human
form—look you, my friend, when you regard this awarely, it must
be clear to you that all would have to be destroyed, except the mere

name, to produce something appropriate to the conventions of our age and our theatre. It would be much more advisable to select subject matter of a smaller specific gravity. . . .

Teplitz, July 19, 1812

To Christiane

The incredible slowness of the postal service delayed the manuscript of the poems until yesterday. It was on the way two weeks. But it turned out very well. The Duke at once sent it over to Her Majesty and right after dinner the Empress asked me most charmingly if I didn't want to read some poems. . . . She has invited me to dine with her on three occasions. She is most cheerful and agreeable at such times. She teases her guests gently and incites them to contradict her, but gives every argument a pleasant final turn. . . .
Tell Prince Friedrich [*of Sachsen-Gotha*] that I can never be with Beethoven without wishing that it were in the Golden Ostrich Inn. I have never seen an artist so concentrated and energetic and spiritually profound. I quite understand that his relation to the world must be strange and difficult.

Teplitz, July 20, 1812

From the Diaries

Drove with Beethoven to a mountain in the vicinity.

◇◇◇◇◇

Teplitz, July 21, 1812

Spent the evening with Beethoven. He played exquisitely.

Summer, 1812

Anecdotes gathered by August Frankl

Austrian poet and novelist, 1810-1894.

The two great masters of poetry and music, **Goethe and Beethoven,** were taking a walk down into the valley one day, in order to converse more uninterruptedly. Wherever they went, the people on the promenades respectfully made way for them and saluted them. Goethe, annoyed by these constant interruptions, said: "What a nuisance; I can never avoid this sort of thing." With a calm smile

Beethoven answered: "Don't let it bother Your Excellency; the homage is probably meant for me."

Karlsbad, August 13, 1812

To Reinhard

The tranquility which I enjoyed here in May and the first half of June enabled me to put the final touches to the second volume of my biographical jest. It will come out at Michaelmas and it pleases me thus to carry out its single intention, that of communication with distant friends in order to avoid the danger of dying to them while I am still alive.

Karlsbad, August 15, 1812

To Charlotte von Stein

I am so glad, dear friend, that you gave so kind a welcome to my poems which I publish not without hesitation in these troublous times. In Teplitz one of the leading statesmen of Bohemia expressed his satisfaction to me in terms of diplomatic praise for having solved so questionable a problem so well. He said that he had some insight into the difficulty of writing in this age as I was writing. . . . Forgive me for seeming to brag. I owe everything more to luck than to talent.

Karlsbad, Summer, 1812

Recollections of F. Schubart

The Weimar gossip that Frau von Goethe's mismanagement went so far that she once offered the family carriage for sale in order to pay for a ball may be taken for what it's worth. But I remember very distinctly what the poet's intimate friend and secretary John told me. He was staying in Karlsbad with Goethe, who had fallen ill. He sat beside him and letters arrived from Weimar which brought news of his household there and revealed to him disturbances and pecuniary embarrassments which had been hidden from him hitherto.

Karlsbad, September 2, 1812

To Zelter

By Michaelmas you'll get another little volume of *Poetry and Truth*.
Regard it with kindness. It is, to be sure, but a thousandth part of
that which hammered down on me in those days and also of what
resisted and counteracted those blows within me. . . .

In Teplitz I made the acquaintance of Beethoven. His talent astonished me; his personality is, alas, wholly ungovernable. He is not
wrong, I admit, in that he finds the world to be detestable, but this
attitude renders it more enjoyable neither to him nor others. Much
is to be excused on the deplorable ground that he is losing his hearing, from which misfortune he takes less harm in his musical career
than in his social character. Originally of a laconic nature, he grows
doubly so through this ill.

October 23, 1812

Müller's Diaries

Walking home from a visit to the French Ambassador, we happened
to discuss his collection of copperplate engravings. . . . He said:
"Possession is necessary to me to get the right notion of the things
in question. Not until I am free of the deceptions incident upon
desire can I judge of a thing calmly and without prejudice. And so
I love possession, not of the thing possessed *per se,* but on account of
the calmer and happier contribution it makes to my development.
Thus, too, it is only possession that teaches me the faults that inhere
in a given matter. For instance, if I buy a bad print and think it a
good one, I gain greatly in insight and experience. One day an expert
sold me an antique, in the genuineness of which he did not himself
believe. It turned out to be genuine. Thus he was punished and I
was rewarded for my faith.

Jena, November 3, 1812

To Zelter

Herewith I send you the second part of my warmed-up and newly
dressed *Life,* as it may be called. May the whole of it remind you of

me and the details not be profitless. . . . How much in this little work is quite immediately addressed to you! Were it not for the thought of my absent friends, where would I have found the mood to write such things?

Jena, November, 1812

To Reinhard

A story was being told that Goethe, sitting at table next to Reinhard's young and lovely daughter Sophie, had attended exclusively to his food.

My charming adventure with Mlle. Sophie gives rise to some serious reflections. The true virtues and failings of a man seem never to be in evidence, and the rumors that abound are silly and empty. I am willing to confess my many faults. Ingratitude toward beauty and voracity have never been among them. Many stories have been told of what I was said to have done and spoken; never was there one among these that gave me any pleasure or had been invented for good or ill, to my advantage or disadvantage, in any harmony with my character or way of life. . . . Do give my regards to the lovely child. . . .

The huge and incalculable disaster, the burning of Moscow, in which you are involved through a brother and sister and I through dear friends, makes us feel in what an age we live and how deeply serious we must be to retain the serenity of our accustomed way of life.

November 14, 1812

Zelter to Goethe

. . . My oldest son whom you may remember, since you were so kind to him in Weimar, committed suicide last night. Why? I have no clear idea. His debts are modest and his accounts in order. He had just begun to be helpful to me. In his relation to those about him he could have been called an able person. And now he leaves me. . . . I am recurrently troubled by the feeling that I sinned against him through strictness and earnestness. I could not approve of the many entanglements into which the senses and the passions caused him to drift. He lived entirely with me, although he was entirely free and had a good income of his own. . . . In a letter to his brother he says, that he had often wanted to write me, but could not bring himself to do so. . . . Write me a word of healing. I must struggle to keep going; I am not what I was in former years. . . . I have sent for his child. It is a silent and depressed creature with eyes that remind me of yours. The little girl keeps gazing at your picture on my wall. I shall probably take her to live with me, in order to have something else to lose.

Jena, November 16, 1812

To Christiane

I am very well satisfied with both the houseman and the cook. It is a pleasure to see the seriousness with which the household is managed. In order to keep everybody in practice I have bought a carp and paid out of my own pocket for the sauce polonaise. . . . Which means that I hope you will bring along enough money to indemnify my accounts for the magnificent banquet which awaits you, and which I have just planned with the cook.
P.S. Last night I saw Minnie again. I left a meeting with her to chance, and chance did very well by me and everything turned out right. Of course, she is several years older now. But her figure and her ways are as lovely and charming as ever and I can hardly blame myself for once having loved her more than was reasonable.

November 26, 1812

To Körner

. . . Since I am glad to confess, it being clear enough from my confessions too, that I wrote all my earlier works for my own sake and my own enjoyment, wherefore I had to wait a dozen or more years before they were appreciated and became effective, so I would now equally confess that I feel differently about *Poetry and Truth*. I would that my countrymen but especially my friends, those of middle age and beyond, might take joy in it now and recall with me a beautiful time not so very far removed.

December 3, 1812

To Zelter

The letter, my very dear friend, which announced the great misfortune that has befallen your house, depressed me, bowed me down, for it arrived amid sombre reflections of my own on life; it is in reality you who are keeping me erect. From the dark testing by death you have come out the purest gold. . . .

Concerning the deed and its moral quality I have nothing to say. When weariness of life takes hold upon a man, he is to be lamented, not reproved. My *Werther* lets no one doubt that all the symptoms of this strange, this at once natural and unnatural sickness, once ravaged me to the very soul. I remember well what it cost me in purposefulness and struggles to escape the waves of death on that occasion, even as I was rescued and revived with great pain and labor from many a later shipwreck.

When one sees how in general the world, but especially our youth, is not alone delivered up to its desires and passions, and also how, at the same time, all that is higher and nobler is contorted and caricatured in the eyes of men through the deadly follies of our age, so that everything that could lead to redemption tends to damnation, not even counting the heavy pressure of outer circumstance—I do not wonder at the ill-starred actions which make man rage against himself and his fellows. . . .

December 13, 1812

Charlotte von Stein to Goethe

The dishes from your kitchen overcame my loss of appetite. I am very grateful to you. What I would now like to know is how you, dear Master, are feeling. Ah, if only you were a child, so that I could trim a tree for you or give you some similar pleasure. . . . I add a taper, as usual, being thus certainly the first to remember you at Christmas. The canary which you gave me proves himself ever worthier of the giver. He sings as though the spring were here.

1813

To Jacobi

People are united by their permanent convictions; it is their opinions that separate them. . . . I, for my part, and in view of the varied tendencies of my character, cannot be satisfied with a single way of thinking. As a poet and artist I am a polytheist; as a student of nature I am a pantheist, and I am the one as definitely as the other. If, as a personality and as a moral being, I need God—that need is also supplied. These heavenly and earthly matters constitute so broad a realm, that only all the organs of all the beings in the universe in combination may seek to grasp its nature.

1813

What were a God who, thrusting from without,
On circling finger spun the All about!
He from within must move the Universe,
Nature in Him, Himself in nature nurse,
So that what in Him lives and weaves and is
Never His spirit nor His power shall miss.

Man's spirit is a universe no less;
Hence 'tis the wont of peoples that each bless
The very best that unto it is known
As God—and call that God its own,
Attribute to Him earth and heaven,
Fear and revere and love Him even.

In His name Who, the self-created, spoke
The words eternal which the world evoke;
In His name Who Himself impregnates dust
With faith, love, power, activity and trust;

In His name Who, though often named He be,
Remains as essence still a mystery:

Far as thy hearing or thy sight may win
Thou findest but the known to Him akin,
And though thy soul on fiery pinions rise
Image and simile must still suffice;
He draws thee on, impels thee forth to go,
And where thou treadest paths and places glow,
Numbers die to thee, time's an empty mood,
And every step measures infinitude.

Weimar, January 25, 1813

From the Diaries

Wieland buried today. . . . In the evening August returned from
the funeral and gave us an account of it.

January 25, 1813

To Reinhard

Our good Wieland has left us. He was worn and feeble rather than
ill for only a brief period. On September 3 we still quite festively
celebrated his eightieth birthday. There was a beautiful balance of
tranquility and activity in his life. With a remarkable deliberate-
ness, without any impassioned striving or crying, he contributed an
infinite amount to the intellectual culture of the nation.

January 25, 1813

Recollections of Falk

On the day on which Wieland was buried Goethe was in a mood
more solemn than is his wont. . . . It was natural that our departed
friend was the chief subject of our conversation. . . . Goethe said:
"Of the destruction of such high spiritual powers there can be no
question under any circumstances in the economy of nature, who is
never so wasteful of its wealth. The soul of Wieland was, from its
origin on, a most precious treasure. Add to that, that throughout his

long life he did not diminish but increased his innate gifts. Consider
furthermore another important circumstance! Raphael was hardly
30, Kepler hardly 40, when they put an end to their lives while Wieland—" "What?" I interrupted Goethe in some astonishment, "You
speak of dying as though it were an independent act!" "I venture to
do that quite often," he replied, "and if you like I'll tell you my
reason, since this is a moment when I may be permitted to express
my thoughts. . . . You have long known that ideas not grounded in
the world of sense experience, whatever their other value, failed to
convince me. In the face of nature I want to know, not merely specu-
late and believe. Now as for the question of the persistence of the
conscious soul beyond death, I conceive of it in my own way. Such
persistence by no means contradicts the very long observations which
I have made concerning the character of man and of all other beings
within the order of nature. On the contrary, it emerges from all this
research with redoubled force. But how much or how little of a
given personality deserves to endure—that is another question and
a matter which we must leave to God." . . .

While he was speaking the barking of a dog was repeatedly heard in
front of his house. Goethe, who had an unconquerable antipathy
toward dogs, almost leaped to the window and cried out: "Do as
you will, vestigial creature, you cannot get the better of me!" This
remark would have seemed strange enough to anyone unacquainted
with the concatenation of Goethe's ideas. To me, who understood it
somewhat, the notion was both humorous and appropriate. . . .

"Strictly speaking," he resumed later, "I can have no knowledge of
God except such as I derive from the limited vision of my sensory
perceptions on this single planet. Such knowledge is a fragment of
a fragment. I do not admit that this limitation which is applicable
to our observation of nature, need be applicable in the exercise of
faith. The contrary is the case. It may well be that our knowledge
must be regarded as a fragment on this planet and that all our observations and contemplations are of necessity imperfect and demand
their supplementation and perfecting through an act of faith."

February 5, 1813

To K. L. von Woltmann

Critic, editor, translator of Tacitus.

. . . Too many things, alas, prevent me from contributing to your magazine. I must concentrate my efforts and dare accept no new obligations. . . . Moreover, the older one grows, the less possible it is to speak to the public from within a group. I would not dream of asking an editor to exclude contributions that contradict my way of thought. But it makes the oddest impression on me to see side by side in a magazine my convictions and the contradiction of them. . . .

I beg of you, however, to accept my warm and sincere thanks for what you have written about my autobiography. . . . As an author I have been quite isolated at every period. What of me was effective usually belonged to my own past and I found but little sympathy with any present effort. From this you can see how much I am bound to treasure the cordial and acute manner in which you introduced my new book to the public.

Naumberg, April 17, 1813

To Christiane

The destruction of the French army in Russia was the signal for Central Europe to seek to throw off the dominance of Napoleon. On March 16 Prussia declared war against France. Goethe did not share the nationalist fervor of the German armies. Conflict and invasion were to be feared for Thuringia. Hence, on the solicitation of his family and friends, and on his own principle that "not everyone can serve the fatherland in the same way; each does his best as God has made him," Goethe left Weimar on April 17, with Karlsbad as his destination. He was accompanied by the secretary, Karl John, 1788-1856, who had taken Riemer's place.

The same kind of "nice people" who drove us from Weimar started by making the morning pleasant to us. A few miles from home we met a regiment of hussars. Next it looked as though we had said farewell to the war forever. The messengers plying to and from Jena carried flowers and packages as usual; immediately beyond, the country seemed at peace or, rather, much quieter than in times of

peace, because the drovers were gone who usually at this time are
on their way to the Fair at Leipzig. . . .

◇◇◇◇◇

Dresden, April 21, 1813

I wrote you on the 17th in Naumberg because I wanted to prove to
you that I'm well. But postal communications were interrupted and
I had to take the letter along with me. On Easter Day on the way
to Leipzig the weather was dark and inclined to be stormy. The road
was good but completely empty, as though we were driving through
the desert. The sky brightened and at noon we arrived at the Hôtel
de Saxe in Leipzig. Not far from there we had met a group of
Russians, playing at some sort of game. A good meal restored our
strength and we wandered through the city in spite of the cold and
cutting wind. . . . The next day, Tuesday, was both agreeable and
instructive. Once more we dined on the carp with sauce polonaise
which we had enjoyed so much the day before.

Dresden, April 21, 1813

Recollections of Ernst Moritz Arndt

Prose writer and author of patriotic songs, 1769-1860.

Goethe was in Dresden, too, on this occasion and visited his friends
the Körners. I hadn't seen him for 20 years. His appearance was as
impressive as ever, but the great man did not make an agreeable
impression. He was nervous and anxious. He had no hope and took
no joy in the things that were coming to pass. Young Körner was
there, a volunteer in the armies of liberation. The boy's father spoke
with enthusiasm and confidence. Goethe seemed to be almost in a
rage: "Rattle your chains," he said, "that man is too great for you;
you won't break them."

Dresden, April 25, 1813

To Christiane

. . . At 11 o'clock last night there was a frightful scene. The street
glared in the light of torches and a wild warlike tumult had awakened me from sleep. A column of soldiery had come to a halt. They

were to be billeted here, but the billeting had not been announced.
It looked like a scene from Hades, when they tore open the gates
of big houses and, 10, 20, 30 at a time plunged into the houses by
torchlight. But the householders are used to that by this time.
They've done their best to prepare rooms and beds and they keep
cooked food on hand and warm it up at need. The chief items of
these feasts are thick oat gruel, beef and sauerkraut, potato salad
with a lot of onion and garlic, and brandy. . . .

Dresden is of course very lively. You must consider that it is a city
of 40,000. This in itself, even in times of peace, means a lot of movement and stir. And consider the needs in food of such a popula-
tion. . . .

Needless to say, when the Cossacks assemble on the market place
everybody runs out to surround them and look at them with astonishment. They themselves remain perfectly calm. And you should
have seen young and old throng the square when they turned up
with a camel, as a symbol of their genuine Asiatic origin.

Dresden, May 21, 1813

To Christiane

Saturday morning the whole town was on its feet running to witness
the arrival of the potentates. I crossed the bridge and watched the
Cossacks and the Uhlans and other cavalry, as well as vehicles of all
kinds from wretched carts to the most costly traveling carriages. The
well-mounted and well-trained Civic Guard of Dresden showed up
well. . . . At last at 12:30 the Emperor and King entered on their
mounts followed by their guards, 8000 infantry men, extraordinarily
well set up and well equipped. It was difficult to get back to town.

Dresden, June 30, 1813

To Riemer

In my last letter I gave you full authority to strike out in the manuscript all words of foreign origin, insofar as it was possible and advisable. . . . I am, as you know, neither stubborn nor frivolous in
this matter. But I must confess to you that experience and conversation with others seem to teach me that the people who are so zealous

for the purity of our language are usually quite stupid people. Since they have no delicate feeling for the precise shading of an expression, they can easily find a substitute.

Dresden, June, 1813

Karl August to a Lady of the Court

Goethe refuses to talk but dictates the story of his life and loves to two secretaries whom he has borrowed from police headquarters here. . . . He often asks my advice whether he is not being too frank in his revelations. I always advise prudence, moderation and restraint.

Teplitz, July 1, 1813

To Riemer

. . . I have used this period to go on working at something which will, I hope, be a source of pleasure to my friends. Be sure that you will be among the first to receive this third volume. . . .
We expect the Duke to arrive here shortly. I am glad he decided to come. He has been tormented by the gout again and the baths here agree with him. His presence will probably persuade me to stay here the rest of the month.

Teplitz, July 26, 1813

To Voigt

. . . The tranquility of this place and my personal well-being could make me very happy here, were it not that the sombreness of the political and military sky and the presence of so many so sorely stricken by fate, robs one of every feeling of comfort, to such a degree that one reproaches oneself for enjoying such pleasant hours as are being granted me among these mountains. . . .

Dresden, August 11, 1813

To Christiane

On his return journey Goethe once more stopped in Dresden. For the hour Napoleon seemed again to have prevailed. Goethe arrived home on August 21. On the 26th he rode to Ilmenau. On the 28th he was surprised by his friends' festive celebration of his birthday.

I arrived here at 3 o'clock on the afternoon of the 10th in time to watch the festivities in honor of Napoleon set for this day. The weather is splendid. At night there were fireworks and the city was illuminated. Now I'm going to watch this for a few days and then come home to you. The prospect makes me quite happy.

◇◇◇◇◇

Ilmenau, August 28, 1813

I awoke early, not realizing what date it was. Nor did I remember until my serving man brought me a wreath of flowers from Voigt. I wasn't dressed yet when I saw the approach of the Duke and his train and hastened to meet him. Hardly were they in my room, when three little girls arrived with bouquets and gold-colored paper on platters. Hidden beneath the paper I finally discovered a poem by Our Serenity. Scarcely had I read it, when three more pretty girls entered, each with a jug of wine. They recited the poem very charmingly and, as the third of them placed a wreath on my head, I kissed her very deliberately and thereafter the two others. . . . It was a very good thing for me to go to Ilmenau. . . . I was on horseback for six hours yesterday and the exercise agreed with me well.

September 21, 1813

To C. H. Schlosser

The nephew of Goethe's late brother-in-law, 1782-1829.

. . . I am very glad that you study my *Theory of Colors* for the sake of the scientific method employed. I do not deny that this work interests me in the last analysis more by virtue of its form than of its content. . . . I would that a happy accident might bring you to our neighborhood. Indeed, I would issue a warmer invitation, were I not conscious of the fact that in the autumn and winter of our lives we tend to grow ruder and more rigid than is reasonable. The effect of these qualities may be mitigated by good will, but even more by distance. Why should I not be frank and say that I belong ever more to that category of people *within* whom one may live with pleasure but *with* whom it is far from amusing to be.

November 20, 1813

To Charlotte von Stein

You are cordially invited, my ever dear friend, to be present at a little party at my house at 11 o'clock tomorrow, Sunday morning. An indisposition taking various forms has prevented me from coming to see you.

◇◇◇◇◇

November 22, 1813

I'm so very happy that I may call on you tomorrow evening. Perhaps you will permit me to bring along some pure poetry to add to the semi-poetry of my biographical essay.

November 24, 1813

To Knebel

I go ahead in my own special way and try to preserve, to create order and to lay foundations in contradiction to the age, I seek friends, like yourself, friends of science and of art, who stay at home, and I demand of them to preserve the sacred fire, which the coming generation will need so sorely, were it only beneath the ashes. . . . It is a quality of the Germans to nurse cleavages among themselves. I have never seen them united except by this hatred against Napoleon. I am waiting to see what they will do when the man has been driven across the Rhine. . . .

I did find young Schopenhauer to be a remarkable and interesting person. You will find that you have less in common with him than I. Nevertheless I want you to make his acquaintance. With a certain acute stubbornness he is determined to introduce new devices into the game of modern philosophy. We shall wait and see whether the masters of the guild will let him do so. I find him brilliant; beyond that I will pass no judgment.

December 1, 1813

Recollections of Friedrich de La Motte Fouqué

The romantic poet and author of *Undine,* 1777-1843, at this time an officer in the Prussian army.

The Battle of Leipzig which cleared the right bank of the Rhine brought us, in our pursuit of the enemy, to the neighborhood of Weimar. I asked for a furlough to ride into the city and pay homage to the poet of poets. . . . Once more I stood in front of that simple handsome house. Ten years had passed since the last time. . . . Inside the house it looked very different. Austrian troops had been billeted all over the reception rooms. Orderlies ran up and down. The beautiful welcoming word *Salve* which adorned the floor at the entrance to the farther room had been almost obliterated by the dust of military boots. The sight made me melancholy. . . . Unobtrusively the door opened and that unforgettable countenance arose before me. . . . He summoned me at once to sit down and sat down opposite me. I spoke my little speech. "I have come, Your Excellency, to thank you for something which you have probably forgotten, the gracious and hospitable reception you granted me in your house about a decade ago." . . . With indescribable charm of glance and voice he replied: "Do you really think that I lost sight of you during this period?" . . .

I now expressed my certainty that his hallowed dwelling would soon be freed of its sturdy but superfluous guests. "Are you so sure of that?" he asked. "Because our military forces have no time to waste on pursuing the conquered conqueror!" . . . Thoughtfully Goethe looked at the floor and then said with a profoundly serious look at me: "And so it was a complete victory, a decisive blow? Well, so much the better."

December 13, 1813

Recollections of Heinrich Luden

Professor Luden had come to ask Goethe's editorial collaboration in a periodical to be founded and to be called *Nemesis*. Goethe refused in view of the extreme nationalist and romantic character of the proposed publication.

"You are not to believe," Goethe said, "that I am indifferent to the great ideas of freedom, nation, fatherland. No, these ideas are in us all; they are a part of our very being, and no one can cast them out. Also, Germany is very close to my heart. I have often been bitterly grieved by the thought that this German people, so estimable individual by individual, is so wretched as a whole. The comparison of the German people with other peoples cannot but arouse painful feelings. I have sought in every way to transcend them and it is in science and in art that I have found the wings to bear me beyond these griefs. Because science and art belong to the world and tend to obliterate the barriers of nationality. Yet the consolation thus derived is but a second rate one and no substitute for the proud consciousness of belonging to a people that is great, strong, respected and feared. The only thing that can console us is a faith in Germany's future. To this faith I cling. Yes, the German people holds promise of a future and has one. The fate of the Germans is, as even Napoleon said, not yet fulfilled."

December 29, 1813

Karl August to Goethe

My dear Friend, I'm very glad that your August has volunteered to join the military formation. His decision does honor to his good will and proper convictions and protects him in the eyes of his comrades. Let him remain inscribed in the list of volunteers but let him accompany my emissary to Frankfurt-am-Main in an accredited position. Afterwards we'll see in what direction his own will takes him, since the first law of the present revolution seems to be to let the young fellows do as they wish.

1814

January 5, 1814

To Friedrich von Trebra

A Saxon mining engineer and Ducal consultant at the mines in Ilmenau, 1740-1819. Karl August had resigned from the Rhenish Confederation and was raising a German military corps to serve with the Allies against Napoleon. August von Goethe had volunteered to join these troops. His father had refused his consent.

These recent days have not only been full of tumult but of varying emotions. Our Lord, the Duke, has gone to join his division which is in the neighborhood of Cassel. Since we have come to the point where the state of war seems not only the most natural but the most desirable, we deliberately drop care in order to enjoy our happy success in good humor. Even my son, though he will not follow the drum, will follow the hunter's horn. In peace or war Diana seems always to be the presiding deity of Weimar. . . .

Correcting this letter in red ink is a symbol of these times. Our young people find it most convenient to go forth to be as much of a nuisance to other honest people as those have been to us. It is a very seductive occupation, especially as it causes you to have the repute of a finished patriot. Nothing is left to us people who are over 60 except to be agreeable to the ladies, who without us would quite despair. How is this to be done? I play cards with the old and I teach the young. God keep you in good humor! I have no higher ambition than that one might say of me:

You are the merriest undone man in Europe.

January 14, 1814

To August

August had gone to Frankfurt on a mission for the Duchy.

I am writing to tell you at once that your letter arrived and gave us much pleasure. Continue quite serenely to pay attention to two things: firstly, what the real intention of people is, secondly, what masks they put on to conceal it. Don't seem to be complacent. People should be given no chance to grudge you your good luck. . . . In the *Literary News* of Jena there is an excellent announcement on the method in which, to begin with, the political broadsides are to be made public. . . . Without quoting it, take the following passage to heart. If copies of the paper reach Frankfurt, you might, however, gently point it out to people: "Our men and women are not to believe that being a German is identical with being a Christian and a mediaeval knight. Christianity was an alien thing to us until the Reformation adapted it to our character; chivalry, likewise, was a foreign product in direct contradiction to our original national liberty.

February 14, 1814

To F. B. von Bucholtz

Historian and pamphleteer,

. . . If I am to be perfectly sincere I must say: it is my belief that the greatest service I can render my country is to continue my biographical essays and to delineate fairly and calmly the changes in our moral, aesthetic, philosophical culture, of which I have been the witness, and to show how every period has sought to eliminate or to cancel the period preceding, instead of being grateful to it for the inspiration and knowledge received from it. . . .

February 17, 1814

To the Sister of Frau von Eybenberg, Wife of the Prince of Reuss

It has happened to me on several occasions that when, after much hesitation, I venture to inform friends of the failure of a promised gift to arrive, that the gift came the minute my letter left. And so it happened with the five exquisite smoked goose breasts which arrived happily in their little basket and which are more delicious, or seem so, than any I have ever eaten. Since the last you sent, no comparable ones have been in my pantry. Riemer is an additional witness to their excellence. He comes to me again nearly every evening and helps me prepare various writings which some day will give you pleasure. He joins me in thanks and begs you not to forget him.

February 23, 1814

To Zelter

A little package containing a poetical miscellany which was sent you about a week ago, must have arrived by now. I want to add in prose the assurance that I have been much troubled by your long silence. . . . I showed your invective against philologists to Riemer. He was delighted with it and wishes to be remembered to you. I wish you could hear his commentary. Since that is his own profession, he knows best whence the original sin of these failings is derived. He curses them because, though he has freed himself of them, they weigh on him through others. . . . I pass over an hundred things today, putting them off to some other occasion. I shall probably stick pretty close to Weimar this coming summer. If you could free yourself for a few weeks, you would bring me a whole world. . . . I

have space left to fill with a few rimes from, as it were, the pocket of
the way of the world:

> Old Age remained a courteous wight,
> He knocked by day, he knocked by night.
> But since none said: Come in! and he
> Out in the draft chose not to be,
> He turned the knob and in he came,
> And now he gets a ruffian's name.

March 9, 1814

To Knebel

Our relations to the English are now becoming closer and our poor
Germans do not realize what trap threatens them from that side.
You can deal with French pride, because it is identified with their
vanity; you can do nothing with British arrogance, because it is
commercial and based upon the dignity of gold. We must wait and
see what will come and, since we are neither rich **nor vain,** try to
get along in the quiet circle of our lives.

March 26, 1814

Recollections of Riemer

Goethe said men are productive in poetry and art only so long as
they have religious faith; after that, all they produce are imitations
and repetitions.

March 26, 1814

To Knebel

. . . Riemer is being very useful. In preparation for a new edition,
he is reading *Wilhelm Meister* with me. Since this little work, like
all my things, was written in a somnambulistic condition, his observations concerning my style are most instructive to me, as well as
pleasing.

Weimar, April 9, 1814

From the Diaries

News of the occupation of Paris. Loud rejoicing all day.

May 30, 1814

Recollections of Müller

Dour rainy weather until evening. We drove to Weimar early in order to prevent, according to Goethe's wish, the proposed duel between his son and the cavalry captain von Werther in some appropriate way. The matter was adjusted. Thereafter a cheerful dinner. . . .

June, 1814

Recollections of Riemer

F. A. Wolf visited Goethe this spring in Berka [*a small health resort in the Harz Mountains*]. Goethe had gone there in order to work on his operatic play *The Awakening of Epimenides*. . . .

SUPPRESSED STANZA

From *The Awakening of Epimenides,* written to celebrate the German victories and later performed in Berlin.

> A curse on the misguided man
> Who, void of ruth or shame,
> Does just as did the Corsican
> Under a German name.
> Let him protest both soon and late
> Unto a lasting right;
> His force and toil prepare a fate
> Him and his kin to blight.

Recollections of Arthur Schopenhauer

Now, twenty-one years later, I quite understand what Goethe said to me in Berka in 1814. I found him reading Mme. de Staël's book on Germany, which had appeared a year before. I said to him that she gave people an exaggerated notion of the honesty of the Germans, which would be misleading to foreigners. He laughed and said: "Quite right! They will not lock their trunks and the contents will be gone." Then he continued seriously: "But if you want to get an idea of German unveracity at its lowest, you will have to get a thorough knowledge of German literature."

Goethe was so thorough a realist that he couldn't get it through his head that objects exist only insofar as they are represented to himself by the subject in the act of cognition. "What," he said to me once with a glare of his Jovian eyes, "you mean to tell me that light exists only insofar as you see it? Oh no! You wouldn't be here if the light didn't see you."

1814

TO HAFIZ

Influenced, perhaps against his will, by the German Romantic Movement and by the liberation of feeling which the renewed peace of Europe brought, Goethe was profoundly impressed by the Persian poet Hafiz, 1320-1389, whose works had recently appeared in a complete German translation by Hammer-Purgstall. "By way of these versions," Goethe wrote, "I seemed with a special predilection to lay hold upon that poet's innermost character and sought to establish a relationship with him by inner productivity of my own." Thus "the foundations were laid of the *West-Eastern Divan*," perhaps the supreme achievement of Goethe as a lyrical poet.

> That thou no ending findest makes thee great,
> And no beginning hast—such is thy fate.
> Thy circling song, like cosmic spheres revolving,
> End and beginning into one resolving,
> And at the center causing us to see
> That which was first and shall forever be—
>
> Thou art the source from which in ceaseless rapture
> The waves pour forth poetic joy to capture.
> O mouth for kisses ever fain,
> Deep bosom from which song comes soaring,
> Throat ever swift the cup to drain,
> And heart its kindness still outpouring—
>
> Let the whole world in chaos perish,
> Hafiz! Henceforth this be my gain,

To vie with thee! Delight and pain
Be one for us, the twin-born twain!
Like thee to drink and love to cherish
Shall now my life and pride remain.

Rise now, my song, with thine own passion,
Both old and new in form and fashion.

1814

PHENOMENON OF NATURE

On July 26 Goethe set out in his own traveling carriage to visit Western
Germany for the first time in 18 years. His destination was Wiesbaden.
Filled with a premonition of fresh experiences and poetic productivity,
he wrote this poem in the carriage soon after setting out.

When through the torrent slow
The sun-god surges,
Straightway the seven-hued bow
Arching emerges.

In mist it does not fail
To crown the even;
And though its lines are pale,
It yet spans heaven.

Thus in thine eld still bright
Let nothing rue thee;
For though thy hair be white
Love will come to thee.

Fulda, July 27, 1814

To Christiane

I have just left Fulda. The sky is at its bluest; I am looking down
into a magnificent valley. The corn is ripe and flax and hemp are
being harvested. . . . The first stork is on the meadow and there
are vineyards by the road. . . . I visited the castle of Emperor
Friedrich, the Redbeard. . . . We'll get to Hanau by evening. . . .

◇◇◇◇◇

Hanau, July 28, 1814

I do want to thank your charming self for persuading me to enter the carriage. Considering the heat and the dust and other such things, I might not have gone. . . . And now, to follow the example of our friend Werner, let me praise the vegetables. Such cabbage and kohlrabi as I have not eaten for years! Now all my hope is set on artichokes. . . .

◇◇◇◇◇

Frankfurt, July 29, 1814

As I drove into Frankfurt I found the city illuminated, and was not a little overcome by the compliment. But my modesty found a proper hiding place, seeing that the King of Prussia, also incognito, had just arrived. . . . I took a walk through the bright city. Where the lamps were not bright, the moon shone all the clearer. . . . At last I went to look at our old house. Our big clock was striking. It was a very familiar sound, for our successor had bought it at auction and let it stand. . . .
Willemer is at his mill. . . . I have to change clothes two and three times a day. . . . Tonight, favored by the full moon, I shall set out for Wiesbaden.

Wiesbaden, July 31, 1814

ULTIMATE ASPIRATION

Let the sages only hear it
And the vulgar jeer in vain!
I extol the living spirit
That for fiery death is fain.

Thee begotten and begetter
In the night of mortal passion
Comes by candlelight to fetter
Feeling of an alien fashion.

Now the night no more a prison
Breaks from shadow to elation,
Wherein new desire arisen
Strives toward loftier procreation.

Distances to thee are shrunken
And thy agile flight is doomed,
And at last, with radiance drunken,
Art thou, butterfly, consumed.

And till thine this deep behest:
Die to win thy being!
Art thou but a sullen guest
Upon earth unseeing.

Wiesbaden, August 1, 1814

To Christiane

The stir of a happy trip, the very warm season, the refreshing waters
that I drink and the warm baths are already having so excellent an
effect upon me that I look forward to the happiest results.

Country estate of the Brentanos, September 1, 1814

Recollections of Antonie Brentano

> The wife of Franz Brentano, the son of Maxa von la Roche, and Bet-
> tina's brother. The estate was situated between Wiesbaden and Rüdes-
> heim near the banks of the Rhine. Goethe had remained in Wiesbaden
> the whole month of August, where Jakob Willemer and the latter's
> ward, Marianne Jung, had visited him for several days. Now he ac-
> cepted the Brentanos' invitation.

Every morning Goethe put on his long white flannel dressing gown,
folded his hands behind his back and walked up and down the long
archway, which reaches nearly to the Rhine. He didn't like to be
disturbed during this walk; he scarcely answered when spoken to.
He would dress very carefully for dinner and would then be rather
condescending. He would heap his plate with food, most of which
he didn't eat. I, being the mistress of the house, had the uncomfort-

able feeling that the cuisine was not at all to his liking. But he did drink what seemed to me enormous quantities of our Rhine wine.

Frankfurt, September 18, 1814

To Christiane

On this day Goethe for the first time visited the Tanner's Mill, the beautiful residence of his old friend Jakob Willemer. In 1800 Willemer had "bought" from her mother the 16-year-old actress and dancer, Marianne Jung, for 2000 gulden. Willemer was undoubtedly in love with Marianne; she may even have been his mistress. There is no doubt that, despite the discrepancy in their ages, Goethe and Marianne were at once attracted to each other. However, Marianne's fate was fixed. Nine days after this first meeting Jakob Willemer, who had been married and widowed twice, married the girl with the approbation of his daughters and sons-in-law.

I drove with Mme. Brentano to Willemer's house. The day was extremely beautiful and our host cheerful and Marianne—whom we had not seen since Wiesbaden—was very well. We saw the sunset over the river from a little tower which Willemer has built on the hill behind the mill. The view is marvelous. So much for this time. A sequel will follow.

September 26, 1814

Christiane to Goethe

Dear, good Privy Councillor, We just want to hurry up and tell you that you will find us all in the best of health. . . . In this fine weather we often drive to Tiefurt and Berka and other places. Yesterday we were in Jena with Mme. Wolff. When we came back, there was your lovely letter. Remember me to all the friends in Frankfurt. Professor Riemer, who is with us, wants to send his kind remembrances to you. Don't let your servant forget about the sugar and the coffee. . . .

Heidelberg, October 8, 1814

To Reinhard

On September 24 Goethe had gone to Heidelberg, accepting the invitation of his young friend Sulpiz Boisserée.

From what place, my dear friend, could I more fittingly write you than from Heidelberg and from the house of Boisserée, whose acquaintance and whose friendship I owe to your introduction and for which I am grateful? . . . I spent eight weeks in Wiesbaden and in the Rhine country and, after a short stay in Frankfurt, arrived here, where dear and understanding people afford me the highest delight that anyone can do.

Late September and Early October, 1814

Recollections of J. B. Bertram

The co-proprietor of the great Boisserée collection of mediaeval art, 1776-1841. Goethe stayed with Boisserée from September 26 to October 9. On that day he returned to Frankfurt and on the 12th visited the Tanner's Mill where he found Marianne, now Frau Willemer alone. He stayed nine days in Frankfurt, of which he spent four in the Willemer house.

A few days after Goethe's arrival at Boisserée's house, Frau von Humboldt was announced, just as Goethe was standing in front of the van Eyck of St. Luke painting the Madonna and the child. "There is a great surprise in store for you," I said, as I entered the room in which Goethe was. "A surprise? Sir, You know how much I like surprises! Who is it?" "Frau von Humboldt." "F-r-a-u v-o-n H-u-m-b-o-l-d-t! Let her come up!" and Goethe assumed an expression of unutterable boredom. Frau von Humboldt opened the door and stretching out her arms, cried: "Goethe!" Calmly he asked her to sit down next to him. "Do you know how to catch salmon?" he asked. "No," Frau von Humboldt answered in mild astonishment. "Well, you catch them with a weir! And you see, that's the kind of a fish trap which these gentlemen have set for me. They have caught me, too. Now you'd better get out of here as fast as you can or the same fate will overtake you. I'm caught and have to stick around and look at pictures. But that's nothing for you. So please hurry and get out."

October 24, 1814

Boisserée to a Friend

. . . You know that Goethe stayed with us for two weeks. . . . I think we have gained his entire confidence and succeeded in having his intimate friendship. . . . "The devil," he said repeatedly, "the world doesn't know what you have here and what your aims are. But we will make it known and we will bring to it these golden apples on silver dishes." . . . He had never seen a van Eyck before and nothing, indeed, of the period, except a few things by Cranach and Dürer. Almost daily he exclaimed: "Ah, children, what we love we must praise and praise again! These creations deserve that princes and emperors, that all the peoples of the earth come to pay them homage."

November 9, 1814

To Knebel

Goethe had reached home on October 27.

I have gotten along very well in the world on this journey, because I have asked nothing of anyone except what he could and would give, nor sought to offer anyone but what was conformable to his nature and have serenely accepted what day and circumstance brought me. . . . For look, each one desires that for which his beak or snout was formed. One needs a thin necked bottle, another a flat plate, one food that is raw, another food that is cooked. . . . And so I have partaken of what was best on many tables. . . .

November 19, 1814

To Boisserée

After so rich a meeting and intercommunication, it is difficult to continue at a distance. But I must not delay to send you a few words of gratitude for so much good received. . . . Give my regards to all and forgive me for having so long neglected the duty of being heard from. I must confess that I was the recipient of so many kindnesses that I am almost insolvent in the matter of making any return.

November 23, 1814

To C. H. Schlosser

It gives me real pleasure to tell you of my almost exclusive preoccupation. With all my power and all possible energy I have taken a plunge into the Orient, into the land of faith, of revelation, of prophecy and of foreknowledge. . . . I have allied myself to the company of the Persian poets and am refashioning their spirit in both jest and earnest. I have chosen as my dwelling place their poetic center which was the city of Shiraz, whence I make my small excursions in all directions.

1814

TO SCHAH SEDSCHAA AND HIS COMPANIONS

The Persian poet of this name is said to have died in 1291 at the age of 102.

Through strain of harp and gong
From Oxus faring
Uprises now our song
Thy music daring!
We fear no taint or wrong
In soul so vernal;
Oh, may thy life be long,
Thy realm eternal.

1814

TALISMANS

Unto God the Orient!
Unto God the Occident!
Northern lands and Southern lands
Rest in the peace of His great hands.

◇◇◇◇◇

He, the one and only just,
Wills right for all He formed of dust.
Of His hundred names be then
This one magnified. Amen.

◇◇◇◇◇

Never question which the gateway
Of God's city closed behind thee;

> Settle tranquilly and straightway
> On the spot therein assigned thee.

December 28, 1814

To Willemer

According to the prevalent fashion Goethe had left his autograph book with the Willemers. It had been returned with some awkward verses by Marianne beginning: "Of the small ones I shall be, Since 'tis thus thou callest me." In the accompanying letter Willemer had written: "Since you called Marianne Little One, she refuses to grow, unless it be in your heart."

Yesterday, on the 27th, the precious case of wine arrived by care of the punctual drover, after I had been rather worried about it in view of the cold that had set in. Whether this molten gold will have the taste and fragrance here in the Thuringian forest that it had where the eye had vision of the happy Main, where the ear was quickened by loving speech and the heart by confiding friendship—that is a problem which remains to be solved. . . . The autograph book has arrived, too, and I hope soon to reply to the dear and happy words. And so I bid you to fare well, as you must in the charming companionship that has been granted you.

December 28, 1814

To Zelter

Before the year ends I would send you a friendly greeting and assure you that I am faring quite well. I hope to hear the same of you. Hafiz has been visiting and inspiring me quite industriously and sundry things have come into being which may suggest lovely melodies to you someday.

1815

January 11, 1815

To Knebel

I must not wait longer to say a word to you, my dear friend. I have spent most of my time recently in the Orient where I have indeed found a rich harvest. On a subject like that, one has general notions

and information about details, but once one applies oneself to it
seriously, it is as though an ocean spread out before one. . . .
The poems which you were inclined to applaud have recently been
doubled in number.

1815

WANDERER'S PEACE OF MIND

Baseness in the rest of us
Is no cause for crying;
For it gets the best of us
Spite of all denying.

In the ill it ruleth us
By victorious stature,
In the righteous fooleth us
To adopt its nature.

Wanderer—to such misery
Offer no resistance!
Spiral dust and ordure dry,
Let them cloud the distance.

1815

In my saddle let me be the master!
Hug your huts and tents against disaster!
And in joy I'll ride to the horizon,
Nothing but the stars to fix mine eyes on.

The masters' works I look upon
And clearly see what they have done.
I look at my own stuff—a thing or two,
And see what I should have tried to do.

February 19, 1815

To C. H. Schlosser

Since you have shown me so much confidence and have conveyed to me your profoundest convictions, the differences in our way of thinking were, of course, sharply defined. . . . Since we are about to throw the strongest light upon these differences, which must not serve to separate us, let me set down my general confession of faith:

    a. Everything that is in the subject is in nature.
    y. And something beyond.
    b. Everything that is in nature is in the subject.
    z. And something beyond.

b can have cognition of a, but a presage of y can be attained only through z. Hence arises the equilibrium of the world and of that realm of existence to which we are assigned. The entity which comprehends these four in the highest clarity is that entity which all peoples of all times have called God.

1815

Yield to the moment that arrives,
When world and history are my station?
Who in the ages sees and strives
Alone can rise to speech and to creation.

<><><><>

Naught that is perishable
Deem thou of worth!
Us to eternalize
Are we on earth.

March 12, 1815

To Count K. F. von Brühl

Brühl, 1772-1837, who had lived in Weimar for several years, was now the managing director of the Royal Playhouse in Berlin, where *The Awakening of Epimenides* was about to be produced.

My very dear friend, How glad old Epimenides will be when, opening his eyes after his long sleep, he sees beside him the energetic and
young and gallant man who gives him his new chance to act and
live! . . .

Sorry as I am, I am bound to tell you at once, that I am not able to
accept your kind invitation to Berlin. My health permits me, nay,
forces me to travel to a watering place each summer, but winter and
spring oblige me to stay at home. I might have been tempted to an
exceptional venture in this unusual instance. But I would have been
prevented in any case by the happy circumstance that our very gracious master has announced his arrival for Easter Day. . . .

April 22, 1815

To Karl August

> A decision of the Congress of Vienna, which had recently ended, had
> created Karl August Grand Duke and augmented the territory of the
> new Grand Duchy of Sachsen-Weimar-Eisenach by some 400 square
> miles.

Your Royal Highness has always enlarged to an infinite extent your
contracted circle by arousing and favoring within each one of your
servants an activity appropriate to his character. May a long series
of years be granted you to continue this beneficent activity in a more
extended area. If Your Highness permits me to continue to be the
happy witness and the honest co-worker in that small department
which remains mine, I know that my later days, like those many
others which I have passed near you and used and enjoyed through
your graciousness and your influence, will not vanish without effectiveness and well-being.

April 24, 1815

To Willemer

. . . The unlovely phantoms with which you are in conflict, are
my adversaries, too. The ground on which you stand is the same
region which my feet seek to tread. But from that point on our individual differences appear; for you strive after the general; my nature impels me to seek the particular and concrete. My tendency is

the incarnation of ideas, yours their disembodiment. Yet in these contrary operations there is a common element.

Late April, 1815

To the Willemers

I have suffered grievously. My good wife was but a hand's breadth from death's door. . . . Will I be able to put all that aside and to forget it in view of a beautiful sunset over the Rhine? . . .

Wiesbaden, May 31, 1815

To Christiane

Goethe left Weimar on May 24. He stayed in Frankfurt the 26th and 27th and arrived in Wiesbaden on the 28th.

I am very well established here now. My lodgings are charming but dear; the food is good but cheap. I have ordered wine from Frankfurt, so that the chief matters are well taken care of. Every morning, having drunk the marvelous waters, I take the healing baths. It all agrees with me well, and I can be active in addition. . . .
The weather is the brightest, which is not so good for the truck farmers. There has been no adequate rain for ten weeks. Yet fresh peas are to be had here and best of all is the salmon of which an excellent portion marvelously jellied can be had at any hour in the halls of the balnearic establishment for 30 kreuzer. It's the best time for the salmon; I must be careful not to overeat. Great baskets of oxheart cherries stand at every corner. . . . Perfect roses bloom, nightingales sing and so it's easy enough to imagine oneself in Shiraz. And so I have indeed fitted my recent poems into the larger form of *The West-Eastern Divan* and written a new table of contents.

◇◇◇◇◇

Wiesbaden, June 4, 1815

Now I've been here a week and all continues well. I am drinking the sulphur water mixed with milk. I bathe daily and dictate between. According to the published list there are 400 guests here by now. But I hardly notice them. The town is big and most of those people are really ill. Moreover I neither dine at public tables nor frequent the public places. . . .

◇◇◇◇◇

Wiesbaden, June 7, 1815

. . . I have your dear letter. I suppose you are in Karlsbad by now.
I am writing to Genast. I think we can let August do as he likes. The
Brentanos came to see me and gave me wine and invited me most
affectionately to visit them.

Wiesbaden, July 20, 1815

To Karl August

The Battle of Waterloo had recently been won. The Heinrich von
Stein mentioned is the Prussian statesman and historical scholar, 1757-
1831, who had pled at the Congress of Vienna for the union of the
German states.

Let me dedicate the first of these happy hours to Your Royal Highness and above all to the expression of my sincere and heartfelt
gratitude for the advancement which you have graciously granted
to my son. May he ever strive to be worthy of your favor! I have
thanks to add on my own account. For as I was getting ready yesterday to drive to Johannisberg to deliver your message to His Imperial
Majesty of Austria, the adjutant entered and congratulated me on
the fact that His Majesty had created me a Commander of the Order
of Leopold. . . .
I have received a very kind invitation from Herr von Stein to visit
him in Cologne. I shall do so within a very few days. It is most agreeable to feel at this moment that the general happiness has opened all
hearts, so that people meet with freedom and sincerity. If the
discords of faction were not heard, one would think oneself in
heaven. . . .

July, 1815

Recollections of Ernst Moritz Arndt

Not long before his second journey to Paris, Stein came to Cologne,
where I happened to be at that time. He sent his man to ask me to
meet him at the Cathedral. I went at once. He saluted me most
cordially—and whom did we see almost beside him, admiring the
Cathedral? Wolfgang Goethe, the greatest German of the 19th cen-

tury. Stein whispered to us: "Good people, guard your tongues. Don't talk politics. He doesn't like it. It isn't entirely to his credit, but he's too great to criticize!" It was marvelous to see these two great men together, each revering the other. It continued to be so at tea in the inn. But Goethe was rather silent and soon withdrew to his room. . . . And so it continued for several days. Never have I known Stein to be so gentle and considerate.

August 2, 1815

Boisserée's Diary

Arrived in Wiesbaden and saw Goethe at noon. He received me with happy cordiality. . . .

We talked that day of the gifts of people; how many talents and even geniuses remain undeveloped and retarded by the force of circumstance; how, on the contrary, many dullards are raised even to professorial chairs by luck, training and charlatanism.

◇◇◇◇◇

August 3, 1815

Took a walk with Goethe from 10:30 till noon in front of the great pavilion. Then had dinner in the restaurant inside. After dinner we walked around the lake behind the pavilion and watched the gay people sail their little boats. . . .

Goethe plans to reissue his works in 20 volumes. Two volumes of poems, instead of one. He now thinks his *Italian Journey* one-sided; too much dislike of the Germans, of Gothic architecture, of the climate, of middle Europe. He possesses complete diaries and has asked back from his friends all the letters he wrote them. He also has account books and receipted bills and notations of tips. . . . The *Italian Journey* is almost finished, but he wants first to complete the fourth part of *Poetry and Truth*.

He's working at the *Divan*. Has absorbed much of the Oriental spirit. Napoleon and our period are rich in analogies to Timur, to Djengis-Khan, men like natural forces. . . .

He read me his significant introduction, an exposition of the Oriental spirit and his own relationship to that spirit. . . . He assumes the name of Hafiz as his own in these poems. . . .

He spoke of *Faust*. The first part closes with Gretchen's death. Now he has to begin all over again, and that is very difficult. . . . What he is able to produce now might not harmonize with the earlier parts. I replied, that he must not entertain such scruples. No man can transform himself into another, but a master can transform himself into that self which wrote the earlier works.—Goethe: "I admit it; indeed much has been written."—I asked him what the end of the poem would be.—Goethe: "I won't tell you that; I dare not. But it's finished and has, I think, real grandeur. It belongs to my best period."—I said that I was sure that the Devil would be seen to have been wrong.—Goethe: "In the beginning Faust makes one condition. All the rest follows from that. The man who retains power over himself can accomplish what is hardest and greatest." . . .

◇◇◇◇◇

August 4, 1815

He has started his report on German antiquities. . . . He expresses himself this way: The Holy Spirit has revealed to him that we must finish our first drafts here and therefore stay another week. In Frankfurt people will overwhelm him; if he visited the Willemers, there would be elective affinities. . . . After dinner he discussed the continuation of the *Divan.* . . .
All the splendor of the Orient has, in the end, nothing higher than the description of loving hearts. He spoke of the pride in their poverty taken by true lovers and read us many splendid and charming things. I told him that the *Divan* reminded me of *Faust,* by reason of its grandeur and boldness combined with naturalness and simplicity in the subject matter, as well as in form and diction. He accepted that appreciatively. . . .

◇◇◇◇◇

August 5, 1815

That evening Goethe complained bitterly of the goings on of Pestalozzi [*Swiss founder of Progressive Education, 1746-1825*]. How those methods might well enough have served their first purpose, when Pestalozzi had in mind poor, humble people, who lived in scattered huts in Switzerland and could not send their children to school. But how corrupting it became as soon as one passed beyond the most elementary things and applied this method to language, art and other departments of knowledge, which necessarily assumed a tradition and concerning which one cannot go to work with unknown quantities and empty forms and figures. And worst of all is the horrible arrogance which this damnable system breeds. I ought to see the insolence of the little boys in the Pestalozzi school here. They are not shy of strangers but frighten visitors. All respect, every consideration that humanizes society disappears. What would have become of me, he asked, if I had not always been obliged to respect others? And these people in the madness of their rage reduce everything to the single individual and produce independent gods.

August 7, 1815

Goethe told me that he had written verses on all the political events of his time. Most of them were lost. His son had saved a few. But he cannot live without expressing whatever moves him, be it to joy or sorrow. . . .
In the evening he read us from the *Divan* again. One of the loveliest of the poems was on Adam and Eve; how the Creator made them and took joy in them.

1815

In Eden in the moonshine wide
Jehovah came on Adam who
Slept deep, and gently by his side
Placed little Eve. She slumbered too.

There lay in earthly limitations
God's two most happy inspirations;
Then knew He He had fashioned well,
Himself fain on that spot to dwell.

No wonder souls are lifted high
When eye melts into answering eye,
As though from earth we had risen far
To Him whose shaping thoughts we are.
And when He summons, nothing loth,

We follow—so it be but both—
O held in my arms' limitations,
Thou loveliest of God's inspirations.

⬦⬦⬦⬦⬦

August 8, 1815

. . . Goethe confessed that his poems came suddenly into his mind
and in their entirety, whenever they are right. Then he has to record
them immediately, otherwise they are irrecoverable. Therefore he
is careful not to think of them on his walks. . . . He rarely makes a
change in them. It is bad, too, when he dreams them; they fade from
his mind. . . .

⬦⬦⬦⬦⬦

August 11, 1815

Today, Friday, at 6 o'clock in the morning we drove to Mainz. . . .
We got to Mainz at 8 o'clock and took rooms at the inn of the Three
Crowns.

⬦⬦⬦⬦⬦

August 12, 1815

Beautiful weather this morning. We set out for Frankfurt. . . . I
went to the inn At the Sign of the Swan. Goethe drove out to the
Willemers at the Tanner's Mill. He promised to drive back to town
on Monday.

⬦⬦⬦⬦⬦

August 28, 1815

Goethe did not return to Frankfurt on August 15. He stayed at the Mill
with the Willemers for five weeks.

Wrote some verses on the occasion of Goethe's birthday. Drove to
the Mill at top speed. The Willemer family was there and several
friends, including an old schoolmate of Goethe's. . . . Willemer
started the dinner with an appropriate address, referring to certain
customs of Free Masonry and drank Goethe's health in a vintage of
1749, the year of his birth. In the morning early a boat with musi-

cians in it had passed the pavilion and the music had begun to play as Goethe was rising.

August 30, 1815

Recollections of August Kestner

The son of Werther's Lotte and J. C. Kestner, 1777-1853, now a Councilor in the Hannoverian service. His brother Theodor, 1778-1847, was a practicing physician in Frankfurt.

This Wednesday was a most memorable day to me. I heard from my brother Theodor that Goethe was probably not in Frankfurt, but staying with his friend Doctor Willemer at the Tanner's Mill on the road to Offenbach. Nothing was left me but to drive out there. . . . A footman received us at the door. We asked whether we might wait upon the Privy Councillor. The footman returned with the message that His Excellency would be honored. Up darkish stairs we were led to his spacious sitting room. . . . He seemed intentionally to assume a high dignity, yet was most friendly and considerate. He himself helped draw up chairs for us. First of all he asked which of us two was the Doctor Kestner of Frankfurt.

I gave him my mother's regards. He asked how she was and whether all my brothers and sisters were alive, adding in quite a kindly fashion that our late father had sent him silhouettes of all of us, when we had still been naughty little boys. . . .

After a brief and varied conversation he asked us to follow him to the garden. . . . The garden was a grove on the river. . . . He stopped for a few moments to speak to a gentleman and then led us to a group of ladies. . . . He seemed to be in a continuous state of slight restlessness. Now and then one of the ladies shared in our conversation; after that he walked up and down under the trees between us. . . . From time to time he raised himself on his tiptoes or else stopped and leaned against a tree. . . . His farewell to us observed all the amenities. . . .

In his expression and demeanor I seemed to catch a constant tendency toward self-observation. Thus he seemed to me to lack the unembarrassed freedom which is necessary for the entire ease and comfort of social intercourse.

Tanner's Mill, August 30, 1815
From the Diaries

Music and gifts on the morning of my birthday. At dinner the
Willemers, Boisserée, others. At supper the family and Boisserée.
Divan. Beginning—end. Magnificent weather.

Tanner's Mill, Early September, 1815
Memorandum by Marianne Willemer

In the morning he would stay alone; at 10 o'clock he would drink
of the wine he had brought with him from a silver cup. At dinner
he had on his formal coat and acted rather formally. His conversation
was easier during our afternoon strolls. He would call our attention
to cloud formations, to the coloration of shadows, to plants and
stones. . . . In the evening, wrapped in his dressing gown of white
flannel, he seemed wholly at his ease and most amiable. He would
read to us and he would urge me to sing. I must not forget to say
that often when he read his own poems, tears would come into his
eyes.

September 12, 1815

HATEM (GOETHE) TO ZULEIKA (MARIANNE)

'Tis not chance that leads to thieving,
Chance itself incurs the sin,
Pilfering my heart and leaving
Not a spark of love within;

Unto thee the fullness giving
That my garnered years have shown,
So that, stripped of all, my living
On thy favor hangs alone.

But already does compassion
Make to gleam thy lustrous eyes;
From thine arms in fairer fashion
Of a fate renewed I rise.

ZULEIKA (MARIANNE) TO HATEM (GOETHE)

By thy grace of love enchanted
How can I that chance disdain
Which from thee took the unwanted
And whose booty was my gain?

But why utter words so frightful?
Free to give thyself thou art;
Let me nourish the delightful
Faith 'twas I that stole thy heart.

What thou gavest without measure
Splendidly rewards thy day,
Since my life and all its treasure
Gladly in thy hands I lay.

Jest not! Dearth cannot disgrace us,
Love has amplest wealth to spare,
Holding thee in my embraces
Blesses me beyond compare.

Frankfurt, September 12, 1815

To Christiane

Goethe went to the Willemers' town house on this date. On the 15th he returned to the Tanner's Mill.

. . . At this moment I am alone in town in Willemer's house. You know what a magnificent view it has. There are crowds under my window all day long. I go about a good deal in the city to see people and collections. . . . So sorry to have missed Fritz Stein. Try to keep his mother and the other ladies in good humor. . . . Concerning my return I would say this: it is fitting and advisable that I meet the Grand Duke on his way home. So I'll stay here until he starts back. I'll probably meet him in Heidelberg. Details will follow. . . .

September 15, 1815

Boisserée's Diary

Goethe gave the Willemer a leaf of a curious East Indian plant as a symbol of friendship. The leaf is so formed that one does not know whether it is one leaf, divided into two, or two leaves joined into a single one.

❖❖❖❖❖

September 19, 1815

It had been agreed that Goethe and Boisserée were to go on to Heidelberg on the 20th and that the Willemers were to visit them there the following week.

During these last evenings Marianne sang with very deep emotion, also more expressively. She sang Goethe's "Know'st thou the land," and ballads and other lyrics of his. . . . After supper Goethe read poems. . . . On the last evening of all Marianne sang folksongs and Mozart. She sang from *Don Giovanni* with such seductive magic that Goethe called her a little Don Giovanni. Thereupon Goethe read a group of his new love poems and Marianne listened silently. She had wound about her head a turban-like scarf of yellow which Goethe had given her. Willemer dozed. This went on until 1 o'clock. I accompanied the poet to the door of his room.

❖❖❖❖❖

September 20, 1815

Set out for Heidelberg. On the way we talked about the continuation of *Faust*. His works. The sequel to *Wilhelm Meister*. The limited number of conceivable love intrigues. . . . At noon we arrived in Heidelberg.

September 23, 1815

FROM ZULEIKA (MARIANNE) TO HATEM (GOETHE)

Western wind, thy pinions flying
How I envy and would borrow;

I would whisper in their sighing
Of this parting's heavy sorrow.

As their beating marks the hours
All my yearning they awaken;
Woods and hills and eyes and flowers
By their breath to tears are shaken.

Yet thy mild and dewy weaving
Serves to cool mine eyelids' fever;
Ah, to death I would be grieving
Were I not to see him ever.

Hasten, then to my belovèd,
Speak unto his heart as bidden,
Guarding well lest he be movèd
By my grief which must be hidden.

Gently whisper near his bosom
That I live to love him only,
And that love and life will blossom
When I am no more left lonely.

Marianne von Willemer

REUNION

On September 24 Marianne and her husband arrived in Heidelberg where Goethe welcomed her with this and the following poem which he had written under the chestnut trees of the terrace of the ruined castle of Heidelberg on the day before.

Star that crowns my constellation,
Do I hold thee close again?
Ah, the night of separation
Is a very chasm of pain.
Yes, 'tis thou, O dear tormentor,
Of my fragile joys the foe;
Who has suffered fears to enter
On a present's other woe.

When the world's unplummed foundation
On God's bosom still reposed,
In the rapture of creation
He the primal hour disclosed.
And He spoke the word: So be it!
From the deeps arose a sigh,
As the universe to free it
Broke into reality.

Light burst forth and separated
Shyly from it moved the dark,
And the elements on their fated
Sundered outer flight embark.
Each, a savage phantom, races
Forth into the bleak expanse,
Rigid in unmeasured spaces,
Void of soul and resonance.

Muted was the desolation;
God Himself in loneliness
Added dawn to His creation,
Pitying that cold distress.
O'er the dimness dawn the wonder
Of its sonant colors spread;
All that had been torn asunder
Were by reborn passion wed.

And in swift, impetuous striving
Every creature seeks its own;
The unmeasured joy of living
Beats in hearts no more alone.
Grasping, clasping, not abating
Steadfast bond from core to rim!
God may cease from His creating,
We create His world for Him.

So the rosy wings of morning
Brought thy lips, my dearest want,
And the night, itself adorning,

Seals our starry covenant.
On the earth we are and see it
As its types of joy and pain,
And a second word: So be it,
Shall not sever us again.

Let, dearest, a rewarding
Glance on those branches dwell,
The clustered fruits regarding
In their green, prickly shell.

For long no stirring eases
Their spheric quietude;
A bough tossed by the breezes
Rocks them in patient mood.

Yet ever the brown kernel
Swells unto ripeness on,
To gain the air eternal
And to behold the sun.

At last the cleft shells alter
And give the cores release:
Thus do my lyrics falter
To thy beloved knees.

FROM ZULEIKA (MARIANNE) TO HATEM (GOETHE)

On September 26 Willemer and Marianne returned to the Tanner's
Mill. In the carriage on the way Marianne composed the following
poem. She and Goethe never met again.

Whence this tumult in me stirring?
Does the East wind bring me token
On its pinions' dewy whirring
That can heal a heart so broken?

In the dust he plays and tiny
Cloudlets raises, mock-alarming,
Drives to refuge in the viny
Arbor insects gaily swarming.

Tempers me the noonday watches'
Fever to my cheeks ascended,
Gently in his fleeing touches
Grapes that on our hills are splendid.

In his murmur, as I hearken,
Words come from my friend to meet me;
Ere the hills before us darken
Will his crowded kisses greet me.

Cease not, wind, thy gentle blowing!
Serve the kind and sorrow-movèd.
Soon where lofty towers are glowing
I shall find the much belovèd.

Ah, the heart's authentic presage,
Breath of rapture to revive me,
Only of his lips the message,
Only they on mine can give me.

Marianne von Willemer

FROM HATEM (GOETHE) TO ZULEIKA (MARIANNE)

On September 28 the Grand Duke finally arrived. On the 30th Goethe
drove with him toward Mannheim. On his arrival there he wrote the
following poem. The failure of the first and third lines of the final
stanza to rime is confessional in character since, in the original, the last
word of line one *Morgenröthe* requires in the third line the riming
word *Goethe*.

Chestnut tresses, hold me captured
Near that magic countenance!
Keep me, serpents sweet, enraptured
In the silence of this trance.

Oh this heart endures forever,
Burgeons as in primal age;
Under snow and frosty fever
Etna's fires renew their rage.

Dawn thou!—Such as puts the weighty
Somber mountain-peaks to shame,
And once more arise in Hatem
Vernal breath and summer flame.

September 30, 1815

To Willemer's Daughter-in-Law

I write you this note, my dear, in the hope that you will communicate faithfully to my beloved friends that of which I am unable to express even the thousandth part. Look, as hitherto, I must take refuge in verse and cry out:

Where's parchment, where the pencil all my woe
To chronicle? Yet so it was—yes, so!

After our friends had left us, the evils that threatened me manifested themselves. There was a pain in my chest which threatened my heart. It was a natural consequence of the drafts and changeable temperature in Heidelberg. . . . I hope for a word from you.

October 3, 1815

Boisserée's Diary

Early Tuesday morning we drove to Karlsruhe. . . . Bright clear weather. . . . We spoke of our experiences in these recent days and how everything had pressed in upon him at once, regretting that the Grand Duke had insisted on this trip to Karlsruhe. He praised the Willemers and women in general. . . . Yet one's relationships with women could not serve to fill our lives and lead to so many complications, to anguish and to suffering which wear us out, or else to complete emptiness. Much to be praised and indeed honored are Willemer's moral principles which had sustained him amid the confusions into which he had plunged himself. Thus the saving of the amiable

little woman was an extremely good deed. . . . Old memories arose
in him. How often had he passed the Tanner's Mill on his way to
Offenbach to meet Lili Schönemann. The story of that passion. His
poems to Lili. How they were betrothed. How they had been gradually separated and drifted apart without quite knowing why. . . .
He spoke of his philosophical development; of his having no real
system of his own. How Spinoza had been the first and most powerful
influence upon him. Next of Bacon and his little tractate on Idols.
. . . We arrived in Karlsruhe and had dinner in his room. More intimate confessions on his part.

◇◇◇◇◇

October 5, 1815

Glad to be in the carriage on the way back to Heidelberg. Recapitula-
tion. Other old memories arise in Goethe. Forty years ago a mounted
messenger from the Duke had summoned him from Frankfurt to
Heidelberg. . . . Later on the drive he spoke of *The Elective Affinities*. He emphasized the rapidity and inevitableness of the catastrophe. The stars had arisen. He spoke of his relation to Minna Herzlieb, the prototype of Ottilie; how he had loved her and how unhappy
she had made him. Finally his speech became strangely mystical and
prophetic. He would intersperse verses. At last, weary, irritated, half
mystic in mood, half sleepy, we arrived in the sharp cold under a
brilliant starlit sky in Heidelberg.

Heidelberg, October 6, 1815

To Willemer

My dear and honored Friend, Surely you must know that my mind
and heart are filled with that beautiful place of yours, the groves you
planted and the house you built—that I see them more vividly in
absence and repeat to myself all the kindness and affection and pleasure and indulgence I enjoyed. I am sure that my image has not been
driven from those scenes and meets you often. I imagine an hundred
things—when and how and where I shall see you again. . . . But
things are so that I must hurry home, comforted by the circumstance
that I am on my appointed way and may therefore direct a purer
yearning toward the friends whom I am leaving. . . . Once more

my heartfelt thanks for all your kindness and affection. Yet this thanks were not just, if it did not assume the form of pain. And I leave it to you, who know the human heart, to convey my message.

October 7, 1815

Boisserée's Diary

Goethe was restless early in the morning. He is frightened of being ill. He wants to leave at noon. I offered to accompany him and even told him I would go with him as far as Weimar. . . . In the carriage he recovered somewhat. He was obviously calmed by the fact that the Grand Duke could not reach him again. Yet he was extremely nervous and spoke of illness and death and determined, whatever came or went, to go straight home. . . . We passed the night in Neckar Elz. The room was cold. Yet Goethe was livelier and forgot about the cold and read me some more of his Orientalizing love poems. We slept in the same room. He was happy to have me near him because he still feared falling ill.

Meiningen, October 10, 1815

To Willemer's Widowed Daughter

Early on the 9th the real parting began. Here I became sensible of the separation; for hitherto all had been, as it were, a continuation of my most happy state. As often happens, the last hours were the most fascinating. You put aside a certain shyness when the inevitable approaches and you attempt by utter openness of heart to find a substitute for the loss that threatens. It moved me to take leave of Sulpiz. Almost he would have gone on to Weimar with me. Suddenly I was alone. . . .

October 21, 1815

To Knebel

Goethe arrived in Weimar on October 11.

I can tell you with great pleasure that rich sources began to flow for the *Divan,* which has been brilliantly enlarged. I have even been practicing learning to write Arabic script. . . .

October 25, 1815

To Zelter

So we have gotten to the point of not hearing from each other for five months. . . . But I do not come back empty from my crusades. . . . Thus I am able to announce to you that many items have been added to the *Divan,* of which a number are quite recent and with the dew on them. . . . Much that is singable is among these pieces, yet reflection is, upon the whole, predominant, as befits both their Oriental character and the age of the poet.

1815

> Folk and clown and conqueror seeing
> This, confess it so to be:
> Crown and core of mortal being
> Is man's personality.
>
> Ways of life need little choosing
> If the self itself sustains;
> Winning is not more than losing
> If what one is—one remains.

October 26, 1815

To the Willemers

When dear Sulpiz left me in Würzburg and I was alone on the endless stubble fields of Franconia, I would bitterly have regretted my hasty return home, had not the necessity of it been so clear to me and had I not been certain that I am ever present in the heart of my friends, as they are present in mine.

You can imagine then with what joyous surprise I received the account sent me on October 18, written, as it was, by so dear a hand; how it brought back to mind and heart the delights of last year as well as of our more immediate past.

As was to be foreseen, the days since my arrival have been busy and restless. I found the theatre in a deplorable condition. . . . Before the departure of the Hereditary Prince and Princess there were an hundred consultations, commissions, tasks, frequent visits from Russian magnates and their beauties, even as to this very day creatures hardly divine, such as Cossacks and other Scythians, seem to chill our air as they go Northward from here.

December, 1815

Thank God for all our benefits!
On Helena the tyrant sits!
But while the single one we banished
Our hundred tyrants have not vanished
Who forge, to cut our peace in two,
A Continental system new.
Germany's to be isolated,
A cordon sanitaire instated,
That in our pure midst be not heard
Least echo of a foreign word;
While on our laurels we repose,
And look no farther than our nose.

1816

January 28, 1816

To Arthur Schopenhauer

How often have I wished you here during these winter evenings. For in this particular instance communication by letter cannot be fruitful. I would propose my theory of colors as the subject of our conversation and we would not need to be in constant agreement. . . . Do let me know from time to time what you're doing. You will always find a most sympathetic auditor in me. For, though I am too old to acquire the opinions of others, yet I am always happy, so far as is at all possible, to be instructed as a matter of record concerning their thoughts and the methods of these thoughts.

February 27, 1816

To Voigt

In connection with the appointment of the philosopher Schelling to a professorship at Jena, the question of his religious sentiments had arisen.

Had Schelling come to me as to an old friend of his and asked me about this matter, I would have answered him: Did you not profit sufficiently from our old master Benedict Spinoza, that we and people like us can thrive only at a distance from all controversy. . . . And I, for myself, would also ask: Is he really known to be Catholic? . . . And if he were still a Protestant and became a Catholic after occupying his professorial chair, what could one do then? And if, in such a case, he sought to make proselytes, which is probable, could one follow the example of the Czar Alexander who drove out the Jesuits in a single night? . . .

March 9, 1816

Zelter to Goethe

I face a heavy trial again. On the 17th of last month my youngest son died of a brain fever in France. He had gone through many bloody engagements unhurt. He was captured during the last battle near Versailles. . . . His horse was shot from under him but he was not wounded. He was only 16 and a handsome lad! How shall I bear it? I have plunged into work; I copy scores. . . .

March 26, 1816

To Zelter

Yes, that was a hard task that fate set you. Alas, one must keep repeating the old tune, that to live long means to outlive many, and yet in the end one hardly knows what it all means. A few days ago I came upon a copy of the first edition of *Werther* and that long-silenced song began to ring again, and it was hard to understand how a man could endure the world for forty years when he had seen its absurdity even in his youth. A part of the riddle seems to be answered by the fact that each one of us has something of his very own which he hopes to develop by letting it exercise itself. This curious element in our being fools us daily and gets the better of us, and so one grows old and knows neither how nor why.

April 14, 1816

To Zelter

The Mendelssohn here mentioned was Abraham, 1776-1835, the son of the philosopher Moses and the father of the composer Felix, 1809-1847.

Your letters came as a delightful surprise to me in my garden and gave me much food for thought and stirred me to many reflections. Then came Mendelssohn and since he was introduced by you, I said to him what I would like to have said to you. He deserved my confidence; his conversation was full of insight and he brought out many important points in science and art and life in the course of our talk. I am sorry not to have seen his family, but they stayed for only one afternoon. Otherwise I would have asked them for breakfast and shown them some of my things.

May 3, 1816

To Zelter

The ceremonies of homage to our Lord as Grand Duke were to take place on April 7 and were to be the completion of the new arch after so much destruction and suffering among us. Well, on April 2 I was seized by a strange and painful, though not dangerous rheumatic attack. I had to take to my bed. I was quite sure that I could not possibly attend the ceremonies. Then, luckily enough, I was reminded of something that Napoleon said: *"L'Empéreur ne connait autre maladie que la mort."* So I said to the physician that, unless I were dead, I would be at my place next to the throne at the proper hour on Sunday. I was also able to perform my duties at dinner. Thereafter I withdrew and went to bed. . . .

May 22, 1816

Christiane to Goethe

Dear Privy Councillor, I must ask your pardon for not having followed right away your well-meant counsel about the bloodletting. Most likely I would have escaped this misery. I thank God that it is happily over. At present I feel pretty well and my head is easier and all my senses clear and cheerful and I don't notice that pressure or heaviness in my head any more. The only thing that bothers me is the mustard plaster. Goodbye and think of me.

P.S. There isn't a bit of champagne in our cellar. The man didn't deliver any. I am sending you two bottles of Rhine wine.

Weimar, June 5, 1816

From the Diaries

> On May 29 Christiane fell violently ill. Goethe hastened home from Jena, but he himself had a sudden attack of violent fever and even the servants fell ill.

Forced to spend the day in bed. My wife in extreme danger. The cook and maid only so-so. My son's help and advice the only thing to cling to in this confusion.

Weimar, June 6, 1816

Slept well and feel better. My wife approaching her end. Her death struggle was dreadful. She died at noon. Emptiness and deathly silence within and without me. . . . Meyer came and Riemer. At midnight my wife was taken to the crypt. Spent the day in bed.

June 8, 1816

To Zelter

. . . When I tell thee, thou harshly tested son of earth, that my dear little wife passed away during these days, thou knowest well what it means.

June 8, 1816

To Boisserée

. . . Let me add that my dear little wife passed away during these days. I am sure that dear friends will sympathize with my situation.

Weimar, June 8, 1816
From the Diaries

My wife buried at 4 o'clock this morning.

June 8, 1816
Recollections of Riemer

Considering his manner of being and living, he will miss his wife often enough. Though he seems composed and talks quite as usual, suddenly grief will overcome him and he will have difficulty in forcing back his tears.

Early June, 1816
Wilhelm Grimm to Achim von Arnim

Riemer told me and Johanna Schopenhauer, too, that her agony had been dreadful. The convulsions were such that the maids could not bear to stay in the room. He wept aloud and it would have been unnatural, had he not done so. He hasn't been out of the house yet and has seen only a few friends.

June, 1816
Elisa von der Recke to Johanna Schopenhauer

What always reconciled me to Christiane was that I never heard her speak evil of anyone. Then, too, her conversation always seemed to me of such a character that I could understand how Goethe might not be displeased by her unassuming brightness and natural good sense. I remember his introducing her to me with these words: "I can give my wife the recommendation that, since she first crossed this threshold, I have had nothing but joy of her."

June 25, 1816
Johanna Schopenhauer to Elisa von der Recke

I saw him for the first time today since the death of his wife. You know his way of not facing his friends until any pain he suffers has been allayed and he can, at least, seem perfectly composed. Yet I did find him changed, depressed in his inmost being. I must say it hurts me that no one thinks of her compassionately, that all her good qualities are forgotten and only her failings mentioned even by those to whom she was kind and who flattered her not a little while she was alive.

June 26, 1816

To Wilhelm von Humboldt

Immersed in this feeling of loss caused by the departure of my good little wife, I find nothing more consoling than to look about me and see how much that is good and loving is still left me. . . . I took to an odd way of entertaining myself these past days. I looked through the papers and manuscripts of my past, where I found so much that had been begun and abandoned, so many purposes and inexcusable disloyalties to them, that I can do nothing but throw myself, in true Oriental fashion, upon the mercy of God.

July 19, 1816

To Zelter

. . . The tempter approached me. He assumed various forms and so he succeeded in persuading me that I must go to Baden on the Rhine. I'll start tomorrow. . . .

July 23, 1816

To the Willemers

At 7 o'clock in the morning of July 20 I set out from Weimar in the company of my friend Meyer. At 9 o'clock the awkward coachman overturned the carriage; the axle broke and my companion was injured in the forehead. I was unhurt.

Nothing remained but to return to Weimar where we arrived around 1 o'clock. The interruption of our plans and the injury sustained by my friend make it uncertain, indeed improbable, that this journey will be undertaken anew.

I wanted to let you know at the earliest moment. I need not assure you that this incident annoys me profoundly.

Tennstedt, August 28, 1816

To Zelter

Early in August Goethe, accompanied by Meyer, went for several weeks
to Tennstedt, a small spa in Thuringia, where he stayed through September 1.

Your dear letter came just at the right time so that I can take pleasure
in it and converse with you a little today. I am celebrating my birthday in unusual solitariness. Meyer was with me for four weeks and
Wolf came for a brief visit. He left today and I am dependent on
myself. Despite their great advantages, these two men are very different when one associates with them. Meyer, though as certain of his
opinions as Wolf, never disturbs his friends. He knows enough to be
silent or to guide the conversation. Wolf, on the contrary, has delivered himself up to the spirit of contradiction. Whatever one says,
he negates it with the utmost stubbornness, and though one is prepared for this, it finally drives one to despair.

September 19, 1816

To August

Without going into the details, my dear son, of the particular case in
which you intend to assume financial responsibility for someone else,
I would like earnestly to commend to you the following considerations. When my good father started me out in life he gave me, among
other examples of good counsel, one which had the force of a command, namely, that never in my life was I to assume a responsibility
of this character. He asked me not to let this warning die with him.
For, said he, if you have cash you may lend it to a friend even without adequate security. If you want to give it away, there is no objection to that either. If you borrow money, you will see to it that
you can pay the interest and gradually, too, the capital. But if you
stand surety for another you deliberately incur an anxiety which is
the more painful in that it reduces you to a passive suffering which
you can do nothing to alleviate. Of course, no one assumes a financial
responsibility for another unless he believes that he is quite safe.
But once the action is completed, he soon begins in nervous moments

to have a sense of a distant threat of evil which is all the harder to
bear because he feels himself unprepared for it, were it to approach. . . .
Such was the conviction of my father and it has remained my own. I
have done a great deal for others in my life, perhaps more than was
quite fair and have forgotten my family and myself in the act. You
know enough of me to know that this is no idle boast. But I have
never assumed a responsibility of this character and you will find no
document involving one among the papers I shall leave behind me.

September 29, 1816

Clara Kestner to August Kestner

> In his *Supplementary Confessions* covering the year 1816, Goethe re-
> calls, among other visitors, who "all aroused memories of early and
> earliest periods" Mme. Councillor Kestner from Hannover. This is, of
> course, the Lotte of *Werther*. She was accompanied by her daughter
> Clara, the writer of this letter. It is upon this incident that Thomas
> Mann's novel *The Beloved Returns* is based.

On September 25 we drove over to dine at Goethe's house. His son
received us at the foot of the stairs. He came to meet us in the antechamber and was quite like the picture you drew of him. His heart
was evidently quite unstirred. He spoke at once as though he had
seen mother yesterday: "How very nice of you not to bear me a
grudge for not calling on you first." It seems that he had a touch of
gout in his arm. Then he said: "You're quite a traveler, aren't you?"
And similar commonplaces. Mother introduced me to him, whereupon he asked me about our journey here and whether I had ever
before been in this part of the country. I answered his questions
calmly. Thereupon we went to the table. He took mother's arm
and, naturally, gave her the place at his side. I was seated immediately opposite him, so that no word or expression of his could escape
me. Unfortunately the entire tenor of his conversation was so com-
monplace and superficial, that it would be presumptuous for me to
say that I heard him speak or spoke to him, for nothing that he said
came either from his soul or from his mind. He was uninterruptedly
courteous toward mother and toward us all. It was the courtesy of a
courtier. After dinner I asked him about a very beautiful drawing

which had attracted my attention. He had it taken down and told me
the history of it very politely and spoke of the great distinction and
talent of the lady whose work it was. Thereupon he sent for a portfolio and showed mother the silhouettes of herself and of our dear
father and of you five older boys. From this you see that he wanted
to be agreeable, yet everything about him was so curiously enameled
by a courtly crust, there was so little that was heartfelt about it all,
that my very soul was wounded. His rooms are sombre and furnished
in uncommon fashion. Vases stand here and there; the walls are
decorated with drawings none of which, in my opinion, are excellent
except the one that had attracted me. After we had seen everything
we drove back to our inn. He once more apologized for his inability
to go out. He had even had to decline an invitation from the Ducal
Court.

October 6, 1816

To the Willemers

Deprivation of good is a wretched thing. It is nothing in itself and
yet it devours what little the day may yet have to offer one. So I have
dragged along for quite three months, no stranger to myself nor yet
myself. So if I do not make my appearance at the Mill nor salute
the miller nor the miller's wife, in brief, if I do not write, it means
simply that I am here and would not seal with words the sad priva-
tion that I suffer by being far away.

October, 1816

To Voigt

. . . I do not deny that I would consider the absolute abolishing of
the practice of anonymity of all printed matter the greatest benefit
that one could confer on any nation, especially on the German
nation, at this time.

October 13, 1816

To Boisserée

My only refuge is continuous activity. The first volume of the *Italian
Journey* will be my next publication. I look up old manuscripts and
edit them as best I can. I find variety enough in this undertaking. It

is incredible and sometimes very funny to see all the groping attempts one has made in the course of life, whence one finally learns to know exactly how the horses, whom one is too old to ride, can be broken in.

To the Willemers

Bereft of any music the winter lies about me. And so the most desirable, indeed the most necessary thing often seems to me the entering into your house in imagination. For although no one can do better than abide in his own place and do the best he can there, yet the temptation is very great to seek with confident assurance the friendly arms and gates that are open far away. . . .

1816

Why is each hour so full of dread?
Long is the day, though life's soon sped!
And ever the yearning heart would flee,
If heavenwards is dark to me;
Far, far it strives, again, again
And from itself to flee is fain;
And if it reach the loved one's breast
Unconscious is that heavenly rest;
Life whirls it onward in its race,
And yet it clings to one sole place;
Whatever its wish or loss or gain,
Self-duped at last it must remain.

November 12, 1816

To Zelter

. . . It seems to be that we grasp the experiences of our youth only in our later years. Never do we learn or apprehend anything once and for all. Whatever affects us is no more than a stimulation and we must be grateful if it causes the inner man to stir and ring out. I have been reading Linné and have been astonished at this extraordinary man. I have learned an infinite deal from him, not only botany. Except Shakespeare and Spinoza I can mention no one among the dead who has influenced me so markedly. . . .

The fact that Wolf continues to tell the anecdote of his behavior toward me points to his bad conscience. I'm sure he doesn't tell how perfectly beastly was my retort. Happily or unhappily, I had drunk more glasses of Burgundy than was reasonable and so my sense of measure was lost. Meyer, who is always so composed, sat beside us, and even he was uncomfortable. . . . That's how it came that I passed my birthday alone and contentedly enough. For Wolf is so maddened by the spirit of contradiction that he would have congratulated me by asserting that I had never been born.

December 16, 1816

To Boisserée

The happy reception you gave to my *Italian Journey* pleased me much; I will go the more industriously at the second part. As, long ago, the older authors wrote for us who were then young, so must we now write for you young people. . . . You had quite the right perception of the book's tempo. You also have a just insight into its frequent lack of fairness. That harsh crudity is perhaps appropriate to the impulse from which the early part of the book sprang. Before the traveler returns home across the Alps you will find it all gentler and more palatable. Did I not possess the accurate diaries and almost all the letters I wrote from Italy, this little work could never have attained its immediacy and its freshness.

December 25, 1816

Charlotte von Stein to Goethe

Permit me, dear Councillor, to send you my Christmas tribute in the form of a wax taper and a tart baked at Kochberg. . . . So soon as the weather is at all endurable I will come to see you in your hermitage.

Weimar, December 31, 1816

From the Diaries

Ottilie von Pogwisch, 1796-1872, daughter of the widowed Frau von Pogwisch, since 1804 lady-in-waiting at the Weimar Court, where Ot-

tilie's grandmother, the Countess Henckel von Donnersmarck, was Lady-
of-the-Bedchamber.

Engagement of my son to Ottilie v. Pogwisch.

1817

January 2, 1817

To Knebel

The New Year begins in rather motley fashion for me. The news
that my son is going to marry the older Mlle. von Pogwisch will perhaps have reached you. It is the desire of both of the young people
who have long entertained kindly sentiments toward each other. I
had expected the matter to become more serious long ago, yet there
can be no more appropriate moment than this. It is easy to see that
this match will consolidate many good and agreeable relationships.
Both the Court and the town seem satisfied and so the young people
may enter upon their venture.

January 8, 1817

Zelter to Goethe

. . . Your New Year's letter contains fine news. The marriage of that
able son of yours with a girl regarded with affection and approbation by everyone cannot but be very pleasing to you.
Now the little woman can come and stroke the old gentleman's
beard and scratch his back and slip off at the right time and taste
the soup and look in the corners and pass her fingers over the furniture after dust and see what the weather will be and go to the stable
to order the carriage to drive up and take the old child out in the
sun and let the air blow about him and then wrap him in his cloak
and put him in the carriage, so that on his return the soup is on the
table and a friendly eye watches him and 'tis Little Father this and
Little Father that. . . . Remember me to the fine son and his sweetheart.

February 23, 1817

To Zelter

Since I first mentioned it to you, a very curious change has taken place in the matter of our theatre. . . . I've got the whole burden on my back again, as I had so many years ago. I am beginning as I did then. . . . All circumstances are favorable. On the artistic side, on the technical one, in the matter of money, the arrangements are all that I might desire. . . . Moreover, it will be easier, because my son has been associated with me in the directorship. I will have unlimited power of decision in all matters of art and will not have to be bothered with the secondary techniques.

Jena, March 31, 1817

To Charlotte von Stein

Karoline Jagemann, the influential mistress of the Grand Duke, insisted on the performance of a farce in which a trained dog appeared. Goethe, concerned for the dignity of art and no dog lover, was horrified. Charlotte von Stein tried to intervene. The Grand Duke was persuaded to permit the performance. Goethe resigned as director of the theatre and his resignation was accepted. Karl August soon went to Jena and apologized. There were tears and embraces. Goethe never entered the theatre again.

I seem to perceive that the mediation of our good Knebel could involve us in misunderstanding. Therefore I turn to you, my dear friend, precisely to you, grateful for your dear and cordial understanding. This is the state of affairs:

In order to render necessary managerial changes useful and fruitful, I drafted a constitution which pleased both Serenissimo and my colleagues. Therefore I drafted resolutions which have been sent off and which I want accepted. . . .

To think all this out and make it practical is my whole concern in my quiet retreat here. If this effort of mine succeeds, a relationship will have been arranged according to which I can continue to influence an institution, from which I can never withdraw my sympathy. Alas, dear friend, I cannot ask you to come to see me. The valley roads are under water and the weather perfectly dreadful.

                                                            April 13, 1817
Karl August to Goethe

Dear Friend, Various remarks of yours which have come both to my
ears and eyes, have tended to inform me that you would be glad to
be relieved of the annoyances inseparable from the management of
the theatre, but that you will be glad to offer your advice and helpfulness to the management whenever the need arises, which is sure
to occur quite often. I am glad to meet your wishes in this matter,
adding my thanks for all the good you accomplished in this confused
and tiresome business, begging you to retain your interest in the
artistic aspects and expressing the hope that relief from these annoyances will improve your health and prolong your days.

I am enclosing an official letter pertaining to the matter and sending
you my best wishes.

                                                            May 5, 1817
Recollections of Riemer

On the subject of his decision to resign the management of the theatre, I found our Goethe who, in these local matters, is usually very
self-restrained, in a state of extreme excitement. This was one evening a few days ago. In the course of the conversation he said: "Actors and public are in the same confusion and this confusion is now
made co-extensive with art. A man would have to go to another
country in order to remember the good that was once here and is
now being destroyed. I've never felt in this place a natural need of
what is good; always and again this lust for the bad breaks through.
I can stand it no longer. I cannot permit disgrace to be added to
annoyance. The least forbearance undermines all my work, until
the whole crashes. . . . If there is no other tendency than that which
must have novelty even on the lowest plane—well, then one must
leap from the carriage that is about to plunge into the abyss. . . .
What we have here is an effeminate mob and the rule of women suits
it exactly."

May, 1817

Anecdotes of Adolph Stahr

   Writer, pedagogue, interviewer and gatherer of anecdotes, 1805-1876.

Goethe's powerful nature survived the blow of his removal from the management of the theatre. But it is quite certain that the matter shook him to his depth and that at the first moment of extreme perturbation he half planned to leave Weimar forever and to accept the splendid offers made him from Vienna. It is equally certain that Karl August soon felt remorse over the affront offered to his old and trusted friend. . . . He wrote him in a conciliatory spirit to Jena at once. But his pressure on Goethe that he resume management of the theatre was in vain. It is a mark of Goethe's greatness and dignity that he made no mention of this matter in his biographical records, although it went so deep that at the first moment he exclaimed: "Karl August never understood me!"

June 1, 1817

To Rochlitz

I don't know whether I ever told you that my fondness for the 16th Century persuaded me to buy a considerable collection of majolica which was found in Nürnberg. It has arrived safely. It is a pleasant thing to see, but I want to add that art objects of a secondary character, such as these are, can be judged only in the mass, from which both its merits and its faults are clear. If you find things of this kind in Leipzig, and they are not too dear, do me the favor of notifying me.

Weimar, June 13, 1817

From the Diaries

Document concerning the conditions of the marriage drawn up.

Weimar, June 17, 1817

Wedding ceremony at 7 P.M. Reception. Supper.

◇◇◇◇◇

Weimar, June 18, 1817

The little couple off on its wedding journey.

June 18, 1817

To Boisserée

From the date of the enclosure you see, my dear fellow, that there was in my house last night a great festivity of an unique kind. The young people are a most original pair; each seems predestined for the other. I have no fear for them at all. . . .

All my friends, physicians and laymen, insist that I go to Karlsbad. It is true enough that the waters have always done me a great deal of good. But I won't go until late July when the flood of guests has ebbed or is about to do so. . . .

This is the first time in my life that I'm letting the printer hound me, and it is odd how one can pull oneself together at need. I have dreamed and simmered away a great part of my life. Looking through my old manuscripts I find so much that is good in intention and significant in detail, but never executed. Everywhere I find impulse to creation and distraction by life.

August 4, 1817

Charlotte's Sister to Fritz von Stein

Papa is terribly fond of the daughter-in-law. While he was in Jena she had to write him once a week and he replied. He reads all his favorite things to her and everything new that he writes. Since she is very clever, it pleases her greatly and her soul nestles very kindly against the paternal one. She was among the young choristers that used to meet at Goethe's house during his wife's lifetime. When she became engaged to August, the old man said to her one day: "Listen, Ottilie, I warn you of one thing—my son just loves to be praised. You mustn't ever contradict anything like that. If you feel like quarreling, come and quarrel with me. I can stand it."

1817

TO OTTILIE VON GOETHE

Come, my dear, ere we continue
Halt thy tread and look about:
For the age attempts to win you
Now by silence, now by shout.

How thy childhood was my profit,
What thy girlhood meant to me,
In thy heart the record of it
Will reveal itself to thee.

This reward thy faith may gather
Even while these songs thou sing'st,
That to us, through son to father
Sturdy, handsome boys thou bring'st.

October 13, 1817

To Knebel

The most remarkable thing that I have recently seen is Byron's tragedy of *Manfred*. A young American presented the book to me. This strange and brilliant poet has absorbed my *Faust* and his own morbidity has drawn the most curious nourishment from it. He has used all my motivations in his very own way, so that none remains the same, for which very reason I must admire his mind. . . . Of course it is not to be denied that the sombre glow of his boundless and manifold despair becomes burdensome in the end. Yet one's very annoyance is never devoid of admiration and respect. All our womenfolk are mad for this man and are devouring the book. When they're through with it, I'll send it to you.

October 17, 1817

To the Willemers

And so once again the Apostles of the Lord [*12 bottles of precious Rhenish wine*] have sought me out. I welcome them, yet how much

rather do I salute those who sent them. I have so often conversed
with you in my thoughts, dear friends, that I can no longer tell what
was written and what only arose in mind and heart. . . .
What shall I say to that most kind of invitations which allures me
more than all feasts? . . . What has happened since the epoch of
our meeting I dare scarcely call to mind, nor dare I compare my
present estate with those beautiful days and hours. For I am more
involved than ever with the undelightful accidents of mortality. I
have been freed, thank God, from one business which was massive
in its evil; now I am enmeshed in other matters which are no better
in detail and which threaten to become massive in their own way.

1817

Chide not my tears! Enclosed by night
In the limitless desert.
The camels rest and also their drivers.
The wakeful Armenian counts his takings.
While I, beside him, reckon the distance
That separates me from Zuleika, rehearsing
The interminable, exhausting serpentines between.
Chide not my tears! They are not shameful.
Good are men who can weep.
Wept not Achilles for his Briseis!
Xerxes bewailed the undecimated host;
Over his self-slain beloved
Did Alexander weep.
Chide not my tears! They fructify the dust
To greenness.

October 18, 1817

Recollections of Victor Cousin

French eclectic philosopher, influenced by Kant, Hegel, Schelling.
He was in Germany to study the system of higher education which he
recommended for French adoption. 1792-1867.

"Very well," Goethe said, "since you love philosophy and want to
acquaint yourself with German philosophy, I could well speak of it
to you, for I have witnessed its rise and development. . . . I have

seen everything in Germany, from rationalism to mysticism. I have
been present at all the revolutions. A few weeks ago I took up Kant
again; nothing can be clearer than the ultimate inferences of each
one of his assumptions. The Kantian system stands. This system or,
rather, this method consists in the discrimination between subject
and object. This 'I' which exercises its judgment upon a certain
matter does so with the reflection that it is this individual 'I.' Hence,
even as the subjects and the guiding principles of judgments are
diverse, so it follows simply that the judgments themselves will be
diverse, too. This Kantian technique is a principle of humanity and
tolerance." He added later that German philosophy is the expression
of very varied intellectual tendencies. "We have had one after another in Germany, rationalism, representationalism, the philosophy
of feeling, finally that of ecstasy." . . .
I cannot render even a faint picture of the charm of Goethe's language. It is all his own and yet approaches the magic of the infinite.
In it are terseness and breadth, clearness and force, fullness and simplicity and withal, I say it again, an inexpressible charm.

Weimar, October 31, 1817

From the Diaries

Jubilee of the tercentenary of the Lutheran Reformation.

December 4, 1817

To Boisserée

Let's leave all other things aside. I am so glad that you immediately
recognized the subject of Nausikaa as fit for tragedy. I knew you
would, and it grieves me anew that I never went on with that plan.
I needn't tell you what touching and heartrending motivations could
be brought out. If these could be followed to their most delicate
fibres, as I did in *Iphigenie* and especially in *Tasso,* how effective
that could have been!

Jena, December 16, 1817

To Zelter

I am living partly in Weimar, partly in Jena. I have pleasant occupations in both places. But in Jena I can study, too. . . .
In this innocent way I preserve my privacy and let that horrid Jubilee Reformation stench and fume dissolve. It sickens all Germany. Here it would have vanished long ago, did not the northeast wind blow it back to singe our faces a second time.

From the Supplementary Confessions

During this year English poetry and literature in general occupied the foreground. The poems of Lord Byron, as the peculiarities of this extraordinary mind became better known, engaged ever greater sympathy. . . . As it became easier to obtain and possess his works, I, too, fell into the habit of paying attention to him. . . . I had heard a great deal about Peter Pindar. . . . He seemed to me, when I read him, to have merely a talent for caricature. It seemed to me that the *Life of John Hunter* was of great import as the memorial of a magnificent mind which had to develop nobly and powerfully by the teachings of nature with very little academic training. The *Autobiography of Benjamin Franklin* came with a message of the same character, though infinitely different in detail.

1818

January 16, 1818

To Antonie Brentano

Since my little ship not, alas, richly laden, weighs its anchor, it is very amiable of my friends to wave their handkerchiefs to me as I depart. . . .
What an innocent and hermit-like life I lead you can see from the fact that I pay no attention to the many flying leaves and leaflets and pamphlets that come with every wind. Injustice and unfairness are the order of the day; how can political parties be considerate of each other? . . . My days are ordered according to the maxim, that where none spares his neighbor, one must spare oneself. . . .

Jena, February 10, 1818

To August and Ottilie

A young artist friend has made me a present, fit for talent and charm to give. It is a portion of the Phigalian frieze; Hercules in combat with the Queen of the Amazons. . . . It is a facsimile in the dimensions of the original. . . . It is a well of wisdom and power. To contemplate it is to become two thousand years younger and better. One cannot say more. Do come and see it!

March 6, 1818

Recollections of the Countess Julia von Egloffstein

The daughter of Henriette von Beaulieu, 1792-1869, lady-in-waiting at the Court and painter.

I spent the evening with Ottilie and Goethe invited us into his rooms. He was very charming in his big white dressing gown and rocked us, as it were, in the gentle up and down of his conversation. . . . He spoke of Wiesbaden and said the life there was marked by such ease and serenity that it spoiled one for everything else. He wouldn't go there very often. Karlsbad was far less dangerous to one's equilibrium. . . . "Look, dear children," he said finally, "how far would I have gone if I hadn't always associated with clever people and learned from them? I want you girls to learn things through the living exchange of ideas in society, rather than from books."

Jena, March 19, 1818

To Zelter

Let me be very frank and console myself by saying to you, that if you are really sincere with me, you won't invite me to come to Berlin. Such is the opinion of all who wish me well. Of course our excellent Wolf—give him my regards, nevertheless—doesn't care. He would have somebody else to contradict. . . . By the way, the other day a man assured me that my prose style was as bad as Xenophon's. I must say that that comforted me. . . .
You yourself have conferred a true favor on me. A delicate feminine

creature sang me your music to my "Midnight Song." Once more
you have stamped upon a piece of work your love and understanding of me most honorably and ably. My son, who is far from musical,
was utterly delighted. His gratitude is such that he will probably
invite you to be the godfather of his first-born.

1818

AT MIDNIGHT

At mid of night I went with no great pleasure,
A tiny fellow, past the graveyard gate
To father's house, the parson's; heavenly treasure
Of radiant stars shone beautiful and late
        At mid of night.

When farther on in life my pathway wending
To some beloved by strong compulsion led,
Northlight and stars above my head contending,
Both back and forth on rapture I was fed
        At mid of night.

Until at last of the full moon the brightness
Made clear and visible the darks of space,
And my thought, too, with meditative lightness
Grasped past and future into one embrace,
        At mid of night.

March, 1818

Recollections of Countess Karoline von Egloffstein

A sister of Julia von Egloffstein, 1789-1868, and also a lady-in-waiting.

Goethe leaves Weimar tomorrow because he wants to avoid the
anxiety attendant upon Ottilie's accouchement. He makes me sing
to him and seems very cheerful. Zelter has set some of his new poems
to music and it is these I sing and play.

From the Supplementary Confessions

All winter the *West-Eastern Divan* had had my devoted and loving
and passionate interest, so that by March there was no further need
to delay the printing. . . . A strange condition of soul, induced in
me by a sublime moonlit night, brought me the poem "At Midnight," dearer and more precious to me because I could not say
whence it came nor whither it tended.

Jena, April 2, 1818

To Karl Ernst Schubarth

Who still a student had published a critical study of Goethe.

The little book you announced has not yet reached me. But friends
spoke favorably of it to me without giving me any details. Since
you seem to be anxious in regard to my reception of it, it is my duty
to allay any fears that you may have.

When a man has passed his life cultivating whatever is in him with
the desire to be relished by and useful to one's world, nothing can
please us better than to know that contemporaries, especially the
younger among them, take a vital interest in our work and its development. . . . If they seek to understand how it was with their
predecessor, how he, definitely gifted by nature, had first indulged
his talent and sustained himself awkwardly enough, but had later
come to the aid of his destiny and, despite the wild waves of life, had
not stranded but entered a beneficent harbor. . . .

If you had this in mind, you have contributed desirable elements to
your own development by what you have written. For it is quite
indifferent whether we apprehend an activity which tries its strength
against the world in the figure of a Ulysses or a Robinson Crusoe,
or in that of a contemporary and his moral, civic, aesthetic, literary
efforts. For everything that happens is a symbol; insofar as it represents itself perfectly, it contains the significance of all else. It seems
to me that this reflection combines the highest presumption with the
deepest humility.

Jena, April 9, 1818

From the Diaries

A military messenger brought me the news of the birth of a boy.

Weimar, April 16, 1818

Arrived at noon. Looked over my garden. Visited the young mother. Had dinner with August. Discussed pressing matters.

Dornburg, April 29, 1818

Müller's Diary

. . . Our conversation rose to a higher plane. Goethe said: "The ability to ennoble the objects of our senses and to bring to life the torpid stuff of earth by marrying it to the idea, such is the handsomest guarantee of our supra-sensual origin. Man, strongly as earth attracts him with her untold thousands of phenomena, yet raises his searching and yearning eye to the heaven which curves its immeasurable spaces above him, because he feels deeply and clearly that he is the citizen of a spiritual kingdom, in whose existence we cannot and may not disbelieve. This presentiment holds the secret of our eternal striving toward an unknown goal; it is at the same time the lever of all our research and reflection and the gentle bond that unites poetry and reality." . . . Suddenly he rose from his seat. "Children," he said, "let me hasten to be alone with the eternal rocks down there. After such speech it is fitting for the old Merlin to draw near again to the primordial elements." Happily moved we looked after him long as, swathed in his light-gray cloak, he took his solemn course into the valley.

1818

> If I but knew the Eternal's way,
> Nothing could ever persuade me to stray;
> If the House of Truth had an open door
> By God, I would leave it nevermore.

◇◇◇◇◇

"You cling to immortality;
Tell me why you refuse to doubt it?"
Gladly! The chief ground is to me
That we dare not to do without it.

Jena, May 1, 1818

To Boisserée

You will forgive the grandfather for your friend's failure to write. The life force works ever more strangely; it uses up one's powers in things near, so that in the end nothing is left to project into the distance. . . . My physicians urge me to go to Karlsbad. I am reluctant to do so, firstly, because I've lost my faith in the cure; secondly, one gets accustomed to suffer inconveniences and is not as impatient as in youth, when one imagines life without obstacles or conditions to be possible.

Moreover, I have been busy in many ways. Did I tell you that I have moved into cheerful quarters here on the right bank of the river immediately by the bridge? There I have a bay window with a beautiful view of river, land and city. Everything is in bloom at this moment. . . .

Fate, which imposed upon me the task of putting in order the library of our university here, seems to revenge itself upon me for that monologue of Faust and that blasphemous disesteem of knowledge.

Jena, June 8, 1818

To Christian L. F. Schultz

Government supervisor of the University of Berlin, adherent of Goethe's scientific theories. He visited Goethe frequently from 1814 on. 1781-1834.

Our Prince is expected on June 20. The accouchement of the Hereditary Princess is likely to take place at the same time. So I am tied down here until about the middle of July. Then I have to go to Karlsbad, which seems most necessary, despite my vaunted unbelief in the cure. After my last catarrhal attack I am barely able to putter around. . . .

I have, on the other hand, nothing but good news of my young people. They are well suited to each other, even if they did not love each other. The child exercises its power of uniting them; they enjoy their happy situation in Weimar and ask nothing better than that I were able to share it with them. . . .

Since recently it's almost impossible to talk to anyone, I'm having various things published. He who reads it may accept it or reject it. That leaves me cold. If I had nothing to say except what people like to hear, I would prefer to keep quite silent.

1818

> If the Lord had wanted me to be
> Different, He would have seen to it.
> But since this talent He granted me,
> To trust me He thought fit.
> I've used it too freely to reckon,
> Nor know the final score;
> When it serves no more,
> Be sure He'll beckon.

Jena, June 11, 1818

From the Diaries

The baby was vaccinated today.

June 19, 1818

To Voigt

Man is a curious being! Since I know how the machine works, I'm no longer interested. God could cause us the keenest embarrassment, if He were to reveal to us all the secrets of nature. For lack of interest and boredom we wouldn't know what to do.

June 19, 1818

Charlotte von Stein to Lotte Schiller

. . . I am truly sorry to hear that our friend Goethe is ill. He ought to hurry and go to Karlsbad. It is rather saddening that he is inaccessible to love and open only to the appeal of art.

Karlsbad, August 1, 1818

To Ottilie

People at first tried to frighten us about finding accommodations in Karlsbad this year. Undeterred we drove there and stopped in front of the Three Moors. They gave us spacious rooms at once. Next morning people vacated my old suite on the third floor. We moved into it and everything goes extremely well. . . .

Since the day is very long, I manage to be well entertained by the work I have taken along. . . .

All this being so, one must put up with the high prices. The old prices of commodities have been retained, but the gulden is quoted at 8 groschen. People are not buying; they need what money they have for their daily necessities. Nevertheless I am sending you chocolate and pins and a few similar things.

August, 1818

Recollections of Genast

Goethe's faithful servant, Karl Stadelmann, was ordered by his master on the morning of August 27 to fetch two bottles of red wine and two glasses and to place one bottle and one glass in each of two windows on opposite sides of the room. This having been done, Goethe began to walk up and down in the room from one window to the other. From time to time he would stop at one of the windows, next at the other, and each time he stopped he drank a glass of wine. After quite a long while the Duke's physician who had accompanied Goethe to Karlsbad entered the room.

Goethe: You're a fine friend! You don't even know what day and date this is!

The Physician: It's August 27th, Your Excellency.

Goethe: Oh no, it's the 28th; it's my birthday!

The Physician: You're wrong. I wouldn't have forgotten that. It's the 27th.

Goethe: Can't be! It's the 28th.

The Physician (Very decisively) : It's the 27th!

Goethe (Rings. Karl enters.) : What is the date?

Karl: It's the 27th, Your Excellency.

Goethe: The devil! Fetch me a calendar! (Karl shows him the calendar.)
Goethe (after a long silence) : Damn it all! Here I got drunk for
nothing at all.

Karlsbad, September 4, 1818

To Knebel

I want to tell you, dear friend, that after my birthday, which I spent
gaily and feeling well, I had a very bad catarrhal attack. Under good
medical care I soon got better, so that I'm planning to leave here
on Sunday, the 13th. I'm writing you this in order that vague rumors
may not cause you anxiety. This monition seems to have been addressed to me so that I may not feel and consider myself too happy.
For the first five weeks of my stay were delightful beyond all hope.
I'll tell you all about it. Remember me to your family and to all
friends and forgive me if I pass through Jena without stopping off
to see you.

September 29, 1818

To Karl August

Will Your Royal Highness graciously allow me to submit the enclosed documents concerning the order by which His Majesty, the
King of France, deigned on the occasion of the Order's anniversary,
to appoint the undersigned an Officer of the Legion of Honor? Since
I can take no pleasure in this distinction without Your Royal Highness' consent, I herewith submit the matter for consideration.

Early November, 1818

Marianne von Willemer to Goethe

Your kind letter and the accompanying pages took me back wholly
to that time in which I was so happy and, if I may say so, youthfully
gay. If I recall that condition now, I might justly compare myself to
a tree which a lovely autumn persuaded to bud once again. The life-
giving sun adorned me once more with the wreaths of youth. 'Twas
my last taste of happiness. My life grows sombre now like a cold
winter; the blossom has fallen to earth. . . .

Let me thank you for the message from the East [*Stitched sheets of the* West-Eastern Divan]. How much that is lovely echoes therein, how much to bring me delight. Raised to greatness by your spirit, every tiny incident, every involuntarily spoken word, enter into a higher sphere. I am astonished at the familiarity of all to myself and rejoice deeply that it was mine, that in a certain sense I may claim it as my own. . . .

November 30, 1818

To Boisserée

My excellent Zelter has been visiting me. As he leaves I am impelled to send you a greeting. A very few days suffice for old and tested friends to come to a perfect understanding again and to rejoice in the constitution of human things. May the fashion of this world pass away, if only friendship fail not, if friends continue to love the same, to detest the same, to follow the same path and to avoid its contrary. This was my experience with my true, old friend; I trust that this coming year the experience may be repeated with you, my younger friend.

1819

January 4, 1819

To Zelter

Elaborate Masques were performed in honor of the visit of the Czarina, mother of the Hereditary Princess.

Your letter and the culinary package arrived. My best thanks for both. The excellent carrots adorned the fish and furnished forth a friendly meal. . . .
Since your departure I have done nothing I intended to do. In view of the Imperial visit I could not well refuse to superintend the Masques and processions. The procession consisted of nearly 150 persons. It was no small task to have them appropriately costumed, to group them, to invent their march and to present the right stage picture. It took five weeks of my time. True, we were cordially applauded, but this applause was bought dearly enough when you consider the expenditure in imaginative energy, time, money, and

that all this in the end was puffed away, like fireworks, within a few minutes.

From the Diaries

Adele Schopenhauer brought me her brother Arthur's book: *The World as Will and Representation*. Read a bit here and there and discussed it.

March 14, 1819

To Fritz von Stein

First of all I want to tell you that my charming daughter-in-law wishes to thank you so much for the excellent and plentiful delicacies. As a housewife and hostess she is now able to offer friends and associates something truly good; also, she herself enjoys these things which, as a rule, we lack during the winter. From time to time, I have been told of good and ill that came to you during these years and always heard the news with a sympathetic heart.

Weimar, March 22, 1819

From the Diaries

Minister von Voigt died at 1 o'clock today.

March 26, 1819

To Marianne von Willemer

Jakob Willemer on his way to Berlin had visited Goethe on the morning of this day.

I experienced a beautiful moment of deception this morning. As my honored friend entered the room, I hoped that you, my beloved friend, would follow him at once. How deeply the moment taught me that I am still all yours! Write me a word. Herewith fragments of the *Divan;* the whole will soon follow to bear witness of the constant intercommunication with my distant friend. And so it shall be forever.

1819

MARCH

There came a sudden snowing,
For it was all too soon
That of the flowers glowing,
Of all the flowers glowing
Should come to us the boon.

The sunshine gleaming nigher
Was false even as it shone,
The swallow was a liar,
Ah yes, he was a liar
Because he came alone!

Can I be glad so lonely,
Although the spring is near?
When we are two, then only,
Oh, when we're two, then only
The summer will be here.

April 14, 1819

To Trebra

Scarcely had I somewhat recovered from the passing of our honored friend and co-worker Voigt, than I hear that another true and admirable friend is dangerously ill and about to bid us farewell. Those of us who survive find the world rather desolate.

May the enclosed poems in which the old swan sings of past times and merits, yet not without some hope for what is to come, reach you at a benign moment and enable you to stay for yet a while with your faithful friends.

1819

BETWEEN TWO WORLDS

(The reference is to Charlotte von Stein and Shakespeare.)

With one only love to tarry,
Reverence to one shrine to carry

Blends the heart and mind in one!
Lida, of all bliss the nighest,
William, of my stars the highest,
All I am by you was done
In the vanished years whose hours
Yet were source of all the powers
In whatever worth I won.

1819

TODAY AND FOREVER

Vain effort which the day its image shows.
The mirror adds confusion from within.
Each in self-righteousness unbridled goes
And yet demands his neighbor's discipline.
This being so, better for lips to close
While stronger pinions may the spirit win.
No yesterday becomes today; but ages
Will rise and falter in alternate stages.

April 18, 1819

To Rochlitz

It is well worth the trouble of having lived to be accompanied by
such minds and spirits as your own; it is not hard to die, if one
leaves such friends and admirers to keep one's memory fresh, to
heighten it, to pass it on. Accept my thanks, then, for your magnificent letter which I regard as one of the handsomest testimonials I
have ever received. Soon you will receive a copy of my *Divan* and I
promise myself its favorable reception at your hands.
My children will probably pass through Leipzig quite soon. Do show
them your country place, in order that they may tell me of the
restoration of that delightful retreat. . . .

May 17, 1819

To Johann Friedrich Schlosser

. . . The news of the death of your venerable mother arrived while
I was contemplating the merits of my admirable friend and co-
worker of more than forty years, Minister von Voigt. . . . In many

ways the memory of your mother will be a blessing to you, even as
on my own way I am often forcibly reminded of my mother's way
of thinking and acting, of her courage and her faith. . . . My children are in Berlin to enjoy the radiance of that royal city. My grandson thrives and I myself feel better than I have done for long.

May 26, 1819

To August

Your letters, up to the one of May 18, my dear son, are all here.
They gave pleasure to us and to all close friends. Thus it is but fair
to let you hear from us. . . .
An English painter, Herr Dawe, has arrived. He has painted my portrait. He worked off and on for four weeks. He became a new uncle
in the family and, as Ulrike [*Ottilie's sister, 1804-1875*] insists, the
most tolerable of them all. . . .
Furthermore, my old friend Cogswell, a free North American, called
on me on his way through here. He brought me handsome books and
told me many fine things about the United States. . . .
Nothing now remains for me to say but to send my love to Ottilie,
to wish you pleasure in all your undertakings, to assure you that the
little fellow grows prettier and better behaved daily and that Ulrike
is cheerful.

May 28, 1819

To a Student in Breslau

I am herewith sending you the list of books in our Grand Ducal
library which I promised you and which may be of interest to you
in your task. . . . Let me add a word concerning these new nation-
alistic affectations. From of old the masses are united by their prejudices and excited by their passions alone; thus the best purposes are
darkened and often contorted. . . . But I would not have you disturbed by these matters in the pursuit of your special aims; the
peculiar character of a nation can be best judged by its behavior
toward the world beyond its own boundaries.

May 29, 1819

To Zelter

Thank you for your kind reception of my children. I don't seem to feel happy any more except in my house. Especially during the summer it possesses all advantages; furthermore, I have at hand in it all the things I have gathered about me these many years and which are both delightful and useful to me.

Have patience with the children and let them drink and enjoy their share of that great spring after their own fashion. I do not find that August mentions Wolf. See to it that he does not neglect our friends.

June 2, 1819

To Karl von Brühl

From my son's letters I perceive with admiration all that you are doing for the performance of *Faust*. It is an undertaking that needed your genial power and devotion. Wolff will tell you why we got stuck in the middle of it here. . . . Unquestionably your stage will open a new epoch in the German theatre.

June 13, 1819

To Rochlitz

. . . Let me add an observation not unfitting for an old author to make. There are three kinds of readers: those who enjoy without any judgment; those who sit in judgment without enjoyment; between these two there is a minority which judges while it enjoys and enjoys while it judges. This minority really reproduces the work of art within itself. . . .

June 18, 1819

To Boisserée

My children are in Berlin and Dresden; I like the thought of their being in the midst of the rich movement of life. They have left their boy in my care; he is 14 months old—well, well behaved and bright. . . .

Going through all kinds of past work is, of course, a very special kind of return to circumstances that are gone. The distraction by life which took me from one object to another and from one task to another becomes very apparent. As I open these notebooks and manuscripts and examine them, I shake my head over and over again.

June 18, 1819

To Charlotte von Stein

If you, my dear friend, and your dear guests would come and take tea with me this afternoon, it would be most delightful for us all.

Jena, July 11, 1819

To Georg Nicolovius

I had no doubt at all, my very dear friend, that my children would be well received by you, as I was equally sure that the remarkable sights of the royal city would be shown by you and disclosed to our young travelers in their search for new experiences. And so it came to be and at the same time there was established a living and familial relationship between our houses which did not arise earlier by reason of the curious development of other years. Do let it grow and become effective and let the children make up for what the fathers neglected.

July 26, 1819

To Marianne

No, my sweetest friend, you shall not be left without a word from me, since you opened your dear lips again to break the undelightful silence. Need I repeat that, on that March day, I thought you inseparable from my friend, so that at the sight of him there revived within me all that he was noble enough to grant us. . . . Now that you speak, now that you say so charmingly that you not only think of me but do so gladly, let me give you the double and treble assurance that I reciprocate your feelings constantly and from the very heart. May this letter reach you in a fruitful hour and cause you to add a long commentary to its brief text.

August 21, 1819

To Schubarth

Your valuable letter and enclosure arrive just as I am about to clear
my desk and pack my things for a journey to Karlsbad. I hasten to
thank you for your continuous sympathy and confidence. . . .
At the time of its discovery I absorbed as much of the *Lay of the
Nibelungen* as agreed with me. Whatever this poem may now or in
future mean to others, I am not able to concern myself with it at
this moment. As once before, I feel like the corpse of Moses for the
possession of which the demons are said to have fought. I hope you
will do your best to see to it that this archfather receives decent
burial among his ancestors in the grove of Mamre.

From the Supplementary Confessions

I must not neglect to record the sympathetic messages that came to
me from many places and from many quarters on the occasion of
my seventieth birthday. Yielding to a whimsical and stubborn sense
of embarrassment, I have always tried to avoid any celebration of
this day. This time I spent it in my carriage on the way to Karlsbad.
I arrived there late and I thought that to a limited degree, I had accomplished my purpose. But a banquet had been planned for August 29. I excused myself from attendance in view of the state of my
health, not quite without good reason. From afar, too, the kindness
of people surprised me. In Frankfurt a handsome and significant
celebration in my honor had been held on August 28 and the German Historical Society had elected me to honorary membership.

Jena, October 7, 1819

To Zelter

How can I thank you enough for the precious letters which offered
me so much companionship and constant converse during my journey. The first batch came to Weimar, the second to Karlsbad, the
third here to Jena, where I arrived ten days ago.
I have nothing to offer you in exchange for your account of your
stirring life. In Karlsbad, where the cure agreed with me very well,

I lived quite isolated. . . . And so the four weeks slipped away, not quite in idleness, for I outlined and reflected upon various things that I mean to work at this winter. Since I haven't been alone for a long time, as I was then, I was able to concentrate and use my own pen, instead of that of an amanuensis. . . . It's a pity that you had to pay such a high price for my *Divan*. I'll charge it to my traveling expenses. On journeys, when money is so necessary, it seems to lose in value. I hope the little book will edify you once again. There's a lot in it, a lot to take out, a lot to put in. A fine copy is being put aside for you.

December 24, 1819

To Reinhard

Karlsbad did me a great deal of good this time, yet a certain moodiness succeeded my journey. I am trying to control it by instant activity. . . . I am seeking to put into final form many ideas and interests of my past and I am almost coming to look upon myself as the editor of someone else's literary legacy. I am sending you my *Divan*. I have already been much pleased by many a pleasant echo it has awakened. The days in which I wrote it will never return. Yet it is a kind of poetry so appropriate to the later years of life that I still from time to time manage to write things which may be interpolated and render the whole more accessible through the filling in of gaps.

1819

His final works to smooth and polish
God sent art, science, order, law,
Drenched with His grace, these were the raw
Antics of mankind to abolish.

From heaven they came in stript distress
Awkward and blundering in their crudeness;
Poetry clothed their nakedness,
And they were no more shamed by rudeness.

◇◇◇◇◇

1819

From whence I came? It is most questionable,
My hither path is scarcely less obscure;

Only this day makes heaven's delight no fable
When pain and joy have made a compact sure.
O happiness, when both such covenant keep!
Who, all alone, would either laugh or weep?

December 27, 1819
To Marianne

At the right time, in the very hour when my children and the small
grandson hastened toward the sweets of the season and left the
grandfather to himself, there arrived the pictures of you, my dear
friend. I had looked forward to them. The expression of the likeness was so happy and contented as though the picture knew how
welcome it was. And so I shall not be lonely even when the winter
snow separates me from the world and I shall salute the returning
sun in the best companionship. . . .

1820

Weimar, January 6, 1820
From the Diaries

Started to reread *The Elective Affinities*.

January 14, 1820
To Boisserée

A committee had been formed in Frankfurt to erect a monument to
Goethe during his lifetime. Boisserée was the committee's chairman.
The matter dragged on for years and came to nothing.

In my estimation the sympathy shown me on the occasion of my
birthday by my dear native city and by the rest of Germany quite
sufficed to mark whatever merits I have and to ease a modest contemplation of the results of my life work. The plan you mentioned
to me, of going even farther, demands the most careful and humble
consideration, lest Nemesis be invoked to take a hand in the matter.
Moreover, my age and state of health do not fit me for daring undertakings. If I am to go on living, it must be according to tradition and

custom. Karlsbad again did me so much good last year, that I am determined from every point of view to go there again in the very early spring. . . .

March 23, 1820

To Zelter

The account of your vacation experiences was very valuable to me. . . . I am proceeding gently to edit, separate, preserve whatever interested me in the past as well as possible and so I rescue a good deal from the Lethean floods and put to use every tolerably comfortable hour. I live in entire isolation, waiting for the first breath of spring; then I return to Karlsbad to the effects of which I owe this tolerable winter. In the garden beyond my window the first lilies of the valley are emerging; soon I expect the crocuses; next I hope to go beyond these beds of flowers.

March 28, 1820

To an Italian Critic

Goethe was an early admirer of the Italian poet and novelist Alessandro Manzoni, 1785-1873, whose best-known work *I Promessi Sposi* was not published until five years after this.

Sir, I must no longer delay the thanks due you for sending me the tragedy of Manzoni, *Il Conte Carmagnola,* although at the moment I can speak of it only in generalities. I recognized Manzoni as a born poet from his beginnings on and commended him as such to my compatriots. He sustains his quality as an original poet in this tragedy, too; he will continue to be a credit to his country.

His failure to observe the unities of time and place will hardly be blamed among us here. We have for many years shared the conviction which he so freely expresses in his preface. It suffices to gain our applause that he has observed unerringly the necessary third unity, that of action and of interest, so that our sympathetic attention does not waver from the beginning to the end.

April 3, 1820

To a Collector of Specimens of Handwriting

There is no doubt in my mind that the handwriting of a given person sustains a relationship to his mentality and character and that from it a perception, at least, of his way of being and acting can be gained. This is analogous to the fact that one recognizes expressions, tones, the very gestures of the body as significantly harmonious with the total individual. But I think these things far more matters of feeling than of clearly conscious knowledge. Details may be discussed with profit; a methodical and integral treatment will hardly succeed.

I myself possess a considerable collection of specimens of handwriting; I have had frequent occasion to reflect on the matter and render myself some accounting of it. And so it seems to me that everyone who applies his mind to it, may well make some little progress and gain some little insight into the way to be pursued, at least for the sake of his own instruction and satisfaction. . . .

I cannot fulfill your wish for certain specimens you desire; I think I'll find one by Herder which I can spare.

Recollections of J. S. Grüner

Grüner, 1780-1864, was magistrate and chief of police in the Bohemian town of Eger, not far from Karlsbad.

Goethe arrived in Eger on April 26 and sent his passport to Karlsbad for validation to the police officer in Eger which was in my charge at that time. Since I knew the great man from his works, I wanted to pay him my respects and I asked his servant to announce me. I was admitted immediately and handed Goethe his passport. . . . His personality made an indescribably deep and agreeable impression on me. . . . He usually wore a dark-blue coat that came down to his calves, occasionally, too, a black swallow-tailed coat and knee breeches of the same color. His garments were cut in the prevailing fashion but not conspicuously so. He wore a delicate waistcoat of white or black silk, a neck cloth of white batiste narrowly folded about the throat; the two ends of it were secured by a stick pin. He was full-blooded, as was evident from his ruddy color and so he was accustomed to wear his neck cloth loosely. In his apartment he discarded it and worked in his dressing gown. On excursions and other drives he took along his cloak even in summer. It had a standing collar lined inside with red velvet which projected about a quarter of an inch above the collar's edge. He wore his decorations only on festive occasions.

To Zelter

I went on an excursion to Marienbad, a new and important balnearic establishment. The situation of the town is admirable. Yet
there were difficulties and discomforts, but they are being removed
in time. The architects and landscape gardeners know their business
and are letting their imagination go to work. . . . It seemed to me
in a way as though I were in some North American wilderness, where
forests are cut down so that a town may arise within three years. The
felled pines are used as foundations, the splintered granite rises as
a wall and is combined with scarcely cooled-off bricks; harmoniously,
industriously, skillfully, painters, stucco workers and decorators from
Prague and other places cooperate. . . .

May, 1820

Recollections of Karl F. von Conta

An official of the Duchy of Weimar, 1778-1850.

In May, 1820, I had the good luck to see Goethe almost every day.
He was in a most cheerful mood and was fond of talking about certain periods of the past and especially about his friend Schiller. . . .
He spoke of Schiller's early death and said that he had been sharply
criticized for not at once having a memorial performance in our
theatre in Weimar. "How could I think of that? I was crushed!" He
attributed Schiller's far too early death to the poet's way of working.
He said: "It was always my opinion that a poet should not set to
work until the creative impulse became irresistible. To the observ-
ance of that principle I owe my serene old age. . . . Schiller was not
satisfied with this. He asserted that a man must be able to act at the
command of his will. He abided by this principle. Let me give you
an example. Schiller determined to write *Wilhelm Tell*. . . . After
he had gathered all necessary material and completed his research,
he sat down to work and"—at this point Goethe arose and brought
his fist down on the table—"quite literally did not get up from his
chair until the play was done. If weariness overcame him he laid
his head on his arm and slept a while. So soon as he awakened he
did not ask—as has been falsely reported—for champagne, but for

strong black coffee to keep himself awake. So the play was written in six weeks."

Karlsbad, May 19, 1820

To Zelter

Let me commend the *Divan* to you again. I know what I put into it. Some of that can be disentangled and put to your use. . . . Meanwhile new verses arise. Oriental religion and myth and custom are the right sources for such poetry as befits my years. Unconditional resignation to God's unfathomable will, a serene vision of this stirring earthly life with its way of circular and spiral recurrence, love, benevolence, the alternation between two universes, the purification of the real until it resolves itself into the symbol. What more can Grandpapa want?

1820

A little lake was bound by frost;
The frogs now at the bottom lost
Could neither croak nor swim nor spring,
But in their somnolence they swore:
If once again they reached the shore
They would the nightingales outsing.
The spring winds came, the ice thawed out,
The frogs landing with courage stout
Squatted complacent in the sun,
And croaked as they had always done.

◇◇◇◇◇

1820

What props in evil days my mind?
Sensible people their bread will find,
Able men will the land sustain
And lovely girls make one of twain.
So long as things like these go on,
Be sure the world is not undone.

Karlsbad, May 11, 1820

To Zelter

Isn't it curious how that fragmentary *Prometheus* of mine which I gave up and had forgotten raises its head again? The well-known monologue which I printed among my poems was to open the third act. You're not old enough to remember that our good Mendelssohn died as a result of the poem's premature publication. Don't let on that you have a manuscript; I don't want it reprinted. It would be welcomed as a very gospel by our revolutionary youth. . . . Strange, nevertheless, how this recalcitrant fire has smoldered these fifty years under its poetic ashes until at last it approaches inflammable matter and destructive flames threaten to break out.

Jena, July 9, 1820

To Zelter

Let me begin this letter with an anecdote. You may remember that the *Prometheus* fragment first appeared in Vienna in very small format. . . . The Duchess of Cumberland, recovering from a serious illness, asked me to recite something to her. The *Prometheus* was at that time closest to my heart. She admired it very much and I presented a little volume to her. At our last meeting she spoke of those days and of the poem and expressed the desire for one of those little copies for a friend of hers. Of course, I hadn't any. Now by good luck I found one of these little lost sheep in Karlsbad. I bought it for her. Naturally, it has to be bound first to be worthy of her most beautiful hands. Since she has spoken to you of me so often, I thought it would be charming if I sent it to her through you. Say nothing about this but tell me how you feel about it.

Jena, July 16, 1820

To Boisserée

Let me first speak of the Frankfurt monument, for it would be a discourteous kind of modesty if I were not to make the inquiry. So

tell me what is planned. Insofar as is seemly for me to give an opinion . . . I would make the following tentative proposal. Rauch of
Berlin [*well-known sculptor, 1777-1857*] enjoys a well-deserved reputation. . . . He could visit me within the next few months and
take his model with him. In view of the enormous amount of work
in marble that is now being done in Berlin, the bust would soon be
finished. . . . I hope your life is beautiful and I want you to think
of the hermit who, from his cell, yet hears the roaring of the sea.
Use what I say concerning the bust with the utmost modesty and
discretion. Whenever I give advice terror overcomes me. For who
knows the far consequences of a suggestion, even though it was a
good one to begin with.

.   Jena, July 23, 1820
From the Diaries

Drove to Dornburg where an East Indian juggler displayed his art
before their assembled Lordships. Dinner. Thereafter conversed on
the terrace with the East Indian and his wife.

Early August, 1820
Marianne to Goethe

And so another year has passed and that day, dear to us all, without
our friend. With both delight and sadness we think of him and of
the beautiful hours we spent together. Will they ever return? I
doubt it; for the same thing does not recur in life and the similar
but rarely, and so each autumn sees the renewed death of a secretly
nurtured hope. . . .

Jena, September 1, 1820
To Boisserée

It gives me pleasure to be able to report to you that on August 15
Herr Rauch came to Jena with several friends and made a bust of
me with which I am thoroughly satisfied, as are all my friends here.
. . . His treatment indeed, has an effect of grandeur and will be
impressive in whatever dimension it is executed.

Jena, September 15, 1820

To Reinhard

Although the condition of society in the world today can hardly be called delightful, yet for my part I confess that I am indeed well situated. A stream of travelers passes through the Duchy. Now the occasion is some holiday in which professors and students are wont to travel; next comes the season when people go for cures; the occasions are countless. No day passes but that strangers ask to be received. I spend a couple of hours a day with them, and these hours are never uninstructive. People of the most diverse kinds, approaching and passing by my solitariness, give me an easier notion of the world beyond than I could gain in any other fashion.

Jena, September 20, 1820

To Zelter

Well, that does look like something! Last time I hear from you you are clinking champagne glasses with an irresistible princess and now I behold you on the salty waves about to put down the vilest swill, to which no toast can be drunk. . . . During the period when you, an Odyssean vagabond, have the audacity to ride the dark and dangerous sea, I have stayed quietly at home. . . . I must now add what I should have begun with. Alas, that our gayest melodies must often turn to the minor key. My daughter-in-law has given birth to a sturdy boy. But her delicate nature made her pregnancy a period of dreadful suffering to her and, if I am to be quite frank, I must say that I am badly frightened. . . .

October, 1820

Recollections of Adele Blumenbach

Daughter of a professor of medicine in Göttingen.

When Mme. Frommann and her daughter left home this autumn for several weeks and the foster daughter, Minchen Herzlieb, was in the house alone, Goethe went to see her almost every day to chat away the lonely hours with her.

Jena, November 3, 1820

To Schubarth

What you say of the dedication to *Faust* and of the prelude is really
faultless. What touched me particularly were your conjectures concerning the second part and the final resolution. You have felt correctly that there will be an approach to the ideal and an enfoldment
within it; only my treatment must take its own peculiar path. There
are upon this earth magnificent errors, both real and imaginative, in
which a poor human being might lose himself in a nobler, worthier,
higher fashion, than takes place in the first and earthier part of the
tragedy. . . . You also had a correct feeling about the final outcome. Mephistopheles may win the wager only by half. If the other
half of the guilt remains on the shoulders of Faust, there is still the
Old Master's prerogative of forgiveness which brings the whole to
the serenest close.

Early December, 1820

Recollections of J. G. von Quandt

Art critic, 1787-1859.

On the return from our second journey to Italy my wife and I had a
great impulse to call on Goethe. My wife was introduced by Mme.
Councillor Schopenhauer to Mme. Chamberlain von Goethe, whose
lively mind and affection for her father-in-law served so well to cheer
his later years.
During our short stay in Weimar we saw Goethe daily. Rauch had
been there recently to make a bust of him and the clay model still
stood in his house. I expressed the desire to see it and Goethe asked
me to come in the next morning. . . . Goethe was jocular on the
fact that nature had played him a trick. The right side of his forehead had an indentation and his right eye was set somewhat lower
in his head than the left. From this anomaly he derived the entire
conformation of his face, speaking as a physiologist, as an artist, as
a poet, as a universal mind. It was especially instructive to me to
hear Goethe say that the artist must stick to the facts of reality and,
especially in portraits, make no conscious changes. . . .

1821

Karl August to Goethe

My dear old friend and comrade-in-arms amid the storms of this world, I send you my best wishes for an easy and comfortable year and my thanks for your expressions of unchanging friendship. . . .

January 22, 1821

Müller's Diary

Just as I entered his study Goethe was arranging some proof-sheets. "Surely that's not *Wilhelm Meister's Pilgrimage?*" I asked, because I had been quite excited by an article in a Frankfurt paper. "And why not?" Goethe asked in return. So I had the certainty without having betrayed my doubt. This started an intimate conversation about the whole of *Wilhelm Meister*. Goethe had re-read the original, except the very first part, for the first time in many, many years. Most of it had been written even before he went to Italy. Today it was a source of joy and of comfort to him to find that the whole novel was symbolic and that behind the foreground personages, a general and loftier action and meaning were hidden. The book had been misunderstood for long; it had even been considered offensive. But Germans always needed a great deal of time before digesting properly a work that deviates at all from the usual, and adjusting themselves to it and reflecting on it. In the days of her bitter exile in Jena, the Queen of Prussia, who at first had not cared for it at all, had become passionately devoted to the book and had read it again and again. Perhaps she discovered that it knocks upon the heart in those deepest places, where true human grief and true delight and true sorrow and true joy are wont to dwell. . . . No doubt, Wilhelm himself is a poor enough creature, but only through such an one was it possible to illustrate the interplay of life's forces and the thousand varying tasks that life sets us, rather than by means of a ripe and well-developed character.

February 14, 1821

To Knebel

At last, my dearest friend, I live to see a great wish of many years realized, namely, to see your translation of Lucretius in print. I am going to express my personal thanks to Herr Göschen. . . . All that is left for me to do now is to wish that your well-thought-out and laborious undertaking be well received by the public. . . .

What causes Lucretius to rank so high and to be of such permanent value is his keen and exact and able vision of the sensuous world which gives such power to his delineations. Next there is at his command a vivid imagination which pursues the scene into the unseeable depths of nature, beyond the reach of the senses, into the most secret hiding places of the universe.

February 28, 1821

To Charlotte von Stein

It made me unhappy to hear of your ill health. May the spring cause us all to thrive. Not too easily have I managed to get through the winter by not leaving the house and by the greatest regularity. But I do not deny that I hope that spring will free me from my prison and that I will then be able to come and salute you once again.

March 7, 1821

Recollections of George Bancroft

The American historian, statesman, and educator, 1800-1891.

I was with Goethe for a half-hour today. . . . He spoke of the progress of colonization in America and of the agreeable manner we have in America of setting before each advertisement a little cut denoting its subject, as a house, a ship, a horse. He thought it a very interesting custom. . . . Goethe is still very industrious. He often dictates for several hours in succession. Professor Riemer says of him, he brings forth like the mice, who carry about in the womb young ones ready for delivery and others just beginning to exist. At present Goethe has finished a volume of *Wilhelm Meister's Pilgrimage*.

1821

TO THE UNITED STATES

America, thy fate is kinder
Than that of our old continent,
No ruined keeps are thy reminder
Of ages misspent.
Thy soul is not shaken
As thou buildest thy life,
Because there awaken
Old cries of vain strife.

Use then thy fortunate present so
That when thy children come to write,
A kind fate guide them to forego
The false romance of ghost and knight.

Weimar, April 23, 1821

From the Diaries

Dug up the first asparagus of the season today.

May 10, 1821

To Brühl

Although, my very dear Sir and Friend, I have reason to be fairly satisfied with my condition, yet your handsome and cordial invitation is calculated to arouse a feeling of disappointment within me. It makes me realize that old age is a burden, in that it hinders us from enjoying many desirable goods. All this winter I didn't leave the house and even spring has seen me no farther than my garden. How should I venture upon such a journey and become involved in the excitements of the great world? Accept my excuses then and convey them to my Royal Friend as well as possible, and be assured that on that festal day disquietude and impatience will stir within me for my inability to join in the great things that are to be done.

Weimar, May 11, 1821

From the Diaries

Happened to pick up *Wilhelm Meister* this evening.

◇◇◇◇◇

Weimar, May 12, 1821

Read *Wilhelm Meister's Apprenticeship* all evening.

June 13, 1821

To Knebel

Rarely have I seen anything, my very dear friend, that pleased me more than the two volumes of your Lucretius. What memories arise and what a series of years opens itself to my view when I think of your steadfast efforts! . . .

I wish you had been with us last night. The Ducal Chief Architect Coudray [1775-1845] happened to pick up the copy of your book that lay on the table. He read from it with excellent expression, which improved as the spirit of the poem got hold of him more and more and as the clarity of your text and the natural charm of your verses made him more and more enthusiastic. If you were to send him a copy without the Latin original, it would be most fruitful. He is a good reader and often reads in society. My Pilgrim will soon knock at your door. The binder is holding us up, or he would have done so already.

Their Lordships are now all gone abroad and there is a great stillness hereabouts. I find it difficult to move beyond my little territory, since the habit of staying at home must first be shaken off. The solicitude of my children assures my comfort at all times and ties me down. Yet I will soon seek to mobilize myself a little.

July 21, 1821

Diary of K. G. Carus

Physician, naturalist and painter, 1789-1869.

Soon after 11 I hastened to Goethe's house. The moderately spacious mansion built in antique style, the gradually rising stairs, as well as the objects in the niche of the stairwell—the dog of Diana and the young fawn of the Belvedere—expressed the inclinations of the master of the house. . . . A vigorous tread in the adjoining room announced his approach. He entered in a long blue coat, boots, short-cut, slightly powdered hair, the features quite as in the bust by Rauch. He held himself erect and approached me and led me to a sofa. . . .

The footman brought in a collation. I was moved to see Goethe pour wine for me and break a roll, keeping one half and giving me the other. He spoke of my two paintings which I sent him through Frommann a year ago; how one of them, the picture of the hut on the Brocken, had long been mysterious to him and how a third person [*the Grand Duke*] had finally explained it to him. . . . Then he sent for his portfolio of drawings concerning comparative anatomy, which he had worked at long ago.

August, 1821

Recollections of Ulrike von Levetzow

Several years before, Goethe had made in Karlsbad the acquaintance of Frau Amalie von Levetzow, the mother of three daughters, Ulrike, 1804-1899, Amalie and Bertha. Now Goethe met the family in Marienbad in 1821 and 1822 and 1823. During that last season his paternal affection for Ulrike flamed briefly into the last great passion of his life.

I made Goethe's acquaintance in Marienbad in 1821. Mother had brought me from my boarding school in Strassburg. . . . Marienbad was at that time a small place; it was just beginning to be built up and the house of my grandparents, City of Weimar, was almost the largest and handsomest. In this house Goethe had hired lodgings. I can remember the very moment of our meeting. Grandmother had me called, and the maid said there was an old gentleman who wanted to see me. I was rather annoyed, because I had just started a piece of fancy work. When I entered the room I found my mother there, too. She said: This is my oldest daughter, Ulrike. Goethe immediately took my hand and asked me how I liked Marienbad. Since I had been for some years in a French boarding school in Strassburg

and was only 17, I had never heard of Goethe and had no idea that
he was a famous man and a great poet. So I wasn't at all shy with
the friendly old gentleman, as I usually was when I met strangers.
The very next morning Goethe asked me to take a walk with him.
I had to give him an account of Strassburg and of the school. I complained to him how lonely I felt separated from my sisters, and I
imagine that my childlike frankness pleased him, for he took a very
great interest in me. He took me along on his walk nearly every
morning. When I didn't go along he brought me flowers. . . . In the
evening, too, he would sit for hours on a bench outside of our door
and tell me of all kinds of informing things. . . . Neither now nor
later did it occur to my mother or anyone else that this constant companionship could mean anything but the pleasure which a man, who
could well have been my grandfather, took in the company of a mere
child. . . . That first summer Goethe made me a present of a copy
of *Wilhelm Meister's Pilgrimage*. . . . He had written on the fly
leaf: To Ulrike von Levetzow, in friendly recollection of August,
1821.

August 30, 1821

Recollections of Grüner

Under Emperor Siegmund the synagogue at Eger had been transformed into a Catholic church. Goethe and I drove out to see it.
Set into the outer masonry we found a box for charitable offerings
with a Hebrew inscription no longer legible. In the nave there was
another Hebrew inscription carved in a column. I was eager to know
Goethe's opinion of the Jewish people. But however much I hinted
around, he remained absorbed in the ancient inscriptions and made
no definite observation.

Eger, August 30, 1821

From the Diaries

Beautiful weather. East wind. We went to see an old, ruined synagogue, notable for its Hebrew inscriptions. We then proceeded to
the castle where the present commandant has reconstructed the
courtyard with vegetable and flower gardens, with paths that rise
and fall and with delightful arbors. We also viewed the so-called
Chapel of the Knights Templars. . . . The remaining hours of the

forenoon and afternoon I was absorbed in the history and language
of Bohemia.

Eger, September 12, 1821

To Karl August

During these early September days, the weather being quite good, I
have been surveying Eger and the vicinity from many angles. My
former pupil, Fritz von Stein, is near here with his daughter from
Breslau and there are many visitings back and forth. I never saw
Eger so lively. On the Sunday of my arrival the feast of the patron
saint St. Vincent was being celebrated. . . . The assembly on the
great square was extremely picturesque. Moreover, I attended a
school examination. Prizes were distributed to the best pupils and I
was honored by being asked to award the first prize to the youth who
won it. . . . They are now putting up booths for a provincial Fair.
I love to see things like that, especially in unfamiliar places, because
they bring home to me the general character of human needs, and
especially those of the region. . . . Chief of Police Grüner is most
helpful in all these matters. A model officer, he amuses and delights
me by playing the policeman as we drive about.

Jena, September 19, 1821

To Zelter

Herewith *Wilhelm Meister's Pilgrimage* comes to you. I hope the
book will rise in your estimation, as you contemplate it more closely.
For I can truly say that it contains no line which I have not thoroughly felt or deeply thought out. The genuine reader is bound to
become aware of that.

Jena, September 28, 1821

To Zelter

I am now in receipt of your very dear messages and letters, for all of
which I thank you. I wish to announce that I have acquired a concert
pianoforte built by Streicher with all eight octaves. I am told that my
choice of an instrument was a happy one, and so I hope that my
winter will be more musical. I trust that both to judge it and enjoy

it, Your Honor will transport yourself to this place, properly announcing your arrival and not surprising me.

Jena, October 2, 1821

From the Diaries

Wrote letter to Eckermann, a student in Göttingen.

Weimar, November 6, 1821

Felix Mendelssohn to His Family

The composer and virtuoso, 1809-1847, who was at that time a pupil of Zelter.

After two hours Professor Zelter came with the announcement: Goethe is here! We dashed down the stairs and over to Goethe's house. He was in the garden and came from behind a hedge. Isn't it odd, dear father, that you had exactly the same experience? He is very friendly but doesn't look at all like any of his pictures. . . . I walked about in the garden with him and Professor Zelter. Then we sat down to dinner. He is much more like a man in his fifties than one in his seventies. After dinner Ulrike, the sister of Frau von Goethe, asked him to kiss her and so I did the same. Every morning the author of *Faust* and *Werther* kisses me once, and every afternoon my adopted father and friend kisses me twice. Just think of that!—In the afternoon I play to Goethe for about two hours, partly fugues of Bach, partly my own improvisations. . . . We also eat supper together; Goethe, too, who usually does not eat in the evening. Well, my dear sister, yesterday I showed your songs to Frau von Goethe. She has quite a good voice and will sing them to the old gentleman. I've already told him that my little sister composes songs and asked him whether he wanted to hear them. He answered: "Yes, yes, very gladly." Frau von Goethe likes them a great deal. That's a good sign. He shall hear them today or tomorrow.

November 7, 1821

To Schubarth

First of all let me send you my blessing on your getting married the moment that your hut is founded and has a roof. I agree with every word you say in this matter. Perhaps I have reason to assert that whatever ills meet us within the realms of law, be it the law of nature or of the state, physical law or economic law, never outweigh by a thousandth part the wretchedness with which we must contend, whenever we try to live outside of or beside the law or even in defiance of law and custom, seeing that we cannot help feeling at the same time the inner necessity of an equilibrium between ourselves and others and the moral order of the world. . . .

I have now given up Jena for the season and moved back into my winter quarters in Weimar, where I hope to be well employed.

Weimar, November 8, 1821

From the Diaries

The two Princesses and the Hereditary Prince came over to my house to hear Felix play.

November 8, 1821

Recollections of Ludwig Rellstab

Novelist and music critic, 1799-1860.

In Goethe's reception rooms there was an excellent grand piano, which Rochlitz had procured for him. There we assembled that evening once again. Goethe had invited a good many guests, in order to introduce to his Weimar friends, especially to the musical ones, the astonishing talent of the child, of whom Zelter had told him so much and had written him for some time. . . .

When the rest of us gathered, Zelter was not yet present, but Felix Mendelssohn was, jestingly conversing with the ladies of the house. . . . Now Goethe himself appeared, coming from his study. . . . A certain solemn mood made itself manifest before the entrance of the poet, for there were always a few in these parties who saw him for the first time or else had had no intimate contact with him. . . . Felix Mendelssohn looked up at the snowy head of the poet with his very bright eyes. Goethe took the child's head in both hands and said affectionately: "Now you're going to play us something." . . .

Zelter sat down at the piano and with his stiff old hands played a very simple song in G major. Felix sat down now and played it over. . . . Almost at once, however, he broke out into a wild allegro. He

transformed the gentle melody into a stormy configuration which he
founded now on the base and now on the treble and carried through
with beautiful contrapuntal variations. . . . With the delicate tact
which characterized him even in those days, the young artist did not
prolong his performance unduly. The impression was all the deeper.
. . . It was evident that Goethe was extremely charmed. He hugged
and kissed the little artist, on whose features were mingled happiness,
pride, and shyness. . . . Goethe was especially fond of the fugues of
Bach and so Felix was asked to play one. . . . Throughout the performance Goethe kept standing near the instrument, his features
suffused with joy.

November 10, 1821

Felix Mendelssohn to His Family

Every afternoon Goethe opens the piano and says: "I haven't heard
you at all today. Come, make a little noise for me!" Then he sits
down next to me and listens. . . . You have no idea how kind and
affectionate he is. . . . I don't think his figure is at all impressive.
He is hardly taller than Father. But his demeanor and his speech and
his name are impressive. His voice has enormous resonance; he can
roar like ten thousand warriors. . . . Saturday night Adele Schopenhauer was with us and, contrary to his custom Goethe stayed the
whole time through. The subject of our departure came up and
Adele decided that we must all go and throw ourselves at Professor
Zelter's feet and beg for a few extra days. So Zelter was dragged into
the room and now Goethe raised his voice of thunder and scolded
Professor Zelter for wanting to take us away. He said that Zelter
could go to Jena and come back alone. . . . Now gratitude to Goethe arose on all sides and the girls and I kissed his lips and hands.
Ulrike von Pogwisch threw her arms about his neck and since she is
very pretty and since he flirts with her all the time, the effect was
excellent.

November 27, 1821

Diary of Adele Schopenhauer

  The philosopher's sister, 1796-1849.

All kinds of annoyances this morning. In the afternoon I called on
Ottilie. August has been gossiping most dreadfully. Thoroughly em-

barrassed and ill-humored, I went down to see Papa. At times I must honestly ask myself where all this business will end.

November 28, 1821

To Schultz

The presence during two whole weeks here of Zelter and his daughter and an extraordinary young piano virtuoso made me feel again as though I were transferred to Berlin. I am hardly able any longer to distinguish whether I have seen what is to be seen there with my own eyes, or have only been told about it. . . . I want to tell you about a little avocation I practiced this summer. A Leipzig professor published the fragments of a Euripidean tragedy, a Phaëthon. The beginning and end are extant. The middle is lacking. Other smaller fragments were known before and so I amused myself by an attempt to reconstruct the play. . . . On this occasion I reread Euripides and I understand better than ever, how Aristophanes could hate him and yet how all Greece could adore him. He was at once the creature and the favorite of his age.

December 5, 1821

To Abraham Mendelssohn

If the gifted, able, and already perfected Felix would sometime turn his head after his dessert and look at the piano, he could not but feel how I miss him and what pleasure his presence gave me. Since the departure of those welcome friends utter silence has fallen about me again. Enjoyable as it was to find my house, after a long absence from it, so full of vivid life, yet is the contrast with the dark and brief days of winter all the more evident. I wish you all happiness in the enjoyment of your little private orchestra and I trust that Mlle. von Pogwisch will give me a lively account of your family circle. Accept my sincerest thanks for entrusting to us the dear pledge of your child for so long a period. Nothing is more consoling to old age than to watch arising talents which promise to fill a long span of life with significant achievements. Commend me to your worthy family and friends and be assured that I shall always be happy to hear good news of our young virtuoso through my excellent friend Zelter.

1822

January 16, 1822

To Knebel

I am delighted and cheered by the fact that you like my introduction
to Lucretius. For who has a surer feeling or judgment in the matter
than yourself who know him so intimately. . . . We gain a tremendous advantage by turning to humorous account that aspect of his
work which has been the subject of such bitter attacks, namely, his
passionate denial of human immortality. Moreover, it will not be
difficult to show that everything for which he can really be criticized,
was due to his century and not to himself.

January 17, 1822

To the Willemers

I would like to announce that your sweet and spicy Christmas gift
arrived duly. It delighted young and old, especially when I threw
fragments of it out of my window into the laps of my grandchildren
playing with their sleighs.
Meanwhile I live the life of a monk, though I am writing and causing
to be printed things which will bring me nearer to my distant friends.
Yet I would learn how you have entered upon the New Year and how
you employed the previous months. If a certain small person were
to devote an hour to writing such a letter, it would once again give
me a truly good day and evening.

June 10, 1822

To Reinhard

Your letter of February 14 arrived duly, but it found me in the
midst of a piece of work, which forbade my looking either to the right
or to the left. Yet have I read and re-read your significant pages which
constantly stir and excite new thoughts. I hate to think of you as
indisposed, seeing that, considering my years and constitution, I seem
tolerably well and equal to my duties and inclinations. May your

dear daughter Sophie remain, as it were, your right hand, so that I may hear from her when I am in Marienbad. . . .

In England a certain Herr George Soane seems to have understood my *Faust* marvelously well and has sought to bring its characteristics into harmony with those of his own language and with the demands of his nation. He sent me the early sheets of his version printed in parallel columns with the original. This persuades me the more that the nations are coming to understand each other better and better and that misunderstandings tend rather to lie within each nation's own body.

June 16, 1822

Marianne to Goethe

The lovely evidence of your remembrance and kindness renews the happiness of hours which we once spent together. When I behold the well-known features, that beautiful past time appears immediately before me and it is as though you spoke to me face to face. . . . Since you would know how it is with us, let me say first that I am going to a watering place next week. Since you, too, are seeking a similar spring of healing and release, I cannot but wonder concerning the cause and origin of all evil. Since all evil, including physical suffering, is a result of original sin, I seek in the watering place an antidote to my first contamination. If I am not cured, I shall turn to you and expect friendly encouragement from that side. . . . Count Reinhard was here yesterday and read us your letter.

Marienbad, June 29, 1822

To August

Now, on the tenth day of my stay here, I must acknowledge your dear letter. The weather is magnificent, though not favorable to the farmers . . . Visitors are still few, though there is daily hope of increase. In the house in which I live everything is as excellent and faultless as last year. I live in the second storey above my last year's quarters. The food is very good and the people courteous and agreeable. . . . Remember me to everyone and do not neglect to say a cordial word to the Schopenhauers. I have read the novel *Gabriele* with much pleasure. The mother is to be praised for having written the book and the daughter for having sent it. It is really quite good. . . .

My way of life is very simple. In the morning I drink the waters in bed, in the evening at the spring. I bathe every third day; I dine in company, and so it goes. The wine did finally arrive; I am having it decanted in jugs. A friend made me a present of six bottles of Würzburger, which also helped me to get along. . . . I am very industrious. Love to all; think of me and give me an account of what goes on from time to time.

Summer, 1822

Recollections of Ulrike von Levetzow

As in former years, Goethe spent nearly all his time with us. . . . He and other learned gentlemen carried on conversations which interested even us young girls, and they were all kind enough to explain whatever we did not understand. My youngest sister Bertha, who was only 14 at that time, was interested in mineralogy and Goethe and the other gentlemen presented her with a nice collection of specimens.—On another occasion Goethe called us to him and showed us on a long table specimens of all the kinds of stone to be found in this region. He led me to a certain spot on the table at which, between the specimens, he had placed a pound of Viennese chocolate. To place the chocolate there for me was Goethe's special little jest, because I couldn't get interested in that sort of thing at all.

All this summer Goethe was very friendly to me and took notice of me on every occasion. Again and again he said to my grandmother, how he wished he had another son, so that I could marry him and so that he could educate me entirely to his taste, because he had a great and paternal love for me. Again, as the year before, Goethe gave me a book which he had sent for. It was the second part of *Poetry and Truth*. He inscribed it to me beautifully. . . . There were many people in Marienbad that summer of '22 and, of course, they all wanted very much to make his acquaintance. Often and often he was not in the mood for new people, and so it would happen that they would ask me to play the intermediary. He never denied me a single time. He used on such occasions to say: "Does it make you happy, little daughter?"

July 27, 1822

Recollections of Grüner

Goethe wanted to see with his own eyes the place where the tooth of the mammoth had been found. "Can you drive me over after dinner?" he asked. I said I would do so with pleasure. We drove over immediately after dinner. There was a view of Franzensbad and of the place where the sacred heathen oak had been found and about us we saw the wreath of mountains which encloses the valley of Eger. . . . I handed Goethe, as I had done before, some little poems which I had composed in former years. They were not of the kind that is fit for publication. But he laughed at them and exclaimed: "How did you manage to write them? They're something for His Serenity!"

Eger, August 10, 1822

From the Diaries

Grüner brought the latest papers. What a confused world!

◇◇◇◇◇

Eger, August 13, 1822

Bought an old tankard bearing the date 1651.

August 19, 1822

Recollections of Grüner

He asked me to lend him my copy of Schiller's *Thirty Years' War.* . . . When I came to him that evening I saw that there were tears in his eyes. In astonishment I asked: "What has happened, Your Excellency?"—"Nothing, good friend, except that I am full of remorse that I lived for a long period misunderstanding this man. Schiller's house was three doors from my own and we didn't see each other because during my stay in Italy I had gone forward along a certain path and could not endure the stuff with which Schiller started out."

September 21, 1822
Frederic Soret's Conversations with Goethe

> Soret, 1795-1866, a Genevese Swiss, student of both theology and science, had just been called to Weimar as tutor of the Hereditary Prince, Karl Alexander.

It was on this evening that M. Meyer took me to see the celebrated Goethe who received me kindly enough, though with a certain coolness. The principal subjects of our conversation were mineralogy, chemistry and physics. What seemed chiefly to interest him was the phenomenon of polarization. He showed me an apparatus partly constructed after his own design and desired me to join him in experiments on this matter. It seemed strange enough to me to see the great poet occupying himself with scientific research and finding pleasure in contemplating the inert stones, after having written so impassioned a book as *Werther*.

September 24, 1822

Spent the evening at Goethe's house with M. Meyer, the young Goethe, Mme. de Goethe and their physician. Goethe was far more animated than he had been that first time. He showed me some superb lithographs of Stuttgart; I had never seen anything so perfect of its kind. After that we chatted about the progress of science again, especially chemistry. . . .
His Excellency is especially preoccupied with iodine and chlorine. He talks of these substances with a kind of astonishment, as though the new discoveries of chemistry had taken him utterly by surprise. . . .
Goethe's judgment is much sounder in the arts than it is in science.
. . . He speaks a very pure French but without ease because he stops to seek for appropriate expressions. It is evident that he is eager not to compromise himself. From time to time he broke into German and then he spoke with equal vivacity and gaiety.

October 7-8, 1822

Recollections of Lea Mendelssohn

The wife of Abraham Mendelssohn and the mother of Felix.

. . . He is so kind and gentle, indeed so paternal toward the boy that I recall the images of these few days with gratitude and happy emotion. For hours he talked to my husband about Felix and begged him to come back and stay with him for some time. . . . Since he is not fond of ordinary music no one had touched his piano since Felix left. He opened it with the words: "Awaken me the winged spirits that have slept so long!" And another time: "You must be my David; if I were to be ill or melancholy, your playing must chase away the evil dreams, nor will I ever, like Saul, throw my spear at you."—He was also most kind to our daughter Fanny. She played a good deal of Bach to him and he was delighted with her compositions of certain of his poems.

He asked Felix to play a fugue of Bach which Ottilie von Goethe had mentioned. Felix didn't know it by heart but he knew the theme which he executed in a long, correctly constructed movement. Goethe was charmed. He came up to me and pressed my hands with much warmth and exclaimed: "What an exquisite and precious boy! Send him back to me quite soon."

October 10, 1822

Soret's Conversations

Instead of the snack which I expected, there was served a kind of supper. I noted the details in my journal because it formed such a contrast to our Genevese customs. First we were served cups which I thought contained chocolate. But it was very strong ice cold bouillon. Next came caviar; next cold meats and venison. Thereafter came three or four ample dishes with anchovies and lamprey, such as salads and sandwiches. Two or three kinds of wine as well as fruits preserved in vinegar (?) and very rich cakes.

October 15, 1822

A little family gathering at Goethe's. I took along my little instrument for exhibiting polarization. Goethe asked to keep it for a little while. I haven't yet seen him as gay as on this occasion and so disposed to jest.

◇◇◇◇◇

October 20, 1822

All the ladies of the family call Goethe Father. They treat him with a deep veneration; they surround him with their attentions and their caresses, as though he were an idol. I believe that few or no great men have enjoyed both glory and life as completely as he. He is sure of the remembrance of posterity and yet enjoys, while he lives, the homage of his contemporaries.

◇◇◇◇◇

November 4, 1822

Goethe's secretary told me that his master, having had his hair cut yesterday, the secretary at once asked for a lock of it. The hairdresser answered that he himself had another use for the hair. Each time it is cut he sends it to Frankfurt. He has done so for long and so Goethe, without suspecting it, has enriched his hairdresser.

November 12, 1822

To George Friedrich Benecke

> Benecke, a professor in Göttingen, communicated to Goethe Byron's dedication of his tragedy of Sardanapalus: "To the illustrious Goethe, a stranger presumes to offer the homage of a literary vassal to his liege lord, the first of existing writers . . . The unworthy production which the author ventures to inscribe to him is entitled *Sardanapalus*."

Your present communication amazes me and I thank you for it with a certain sense of shame. Since he first rose above the horizon, I have followed, together with friends far and near, with the unanimous

agreement of Germany and of the world, all the ways of that powerful, endlessly productive, irresistible and exquisite poet. . . .

It is with great reluctance that I return to you the autograph of
the man so dear to me. Who would willingly renounce the possession of so precious a document? Old age which may be pardoned for
occasionally doubting itself, stands in need of such evidence of admiration which the stirring power of a younger man might not, perhaps, be able to endure.

December 14, 1822

To Knebel

Manzoni, whose "Ode on Napoleon's Death" will certainly please
you, has written a new tragedy on a theme from the history of Lom-
bardy. . . . I shall take great pleasure in giving a report on this
work. Ah, that there were a German contemporary whom one could
offer a similar service of love! But in order to be quite clear on this
entire subject, it is necessary to renounce all national advantages in
the higher reaches of art. Are not the works of Byron and of Walter
Scott in the hands of all Germans? . . . We must do our best to promote the study of languages and the appreciation of our neighbors,
in order that there be finally gathered a single flock guided by a
single shepherd.

1823

January 9, 1823

To Ulrike von Levetzow

Your charming letter, my dear one, gave me the greatest pleasure, a
double pleasure on account of a special circumstance. For, though
the loving Papa is always mindful of his faithful and loving daughter,
yet recently your welcome form lives more clearly and vividly than
ever in my inmost mind. But now observe, that this took place precisely during the days and hours in which you, too, thought of me
with a higher intensity and felt the inclination to send me a word
from afar.

A threefold thanks, therefore, my dear one, and at the same time convey my best wishes and greetings to your excellent mother, whom

I remember with pleasure as a radiant star upon my former horizon. . . .

And so be much assured that it is my fairest hope of the whole year to re-enter once again into the lovely circle of your family and to find all its members animated by the same kind and friendly sentiments as they were when I said farewell. . . .

Herewith, my dearest, I lay claim to your daughterly feelings for the immediate future. May that mountain valley with its springs be and remain as beneficent and healing to me at your side, as I hope to find you again in cheerfulness and happiness.

January 18, 1823

To Zelter

In my solitary smithy I am forging many a thing. I do not leave the house, scarcely my room. In this way I hope to be and to produce something for my friends.

1823

EACH AND ALL

Himself in vastness to recover
His rigid self will man give over
And leave satiety behind.
Void of wild whim or hot sensation,
Of harsh demand and obligation,
Renunciation's self grows kind.

Come, soul o' the world to penetrate us!
Our highest powers will elevate us
With the world-spirit to contend.
Influences benign will lead us,
High gentle masters who have freed us,
To Him Whose shaping knows no end.

Still to transform what was created,
That no rigidity be fated
Demands the endless living deed.
And what was not, now it arises,

With greener earths, purer sunrises,
From stagnancy forever freed.

Its acts are permanent creation,
First it is form, then transformation,
And only momently seems still.
The eternal force in naught is bated:
For each must be annihilated,
If to duration be its will.

February 2, 1823

To J. S. Zauper

A college professor in Pilsen, 1784-1850, who published several analytical studies of Goethe's works.

. . . Since we are speaking of aesthetic matters, test yourself continually in the diamond mirror of the Greeks; it will show you your merits and your faults with uninterrupted clarity. Regard the works of your contemporaries only in order not to be ignorant of them, to be aware of what in them is akin to you or is alien to you, what can promote or obstruct your development.
Have no fears on my account. Of what is being written in my favor or against me I know as little as I hear the storms of the North or the Baltic, the Mediterranean or the Adriatic seas. . . . Furthermore, I can well say that I have derived great benefit from the hostility directed against me these 50 years. It taught me to know my nation, and this continues to be the case, insofar as the voices of my more recent adversaries reach my hermitage. . . .

1823

To form, reform, transform me have they striven,
For fifty years to change me have been fain;
Time long enough to know what to attain
In his own land unto a man was given,
Whose festive youth joined him from morn to even
With a daemonic and a genial train,
But whom the lessening years urged to attain
A sage's wisdom, mild and nearer heaven.

February, 1823

Soret's Conversations

Goethe was very ill in the course of this month.

Weimar, February 12, 1823

From the Diaries

Bloodletting ordered on account of increasing catarrhal condition. Spent the rest of the day as well as I could.

◇◇◇◇◇

Weimar, February 13, 1823

Restless night, yet somewhat better. Preparations for work.

◇◇◇◇◇

Weimar, February 18, 1823

Very much worse. Violent pain in the region of the heart. Bled again at 11. Another sleepless night. The physician stayed with me all day.

◇◇◇◇◇

Weimar, February 19, 1823

Continued pain, though somewhat less acute. Leeches used on me at 9 o'clock. Violent fever that evening and very restless night. Pain too great to sleep.

◇◇◇◇◇

Weimar, February 20, 1823

Almost the same condition as yesterday, only the pulse was a little better. Consulting physician came twice, while my own stayed all day. Slept only about an hour and a half all night.

February 22, 1823

Müller's Diary

For several days his condition varied. He often acted half unconscious, next was half delirious. Yet in between he would speak quite rationally. Thursday he still played with his older grandson and even sang him a little song. . . . One night he said to Stadelmann: "You have no idea how wretched I feel and how ill I am!" Again and again he warned his physicians to give serious thought to his state and implied that he had but little faith in them. "Use all your tricks! It's well and good, but I don't believe you'll pull me through!" . . . Once when the physicians were in whispered consultation, he said: "Look at those Jesuits! They can consult each other, but they don't know enough to save a man's life." He complained that they intentionally gave him the most revolting mixtures to choke down and misused the dear girls, Ottilie and Ulrike, to make him take them. The moment he was the least bit better, he insisted that his daughter-in-law resume her accustomed social life and go to Court and to the theatre. . . . Saturday noon he was permitted a glass of champagne, which had no visible effect. But with great relish he ate a bergamot pear and some pineapple jelly. Once he said quite to himself and under his breath: "What I want to know is whether this tortured and riven entity will be able to reappear and assume its form as a new entity!"

◇◇◇◇◇

February 23, 1823

Today, Sunday, was his worst day. Early in the morning he said to his son: "Death is in every corner of the room." And to the physician he said several times: "It's all over with me." . . . In the morning I was in Stadelmann's chamber next to his bedroom and in the evening I was in the house for a while. The physician said to him: "Your inhalation is easier than your exhalation." "Certainly it is," he said. "I know that better than you do, you scoundrels." [*To me he said:*] "I have no wish to live; I have no wish to die. God knows what will become of me."

Weimar, February 24, 1823

From the Diaries

Toward evening an irresistible longing for Marienbad water. I drank a quantity of it. Later I drank a cup of arnica tea, after which my condition seemed to undergo a radical change. The first quiet and refreshing sleep that night.

◇◇◇◇◇

Weimar, March 13, 1823

Examined thoroughly the writing machine for the blind which
arrived from Vienna. Watched after dinner how the machine could
be made to write letters.

April 10, 1823

To Reinhard

Quite in confidence and with utter unassumingness I dare to communicate to you a most significant thing. On the tenth day of my
illness, when the physicians thought that my physical being could be
sustained, I silently asked the question, whether the Almighty Being
was preserving me for a definite destiny. Convinced that no one but
myself could answer this question, I began at once, without the least
anxiety or diffidence, to will that my spirit take over the rulership of
the situation, as it could and would. From that day on I felt daily
freer and more serene in mind, far happier and more capable of de-
cisions than before the onset of my illness, of which I had a not in-
definite presentiment without knowing how I was to escape it or
prevent it.

April 17, 1823

To Countess Auguste Bernstorff (Née Stolberg)

At last and once again to see the evidence of intimate memory in the
handwriting of that dear earliest friend of mine, whom my heart
knew so well, though my eyes never saw her—how could it but give
me joy and move me deeply? Yet I dwell in a state of indecision as to
what reply to send. Let me remain in the sphere of the general, for
neither of us knows the particularities of the other's life.
To live long means to survive many and much, the beloved, the
hated, the indifferent, kingdoms, capitals, forests and the very trees
we ourselves planted in our youth. We survive ourselves and must
be grateful if some gifts of body and of mind remain to us. We can
endure this mortal mutability, if we remain aware at every moment
of the eternal, for thus we escape the suffering due to the transitori-
ness of time.

All these many years my intentions toward myself and others have been honest; whatever I have done has been a striving toward what was high; you and yours have done the same. Let us continue to do so, while the sun shines for us; it will shine for others, too; they will act out their lives under his warmth and light a brighter light for us. And so let us have no anxiety concerning the future. In our Father's Realm are many provinces and since He permitted us to settle so happily upon these mortal shores, He will surely have seen to it that we are taken care of in that other country. Perhaps we shall then attain what here we never did—to know each other face to face and so to love each other the more deeply.

The above was written soon after your letter came. But I didn't dare send it because I remembered that a similar expression of mine seemed to wound your admirable brother without any conscious will on my part. But now, that I have just returned to life after a mortal illness, this shall go to you with the immediate message that the Almighty has granted me to continue to behold the beautiful light of the sun. May the light of day seem equally friendly to you, and may you think of me in kindness and in love, even as I never cease to remember those days when those were at one whom life afterwards put asunder, and may we all be reunited in the arms of the All-Loving Father.

June 2, 1823

Soret's Conversations

A little party at Goethe's. Just Riemer, Müller, Meyer. The conversation went from subject to subject. First we talked about the varying difficulty of understanding a foreign language according to the subject matter. "When you come to sermons," Goethe said, "you have more trouble following their meaning than anything else, because you so rarely agree with the speaker." Next we spoke of the popular poems of Béranger. Goethe commented on them and paraphrased several of them in German with an altogether pungent originality.

June 11, 1823

Eckermann's Conversations with Goethe

Johann Peter Eckermann, 1792-1854, came to Weimar in the spring of 1823. He was a young man of the humblest origin and of more

zeal than literary equipment. Goethe at once and instinctively knew
Eckermann to be his man and kept him in Weimar as secretary, friend,
collaborator. By virtue of the purity and plasticity of his nature, Eckermann was enabled to produce those conversations which stand alone in
their kind. He had first seen Goethe on June 10.

This morning I found a hand-written card from Goethe asking me to
come to see him. I spent an hour with him. He was utterly different
from the day before, swift and decisive as a young man in all matters.
He brought two big volumes with him as he came in. "It is not well,"
said he, "that you should just pass by here; it will be much better
for us to know each other well. I want to see you and to talk to you.
But since generalities are futile, I have thought of something specific
which will establish our relationship and give us something to discuss. In these two volumes you will find the file of the *Scholars'*
Journal of Frankfurt of 1772 and 1773. All the short reviews I wrote
during those years are here. But none of them are signed. Since you,
however, have entered so sympathetically into my style and ways of
thought, I would like you to look at them carefully and tell me
what you think of them. I'd like to know whether they are good
enough to be included in future editions of my works." . . .
I answered him that I would be very glad to make the attempt and
desired nothing better than to succeed in following his directions. . . .
He now told me that he was leaving for Marienbad in about a week,
but that he very much wanted me to continue to stay in Weimar, so
that we could see each other from time to time and get to know each
other better. "And I would like it, too," he added, "that you stay in
Jena not just for a few days or weeks, but that you settle down there
comfortably for the whole summer until autumn, when I come home.
I have already written to Jena to get lodgings for you, so that you
will find everything comfortable and agreeable."

Weimar, June 20, 1823

From the Diaries

Eckermann. A secretary brought me my authorized passport. A merchant came to see me, Castro of Altona, probably a Portuguese Jew.

Marienbad, July 8, 1823

To August

I feel incomparably better and I hope to stay that way, so that I may engage in some satisfying activity. I am sending an engraving of Marienbad. . . . I live in the corner house which you observe within the shadow just to the left of a row of bigger buildings. The bird in the engraving flies straight across the house. The Grand Duke is housed in the biggest of those buildings. From my windows I can see whatever takes place on the terrace. . . . To turn to a prime necessity, I can say that my food is good. I have it fetched from the inn. They send me six dishes, from which I can choose enough to content me. Everything is well and tastily prepared. The Graves is excellent, as it was last year; there is also an agreeable Hungarian wine. I am often tempted to accept invitations to dine with the Grand Duke and with other people. But I avoid all public appearances, so as to remain my own master.

Marienbad, July 11, 1823

From the Diaries

Frau von Levetzow and her daughters arrive.

Marienbad, July 24, 1823

With the family. . . . In the evening an impromptu ball. Then a little supper which lasted until midnight.

Marienbad, August 4, 1823

To Ottilie

Some serious and important men here decided to raise a considerable sum to add to the endowment of the new hospital; others, of a more worldly temper, gave a big banquet at the new inn. But far more charming was our entertainment up here, where many ladies and gentlemen attended a *thé dansant*. We drank tea and danced. Later, however, a cold supper was served at small tables, exquisitely prepared and accompanied by good wine. . . . I didn't get home till midnight, whence you will guess that, in addition to dancing and tea and supper and champagne, of which I did not partake, a fifth element must have been present, of the kind that has never failed to have its effect upon me. The dance was charming and vivid; splendid and dainty dancers of several nations were conspicuous. . . . The presence of the Grand Duke naturally lends distinction to our terrace here. . . . He found what attracted him, nor did other great gentlemen refrain from picking out agreeable partners. . . .

And so I come to the end of my comedy. . . . I need say nothing of my health. It is clear from what I have written that my infirmities do not prevent me from being gay, nay, almost happy. Remember me to Ulrike, whose name approves itself daily as the most admirable ingredient of my situation here. Kiss the children. . . .

August, 1823

Recollections of Ulrike von Levetzow

. . . Goethe once said to me that he had written something which described his relationship to me and asked me whether I wouldn't like to read it. I said: "No, I don't want to read it; I'd rather have you tell me about it." "That's just like my little daughter," said Goethe. . . . My sister once asked him how he liked her dress. "It's very pretty," he replied, "but Ulrike's is prettier." Whereupon my sister said: "Oh I know, I needn't have asked; everything that Ulrike has is prettier."

Marienbad, August 14, 1823

From the Diaries

Marie Szymanowska, 1795-1831, Polish pianist, attached to the Russian Court.

Went to a neighboring house where Mme. Szymanowska played. One piece by Hummel, one of her own and two others. Altogether magnificent. Took a walk with her in the direction of the Mill. Overtaken by rain. Later went to the spring with umbrellas. Evening on the terrace.

◇◇◇◇◇

Marienbad, August 15, 1823

Walked down the street. Found all the ladies assembled. The mothers drove back to the terrace. I walked back with the Levetzow daughters.

◇◇◇◇◇

Marienbad, August 16, 1823

Went to Mme. Szymanowska at 4 o'clock. She played exquisitely. The Levetzow ladies still here. All kinds of oddities and jests concerning misunderstandings and losing each other on the way. Everything smoothed out at supper.

1823

TO ULRIKE

Thou didst pass by here? How? I saw thee not?
Thou camest back? The sight did not pursue me?
Unblessèd moment and accursèd spot!
Have I gone blind that this could happen to me?

I will be comforted. Thy gentle heart,
Quick to forgiveness the blame will banish:
I see thee howsoever far thou art!
And in my very presence thou couldst vanish.

Marienbad, August 17, 1823

From the Diaries

The Levetzows are preparing to leave. We all gathered at breakfast and before saying farewell planned to meet within a few days, and so we all parted quite gaily.

◇◇◇◇◇

Marienbad, August 19, 1823

Phlebotomy this evening. . . . Considered what has passed, meditated on what is now to be.

1823

TO ULRIKE

Let them frown upon our loving,
Grieve we not at their reproving;
Scatheless by their blame are we.
Other things may yield unto them,
Nothing that may irk or rue them
Can make love less lovely be.

Marienbad, August 20, 1823

From the Diaries

The Levetzows had gone to Karlsbad on August 17. Goethe, having stopped at Eger on the way, joined them there on August 25.

Passed a calm night. Ingratiating dreams. Drove off around 3 o'clock. Magnificent clear day.

Eger, August 24, 1823

To Zelter

Political news is utterly depressing. In order to liberate myself from such, as well as from aesthetic conversations and discourses, I made myself the servitor of a very pretty girl for the space of six weeks. Thus I was wholly secure from all the ills of the world. But now comes the most marvelous circumstance, namely, the enormous power that music has upon me nowadays! A singing voice, the resonant performances of Szymanowska, even the public playing of a military band release my tensions, even as a clenched fist relaxes gently.

◇◇◇◇◇

Karlsbad, August 25, 1823

Arrived at 4 o'clock. Announced myself to Frau von Levetzow. My lodgings in the second storey directly above hers. Beautiful rooms. Beautiful view.

◇◇◇◇◇

Karlsbad, August 26, 1823

Breakfast with the Levetzow family. By myself till 1:30. Then went through almanachs and small copperplate prints with Ulrike.

❖❖❖❖❖

Karlsbad, August 27, 1823

A *thé dansant* in the Saxon Hall where tea was drunk and sweets and pastries served. The really good dancers of both sexes, of whom there were not many, went on and on. A Polish lady invited me to dance the last Polonaise with her and so I crept through it and when the moment came to change partners, most of the pretty girls in the room passed through my hands.

Late Summer, 1823

Recollections of Ulrike von Levetzow

He spent his birthday in Karlsbad with us. But my mother noticed that he didn't want to let on that it was his birthday, and so she forbade us to mention it. He said the day before, that he wanted us to go on an excursion with him and that we were to be his guests for the day, even as he had been ours. Mother accepted and gave instructions to the cook. When Goethe came down to breakfast at 7 o'clock he found at his place a lovely cup on which a wreath of ivy had been painted. He turned to mother and asked: "What is the meaning of this?"—"It is to remind you of our friendship, of which evergreens are the symbol." Goethe took mother's hand: "How lovely! I shall keep it as a dear souvenir." Soon after that we drove off. Goethe was very cheerful and told us many amusing incidents. He also showed us the various points of interest of the place to which we had driven. Now the dinner hour approached. It turned out that he had sent his serving man ahead to make all preparations. But mother, too, had brought along a wonderful cake, a real birthday cake, and two bottles of a precious Rhenish vintage, of which Goethe was particularly fond. These were on the table and Goethe noticed them at once: "What a wonderful cake!"—"Well," my mother replied, "I did have to make my contribution to the meal,

and I chose cake and the wine which you like."—"What an attentive little friend you are! And what a beautiful glass is that with your
and your dear children's names inscribed on it!" And again my
mother said: "We don't want you to forget us; that is the chief thing.
You are to recall this beautiful occasion and think of us when you
do so!" . . .

So we drove happily back to Karlsbad. From afar we saw people with
a band on the meadow in front of the house. The moment we descended from the carriage Goethe was surrounded. Mother beckoned
to us and said good night to Goethe and we went upstairs. Since it
was quite late, we didn't see him again till morning. . . .

It was a lovely time that we spent with this amiable man. Goethe
contributed greatly to my sister's and my own instruction and culture. He talked to us about many things and he also gave my mother
clever hints and good advice.

Karlsbad, August 30, 1823

From the Diaries

Dined. Drove out after 4. Continued merriment on our excursion.
Latish coffee at a roadside inn. More occasions for jest and gaiety.
Magnificent drive back.

◇◇◇◇◇

Karlsbad, August 31, 1823

Went to the play. Afterwards sat for long with Frau von Levetzow
and Ulrike exchanging manifold reminiscences.

◇◇◇◇◇

Karlsbad, September 1, 1823

This evening Bertha von Levetzow read us aloud the first chapter of
Walter Scott's *The Black Dwarf*. She read nicely. . . . We were all
tired and said good night early.

◇◇◇◇◇

Karlsbad, September 2, 1823

We called on Frau von der Recke, whom we found far from
well. . . .

Anecdotes of a former tutor of the Levetzow girls and the incredible tricks they played on him.

❖❖❖❖❖

Karlsbad, September 3, 1823

Ulrike now continued reading from *The Black Dwarf*. She does it naturally and well, but she ought to try for more energy and dramatic liveliness. We stayed together late.

❖❖❖❖❖

Karlsbad, September 4, 1823

Spent the evening with the family. Details from the childhood of the daughters brought out.

❖❖❖❖❖

Karlsbad, September 5, 1823

Packed early. Grüner's carriage came to fetch me. Stadelmann paid some farewell calls for me. . . . After he went out, general, tumultuous farewell. Drove off at 9 o'clock. Arrived at Castle Hartenberg [*seat of a Bohemian nobleman and admirer of Goethe*] at 5 o'clock. Began to copy a poem.

❖❖❖❖❖

Castle Hartenberg, September 6, 1823

Continued with the poem. Took a drive with the Count. . . . Spent the afternoon alone.

❖❖❖❖❖

Castle Hartenberg, September 7, 1823

Continued to work at the poem all day Sunday. Bade farewell to the Count and his family. Drove to Eger. New stanzas came to me and I wrote them down.

September 10, 1823

TO ULRIKE

That 'tis still given thee by those springs to tarry
Cleaves me within with hurt I scarce can bear,

For since thyself in my whole heart I carry,
I cannot grasp that thou art otherwhere.

                                          Eger, September 10, 1823

To Frau von Levetzow

I am about to leave Eger. I place a sheet of paper before me and take
up my pen and discover at once how much is to be said and how
little may be expressed. If, my most dear friend, you will go over the
past several weeks, especially the very last in your mind, you will
find each day a very web of my gratitude. . . .
May I now address myself to your daughter? But I am in the same
case. Yet since she is herself sparing of words, she will surely forgive
me for being reticent at this moment as well. For if my darling
(which she can hardly refuse to be) will repeat to herself what,
indeed, she knows by heart, that is to say, the innermost quality of
my sentiment toward her, she will be able to tell herself better than
I can tell her, what my present condition must be. And while she
indulges in these thoughts, I trust she will admit that it is a goodly
thing to be loved, even if the friend is sometimes troublesome. . . .
I must, must close! If I were to take a new sheet, all bounds would
be passed. But I must thank you, however briefly, for the insight
which you permitted me to have into your earlier life. By virtue of
it I feel the more akin and united with you. And I would say to your
daughter, that I loved her more dearly the better I came to know her
and that I desire to prove to her personally that I do know her and
know what pleases and displeases her and that in the hope of proving this, I am, at the end, as at the beginning, devotedly, G.

                        On the journey home, September 12, 1823

From the Diaries

Went over the poem again and made many improvements.

Jena, September 14, 1823

Müller's Diary

When I joined him at 7 o'clock in the evening, the conversation immediately turned upon the betrothed of our friend, his physician, who had just left town to fetch her home. Goethe used this occasion slyly enough for a confession of faith. He spoke of the lady in terms of the highest praise; nevertheless, he called this hasty marriage a silly trick. "You know," he said, "how I hate all extemporary action; an impulsive betrothal or marriage always seems to me especially horrible. Love can be born on the instant and every genuine inclination must once have flamed up with the suddenness of lightning across the skies. But who is going to follow up love by immediate marriage? Love belongs in the realm of the ideal, marriage in that of the real, and never are these two realms united with impunity."

Jena, September 15, 1823

Eckermann

Goethe has come back from Marienbad, but since his lodgings in the garden here are not sufficiently comfortable, he is staying for but a few days. He is well and vigorous. . . .
"I must tell you frankly," he said, "I want you to spend the winter with me in Weimar." These were his very first words. . . . "I shall arrange to have you lodged quite near me," he added later, "you are not to have a moment without significance all winter."

◇◇◇◇◇

Jena, September 18, 1823

"The world is so great and rich and life so manifold, that occasions for poems can never fail. But they must indeed be poems of occasion, that is, reality must indeed furnish their substance and be their cause. The special theme they treat rises into poetic generality by virtue of the fact that a poet has written them. All my poems are poems of occasion; they were inspired by reality and therein lies their firm foundation. I think little of poems snatched, as it were, out of the empty air."

Weimar, September 19, 1823
Müller's Diary

At 6 o'clock Riemer called on Goethe who had arrived at noon from Jena where he had, as it were, quarantined himself for several days after the extraordinary agitations of his stay in Marienbad. I gave him the birthday present sent him by the city council of Bremen, consisting of a dozen bottles of the famous old Vin Rosé. . . . Ottilie was still very weak but most amiable. . . . Goethe told us that in Marienbad and Karlsbad nobody talked about any authors except Byron and Walter Scott. But the magic of Scott, he thought, depended upon the splendor of the United Kingdom and on the inexhaustible variety of its historic past, whereas in Germany there was hardly to be found a fruitful field for the novelist, so that in *Wilhelm Meister* he had had to delineate life and its movement through the adventures of wandering players and poor country squires.

Late June 1823
Recollections of Ulrike von Levetzow

It was Karl August who said to my family and to me, too, that I might better marry Goethe. First we took it as a joke and were of the opinion that he could not possibly mean it, but he denied this over and over again; he went on to describe to me the very alluring prospects; how I would be the first lady at Court and in town; with what distinction he, the Grand Duke, would treat me; he would at once furnish a house for my family in Weimar and present it to them, so that we need not be separated and that he would secure my future in every way. He did his best to win over my mother and I heard later that he had promised her, seeing that in all likelihood I would outlive Goethe, that he would assure me after the latter's death an annual pension of 10,000 thaler.

A Last Echo

In 1947 there died in Quito, Ecuador, Dr. Wladimir Schiller, a Jewish refugee from the Hitler terror. He had been an attorney in Prague and had passed his early youth on his father's estate in Bohemia near which Ulrike von Levetzow lived in her ancestral chateau to an extreme old age. The young collegian visited her often. She told him stories of her youth.

Ulrike said: "It is like a dream to me today. And it was equally like a dream to me in those days when the aged Minister of State von Goethe asked for my hand in marriage. I was only 19. But my mother, too, though she had long been widowed, did not wish to marry him either."

From *The Aufbau,* New York

(Written between September 5 and 19, 1823)

MARIENBAD ELEGY

What hope were there in yet another meeting
When once the blossom of this day uncloses?
Heaven's gate and hell's gape for an hour fleeting
While the irresolute spirit still opposes.
Be gone all doubt! She's at the skiey gate
And lifts me upward to her own estate.

And so thou wert received, of Paradise's
Beautiful life deemed worthy, the eternal
Wherein no wish, hope nor desire arises
Of all that throng the heart in hours diurnal,
And having that one beauty to adore,
The spring of tears and longing flowed no more.

How irresistibly the day went winging
With minutes like swift coursers forward driven!
The good-night kiss, a seal of union, bringing
Promise of sunshine in as kind a heaven.
The delicate hours trod with a single gait,
Like sisters, yet none quite the other's mate.

That kiss, the last, cruelly sweet, dividing
Exquisite webs of tenderness that move thee.
Then the foot halts or hastes as though a chiding

And fiery angel from that threshold drove thee.
To the dark path the eye turns in dismay
And gazes back. The door is closed—to stay.

The sullen heart now shuts, as though the flying
Immortal hours had not unlocked it ever,
As though with every star in heaven vying
Beside her it had radiated never;
And spleen, rue, self-reproach and heavy care
In sultry circumambience it must bear.

Is not the whole world left me? Do the mountains
No longer wear their crown of sacred shadows?
Are harvests no more gold? Rivers and fountains,
Do they no more make green the fruitful meadows?
Does not the vaulted and divine creation
Transform the formless in renewed formation?

Exquisite, light and delicate floats hither,
Seraphically from the cloudland there,
So like to her along the azure aether,
A slender image wrought of light and air!
Thus was she seen in happy dances moving,
Loveliest of all the lovely made for loving.

But only for an instant dar'st thou bind her
Unto a fancied image, light and aery!
Look in thy heart where better thou canst find her,
For there she stirs in many forms that vary,
Her single self in shifting shapes grows clearer,
And each new form is than the other dearer.

How at the door to welcome me she waited,
On rising rungs of happiness to bless,
After night's last kiss hurried a belated
More ultimate one upon my lips to press:
So clear and mobile does her image start
From flaming letters writ on my true heart.

That heart which, like a battlemented tower,
Itself in her, her in itself has guarded,
Bless'd for her sake its permanence and power,
And by her revelation is rewarded,
Finding its freedom in that dear and fateful
Service of her for which each throb is grateful.

If potency of love, if the attention
To answering passion had been quenched, had faded,
How was my soul to hope and blithe invention,
To daring and to deed anew persuaded!
If ever love the loving did inspire,
'Twas on me proved by a rekindled fire.

Through her! Through her! Heavily dread and terror
Dulled soul and body with abhorred frustration;
Dire phantoms dimmed the eye with hate and error
In wastes of empty-hearted desolation!
New dawn of hope upon that threshold waited
Where she glowed in the light she had created.

The peace of God which upon earth is able
To bless us more than reason—as is proved—
To love's serener peace is comparable
In presence of the one who is beloved.
There rests the heart which now no discord stirs
In the deep certainty of being hers.

Pure in our breast there dwells an aspiration
Unto a loftier power still the same,
To give ourselves in grateful dedication,
Unriddling us to that which has no name.
Call it devoutness, if you like. That height
Blessedly I attain when in her sight.

Under her glance, like summer sunshine glowing,
Before her breath, like airs by springtime bidden
Melts, for so long in icy hardness growing,

The sullen self in wintry caverns hidden.
No avid greed, no stubbornness remains:
Her coming scatters them like vernal rains.

It is as though she said: "In friendly fashion
Life grants its measure to us hour by hour;
Perished of yesterday the grief or passion,
And o'er tomorrow we have little power.
If ever evening's coming did affright me,
The setting sun brought something to delight me.

"Do as I do! With happy resolute glances
Look in the moment's eye, let no delaying
Thy courage curb as blithely it advances,
Whether for act or joy or love or playing!
Move simply as a child, where'er thou be,
And the whole world will yield itself to thee."

How true of thee, I thought. Thy motion guiding,
A very god grants thee each moment's grace,
And fortune's favorite near thee abiding
Hourly beholds the heaven of thy face;
To go from thee leaves me in fear and pain,
For that high wisdom seeks me out in vain.

And now I am afar! The desolate minute,
That's mine—what of its fate? I cannot say.
Though much of beauty and of good be in it,
'Tis but a burden to be cast away.
Restless with bitter longing I consume
My heart and boundless weeping is my doom.

Flow then, resistless tears, flow without rest,
Even though the inner fire ye cannot quench!
For death and life in my tumultuous breast
In fatal combat each the other clench.
Ah, there are herbs the body's hurt to still;
The spirit can command nor deed nor will,

Nor the idea how to sustain this loss!
Her likeness rises in its very seeming,
Hither and yon my thoughts her image toss,
Now dim and faint, now with true radiance streaming!
But there's no comfort in this ebb and flow
Of vain appearances that come and go.

So leave me here, true comrades of my faring!
Leave me alone with crag and moor and time.
The world is open to your spirit's daring,
Wide is the earth and heaven's arch sublime.
Contemplate, seek, and gather the rewarding
Secrets which nature in her deeps is guarding.

Together with my whole world I go under
Who seemed the darling of what gods there are.
They tested me, lent me Pandora's wonder,
So rich in gifts, in dangers richer far.
They offered me the cup of all delight,
And dashed it down and plunged me into night.

Weimar, September 23, 1823

From the Diaries

Filed the poems and letters received on the occasion of my birthday.
In the evening Chancellor von Müller came in. A most disagreeable
conversation about mixed marriages between Jews and Christians.

September 23, 1823

Müller's Diary

It was barely 6 when I entered Goethe's room. In general, he cried,
so many follies were being advocated here that only his personal
dignity would prevent his being insulted were he to travel abroad.
He was ashamed to be from Weimar and would like to emigrate
from there, if only he knew whither.

His ill humor at being cooped up here after his cheerful stay in
Marienbad was noticeable all evening. I urged him to take daily
drives. He answered: "With whom am I to drive without being bored
to death? De Staël quite rightly said to me once: '*Il vous faut de la
séduction!*'" I mentioned Ottilie and Ulrike. He said: "You can't
be seduced by people you see from morning until night. Yes, I came
home well and in good spirits. For three months I was most happy;
I was tossed, as it were, like a ball from one interesting thing to
another and attracted by alternate magnets. Now the ball has been
thrown into a corner. Here I am for the winter, buried like a badger
in its hole, and must do my best to scrabble through."
It was truly painful to see the conflict and confusion in the soul of
such a man. Neither science nor art served to restore his equilibrium.
His inner struggle was dreadful, and not his rich experience of life
nor his brilliant vision of the world seemed able to protect him.

                                                September 25, 1823
Müller to Countess Julie von Egloffstein

From the verses which he wrote in Mlle. W.'s autograph book you
can see, I think, that his passion for Ulrike Levetzow is not wholly
exclusive and that I am right in my assertion, that his present condition is due to a heightened, more general need of his heart for
communication and sympathy.
The crude and hateful attitude of his son, and Ulrike von Pogwisch's
rude one-sidedness and empty naïveté were hardly calculated to help
him over his crisis gently and considerately. As for poor Ottilie, she
has been ill the whole time since he came home and so he sees next
to nothing of her. So he feels the sharp contrast between the happy
weeks in Marienbad and his environment here very keenly and is at
times extremely irritable and bowed down. . . . I myself have always
managed in spite of this to cheer him up and make him talk. The
worst element in the situation comes from his son. That crazy fellow
acts as though he had been injured by his father and threatens to
take Ottilie and move to Berlin.

October 2, 1823

Müller's Diary

With Goethe from 5 to 11. . . . S. played, Ottilie sang; Soret came in and Goethe discussed mineralogy at length and most poetically. . . . Soon he asked me to sit down with him in a corner of the blue room. "Look," he said, "if you want me to feel well among you this winter, I must not lack some vivid society and cheerful stimulation after the great wealth of both which I had in Marienbad. Wouldn't it be possible to have regularly invited guests, now fewer, now more, to come daily to my house? Each one could come and stay as long as he wanted to and bring guests with him, if he pleased. The rooms would be open and lit from 7 o'clock on and tea and other refreshments be prepared. One could play music or read aloud or chat. I myself would appear and disappear, as the spirit moved me." . . . Next he confided to me the most intimate facts concerning his relation to the Levetzows. "It's an inclination that will still give me a great deal of trouble, but I'll get over it. It's a theme, you know for a charming comedy: the old uncle who loves his charming niece." . . . He complained that he had made no tolerable drawings since 1810 and that this diminished his satisfaction with himself immeasurably. The heavier the wine made his tongue, the wittier and more humorous were his notions. We joined the others who were very gay in the dining room. He teased Ottilie charmingly. . . . He made keen fun of his son on account of the latter's indolent sensuality. From time to time the latter growled back. . . . He gave an exquisite delineation of his lovely little friend in Marienbad and told of his acquaintance with a pretty girl from Regensburg, who had worshiped him from afar.

October 14, 1823

Eckermann

I attended one of the big teas at Goethe's house for the first time today. I was the earliest to arrive and took pleasure in the long flight of brilliantly lit rooms. . . . Later Riemer came and Meyer and the Chancellor von Müller and other distinguished ladies and gentlemen. Goethe's son was there, too, and Frau von Goethe, whose acquaintance I made on this occasion. . . .

Goethe seemed most amiable. He went from one guest to another but seemed to prefer to listen to what they had to say, rather than to talk a great deal himself. Repeatedly Frau von Goethe joined him and took his arm and nestled close to him and kissed him. . . .

◇◇◇◇◇

October 19, 1823

Today I dined at Goethe's for the first time. Only Frau von Goethe and Ulrike and little Walter were at the table. It was comfortable and intimate. Goethe acted quite the father of the family. He carved the roast fowl with very special skill and served everyone, nor did he fail to fill their glasses from time to time.

October 20, 1823

Müller's Dairy

I went to Goethe's between appointments. At first he was taciturn. Later, after Riemer had joined us, he was very lively. . . . He gave a remarkable characterization of ecclesiastical history as a union of error and brute force. He said that the doctrine of the Divinity of Christ, first decreed by the Council of Nicaea, had always tended to promote despotism and was, indeed, necessary to it. Reinhard had sent a present of his edition of Tibullus and the poem *Ecce jacet Tibullus* [*Here lies Tibullus*] occasioned a discussion of faith in personal immortality. Goethe expressed himself with the utmost decision. According to him it was inconceivable that a thinking being could imagine non-being, the cessation of thought. Insofar, then, every man involuntarily carries within himself the proof of immortality. To be sure, so soon as an attempt is made to objectify this conviction, to grasp it and prove it dogmatically, to treat in Philistine fashion this perception of the soul, doubtless one would be lost in contradictions.

◇◇◇◇◇

October 24, 1823

Goethe gave a great evening reception in honor of the Polish virtuosà, Mme. Marie Szymanowska, of whom he had told us so much and who had arrived here for a visit. It was to her that he had written those profoundly felt and beautiful stanzas, which he had read to us a few days before. . . . Goethe was in high spirits and very gallant the whole evening. He took an immense pleasure in the general approval which was given to Mme. Szymanowska, not only on account of her inspired playing, but quite as much on account of her personality.

1823

RECONCILIATION TO FATE

To Madame Marie Szymanowska

Passion means suffering!—Ah, who assuages
The heavy heart by fatal losses riven?
Where are the hours now vanished with the ages
Wherein vain beauty was as vainly given!
Dark is the mind, all action faltering,
And dull the sense and the world void of sting.

But music rises on angelic pinions,
A myriad tones into each other weaving,
Lifts up man's being to its own dominions,
Eternal beauty's fullness in him leaving.
The eye grows moist, to the strained heart appears
The divine unison of tones and tears.

Swiftly henceforth it feels its burden lighten,
And knows its beating will not soon be stilled,
And for these splendid gifts it takes delight in,
The grateful offering of itself is willed.
Deeply it feels—oh, that it never ended!—
The bliss of love and music doubly blended.

October 27, 1823

Eckermann

Goethe asked me to join him in his study until it was time for the other guests to arrive.
Stadelmann brought in two candlesticks with lit candles and placed them on Goethe's desk. Goethe asked me to sit down facing the

candles. He wanted me to read something. What he handed me was his new and favorite poem, his *Marienbad Elegy*.

An observation is in place here. Immediately after Goethe's return from Marienbad the report spread that he had made the acquaintance of a young lady there, equally attractive physically and spiritually, and had formed a passionate attachment to her. Whenever he had heard her voice on the Promenade beneath his window, he had snatched his hat and run down. He had neglected no chance of being with her and had experienced very happy days. The report went on to say that the parting had been very difficult and that out of this impassioned circumstance there had arisen an exceedingly beautiful poem which he was keeping secret from all eyes, as something sacred to himself alone.

I gave credence to this report, not only on account of his bodily sturdiness but by reason of the creative power of his mind and the great freshness of his emotions. I had long wanted to see the poem, yet delicacy forbade me from asking to see it. I congratulated myself on my good fortune now that I held the manuscript in my hand. He had himself written the verses in Latin script on heavy vellum and attached the sheets to a red leather portfolio with a silken cord, so that even the physical appearance of the manuscript betrayed his preference for it over all else that he had written.

October 29, 1823

I had sent him some poems of my own. Walking up and down the room he began to talk about them. "Two words I want to say to you about your poems. You are at a point where you must seek to break through to what is really the high and difficult aspect of art— the apprehension of the individual phenomenon. You must try your best to break with the ideational. . . . I know very well that this is difficult, but the grasping and representation of the concrete is the very lifeblood of art. . . . In addition, be sure to write down at the bottom of each poem the date on which you wrote it. You will then possess a diary of your varying situations in life. And that is no small thing. I have done it for years and I know how much it means."

November 4, 1823

Müller's Diary

Today, at last, after many efforts and simultaneous obstacles, Mme. Szymanowska's public recital took place. Only a few hours before the time set the whole thing was doubtful, for lack of a good concert piano. Then the Grand Duchess sent her own. After the concert the Egloffsteins and a few others and myself had supper at Goethe's house. He was in a charming and intimate mood. Many toasts were proposed, among them one to memory. He spoke on the matter with almost violent passion. "I do not admit of recollection in your sense. That is an awkward way of talking. Whatever we meet of goodness and greatness and significance need not first be recollected and hunted down again. From the very beginning it must be woven into the texture of our being; it must beget a better soul in us and thus live on to a creative eternity. . . . True yearning must always be productive and create for us a new and better life." With deep emotion he added: "Have we not all experienced that during these past few days? Do we not all feel profoundly refreshed, improved, enlarged by the amiable and noble figure who is now preparing to leave us? No, she can never vanish from us; she has passed into our inmost selves and will continue to be with us and be our own."

Weimar, November 4, 1823

From the Diaries

A letter from Bohemia. Wrote a reply.

November 5, 1823

Müller's Diary

I dropped in in the afternoon and found Goethe still at table with Mme. Szymanowska. She had given the most charming little farewell gifts to every member of the family, especially to the younger grandson, Wolfgang, who was her special favorite. . . . Goethe tried to be not only cheerful but humorous. Yet the pain of parting stuck out all over him.

After everyone got up from the table there was a great hurrying back

and forth. Goethe disappeared and came back. . . . At 5 o'clock
Mme. Szymanowska had agreed to an audience of farewell granted
her by the Grand Duchess. Since the Court was in mourning, the
musician was all in black, which intensified Goethe's emotion. The
carriage drove up. Suddenly she was gone. It seemed doubtful
whether he would see her again. Goethe broke down and became
very human. He besought me to see to it that she come back once
again and not part so abruptly. Several hours later August and I
brought her back. . . . But all attempts to be of good cheer did not
avail him. He could not restrain his tears. Silently he pressed her to
his bosom and his glance followed in her direction, long after she
had disappeared down the long flight of rooms.

                                        Weimar, November 9, 1823
From the Diaries

Though quite indisposed, tried to work as hard as possible.

◇◇◇◇◇

                                        Weimar, November 12, 1823

Dozed in an armchair. Walter told little stories very sweetly.

                                        November 16, 1823
Eckermann

Remembering his promise to show me his Elegy once more at an
appropriate moment, Goethe got up and placed a candle on his desk
and gave me the manuscript. . . . After I had read for a while I
wanted to make an observation. But it seemed to me that he had
dozed off. . . . Presently I said that it seemed to me as though the
feelings expressed in this poem were more powerful than in any
other of his works. He said: "You do indeed see the product of a
most passionate condition. While I was in that state I would not have
renounced it for all the world; now I would not summon it back for
anything. I wrote it immediately upon my departure from Marienbad in the first, full flush of that experience. At 8 o'clock in the
morning I wrote the first stanza; I composed in the carriage and

wrote down from memory the stanzas at each stopping place, so that by evening the poem had been reduced to paper. It is for this reason that it has a certain immediacy and is as though it had been poured from the mold with a single gesture."

November 17, 1823

Müller's Diary

With Goethe from 7 until 10. Ottilie was with us most of the time and spoke with great purity of her friend W. She had just received a letter from Mme. Szymanowska who was in Berlin. When Ottilie left the room, Goethe gave vent to his irritation over Ottilie's friendship for her Englishman. Her goings on, he said, were hollow and empty, the result of neither passion nor inclination nor true interest, but of a mere lust for excitement.

November 24, 1823

Recollections of Zelter

The agitations of these months led to Goethe's falling into a violent illness. When the crisis had been passed, Zelter came to visit him in Weimar.

My business in Erfurt was soon accomplished. I washed and dressed and hired a coach and drove to Weimar and stopped at Goethe's door. I lingered for a moment in the coach; no one was to be seen. I approached the door. A woman's face appeared at the kitchen window—then disappeared. Stadelmann comes out with a hangdog look and shrugs his shoulders. I make an inquiry. No answer. There I am at the door. Am I to go again? Does death dwell here? Where is your master? He stares dimly. Where is Ottilie? In Dessau. Where is Ulrike? In bed. I had an evil dream which now comes back to me. At last Goethe's son turns up: Father is not well; he is ill, very ill. Is he dead? No, not dead, but seriously ill. I enter—"And marble statues stand and gaze at me." I mount the stairs and those comfortable stairs seem to withdraw from me. What will I find? What do I find? I find a man who looks as though he had swallowed all the passion and anguish of all the youth in the world. Well, if it's that, he'll get over it! Nay, rather let him hold it within him and let him continue to glow with that fire. Twice before had I seen my friend in a comparable condition, apparently near death, and each time I had seen him revive under my very eyes. This time, commanding himself, as it were, to recover, I saw him improve so swiftly that, to the utter astonishment of his physicians, I could leave him by the middle of December completely restored.

November 29, 1823

To Frau von Levetzow

Your dear and precious letter, though I awaited it and hoped for it, surprised me nevertheless. But it is so with all the joys after which we yearn. If they delay, it seems for an eternity. . . .

And so I seem once more, after the long want of it, to enter into the midst of your family and to rejoice in that free air, in those vineyards and orchards, though it be only in imagination, where I was so happy under those brief but golden wings. To this moment I feel as though that happy past were present to me and as though those charming influences were uninterruptedly active.

Weimar, November 30, 1823

From the Diaries

Long talk with Zelter. Read and re-read the Elegy. Went over it once more with Zelter in the evening. Moved into my rear rooms and slept in bed for the first time in many nights.

December 1, 1823

Eckermann

Goethe invited me to dinner today. When I came in Zelter was sitting with him. They got up to welcome me and gave me their hands. "Here," said Goethe, "you have my friend Zelter—a good man to meet." . . . Little Walter came leaping in and asked his grandfather and Zelter many questions. "When you come in, you restless little soul," said Goethe, "you immediately interrupt the conversation." But it was evident that he loved the child and was tireless in doing what the little fellow wanted. Next Frau von Goethe and Ulrike came in, as well as the young Goethe in uniform and sword ready to go to Court.

December, 1823

Recollections of Zelter

Once I told Goethe the following anecdote. Haydn was asked why his Masses were so gay and their mood so happy. Haydn answered: "It is because when I think of God an indescribable sense of happiness comes over me." The tears ran down Goethe's cheeks.

Weimar, December 14, 1823

From the Diaries

Riemer came in the evening. We talked about a number of my poems still kept secret. But I read him the Elegy. Discussed it. Afterwards a long conversation with my son concerning the past and what had been accomplished and enjoyed and suffered in that past.

December 30, 1823

Soret

For the first time, so far as I remember, we talked about *Werther*. Goethe had never re-read it until ten years after publication. He does that with all his works. Next we discussed the problems of translation. He said that he found it extremely difficult to translate English poems into German, because English was so largely monosyllabic and so its terseness vanished when one had to substitute compound words.

December 31, 1823

To Frau von Levetzow

I shall not let this Old Year, which gave me so much good and beauty, pass away without sending my dear friends a word of greeting and of gratitude. . . . If a lovely, slender girl were to be seen bending over and picking up a little specimen stone in memory of me, it is but one out of an hundred gestures in which I see her before me. . . .
Yonder hangs the new wall calendar of 1824. The twelve months are blank and look upon me with complete indifference. In vain do I

ask which days will be red letter days for me, the while my hopes and wishes flutter up and down. Oh, may they coincide with yours! May nothing, nothing oppose their fulfillment and fruition. Do you two say to each other in some intimate hour those things that can be further discussed on a certain terrace, the while we walk up and down. And do not disappoint me of my most intimate expectations which depend so utterly on you. Where and how is it to be? Where may my thoughts seek you out? . . . In yearning hope and longing and devotion . . .

Book Seven

PRINCE OF POETS

1824—March 22, 1832

WEIMAR

1824–March 22, 1832

1824

Eckermann

We were all at the table. The conversation turned to a young beauty in Weimar society. A gentleman who was present said that he was about to fall in love with her, although you couldn't exactly call her brilliant. "Nonsense!" said Goethe and laughed. "As though love had anything to do with the understanding. In a young woman we want quite different things. We love her beauty, her youth, her little ways, her clingingness, her character, her very faults and caprices and God knows what all else which is difficult to define. But we don't love her mind. We may respect it if it's really good and it can make a girl's value rise very greatly in our estimation. Also, if we already love her, her mind may bind us to her. But mind is not what inflames us and awakens passion."

January 4, 1824

"It is quite true that I was no friend of the French Revolution. Its horrors were too immediate and stung me to indignation daily and hourly, while its beneficial effects were not yet visible. . . . But I was just as little a friend of the arbitrary rule that had preceded it. I was completely convinced even then that no revolution is the fault of the people, but always the fault of the government. Revolutions are quite impossible if governments are steadily just and steadily aware and meet the necessity of timely improvements without resisting them so long that amelioration must be wrung from them by the people.

"But because I hated revolutions, I was called a friend of things as

353

they are. But that is an equivocal phrase and I repudiate it. If all
that is were excellent and good and just, I would have nothing
against it. But since what is contains as much evil and injustice and
imperfection as it does of good, a friend of things as they are may
easily be a friend of the outworn and the ill."

January 18, 1824

To Ottilie

If I were to report quite sincerely on our situation here, my dear
daughter, I would have to say that both the house and the town are
quite as confused as though you were here. Charades and masquer-
ades, picnics and balls give people no rest on this restricted scene as,
I suppose, they give you none on that greater scene where you
are. . . .
I want to commend you for keeping your diary so industriously and
so recompensing us for your absence through a good employment of
your time. August, though more laconic, will try to do his share. . . .
I want you, my dear, to convey my sincere thanks to those who sent
me that generous quantity of marvelous asparagus. I am eating it
with particular relish because it shortens the time until August's
harvest this spring. He tells me how copious it will be. And this
leads me to add that Ulrike's culinary rule is marked by care and
skill. The carp with sauce polonaise is better than it has been. But if
you can send her a more authentic recipe from Berlin, her attempts
may be even more successful.

January 27, 1824

Eckermann

"I have been called a great favorite of fortune, and I am unwilling
to complain or to criticize the course my life has taken. But at bottom
I have had nothing but trouble and toil and I can truly say that in
my seventy-five years I have not had four weeks of entire ease.
Eternally I rolled a stone up the mountain; eternally it had to be
done anew. . . .
"I have found my true happiness in creative meditation and ac-
complishment. And yet how that was always interrupted, limited and
hindered by my position in the world. Had I refrained from public

business and lived in greater solitariness, I would have been happier and more productive. . . .

"A wide renown and a high position in life are good things, yet even these have advanced me no farther than that I must be silent when others speak their mind, in order not to wound them." . . .

February 25, 1824

"If attention to the spirit and a high degree of culture were the possession of all, the poet would have an easy time. He could be utterly veracious and would never need to hesitate to say the best he had to say. . . . Time, too, has a curious influence on these matters. It is a tyrant and has its whims. . . . We are not supposed to say things permitted the Greeks. What pleased the virile contemporaries of Shakespeare is unendurable to the English of 1820, so that recently a 'family Shakespeare' [*the Bowdler edition which has become proverbial*] satisfies a need that was felt.

"Much, too, depends upon the form," I said. . . . "You are right," Goethe replied, "mysterious and powerful effects inhere in the various poetic forms. Had I embodied the content of my Roman Elegies in the measure and tone of Byron's *Don Juan,* what was said in them would have seemed infamous."

February 26, 1824

"There is not in the whole of *Faust* a single line," I said, "which does not bear witness to a careful research into reality." . . . "It may be so," Goethe replied, "yet I bore the world within me by anticipation, otherwise I would have remained blind for all my peering, and all research and experience would have been lifeless and vain. The light exists and colors surround us, but if the eye did not already possess light and color, we would perceive neither in the world without us."

February 28, 1824

"It is, in general, the personal character of the writer which impresses the public significantly and not the display of his talent. Napoleon said of Corneille: *'S'il vivait, je le ferais prince'*—and didn't read him. He read Racine, but said nothing comparable of him."

Weimar, March 16, 1824

From the Diaries

Drove to the Garden House with Walter, the while the house was opened and aired and cleaned.

◇◇◇◇◇

Weimar, March 22, 1824

This evening Walter told me the story of *The Magic Flute* vividly and well. . . .

◇◇◇◇◇

Weimar, March 24, 1824

Alone at night considering a new edition of *Werther*.

March 31, 1824

Müller's Diary

Riemer observed that it was a great error to separate knowledge and character. . . . "Yes," Goethe commented: "Character does not take the place of knowledge but complements it. In all business affairs and intricacies the absolute quality of my character was of great help to me. I could be silent for many months and suffer like an animal and yet stick to my purpose. . . . Yet I have often been maligned, especially in regard to my best actions. . . . I joined the War Commission in order to improve the Ducal finances. . . . I sent an Ilmenau tax collector to the penitentiary because his books had been falsified to cover his shortages of 4000 thaler. I showed him up, although Fritsch and other ministerial gentlemen tried to protect him. . . . But, of course, a parvenu like myself could sustain himself only by complete disinterestedness. I was often admonished to act in contrary fashion. Instead, I used up here all my literary earnings and two-thirds of my patrimony on a salary of 1200 thaler a year to begin with and on 1800 up to 1815.

◇◇◇◇◇

April 3, 1824

Today there was a bitter outcry at the Goethe house. Ulrike had had an accident and the domestic routine was upset. But—Goethe averred—he who dare not despair must not live. The one thing he hated was cowardly surrender. I asked him whether this belief made him happy. It's not a question of happiness; it's a question of life itself and of the true constitution of things. He finally added that he refused to be tossed back and forth between hope and fear like any common Philistine.

April 13, 1824

To Frau von Levetzow

At last March is finished, the sun is higher in heaven and from my window I see lilies of the valley and crocuses . . . and can easily believe that my friends would like to keep a little place for me at their cosy evening table. . . .
So spring is here. What will the summer bring? I am not happy when I ask this question. . . . Tell me, nevertheless, dearest friend, more definitely of your prospects, plans, purposes for the next few months. In the general uncertainty that might give me a point toward which to steer. . . .

May 2, 1824

Eckermann

"When a man is 75," he said very cheerfully, "he is bound to think of death from time to time. The thought does not disturb me at all. I am firmly convinced that our spirit is in essence indestructible and is active from eternity to eternity. It is like the sun, which seems to sink in our mortal vision but which, in fact, never sinks but shines uninterruptedly on."

◇◇◇◇◇

May 6, 1824

He showed me this morning an enormous stack of correspondence which was being classified and filed. "These are all the letters," he

explained, "received by me since 1780 from the most significant
people of the nation. There is a very treasure of ideas here. The
publication will take place at some future date. I am now having a
cabinet made in which these letters will be deposited together with
my literary remains." . . .

Weimar, May 23, 1824

From the Diaries

News of the death of Lord Byron.

June 6, 1824

Müller's Diary

After dinner at Court he sat at home in shirtsleeves, drinking with
Riemer. He refused to receive Countess Egloffstein. He said to
Ottilie, the lady might come later when there were no friends present
with whom he could be profound or sublime. . . .
"Only he who has neither conscience nor a sense of responsibility can
make a business of being humorous. . . . Everyone naturally has
moments of humor, but it must not be a continuous mood which
pervades life." . . . I adduced the saying of a certain writer, that
humor was nothing but the wit of the heart. Goethe flew into a
violent rage over the phrase—nothing but. "Thus," he roared,
"Cicero once said that friendship was nothing but etc. O thou ass,
thou simpleton, thou luckless fellow, who runs to Greece to fetch
us wisdom and brings back nothing but that senseless phrase.
Nothing but! Pure negation and leveling downwards! It enrages me
to hear such nonsense. . . . And wit of the heart—what folly! . . .
The reason finds no content in such stuff; it is utterly hollow." . . .
"The contradictions between the religions of heathendom and
Christendom," he said later, "offer a rich mine of material for poetry.
But fundamentally neither religion was any good." . . .
"The tragic is founded on an irreconcilable opposition. So soon as
reconciliation is possible the tragic fades."

London, June 24, 1824

Carlyle to Goethe

Carlyle, 1795-1881, had begun an intensive study of German in 1819.
Awareness of contemporary German thought and writing was steadily

increasing in England at this time. Carlyle revered Goethe specifically as one who, escaping from dogma, had remained a practical idealist. While Carlyle was a private tutor, from 1822-1824, he wrote his *Life of Schiller* and his translation of *Wilhelm Meister*.

Permit me, Sir, in soliciting your acceptance of this Translation to return you my sincere thanks for the profit which, in common with many millions, I have derived from the Original. That you will honor this imperfect copy of your work with a perusal I do not hope; but the thought that some portion of my existence has been connected with that of the Man whose intellect and mind I most admire, is pleasing to my imagination. . . . Four years ago, when I read your *Faust* among the mountains of my native Scotland, I could not but fancy I might one day see you, and pour out before you, as before a Father, the woes and wanderings of a heart whose mysteries you seemed so thoroughly to comprehend and could so beautifully represent. . . . That your life may be long, long spared, for the solace and instruction of this and future generations, is the earnest prayer of, Sir, your most devoted servant, Thomas Carlyle.

June 26, 1824

To Zelter

I am so glad that you succeeded with your music for *Troilus and Cressida* or, rather, that the play succeeded in having its effect on you. I have never denied my bitter enmity to parody and travesty, because the horrid race of parodists seeks to degrade beauty and nobility and greatness in order to destroy them. . . .
The ancients and Shakespeare give us in place of what they seem to rob us of, things estimable and worthy and delightful. It is in this way that a play as equivocal as *Troilus and Cressida* has captured and delighted and satisfied you. . . .

August 13, 1824

To Ottilie

. . . The children are well and happy. Walter is kept busy and interested with his lessons, his piano practice and his visits to Court. Little Wolf sticks to me closely. He has possessed himself of a drawer in my desk in which he keeps all kinds of small objects and toys. He rearranges them every day, but with a carefulness and sense of symmetry which are pleasant to observe.

Dresden, August 28, 1824

Frau von Levetzow to Goethe

Weeks and days have passed in the silent hope that we might still see you in our midst before the summer faded. Thus it was that up to this very day we hope, by some strange faith within us, to see you, dear Privy Councillor. But this day, too, is nearly gone. Thousands of people celebrated; none, assuredly, with a deeper concern for your welfare. . . .

P.S. by Ulrike: Dear Privy Councillor, A year ago today we had the pleasure of spending almost the whole day with you. We were careful, you remember, not to desecrate the open secret by words, though you could read our feelings on our faces. Today it is different, but not better, because we lack the happiness of your society. . . . Your devoted friend, Ulrike.

Weimar, October 2, 1824

From the Diaries

Heine from Göttingen was here.

Heinrich Heine: the Romantic School

I was tempted to address Goethe in Greek. I observed, however, that he understood German and so I told him in that language how excellent were the plums which grew on the road between Jena and Weimar. In many long winter nights I had meditated concerning the sublime and profound observations I would make to Goethe, if I ever saw him face to face. And when I finally did see him, I told him how excellent were the plums of Saxony. And Goethe smiled.

October 19, 1824

Bettina (Brentano) von Arnim to Her Cousin

Arrived in Weimar at 6 o'clock and surprised Goethe in his white dressing gown over a bottle of Karlsbad spring water with an iron kitchen candlestick beside him. . . .

I told him that the Brentanos had expected him this year and had broached a special keg of wine on his account. That made him feel thoroughly dry and he ordered brought in a very acceptable vintage, which did not fail of its effect. He drank to the health of every member of my strange and amiable family. . . . Thereafter he ordered me to the piano to sing the songs which I had composed to words by him. He bade the chambermaid bring in a pair of the handsomest silver candlesticks from his cabinet and she and he and I then formed a procession, I holding the kitchen candlestick, Goethe his glass of wine and the maid the silver candlesticks . . . To my mortification a song composed by somebody else which I sang to him, too, pleased him best. "Well, that is a melody! It is beautifully and nobly done and the tune impresses itself upon my ear." He made me sing it twice over and copy it out for his daughter-in-law.

October 30, 1824

To Thomas Carlyle

If I did not, my very dear Sir, acknowledge without delay the happy arrival of your welcome gift, the reason was that I did not want to send you a mere empty receipt but had the intention of adding a well-considered word to the piece of work by which you honored me.

Unfortunately my great age, not unburdened by inescapable obligations, prevented me from a calm comparison of your version with the text of the original—a more difficult task for me than for some third person thoroughly acquainted with both German and English literature. A moment arrives at which I am offered the opportunity to send you this letter to London through Lord Bentinck [*William, 1776-1839, British statesman*]. There is the added advantage of establishing an agreeable relationship between him and yourself and therefore I delay no longer to thank you for your profound appreciation of my works and my personal fortunes and to express to you cordially my prayer for a continuance of both in the future. Perhaps I may be so fortunate as to hear from you again, and so I add to this letter a group of poems, which you will scarcely have seen but which, I dare hope, will not be without interest to you.

November 24, 1824
Eckermann

"The French," said Goethe, "do well to study and translate our writers. Limited as they are in both form and variety of motivation, they need badly to look beyond their boundaries. German writers may be reproached with a certain lack of form; in substance we excel the French."

◇◇◇◇◇

December 3, 1824

"What you must do," Goethe said to me, "is to found for yourself an inexhaustible intellectual capital. You will do that by continuing your study of the English language and its literature. Stick to that and use to your advantage the presence of young Englishmen here. Since in your youth you largely missed the study of the ancient languages, seek the support of the literature of so able a people as the English. Moreover, our own literature has been profoundly influenced by theirs. Whence do our novels and our tragedies derive but from Goldsmith, Fielding and Shakespeare? And to this very day, where will you find in Germany three heroes of literature who can be placed beside Byron, Moore and Scott?"

December 24, 1824
To Knebel

I have been both entertained and instructed by going over my correspondence with Schiller, now almost completely arranged. It ends in 1805, and when you consider that the French invasion took place in 1806, you see at a glance that it closes an epoch, of which scarcely a vestige remains. The cultivation developed and heightened in this part of the world by a long peace was violently interrupted. . . . All the more purely does there arise from that correspondence an epoch which is gone, which will not come again and which, nevertheless, is effectual to this day and reveals its living influence not only in Germany. Let us be glad, you and I, that we had our share in it, that we still are what we were then, and that our friendship has proved equally durable. May the New Year grant us its favors once again.

1825

January 11, 1825

To the Assembly of the German Confederation

In the year 1815 I made a seven years' contract concerning all my poetic and aesthetic works with the publishing house of J. G. Cotta. At the expiration of this period the question arose concerning the publication of an enlarged edition, far more extensive than the previous one of 20 volumes. . . . In planning such an edition, which contained the efforts of an entire life, the desire naturally arose to obtain that proportionate advantage and reward therefrom, which a German author usually receives in but a penurious measure. . . . Soon after the invention of printing means were sought to preserve an author's right to his acknowledged intellectual property. Since there were no general laws, special privileges were used. In the beginning of the 16th century Imperial letters of protection were quite efficient; kings and princes issued letters of the same kind. Such has been the custom to this day.

Were it not well, however, if the Assembly of the Confederation, combining all German sovereignties, were to exercise a similar function in its corporate capacity? . . . An enactment of this character would be decisive in its influence upon German literature and intellectual development. . . .

I respectfully petition, therefore, that the Assembly of the German Confederation grant me the rights of a new complete edition of my works and secure me protection against reprints in all the states of the Confederation, under pain of confiscation and other penalties. . . .

January 18, 1825

Eckermann

"Scholars," I said, "always seem to me very odd. They seem to think that creative literature is drawn not from life but from books." . . . "Yes, indeed," said Goethe, "that is quite absurd." "Thus, too," I continued, "Byron isn't very clever when he takes *Faust* to pieces and

Goethe: The Story of a Man

says that you imitated one bit here and another bit there." "I never even read the various writings which Byron cites," Goethe said, "nor did I even think of any such thing when I wrote *Faust*. But Byron is great only as a poet; so soon as he reflects, he is a mere child. He wasn't able to defend himself against similar attacks at home. He ought to have spoken much more vigorously and said: What is here is mine, whether derived from life or a book. The important question is, what I made of it. Scott, for instance, borrowed a scene from my *Egmont*. He did it with true understanding and justified his right and is to be commended. Similarly he imitated Mignon in one of his novels, whether with equal wisdom remains a question. . . . Mephistopheles, to give another instance, sings a song of Shakespeare's, and why should he not? . . . Has not my Prologue to *Faust* a definite similarity to that of the Book of Job? And that again was right, and I am rather to be praised than criticized."

Weimar, February 20, 1825

From the Diaries

The children found the first lilies of the valley in the garden.

◇◇◇◇◇

Weimar, February 27, 1825

Received the *Venetian Sonnets* of Platen [*a poet characterized by perfection of form, 1796-1835*]. They are admirable.

March 22, 1825

Eckermann

Near midnight on this night I was awakened by a fire alarm. I heard cries in the street: The theatre is burning! I slipped into my clothes and ran to the place. . . .
There was no lack of proper provision against fire. The building was surrounded by pumps, which poured water into the flames. But it was quite in vain. . . . A little to one side, but as near the fire as was safe, there stood a man in a military cloak and cap, calmly smoking a cigar. At first glance he seemed to be merely an idle onlooker. But I observed him giving brief orders to people who went back and

forth and saw that these orders were instantly obeyed. It was the Grand Duke. He had soon seen that the building could not be saved; hence he commanded the pumps to turn the water upon the surrounding houses in order that they might not catch on fire. . . .

I went home and rested a few hours. In the course of the forenoon I went to Goethe's house. The servant told me that his master was not well and in bed, but that he wanted to see me. He held out his hand to me. "We have all been losers in this matter," he said, "but what can one do? My little Wolf came to my bedside this morning and took my hand and made big eyes at me and said: 'That's the kind of thing that happens to people!' That sums up everything that can be said in consolation. There the scene of my loving pains of thirty years lies in ruins and ashes. I slept very little all night. From my windows I could see the flames rise and spread. You can imagine how memories of old times and of the long years of my work with Schiller passed through my mind and, naturally, moved me a great deal. Therefore I think it is prudent for me to stay in bed today."

I wanted him to take care of himself. But he wasn't in the least feeble or tired; he seemed rather comfortable and cheerful. But, indeed, this lying in bed is an old piece of strategy of his which he uses when extraordinary events threaten to bring too many people to his door.

April 11, 1825

To Zelter

The papers will have brought you and all my Berlin friends the news that the Assembly of the German Confederation views my petition affirmatively and with favor. We shall now see how the matter develops further.

April 20, 1825

Eckermann

"The trouble in the State is," said Goethe, "that no one wants to live and enjoy himself. Everyone wants to rule. The trouble in art is that no one wants to rejoice in what is being done but desires to be productive himself. . . . There is furthermore no pervasive seriousness, no desire to serve the community. Everyone seeks merely to emphasize his own self and to render that self conspicuous. This false tendency is universal. They are all like those modern virtuosi who do not choose pieces in order to give their hearers a pure musical pleasure but only such as will win admiration for the skill of the performer." . . . Later he said: "I have spent too much time on occupations which were not really appropriate to me. When I think of the work that a man like Lope De Vega [*extremely prolific Spanish dramatist, 1562-1635*] produced, the number of my own productions seems very small. I should have stuck to my proper business."

April 27, 1825

"It is extremely curious," said Goethe, "how easy it is to get into a false position in the mind of the public. I'm not conscious of ever having sinned against the common people, yet I am said to be its enemy. To be sure, I am no friend of the revolutionary mob which is out for theft and murder and arson and the most vulgar personal profit in the name of the public weal. I am no friend of such people, but neither am I a friend of Louis XV's. I hate violent overthrow, because it always involves the destruction of good, whatever be its gain. I hate those who bring it about and equally those who made it inevitable. Well, does that make me an enemy of the people?" . . .

May 12, 1825

We talked about Molière. "Molière is so great," said Goethe, "that one is astonished anew every time one reads him. He is unique. His comedies border on the tragic; they embody every hint of fate. No one has had the courage to imitate him. His play *The Miser* in which vice abrogates both filial and paternal piety is especially remarkable and tragic in a high sense. . . . I read several of his plays every year. . . .
"People talk about originality. What do they mean? So soon as we are born the world begins to affect us and that continues to the very end. What is our own after all, except our energy, our force, our will? . . .
"Everywhere and always one can learn only from him whom one loves." . . .

May 31, 1825

To Schultz

With the destruction of the theatre all the physical memorials of my former activity of this kind have disappeared. For not only the building itself, but the library and the very property room contained many traces of my former share in the institution. Everything from now on will be new and different. I am not dissatisfied that my accounting and that this chapter are both closed.

June 6, 1825

To Zelter

Nowadays young people are fed on excitement far too early and plunged into the whirlpools of life. What the world admires and what everyone strives after are wealth and speed. Even educated people rival each other and try to surpass each other in order to establish railroads, express postchaises, steamboats and all kinds of facilities for communication, and thus they are bound to remain in their original mediocrity. But this is the result of all attempts to render everything common. It is a mediocre culture that becomes common; and this is indeed what the Bible Societies and the Lancaster pedagogical methods seek to attain.

In reality then this is the century of the capable, of agile, practical people who, provided with a certain adroitness, can attain a superiority over the mass without being in any sense highly endowed. Let us, then, cling to the convictions at which we have long arrived. We and a few like us will be the last of a period not likely soon to recur.

June 17, 1825

To Marianne

You have probably heard, my sweet friend, that I am employed in arranging in strict order all that I have recorded black on white. I would not mention this, did I not need an excuse for not having been heard from in so long a period. May I hope that the lines once graven into your dear heart will remain forever fresh and stand in need of no renewal. . . .

June 18, 1825

To Felix Mendelssohn

Who had sent him his Quartet in B Minor.

My very dear Felix, You have given me a true pleasure with your rich gift. Although it was announced, yet it took me by surprise. The title page, the beauty of the engraving, the magnificent binding all vie to render your gift the more splendid. . . . Accept, then, my warmest thanks and let me hope that I shall soon again be able personally to admire your marvelous activities. Commend me to your worthy parents, your equally gifted sister and your admirable teacher.

July 8, 1825

Varnhagen von Ense's Diary

I spent the afternoon and evening with Goethe. I found him much aged since last I saw him some years ago, but still very vigorous and cheerful. He was unusually amiable and sympathetic, frank and kind. His glances were earnest and attentive and vividly accompanied all that he said or heard.

July 11, 1825

Charlotte von Stein to Goethe

How are you, dear Privy Councillor, after sitting so long yesterday on my hard bench? I reproached myself for not having a chair brought for you to sit on, but your dear visit was so unexpected. Do try to answer me and to assure me of your well-being. That's all I want to hear.

August 19, 1825

To Boisserée

Since, at my age, the profit from the business transaction in question will be entirely for the benefit of my family, I think it fair that the family should assume the trouble and labor connected therewith. I would therefore appreciate whatever you can do to bring my son together with Herr von Cotta. Whatever final arrangements are made, I would like, naturally, to be able to approve while I am still alive.

ENCLOSED MEMORANDUM: When my former contract made with Herr von Cotta in 1823 expired, I offered him another for a new complete edition of my works at once. The matter was discussed on several occasions, but no progress was made. . . .

I have transferred the technical and pecuniary and mercantile management of this matter to my son. The latter, more irritated than myself by the delay, as well as by the continuous pirating of my works in Vienna, took council with business friends and was urged by wise and well-meaning men to that appeal to the Assembly of the German Confederation. . . . The public and unconditional approval of the Assembly has made this matter one of national import. More than one publisher was ready hopefully to engage in this undertaking. A number of offers were made to my son. . . . Fifty thousand thaler with the proviso of an increase upon the signing of the contract have now been offered. Herr von Cotta increased this offer and so the present price seems to stand between 60,000 and 70,000 thaler. My son and his advisers are of the opinion, however, that the rights to an edition in 40 volumes for the space of twelve years may be properly estimated as being worth 100,000 thaler. A considerable sum should be paid during the first year as the greater part of the copy is delivered. The rest should be pro rated over the following years, so that my family enjoys a continuous share and profit. . . .

Considering that Herr von Cotta is best equipped both by experience and ability for such an undertaking, I desire him to give his opinion and to put an end to this hesitation which, naturally, is disagreeable to a man of my age.

Weimar, September 3, 1825

From the Diaries

Went at 6 o'clock in the morning to pay my respects to His Serenity. The highest ranking persons of the Duchy were there. Back at 8 o'clock. Thus began the fiftieth anniversary of his reign.

September 3, 1825

Müller's Diary

The early morning meeting of the Grand Duke on his day of jubilee
with Goethe was the moment which quite evidently moved him
most deeply. With both hands the Grand Duke grasped Goethe's
who was himself too moved to speak and only murmured at last:
"Together to the last breath!" The Grand Duke recovered his composure and I heard him exclaim: "Oh to be 18 again and in Ilmenau!" Thereafter they exchanged reminiscences concerning their
youth and with eloquent feeling the Grand Duke closed his first
remarks as follows: "But let us be particularly grateful for this, that
we are still as fulfilled as ever by the sentiment that we once heard
in a song at Tiefurt:

> O air and light
> 'Twixt friend and friend!
> This shall not fade
> Until our end.

Goethe was still deeply moved. The Grand Duke put his arms about
him and drew him aside to a window niche, where they conversed
softly. I did, however, catch the last words of the Grand Duke: "Well,
I'll live to see it!" As I was told later, he was thinking of the celebration of the fiftieth anniversary of Goethe's arrival in Weimar, concerning which the Grand Duke gave certain orders on this day.

1825

INTERLUDE

Written to commemorate Goethe's entrance into the Masonic Lodge at
Weimar.

> Cling not to the too transitory,
> Nor counsel ask; there's no reply.
> The brave in our recorded story
> Begets the good that cannot die.
>
> And so from life itself unfolding
> Evolves forever strength renewed,

For man, his changeless faith upholding,
Is thus with permanence endued.

No need to question if a portal
Unto a second life there be;
The enduring groundwork that sustains the mortal
Assures our perpetuity.

November 7, 1825

Karl August to Goethe

This letter was used as a public proclamation and copies were affixed
to hoardings in Weimar. A banquet in Goethe's honor was held in the
City Hall and August and his posterity made honorary citizens of the
municipality. The day ended with a gala performance of *Iphigenie* in
the new Court Theatre.

With profound pleasure I would mark the fiftieth return of this day
as the jubilee not only of the premier servant of my state but of the
friend of my youth who has accompanied me through all the mutability of life with unchanged affection, loyalty and steadfastness. I
owe the happy outcome of my most important undertakings to his
circumspect council, his ever living sympathy and beneficent service-
ableness. To have attached him permanently to myself I regard as
one of the highest ornaments of my reign.

Weimar, November 7, 1825

From the Diaries

Most solemn day.—Letter from Serenissimo.

Weimar, November 8, 1825

Last echoes and recuperation.

November 7, 1825

Zelter to Goethe

So this is the day and they've got you cornered. Hold on, old fellow,
and let them do their worst! Once more the strong old heart must

hold out. . . . What saved me on a similar occasion was the thought
that I was the innocent cause of other people having a good time.
Your jubilee is like a wedding. Nothing more so—thou bridegroom
of time and eternity. . . . The amount of champagne consumed
here is now a matter of history.

November 29, 1825

To Zelter

Even as the impression of misfortune needs time to allay it, so does
good fortune require the same beneficent influence. I am gradually
recovering from the seventh of November. . . .

December 25, 1825

Eckermann

Goethe showed me an important English work of copper engravings
illustrating the whole of Shakespeare. "It is frightening," said
Goethe, "to examine these pictures. They make one aware of Shakespeare's infinite wealth and greatness. There is no human motive
which he did not delineate and express. You can't talk about him;
whatever you say is inadequate. . . . In fact, he is so wealthy and so
powerful that a creative artist should read only one of his plays a
year or he will be overwhelmed. . . . I consider *Macbeth* Shakespeare's theatrically most effective piece; it is done with the best
understanding of the stage. But if you want to be acquainted with
the freedom of his mind, read *Troilus and Cressida,* where he treats
a subject from the *Iliad* after his own fashion.

1826

January 21, 1826

To Zelter

He who wills, must! And I continue: He who has insight, wills, and
therewith we have returned to the point from which we started out,
namely, one must will one's obligations out of conviction. . . .
Everything comes right so long as he who knows both what he wants
and what he can do is undeterred in his doing of it. You know that
best of all and experience it every day.

January 24, 1826

To the Author of a Treatise on Crystallography

Your important treatise, my dear Sir, came at a very favorable hour. At once and with pleasure I read and re-read it up to page 45. At that point I reached the limitation which God and nature have assigned to me as an individual. I am restricted to word, speech and, in its real sense, image, and wholly incapable of operating in any way with those symbols and figures with which highly gifted minds seem to come to so easy an understanding.

January 29, 1826

Eckermann

"I'll tell you something which, I think, you will find to be borne out throughout life. All historic periods which are retrogressive and in process of dissolution are subjective in character, whereas progressive periods have an objective tendency. You can see that not only in poetry but in painting and in many other departments. Yet every truly able effort fixes the inner attention upon the world, as you can mark in all great periods. . . .

"The trouble with us today is that a certain poetic culture is so widespread that no one writes bad verses any more. The young poets who send me their manuscripts are not worse than their predecessors. Since those were highly praised, they do not understand why they are not equally praised. Yet one dare not encourage them. There are too many hundreds of them. . . . Were there a single one pre-eminent above the others, that would be excellent, for the world can be served only by the extraordinary."

February 3, 1826

To Cotta

. . . It is years since I have felt as truly satisfied as in these hours, in which the certainty has come to me that the results of my literary activity are definitely in your hands. A more valid evidence of mutual confidence cannot well exist.

Weimar, February 27, 1826

From the Diaries

Went into the garden with the children and found the first lilies of
the valley.

March 26, 1826

Eckermann

Goethe was in a very gay and happy mood at dinner today. He had
just received the autographed copy of Byron's dedication of *Sar-
danapalus*. He showed it at dessert and nagged his daughter-in-law
to give him back Byron's letter from Genoa. "Look, dear child," he
said, "I now have gathered everything that illustrates the relationship between Byron and myself. As by a miracle the dedication came
today, and now all I lack is that other letter."

May 12, 1826

To Reinhard

Generally speaking, I must concentrate more than ever and let all
that is polemical simply pass me by. A man really has quite enough
to do to carry out his own positive aims to the very end. Fortunately
I entertain the conviction that many things can co-exist side by
side, which would like, as a rule, to eliminate each other. The world
spirit is much more tolerant than people think. . . .

May 17, 1826

Müller's Diary

On this day I found Sulpiz Boisserée with Goethe, who enjoyed his
friend's visit. Ottilie, who had had the smallpox, did not yet appear.
Goethe had hesitated up to this time to look at her disfigured face:
"For," said he, "I never get rid of disagreeable impressions like that;
they ruin my very memory of things. I am so strangely made in respect of my power of sensuous visible perception, that I retain out-
lines and forms sharply and definitely in my mind. Well, I am
equally affected by deformities and infirmities."

May 20, 1826

Boisserée's Diary

Today he was in one of his condemnatory moods. Paris. German and
French party intrigues. The whims of princes. The corruption of
taste. The folly of priestcraft in France and the lust for so-called
enlightenment and heresy in Germany. Philo-Hellenism as a cloak
for petty politics. Etc. Etc. . . . I finally felt as though I were with
the witches of *Faust* on their mountain. I said so. "Aha, and we're
not coming down again so soon—so long, at least, as we haven't thoroughly discussed the whole world."

July 20, 1826

To Karl August

. . . You have had the kindness to lend me your ancestor, Duke
Bernhard's, accounts of his travels. I am returning them with appreciation. . . . It is remarkable how he avoided no discomfort. Rather
did he seek to utilize these frequently difficult excursions as a source
of instruction and of social life. I had to leave him in Philadelphia
on the important anniversary of William Penn's first arrival at that
well-wooded shore where now, at the confluence of two rivers, a
wealthy and remarkable city has arisen. . . .
Now I would like to make a request. In the first part of the manuscript there is a passage, of which I would like very much to possess
a copy. On the road between Boston and Albany our traveler came
upon a most curious colony inhabited by a variety of Quakers, who
call themselves Shakers. They live in a state of celibacy; in their religious assemblies they wait for the outpouring of the spirit; they
end the celebration of their cult with a grotesque dance. . . .

July 26, 1826

Eckermann

I asked him how a play must be made in order to be theatrically
effective. "It must be symbolical," Goethe replied, "that is to say:
every action must be significant in itself and at the same time aim
implicitly at an even weightier one. From this point of view Molière's *Tartuffe* is the perfect model. Just think of the exposition in

the first scene! From the very start everything is full of meaning and yet forces you to infer the more significant action to come. The exposition in Lessing's *Minna von Barnhelm* is admirable, too, but that in *Tartuffe* is unique." . . .

"It is curious," I said, "that Shakespeare's plays are not really made for the theatre in that sense."

"Shakespeare," Goethe explained, "wrote his plays out of the depth of his nature and his period, and the character of the stage of that time made no demands upon him. People were pleased with what Shakespeare gave them. Had he lived at the Court of Madrid or written for the theatre of Louis XIV, he would probably have used a tighter theatrical form."

August 28, 1826

Charlotte von Stein to Goethe

This is Charlotte's last letter. She died on January 6, 1827.

All my best wishes and blessings on this day. May the Guardian Angels in the heavenly parliament command that all that is good and lovely be granted you, my very dear friend, and continue to remain yours in hope and without fear, the while I beg of you for myself your freely given kindness during the brief span that remains to me.

Weimar, September 18, 1826

From the Diaries

We celebrated little Wolf's birthday. The children dined with us. Then Ottilie and I took a drive. A crowd of boys in the garden were very noisy.

September 29, 1826

Franz Grillparzer's Recollections

The illustrious Austrian dramatist, 1791-1872.

I finally got to Weimar and stopped at the inn At the Sign of the Elephant, which was then known throughout Germany. It was, so to speak, the anteroom to Weimar's living Valhalla. I sent the waiter to Goethe with my card to ask if I could come to pay him my respects. The waiter came with the answer that the Privy Councillor had guests and could not see me now. He would expect me for late tea. . . .

There was quite a crowd in the salon waiting for Goethe. He had not yet appeared. . . . At last a side door opened and he entered. He was in black with the stars of his orders on his breast. Stiff and straight he approached us like a monarch granting an audience. He said a few words to one person and then to another and finally came to me, who stood at the opposite side of the room. He asked me whether Italian literature was much studied in Austria. I was obliged to tell him that, since all Imperial officers had to learn Italian, a knowledge of the language was frequent enough. I added that Italian literature was totally neglected. The fashion was to read English books and that I, for one, considered the comparative coarseness of English literature, despite its excellence, no good influence upon our German culture, especially in its poetical aspects. Whether this remark displeased him or not, I cannot say. . . . He left me and chatted with others, came back to me once more and talked I hardly know what about, and then we were dismissed.

I confess that I went back to my inn with a most disagreeable impression. It was not that my vanity was offended. . . . What disillusioned me was to see the ideal of my youth under the aspect of a stiff ministerial personage. I think I would have been happier if he had insulted me and thrown me out.

Weimar, September 30, 1826

From the Diaries

I continued reading a book on the sources of the Susquehanna River.

◇◇◇◇◇

Weimar, October 1, 1826

I started to read a novel of Fenimore Cooper's over again. I wrote out a list of the characters. I also gave closer attention to its artistic aspects. . . .

October 22, 1826

To Boisserée

. . . Forgive me if I seem to be in an exorbitant mood. But since God and nature have permitted me to possess myself for so many years, I know no better way to show my gratitude than through an activity comparable to that of youth. I want to show myself worthy of what is granted me and so I spend night and day—and this is almost literal—in reflection and in action.

1826

What place thy friends may moulder,
Uncaring let it pass;
If under granite boulder,
If under wind-swept grass.

But while in life thou bidest,
See that, though dour the day,
For them thou still providest
What shall not know decay.

October 22, 1826

To Wilhelm von Humboldt

I've spent the whole summer in the house and continued to work at the new collected edition of my writings. Perhaps you will remember a dramatic fragment called Helena, which was to appear in the second part of *Faust?* . . . It is one of my oldest notions; it derives from the tradition of the mediaeval puppet play to the effect that Faust forces Mephistopheles to provide him Helen of Greece as a bedfellow. I have worked at it from time to time. But it could not be finished until the fullness of ages, seeing that its time is 3000 years, from the fall of Troy to the taking of Missolunghi. In a high sense, then, the play has unity of time; unity of place and action are exactly observed in the quite ordinary sense. . . .

I have no hostility to the Hindu philosophy. I am afraid of it. It draws my imagination into the formless and unformed, which I must guard against more than ever.

November 29, 1826

Eckermann

The illustrations to *Faust* by Eugène Delacroix, 1798-1863, accompanied the French translation of the play which appeared a year later.

"Herr Delacroix," said Goethe, "is a great talent, which came upon the right subject in *Faust*. The French criticize his savage extravagance, but he is in his element here. I am told that he will execute the whole series of designs and I am looking forward with special pleasure to his pictures for the Witches' Kitchen and the scenes on the Brocken."

December, 1826

Recollections of Karl Vogel

Doctor Karl Vogel, 1798-1864, the body physician of the Grand Duke also attended Goethe and his family during these later years.

Soon after I became his physician, he said to me one day: "Your practice takes you around among humble people. If you come across a family that has had much illness and has innocently fallen into destitution and that could be helped by something more than ordinary alms, do let me know. I like to help such people to the extent of my ability." Soon thereafter I came to him and told him about a good, industrious carpenter who had supported his numerous family well but who, on the point of convalescing from a long illness, had reason to regard the future with great distress. Quietly Goethe went to his desk and took out 15 thaler and put them in my hand. "Here is what I can spare; make sure that neither the carpenter nor anyone else know who the giver is."

1827

January 4, 1827

Eckermann

Goethe highly praised the poems of Victor Hugo. "A very remarkable talent who was influenced by German literature. The pedantry of the classicizing critics constricted his poetic youth. But now he has liberal criticism on his side and will win through. There is much objectivity in his writing and he seems to me quite as important as Lamartine or Delavigne. Closely regarded, it is clear enough where he and other new talents come from. They derive from Chateaubriand, who was certainly a man of notable rhetorical and poetical gifts. If you want to see just how Victor Hugo writes, read his poem about Napoleon, 'Les deux îles.' "

January, 1827

According to a Friend of Charlotte von Stein

I had often written him in Charlotte's name. When I went to call on him shortly after her death, he tried to master his grief. But he failed and exclaimed: "It's disgusting of a man of 80 to wail like an old woman! But her loss is a heavy trial to me!" And with these words he fell upon my neck and wept.

January, 1827

Müller to Reinhard

The stormy days of winter have done him little good. I am glad that he was cheered by a two weeks' visit of Humboldt. In addition to everything else, his oldest friend, Charlotte von Stein, died quite recently at the age of 84. He never mentioned the fact, yet it is evident that he suffered keenly.

January, 1827

Recollections of Henriette von Beaulieu

When I first came to Weimar in 1787 I was told that Frau von Stein was the best friend of both the Duchess Louise and of Goethe. People added that she was worthy of this double distinction. Later on I convinced myself of the truth of this. This woman's character was undoubtedly a very noble one. Her understanding, though it never seemed a distinguished one to me, somehow led her happily to escape the manifold pitfalls of her career at Court. . . .
It is not to be denied that though her heart was good, Frau von Stein must have possessed her own share of shrewdness and worldly prudence. Otherwise it would have been impossible for her during so many years without any interruption to sustain her position so

close to both the Duchess Louise and to Goethe. Death alone could sever this relationship which is still hidden, as I write these lines, by an impenetrable veil. Goethe alone could reveal what that veil concealed; he is hardly likely to do so. Hence posterity will have no means of a clearer judgment concerning this matter, which always remained a mystery to the great man's contemporaries.

January 12, 1827

Eckermann

"It often happens that my own stuff seems completely strange to me. The other day I was reading something in French and I thought to myself: that's very sensibly said; I would have said it more or less like that. I regarded the page more closely and found that I was reading a passage translated from one of my books."

January 18, 1827

Goethe said: "It does not constitute freedom to acknowledge nothing higher than ourselves; we are free precisely by giving it our reverence. For by doing so we raise ourselves to that higher level and by acknowledging its character we give evidence of the fact that we are akin to it and worthy of being held equal to it. In my travels I used to meet merchants from the North of Germany who thought to display their equality by sitting down rudely at my table. Of course they were not my equals. They could have become so, had they known how to esteem me and treat me rightly."

January 19, 1827

To Boisserée

Here, my friend, is a last piece of the Helena. It takes you directly to the axis, about which the whole play turns. The complete manuscript will be sent to you before the month ends. . . .
The year began in common earthly fashion between joy and sorrow. Since the former prevailed, let us be grateful. May the Providence that rules us grant that in the final balance the affirmative predominates. . . .

Eckermann

"I see more and more," Goethe said, "that poetry is a universal possession of mankind and manifests itself in all ages in hundreds and hundreds of people. One does a little better than another and so remains visible a little longer. That is all. . . . Poetic talent is not so rare a thing that a man has reason to be specially vain, because he has written a good poem. To be sure, we Germans are apt to be befogged by pedantry, if we do not look beyond our immediate environment. I am fond of seeing what other nations are doing and I advise everyone to do the same. National literatures are no longer so significant in themselves; the epoch of world literature has arisen and it behooves each of us to promote its development."

◇◇◇◇◇

March 1, 1827

"There is no objection," Goethe said, "to a dramatic poet who aims at a moral effect. But in the task of presenting his subject clearly and strongly before the eyes of spectators, his ultimate moral purposes can help him but little. To know what to do and not to do, he must possess a vivid power of representation and a knowledge of the theatre. If a moral effectiveness is inherent in his subject, it will patently arise, even though the playwright had thought exclusively of the effective and artistic treatment of his subject matter. If a poet has the soul of a Sophocles, his effect will always be a moral one, whatever he may do or intend."

March 11, 1827
Zelter to Goethe

I have just received the news of the death of my last son Georg. I know nothing more at present than that he died on the 5th of this month in the town in which he lived of a gall bladder trouble. He was 38 and leaves his beloved young wife and a son of 6 months. Although there are people who, in the face of such experiences, can be their own helpers and counselors, you must admit the blow to be hard. . . .

March 19, 1827

To Zelter

What can a friend say to another in such a case? A similar tragic misfortune first deepened our friendship. It cannot be closer than it is. Tirelessly the Fates repeat a thousand times a thousand times the old story of the falling night. . . . Let us continue to strive until we, too, one after the other, are recalled to the aether by the World Spirit! May the Ever Living One not deny us on that other shore activities analogous to those in which we have approved ourselves here.

March 29, 1827

To Zelter

If the time were calmer and I had but a remnant of the powers of youth, I would dedicate myself wholly to the study of Greek, although I know all the difficulties. I would fix my vision upon nature and upon Aristotle. It is unimaginable what that man saw, observed, noticed, envisioned—granting that many of his explanations were premature.

April 18, 1827

Eckermann

"The artist sustains a double relationship to nature: he is nature's lord and slave at the same time. He is nature's slave, insofar as he must use earthly means to make himself understood; he is nature's lord, insofar as he subjects these earthly means to his higher intentions and makes them serviceable to these."

◇◇◇◇◇

May 6, 1827

"They come and ask me, what was the idea that I meant to embody in *Faust*. As though I knew it or could express it! 'From Heaven through the world to Hell'—that's something of an indication. But that's no idea; it's the course of the action. Furthermore, the fact that the Devil loses the wager and that a man who never ceases to strive to something higher from the midst of dreadful errors, *can* be redeemed, that is a very effective notion and it explains a good deal, but it is not an idea in the sense of being fundamental to the whole and to each scene individually. But, then, can you imagine so rich and colorful and varied a delineation of life as I have in *Faust,* strung on the thin thread of a single pervasive idea? . . .

"If ever I wanted to project an idea poetically, I did it in small poems, where a terse unity of effect could be achieved. The only extensive work of mine, in which I consciously aimed at the delineation of an all-pervasive idea was *The Elective Affinities.* That brought the novel closer to the grasp of the understanding. I am not prepared to say that it is a better book on that account. Rather would I give it as my opinion, that a poetic work is better insofar as it is incommensurable and inaccessible to the mere understanding."

1827

Poems, look you, are stained-glass windowpanes.
If from the square into the church you peer,
All is sombre, darkness enfolds it;
And thus the Philistine beholds it.
Annoyed by anything so queer,
Vexed for a lifetime he remains.

But once you enter and behold
And give the holy nave your greeting,
Suddenly gleams and glints unfleeting
Burst into radiances beating
On serried treasures' glow and gold.
Children of God, this edifies
The heart while it delights the eyes.

May, 1827

Recollections of Karl von Holtei

A writer, actor, and theatrical director, 1798-1880.

Goethe's daughter-in-law, Ottilie, wasn't feeling well. Her sister Ulrike von Pogwisch acted as hostess at the table. Besides there were present August von Goethe, the Chancellor von Müller and Professor Riemer. The old man talked a lot and drank not a little. The conversation was lively, free and without pretension. Hardly had the dessert appeared, when I felt quite at home. I said what came into my mind, without considering whether it harmonized with Goethe's notions or not. I continued to do this later on, when I was often invited to dine in large gatherings. . . . When we had finished, the two grandsons, Walter and Wolfgang, came in. They were two lively boys. Encouraged by their grandfather, they told jokes and sang songs. Some of the latter were from plays of mine. Handing the boys sweets, the old man said: "You see that man. He's the one who wrote those silly things."

May, 1827

Recollections of Moritz Oppenheim

Portrait and genre painter, chiefly of Jewish subjects, 1799-1882. Goethe had recommended him for the distinction received.

When the Grand Duke made me a titular professor, I went to Goethe to thank him as well. He said to me: "A title and a decoration stand between a man and many a hard jolt in such a world as this."

May 24, 1827

To Zelter

I want you to know, my very dear friend, that on Saturday, May 12, I drove quite innocently to my old Garden House, with no thought but of spending an agreeable hour there. But when I got there I liked it so much and the spring was so incomparable there, that I stayed, without meaning to do so and am still here, ever active and, I trust, as pleasing to others as to myself. The second part of *Wilhelm Meister's Pilgrimage* is completed; it needs but a few withes to bind the wreath completely. . . .

And now I want quietly to confess to you that, with the aid of kindly spirits, I have gone to work at *Faust* again. I am taking up the poem at that passage where, emerging from the cloud of antiquity, he meets his evil genius again. Tell no one; but I want you to know that I now intend to fill the gap between that point and the close. . . .

From the Diaries

Read another novel by Cooper almost to the end and admired the wealth of substance and the clever treatment. There are not many works executed as awarely and as consistently as these novels of Cooper's.

July 5, 1827

Eckermann

"Our German aestheticians," said Goethe, "talk a good deal about subjects fit or unfit for poetic treatment. In certain respects they may not be wholly in the wrong. But at bottom no real subject is unpoetic, if only the poet knows how to treat it properly. . . .
"If the imagination could not create things eternally problematical to the mere understanding, the imagination wouldn't amount to much. It is by this element that poetry is distinguished from prose, in which the understanding is at home and ought to be."

◇◇◇◇◇

July 9, 1827

Goethe laughed. "Yes," he said, "there are times when coarseness can be tamed only by still greater coarseness. I remember a case in my extreme youth. At that time there were still quite beastly types among the aristocracy. At dinner in excellent society and in the presence of ladies, a wealthy gentleman used such vile expressions that all who heard him were embarrassed and angry. You couldn't get at him by talk. A determined and personable gentleman, who sat opposite him, chose another means. With great noise he perpetrated an indecency so foul, that everyone was frightened, including the ruffian in question who felt subdued and said no more."

◇◇◇◇◇

July 16, 1827

"People talk about aristocracy and democracy. The matter is simple enough. In our youth when we have nothing or are unable to appreciate the calm of possession, we're democrats. When, in the course of a long life, we have acquired some property, we not only wish that it be secure, but that our children and grandchildren might quietly enjoy the fruit of our labors."

July 20, 1827

To Carlyle

. . . It is clear that for some time past the efforts of the best poets and creative artists of all nations are directed toward the generally human. This element will be seen to gleam through or glimmer through every particularity, be it historical, mythological, fabulous or freely invented in the works of persons of every nationality.

Since a similar principle is making itself felt in practical life, penetrating it all and spreading its mildness through the rude, wild, cruel, false, selfish, unveracious, therefore, though it is not yet to be hoped that universal peace will ensue, yet, at least, that inevitable conflict be less tense, war less bloody, victory less arrogant. . . .

A true and general tolerance will be best attained if you grant individuals and peoples their specific characteristics and yet cling to the conviction that what is most truly meritorious is distinguished by the fact that it belongs to all humanity. . . .

Let me not end without sending my greetings to your wife. In return for her charming attention I am adding some trifles with great pleasure. May your happy marriage continue for many years to come.

July 26, 1827

Eckermann

"I am rather surprised," Goethe said, "that Walter Scott doesn't mention Carlyle in his letter to me. . . . And Carlyle is a moral force of great significance. He has an important future ahead of him and it will be difficult to estimate all that his influence will yet accomplish."

Tanner's Mill, August 28, 1827

Marianne von Willemer to Goethe

We took a trip by steamship to Cologne. . . . I didn't believe it possible to see so many beautiful landscapes in so few days, and to become so comfortably acquainted with so many members of so many nations. . . . How often did I hear your name stammered in foreign languages, for you were a presence even in this small and varied group. I had to sing one of your songs to an Englishwoman, who knows no syllable of German. First I had to give her an idea of the content of the poem in French. . . . She visited us at the Mill later and we gave her one of my step-daughter's little drawings with a stanza of yours written on it. She will hang it up in her room in Richmond. . . .

Edinburgh, August 20, 1827

Carlyle to Goethe

. . . If the best return for such gifts is the delight they are enjoyed with, I may say that you are not unrepaid; for no Royal present could have gratified us more. . . .
This little drawing room may now be said to be full of you. My translations from your Works already stood, in fair binding, in the bookcase, and portraits of you lay in portfolios; during our late absence in the country, some good genius, to prepare a happy surprise for us, had hung up, in the best framing and light, a larger picture of you, which we understand to be the best resemblance. . . .
It is thus that good men may raise for themselves a little sanctuary in houses and hearths that lie far away. . . .

August 28, 1827

Frau von Levetzow to Goethe

Once more I am in Karlsbad on that day which gave you to your friends and to the world to which you belong, that day on which my daughters and I were so happy and so gay four years ago. That day of the open secret has come again and, although hills and valleys separate us, our feelings and our wishes for you are unchanged from what they were when the presence of your mind and heart made us so happy.

September 7, 1827

Recollections of Wilhelm Zahn

Architect and painter, 1800-1871.

I accepted his renewed invitation and arrived at the proper hour. I passed through a long flight of rooms all furnished in the same artistic taste and entered the dining room, where I found Goethe and his guests. . . . They were all in full dress. . . . I found the dishes extremely tasty and the wine at least equally good. In front of each guest stood a bottle of either red or white wine. I wanted to keep my head clear that evening and so mixed my wine with water. Goethe observed this and turned on me curtly: "Where did you pick up that bad habit?" The conversation was general and vivid and never came to a dead stop. Goethe guided it in masterly fashion without, however, limiting anyone's expressiveness. . . . Goethe had finished a whole bottle and was filling his glass from a second one, while the rest of us were already at our coffee. Then we rose from the table. . . .

September 24, 1827

Eckermann

Goethe took me to drive with him to Berka. . . . About a stone's throw beyond the bridge, where the road begins to rise toward the hill which separates the traveler from Berka, Goethe ordered the carriage to stop. "We'll get out here for a little," said he, "and see whether we won't enjoy a little luncheon in the open air." We got out and viewed the scenery. The servant spread a napkin over a square stone and fetched from the carriage a basket woven of rushes, from which he produced roasted partridges and fresh-baked rolls and dill pickles. Goethe carved a partridge and handed me half. I ate standing or walking up and down. Goethe had sat down on the edge of the square stone. I thought that the cold stone, still moist from the dew of night, could hardly be good for him. I expressed my anxiety. He assured me that he was perfectly comfortable. . . . Meanwhile the servant had produced a bottle of wine from the carriage and glasses and filled them for us. "Those of our friends," said Goethe, "who take a weekly excursion to the country are very sensible. Let us follow their example. If the weather holds out, this must not be our last picnic."

September 27, 1827

To an Otherwise Unknown Correspondent

Let me tell you of the pleasure which your understanding sympathy
for Helena afforded me. . . . I never doubted that the readers, for
whom I was really writing, would immediately grasp the chief meaning of this work. It is high time that the passionate opposition between classicists and romanticists end in conciliation. For the chief
demand is that we develop our culture, whence that development
derives is indifferent, so long as we are careful not to contort ourselves by using false models. . . . I would like to add the following
concerning obscure passages in earlier and later poems of mine. Not
all our experiences can be expressed in the round and directly communicated. For this reason I have long chosen the means of revealing
the more secret meanings to attentive hearts by creative formations
which face each other and mirror each other.

Since everything that I have written is the immediate product of
experience, I have the right to signify my hope that my works will
and must be re-experienced.

October 2, 1827

To Alfred Nicolovius

> The grandson of Goethe's sister Cornelia, who had written a study of
> Goethe criticism up to this time.

My friends here assure me that you have made a real contribution
to literary criticism in Germany in that you have thrown a great deal
of light on the character of those critics who have written about me
in the course of the years. Ought you not now to edit a similar collection of all that has been written *against* me? . . . Rightly or
wrongly, I have been harshly criticized, and since it is your purpose
to reveal my character and that of the century, the *contra* is as necessary as the *pro*.

October 21, 1827

To Christian Rauch

In my long life events occurred which, though my situation was brilliant, gave rise to misfortune in others which involved me deeply.

Thence came moments so cruel, that I was tempted to consider the shortest life the highest kindness of fate, in order not to experience unduly an intolerable anguish. Many of those who made me suffer have preceded me into eternity. The duty was laid upon me to endure and to bear a series of both joys and sorrows, each of which was violent enough to be mortal. . . .

October 24, 1827

To Zelter

. . . I have written a poem on the remains of Schiller, which I spoke when they were found upon their Calvary. I have also written a most peculiar short novel and sundry shorter poems. Among the latter is a series called Chinese Seasons and still other things growing out of those I mentioned.

1827

> From above the twilight drifted,
> All things near receded far;
> But at once on high uplifted
> Shone in grace the evening star.
> In the swaying world uncertain
> Faltering mists the uplands take;
> Solidly a sombre curtain
> Crowds the mirror of the lake.
>
> Presage comes when eastward facing
> Of a radiant lunar glow,
> Willow branches interlacing
> Dance where nearer waters flow.
> In the shift of shades abiding
> Magical the moon-rays start,
> Through the eye the coolness sliding
> Unto peace persuades the heart.

October 29, 1827

From the Diaries

A granddaughter has arrived.

Late November, 1827

Recollections of Ottilie von Goethe

Since my first son had been called August Walter after his father, I really wanted the second son to be called by an Italian name. Somehow, I don't know why, I had hit upon the name Flaminio, which would have admirably suited the lively character and fiery eyes of the second boy. But Papa objected strongly and asked, whether one of his grandsons was not to be named after him. This was done. In return he himself chose a beautiful Italian name, quite unfamiliar in Germany at that time, for my daughter. The first time he came upstairs to see her, he stood there, as was his habit, bending over her with his hands folded behind his back and looked down at the cradle with a long, friendly, contemplative glance and said: "She shall be called Alma."

December 4, 1827

To Zelter

Concerning Walter Scott's *Life of Napoleon,* I have this much to say: if you have the time and the desire to re-experience reflectively the significant course of world history, which has carried us along on its torrent these last fifty years, I can give you no better advice than to read this work quietly from beginning to end. A sensible, excellent, reasonably conservative man, whose youth coincided with the French Revolution, and who, as an Englishman, was bound, in his best years, to observe and contemplate and discuss these important events and who is, finally, the best narrator of our time, makes the effort to present to us clearly and distinctly that whole series of events.

1828

Weimar, January 19, 1828

From the Diaries

Went over the calendar and the constellations with little Wolf and taught him to recognize Orion and Sirius.

January 24, 1828
To Zelter

Although I have never been hostile to the Maccabaean family but have, on the contrary, been of the opinion that our good Jews appear under their most favorable aspect at that point of their history, yet I really have cause to complain because you, busy over the musical splendor of the opera of that name, have neglected for two whole months to think of your friends. . . .

I have kept going very well during this period and used my hours for some good and some even important purposes. I have sent three to four scenes of the second part of *Faust* to the printer. When they are printed I hope you will be able in the torrent of your life to devote a few minutes to these delineations. I continue this effort, for I am most eager to complete Acts I and II, in order that Helena may be naturally joined on as Act III. . . .

January 28, 1828
To Reinhard

I closed the last year in unimpeded activity. I might almost venture to say that by some accident I have returned to a mood of youth. . . . I again take delight in using those old, light, easy metrical measures, agreeably linked by recurrent rime and, in this form and through this music, I rehearse after the genuine manner of poets, what delights and saddens, what depresses and cheers us on this mortal scene.

Weimar, February 29, 1828
From the Diaries

Had the children dine with me. Jestingly invited them, that they might make note of the leap year and remember it.

March 12, 1828
Eckermann

"It is a curious thing," Goethe observed, "but Englishmen seem to have an advantage over others. We see only a few of them here in Weimar and probably not even the best. But what able, handsome

fellows they are! The good fortune of personal liberty, the consciousness of the English name and the significance attached to it among
other nations—these advantages accrue to them even in their childhood. Within their families and at their schools they are treated with
much more respect than children are elsewhere, and thus they enjoy
a happier and freer development.

"Take our dear Weimar on the contrary. I look out at the window
to see what's going on. The other day there was a fine snow and the
children of my neighbors wanted to try out their sleighs on the street.
Instantly a policeman turned up and I saw the poor little things
escape as fast as they could. Now the spring sun is here and brings
them out of the houses and they would like to play their little games
in front of their doors. But I see them hesitate, as though they
weren't sure of themselves and as though they were afraid of the
approach of some limb of the law. Let a boy but crack a whip or
sing or raise his voice—there's the police to forbid him to do so.
Everything among us is directed toward the purpose of taming youth
early, of stamping out nature, originality and any touch of wildness,
so that in the end nothing is left but the Philistine."

1828

> The strict original mind
> Never abandon!
> Ground that the mob picks blind
> Is plain to stand on.
>
> The highest reason use
> And be its warder;
> The lore that sages choose
> Is always harder.

Weimar, April 15, 1828

From the Diaries

Took a drive with Ottilie and Alfred Nicolovius. Dined together. He
repeated many characteristic Berlin jokes and witty replies. The
notion one gathers from them is that of an extremely drab kind of
life and a lack of genuine intellectual activity.

Edinburgh, April 18, 1828

Carlyle to Goethe

. . . Ere long, I expect to see Sir Walter Scott, and present him your Medals in person. I know not whether you are aware that he translated your *Götz*, to which circumstances many of his critics attribute no small influence on his subsequent poetical procedure. . . .
On the whole, our study and love of German literature seem to be rapidly progressing: in my time, that is, within the last six years, I should almost say that the readers of your language have increased tenfold. . . .

May 1, 1828

To a Russian Critic and Translator

The opportunity presents itself of sending a word to you to St. Petersburg. . . . I must not neglect it. . . . When a man has seriously spent many years on his own development and has sought to embody the traces of the progress of his own thoughts in written form, in order that those who come after him may be attentive to what all must expect and what may either promote or obstruct their interests, and when such a man learns toward the end of his days that his distant purpose has been achieved and his bold desire fulfilled, it cannot but stir the most agreeable feeling within him.
I have not ever yielded to any extent to the didactic. A creative representation of conditions, partly from the realm of the real, partly from that of the ideal, always seemed to me the most profitable way. A thoughtful reader can mirror himself in these images and, as his own experience grows, draw from them his own manifold inferences. . . .

May 27, 1828

Müller's Diary

I had been invited by the Grand Duke for 1 o'clock. He asked me to sit down beside him on the balcony and we chatted quite intimately until 3 o'clock. A thousand memories of former days in connection with Goethe awakened in him. He spoke of the great drinking bouts at Jena in the winter of 1805-06; of Goethe's former generosity to-

ward young talents. . . . He said that, in his opinion, Goethe had
always put things into women that were not there and had really
loved his own ideas in them. He hadn't ever really experienced a
great passion. His longest love affair had been with Frau von Stein,
who had been a good enough woman, but certainly no shining light.
Then the Vulpius girl had spoiled everything by alienating him
from the society of his equals. Much, too, had been spoiled by the
death of his own mother, the Dowager Duchess, whose house had
been an easy center and meeting place. His wife hadn't had the temperament to continue this. Soon, too, Goethe had quarreled with the
Jagemann—of course on account of that woman of his. . . . In addition to everything else, the French Revolution had muddled many
minds. Even Goethe had not been quite free of that influence,
though he had shown more restraint and circumspection. . . .
Goethe junior, he finally said, was not without brains nor without
good abilities. The pity was that he had taken to drinking and had
had a rather wild bringing up.

June 6, 1828

Soret

> The portrait painted by Johann Karl Stieler, 1781-1851, of the old
> Goethe is the one that has been most often reproduced.

The King of Bavaria sent the painter Stieler here as his personal
representative to execute a portrait of Goethe in oil. Stieler brought
along a portrait he had done of a Munich actress, which was to serve
as his letter of recommendation.
The portrait was completed in the early days of June. He showed it
to me one day after we had dined alone together. Then he took me
to another room to show me the portrait of the handsome actress.
He closed the doors of both rooms. By and by Herr von Müller came
in, very curious to see the portrait and also to admire the actress.
Even a smaller display of curiosity would have aroused Goethe's displeasure. However, Müller was given permission to go into the first
room and come back and give his opinion. Müller went but didn't
come back. Goethe suspected that he had gone farther and got up
and surprised him in the second room. "Get out of there!" he cried
in an extremity of rage, "I can't leave you alone for a moment with-

out your curiosity betraying you into an indiscretion!" He continued his devastating rebuke, which was very painful for me to hear. When he had finished pouring out his wrath in the most violent terms, he went into the salon and, to our consternation, slammed the door behind him.

I walked out with poor Chancellor von Müller and consoled him as best I could. Nevertheless, it wasn't the first storm he had suffered, nor the last that threatens him. For he is the usual object of the master's rages and he is quite used to being so and their friendship does not suffer the least interruption. Next morning they meet again, as though nothing had happened. It seems to me as if I am the only one who has never incurred Goethe's wrath, although in the ten years of our close relationship my opinions were often not his and might easily have occasioned an outburst.

June 15, 1828

To Carlyle

The English translation of *Wallenstein* [*by Samuel Taylor Coleridge, 1772-1834*] made quite a strange impression upon me. I was intimately associated with Schiller the whole time he was writing the play and, of course, cognizant of every detail in it. Together we staged it. I attended every rehearsal and went through the necessary anguish, nor dared I miss the subsequent performances, because I was intent on raising each to a still higher level. So you can imagine how trivialized and how revolting this magnificent play was bound to become to me. Nor have I seen it or read it for 20 years. Now that I see it again so unexpectedly in the language of Shakespeare, it arises before me in all its parts once again like a freshly varnished painting. I rejoice in it as of old and in a new and peculiar fashion. Remember me to the translator and tell him that I am much pleased, too, by his preface written with so pure and sympathetic an attitude. And name his name to me. . . .

P.S. Just as I finish this letter there comes to me the melancholy news of the demise of our excellent prince, the Grand Duke of Sachsen-Weimar-Eisenach. Yesterday on the return journey from Berlin near Torgau the end overtook him.

Weimar, June 15, 1828

From the Diaries

There was a dinner party and the Tyrolese Singers came in to sing for us. The festivity was broken by the news of the death of the Grand Duke.

June 15, 1828

Report of a Chamberlain of the Court

Accompanying the first Minister of State, I officially brought Goethe the news of the death of our sainted Grand Duke, with whom he had lived on terms of the most intimate friendship for fifty-three years. His expression did not change and he insisted on giving a happy turn to the conversation by speaking of the many magnificent things which our late Lord had initiated and founded. Nevertheless, it is certain that he felt this loss deeply and mourned sincerely.

Summer, 1828

Eckermann

A few days after the Grand Duke's death Goethe went to stay in the castle at Dornburg in order to escape the daily melancholy impressions in Weimar and to resume his literary activity in new surroundings. . . . I called on him there several times in the company of his daughter-in-law and of the children. He seemed very happy and again and again expressed his delight in his condition and in the magnificent situation of the castle and its gardens. And, indeed, from the windows at that height the view was enchanting across the valley full of life to the Saale River pursuing its serpentine course across the meadows. To the east rose the wooded heights. . . .

"I am passing truly good days and nights here," said Goethe. "Often I awake before dawn and sit by the open window to contemplate the splendor of the three simultaneous planets and to revive my soul by the growing glow of dawn. I am in the open most of the day and hold spiritual converse with the branches of the vines. They inspire me with good thoughts, whereof I could report strange things. Once more I write poems, too. They are not bad. Would that it could be granted me to continue to live in this condition!"

Dornburg, July 10, 1828

To a Former Valet

Since there is no well-supplied cellar in this charming little castle, and since I know of none near except yours, I request you to supply me with wine during my stay here. Give the bearer of this letter six bottles and continue to send others from time to time. What I want is a light, pure Würzburger vintage. After the completion of my pilgrimage here I shall show my appreciation to you in some appropriate manner. If you will add one bottle of genuine *Stein* wine, it will be welcome, too.

If you should happen to ride in this direction and are willing to be satisfied with a glass of wine and a roll, you will be welcome. Frugality is the watchword of this place and little is to be expected. Therefore if you could also give the bearer of this letter a genuine Jena cervelat sausage, it would be most agreeable.

Dornburg, July 11, 1828

From the Diaries

> Gaudeat ingrediens laetetus et aede recedens
> His qui praetereunt det bona cuncta Deus. 1608

"Let him rejoice who enters this house and him who leaves it; may God grant pleasant paths to those who pass by here."

Thus runs the inscription over the gate of the little castle in which I dwell. It is architecturally and plastically set in and executed in the taste of that age.

◇◇◇◇◇

Dornburg, August 7, 1828

Six Englishmen, coming hither from Naumburg, left their horses at the posthouse and came up my mountain. They announced themselves. They were taken into the castle and visited me. They left soon and I continued with my work.

Dornburg, August 17, 1828

Tried to read Walter Scott's *St. Valentine's Day*. Made no progress. The substance seems interesting, but to me there is too little inner content.

❖❖❖❖❖

Dornburg, August 18, 1828

Arose before the sun. The valley of a crystalline clearness. Deeply felt the expression of the poet—*the sacred dawn*.

Dornburg, August 26, 1828

To Zelter

A History of German Literature had appeared by Wolfgang Menzel, containing a violent attack on Goethe.

. . In age and in youth it is my privilege to pay no attention to polemics against me. The world offers me room enough in which to move about and it need not concern me when today someone tries to block the road at a point where I once passed on my way. . . .

Dornburg, September 7, 1828

When at dawn the vapors fleeing
Clear the hills and gardened valleys,
And unto our famished seeing
Flowers turn each brilliant chalice,

When the clouds that throng the heaven
Struggle with the rising clearness,
And by east winds outward driven
Smooth the azure sun-path's nearness,

Then thou, watching, art beholden
Purely to the great and gracious,

While the orb fires with his golden
Glory the horizon spacious.

Dornburg, September 8, 1828

Whether day my spirit's yearning
Unto far, blue hills has led,
Or the night lit all the burning
Constellations at my head—
Hours of light or hours nocturnal
Do I praise our mortal fate:
If man think the thought eternal
He is ever fair and great.

September 11, 1828

Eckermann

Today at 2 o'clock Goethe returned from Dornburg. The weather is magnificent. He looks vigorous and has a fine tan. We sat down to dinner in the room which gives immediately on the garden. The door was open. He told us of people who had come to see him and of presents sent him on his birthday and seemed to delight in jests and quips. But if one regarded him closely a certain embarrassment could be observed, as of one who returns to a previous situation which involves a variety of relationships and considerations and demands upon him.

September 23, 1828

To Marianne von Willemer

While Goethe was at Dornburg Marianne and her husband had taken a trip through Switzerland. In the third night before his seventy-ninth birthday, Goethe had written a poem commemorating an old promise between him and Marianne, that they were to think of each other with especial intensity at the rising of the full moon.

Bidding them a friendly welcome home, may I ask where the dear travelers were on August 25, and whether, observing the clear full moon that evening, they thought of their distant friend? The enclosed provides incontrovertible evidence so far as he is concerned.

TO THE RISING MOON

Art thou on the instant leaving
Who but now to me wert near?
Sombre mass of cloud upheaving
Hides thee and thou are not here.

Yet that I am sad thou knowest;
By thine edge's starry ray
That I still am loved thou showest,
Though my love be far away.

Rise then! Let thy splendor quicken,
Pure of path, in fullness bright!
Though the anguished heart be stricken,
All-ecstatic is the night.

October 3, 1828

Eckermann

"Isn't Walter Scott's *Fair Maid of Perth* good?" Goethe asked enthusiastically. "What technique! What a grip! First you have the un-
erring plan; next there is no stroke that does not contribute to the
end. And consider the details, both in the dialogue and the descrip-
tions. How excellent are they! The scenes and situations are like
pictures by Teniers!"

October 9, 1828

Marianne to Goethe

Concerning that 25 of August, I can offer you complete confirma-
tion. . . . In the inn at Freiburg our room had a balcony that gave
on a broad, cheerful and busy street. . . . When the moon appeared
above the gables of the old houses we joined the promenaders in the
street and took our way to the Cathedral which was indescribably
beautiful in the moonlight. . . . Back at the inn I lingered long on
the balcony and let the words and emotion of your incomparable
"Song to the Moon" echo in my soul. I remembered the days in
which I had so often sung it to you and felt "the strain of gay and

sombre days" within me. Could I have dreamed how at that very moment the eye of my friend kept its dear vigil over my destiny, how gladly would I have cried with him: "All-ecstatic is the night!" . . .

October 9, 1828

Recollections of a Friend of Ottilie's

Ottilie gave a tea, which Tieck attended, too. The company waited for Goethe in vain. Finally they sent a young girl to lure him from his study.

Goethe stood at his tall desk dressed in a long open dressing gown. Before him there was a stack of old manuscripts. He didn't notice me. Shyly I said: "Good evening!" He turned his head, looked at me with big eyes and cleared his throat, the characteristic sign of suppressed rage. I raised my hands in a beseeching gesture. "What does the little lady want?" he growled. "We're waiting for the Privy Councillor, Sir."—"Aha," he roared. "And do you think, little girl, that I run at the beck of anyone who chooses to wait? What would become of all this?" He pointed to the manuscripts spread out before him. "When I'm dead, there's none to complete this. Tell them that upstairs! Good evening." I trembled at the sound of that ever more mightily resonant voice and said very softly: "Good evening." That must have sounded sad to him. He called me back and regarded me kindly and said in a wholly changed tone: "An old man who still has work to do mustn't be influenced just to please someone. If he does so, posterity will not think it nice of him. You run along, my child. Your cheerful youth will please those upstairs better this evening than my meditative age."

October 11, 1828

Eckermann

"Carlyle studied *Meister*," I said, "and was so penetrated by its value that he would like to have seen it in general circulation."
Goethe drew me into a window niche. "My dear child," he said, "I will confide something to you that will be of great help to you at once, as well as for the rest of your life. My writings can never become popular. Whoever thinks differently and makes attempts in that direction, makes a great mistake. Nor were they written for the

mass, but for individuals who desire and seek similar ideals and are in the process of a similar development."

October 20, 1828

"Everything depends on one circumstance," said Goethe. "A man must *be* something in order to create something. Dante seems very great to us. But he had the culture of centuries behind him. The House of Rothschild is very rich. But it took more than the span of a life to attain such wealth. These things all lie deeper than is commonly understood."

October 22, 1828

Today at table the conversation turned on the fair sex. Goethe spoke very beautifully. "Women are silver vessels into which we place golden apples. My idea of women is not derived from the appearances of reality. It was innate in me, or arose in me, God knows how. Consequently the female characters in my works all have the advantage of this circumstance and are better than the women whom reality supplies."

October 30, 1828

To Zelter

I am now busy with *Wilhelm Meister's Pilgrimage,* the rest of which is about to go to the printer. It will stimulate me to think and that is the chief thing. The fourth section, which will appear in the course of November, contains nothing that will be new to my old readers and admirers. But I trust that its content will reach and permanently engage the interest of those to whom all this is still unknown. Of course, I know that the reading public is so blunted by distractions and so emptily busy, that there is more reason than ever to put one's trust in posterity.

December 16, 1828

Eckermann

"It oftens happens in the literary world," I said, "that the originality of a famous man is placed in doubt through research into the sources, from which his culture is derived." Goethe replied: "That is utterly absurd. One might as well inquire of a well-nourished man after the oxen and sheep and swine he has consumed to give him strength. We bring our abilities into the world with us, but we owe our development to the thousand influences upon us of that great world whence we draw what we can and what suits us. I owe much to the Greeks and the French; I am infinitely indebted to Shakespeare, Sterne and Goldsmith. But these do not begin to exhaust the sources of my culture. I could go on into infinitude, but it isn't necessary. The chief thing is that a man has a soul which loves the true and incorporates it wherever it is found. . . . And the true must be repeated over and over again, because error is continually propagated all about us, not only by individuals but by a massive effort. In newspapers and encyclopaedias, in schools and universities, everywhere error is on top and error agrees happily and comfortably with the feeling of the majority, which is always on its side."

1829

Weimar, January 1, 1829

From the Diaries

The children brought me their New Year's wishes in writing.

◇◇◇◇◇

Weimar, January 4, 1829

Didn't feel well on rising. Went back to bed and stayed there all day and all night, recapitulating what is next to be done.

January 10, 1829

To Schultz

God forbid that somebody should seek to revive the condition of German literature of 30 years ago. . . . I had put my utmost into the last volumes of that old Göschen edition and, for instance, transfused my very heart's blood into *Tasso*. Yet that excellent publisher, whose word was his bond, had to tell me that the edition had a very poor sale. My experience with *Wilhelm Meister* was worse. The

educated thought the puppets beneath them; gentlemen considered
the comedians unworthy company and the girls too loose in their
morals. But the chief objection to it was—it was not another
Werther. I don't know what would have become of me without
Schiller's encouragement, to which our correspondence bears such
notable witness.

Weimar, January 14, 1829

From the Diaries

Ottilie gave me a circumstantial and subtly intelligent description of
Weimar society at present.

◇◇◇◇◇

Weimar, January 18, 1829

This evening came little Wolf and I was persuaded to play games
with him. He was sweet and amusing.

February 4, 1829

Eckermann

"Man must believe in immortality; he has a right to do so; it is conformable to his nature and he may also lend due weight to the
affirmations of religion. But when a philosopher tries to derive the
proof of the immortality of the soul from a mere legend, that is feeble and meaningless. The conviction of our permanence arises from
the concept of activity. If I am tireless to my very end, it is the duty
of nature to assign me another form of existence, when the present
form is no longer capable of sustaining my spirit."

◇◇◇◇◇

February 9, 1829

Goethe said: "In the whole of *The Elective Affinities* there is not a
line which I myself did not actually live, and there is far more behind
the text of the book than anyone can assimilate at a single reading."

◇◇◇◇◇

February 12, 1829

Goethe read me the magnificent poem: "No creature is annihilated," which he had just composed. He said: "I wrote this to contradict the verses:

> For each must be annihilated,
> If to duration be its will.

Those old verses are stupid and it annoyed me terribly that some Berlin friends of mine inscribed them in golden letters in the hall on the occasion of a scientific convention."

1829

TESTAMENT

No creature is annihilated!
The eternal power stirs unbated,
And being is our happiness.
'Tis everlasting. Laws of measure
And form preserve the living treasure
Which is the universe's dress.

The true was found in distant ages,
Uniting companies of sages;
That ancient truth—be it thy stay!
To Him, thou son of earth be grateful,
Who round the sun commands her fateful,
With sister-planets circling way.

Now on the instant turn within thee:
There is the center that will win thee,
As no high spirit will gainsay.
There rules are present for thy gaining,
For conscience, free and self-sustaining,
Illuminates thy mortal day.

Next trust the witness of the senses,
They will pierce falsehoods and pretenses,
While reason keeps a vigil bold.
Use unspoiled observation surely,
And wander agile and securely
Through earth's rich field and wood and wold.

Enjoy the measure of each season;
Under the watchfulness of reason
Life unto life delight can be.
Then is the past no more mere dying,
The future's clear beyond denying,
The moment an eternity.

And when at last by stern endurance
Thou hast attained the firm assurance
That truth from fruitfulness is won—
Then can'st thou test the general striding
Which will not alter for thy chiding,
And with the chosen be at one.

And even as from of old, in quiet
Works willed by love and fashioned by it,
Issued from sage and poet's breast,
Thus grace and good will be thine ever:
For prophecy of high endeavor
Of our vocations is the best.

February 13, 1829

Eckermann

"Everything that is great and wise," Goethe said, "is confined to a minority. It is unthinkable that wisdom ever be popular. Passions and prejudices may be, but reason will always be the possession of the excellent few." . . . After a while he continued: "The true liberal seeks to accomplish as much good as he can with the means at his command. He guards himself against the impulse of destroying inevitable faults with fire and sword. By means of prudent procedure he seeks gradually to eliminate public ills without the use of such force as is likely to ruin the good at the same time. In this imperfect world he is contented with the good until time and circumstances favor the creation of something better."

◇◇◇◇◇

March 5, 1829

"So long as it is day," said Goethe, "let us hold our heads high, and so long as we can be productive, let us not cease from our efforts."

◇◇◇◇◇

March 14, 1829

"I owe my ballads largely to Schiller; he impelled me to write them," said Goethe. "But I had had them in mind for many years. . . . So when at last they were written down, I regarded them with a sense of sorrowful loss, as though I had to part from a beloved friend. The matter is wholly different with my lyrical poems. No impression or presage preceded their creation. They came to me suddenly and had to be written at once. Instinctively and, as it were, in a dream, I was impelled to write them down. In this somnambulistic condition it often happened that the piece of paper which lay before me was placed at a crazy angle. I didn't notice that until I found there was no more space to write. I still have several of these diagonally written manuscripts. . . ."

◇◇◇◇◇

March 15, 1829

"As you know," I said somewhat tactlessly, "you have been reproached for not taking up arms in the heroic days of our wars of liberation and for not even cooperating as a poet."
"Don't let's worry about that, my dear fellow," Goethe replied. "The world is absurd; it doesn't know what it wants, and we must let it talk and do as it likes. How could I have taken up arms without hatred? How could I have hated without youth? . . . Nor need all people serve the fatherland in the same way. Let each do the best with the gifts God gave him. I have slaved hard enough for half a century. . . .
"I don't like to say what I really think," he added. "Behind all that

talk there is more hidden ill will against me than you can imagine.
It is a new form of that old hatred which pursued me for years and
which still tries tacitly to injure me. I know very well that I have
been a thorn in the side to many. They wouldn't mind getting rid
of me at all; and since it's hard to attack my talent, they go after my
character. So I am said to be proud or egoistic or envious of young
talents or sunk in sensuality or devoid of Christianity and finally
they said that I am lacking in the love of country and of my countrymen. . . . A German writer—a German martyr!

"Moreover, to write war songs while sitting safely in a room—that
could never have been my way of doing. . . . I have never affected
the feelings in my poetry. I have never written or expressed anything
that I have not experienced, that was not a burning issue and trouble
in my own heart. I wrote love poems only when I loved. How could
I have written songs of hate without hatred? And, between ourselves,
I never hated the French, although I thanked God when we were rid
of them. How could I, to whom the only significant things are culture and barbarism, hate a nation which is among the most cultivated in the world and to which I owe so great a part of my own
culture? Anyhow, this business of hatred between nations is a curious thing. You will always find it most powerful and barbarous on
the lowest levels of civilization. But there exists a level at which it
disappears wholly and where one stands, so to speak, above the nations and feels the weal or woe of a neighboring people as though it
were one's own. This level was appropriate to my nature; I had
reached it long before my sixtieth year."

March 17, 1829

"Look," said Goethe. "There Sömmering, the well-known anatomist,
died. He was a bare, miserable 75 years old. What poor creatures men
are that they haven't the courage to hold out longer! Look, instead,
at my friend Jeremy Bentham [*British founder of the Utilitarian
philosophy, 1748-1832*], that highly insane radical. Look how he
keeps going and he is several weeks older than I am."

◇◇◇◇◇

March 18, 1829

The conversation turned on novels and plays and their moral or immoral effect upon the public. "It would have to be a pretty drastic book," said Goethe, "to have a more immoral effect than life itself, which daily floods, if not our eyes, then our ears, with scandalous scenes. We need have no anxiety concerning the effects of a book or play even upon children. Daily life, as I said, is more instructive than the most revealing book."

April 2, 1829

We began to talk about the latest French poets and the meaning of the terms classic and romantic. Goethe said: "A fresh definition has occurred to me, which does not define the relationship of the two at all badly. I call the classic the healthy and the romantic the sick. Thus both the *Lay of the Nibelungen* and Homer are classic, for both are healthy and vigorous. Most recent literature is romantic, not because it is new, but because it is feeble and morbid and sickly. Ancient literature is not classical because it is old, but because it is strong, fresh, glad and healthy."

April 29, 1829

To Zelter

I have the impulse to announce to you and to confide to you a very curious circumstance, namely, that according to a powerful and instantaneous resolution I have stopped reading newspapers. I content myself with such news as is conveyed to me in my social life. I consider this a matter of the highest importance. Closely looked upon, it is mere Philistinism on the part of private individuals to pay so much attention to what does not concern them. I can't begin to tell you the time I have gained and the things I have accomplished during the six weeks that I have left all French and German papers with their covers unopened.

May 10, 1829

To K. E. Schubarth

It is your intention, as I see it, to survey the circle of interests open
to the human spirit, to wander through the avenues of philosophy,
and to pitch your tent at the place which will please you best. I
cannot but approve the path you have thus taken since I, too, have
no other aim than to cultivate myself as much as possible in my own
fashion, in order that I may attain my share of that infinite world in
which we are placed in an ever happier and purer way.

I must, however, admit that my polemical tendencies grow ever
feebler and that everything within me concentrates itself to oneness.
True, antitheses are so unavoidable, that if one were able to cut a
single individual into two halves, the right side would immediately
pick an irreconcilable quarrel with the left and, therefore, do not
think that I blame youth when it polemicizes out of the perception
of the antithesis between itself and others.

Weimar, June 8, 1829

From the Diaries

Saw a play this evening. Two acts called *Oberon,* very well performed. Yet the play could be truly called Much Noise About
Nothing.

◇◇◇◇◇

Weimar, June 11, 1829

Dined with my son and Eckermann. Talked about Platen's play
Oedipus, which gave rise to many reflections.

June 25, 1829

To Carlyle

    The Carlyles had left Edinburgh and moved to Craigenputtock.

I would be so pleased if you would grant me a request which I often
address to friends who are far away. When I visit such friends in my
thoughts I don't like my imagination to wander about in the void.
And so what I ask for is a drawing, a sketch, of their dwelling and

its environment. . . . Since your move to the country I have tried
to bring before my mind's eye your valley through which the river
flows with the town of Dumfries on the left bank. . . .

I know enough about the work of your countryman Burns who, were
he alive, would now be your neighbor, to esteem it. Your mentioning him in your letter caused me to take up his poems again and,
above all, to re-read the story of his life which, like the story of
many conspicuous talents, is melancholy enough. Poetic talent is
rarely combined with the talent for a proper approach to life and the
securing of a steady situation in it.

July 28, 1829

To Rochlitz

I was very grateful to you for pointing out to me in *Meister's Pilgrimage* the passages which you have made your own. . . . For I
may well say this: whatever is recorded in my writings does not belong to the past. I see it, when my attention is called to it again, as
something continuously evolving. The unresolved problems that are
woven into it continue to employ my mind in the hope that, whether
in the realm of nature or of our moral being, much will yet be revealed to a faithful inquirer.

Garden House, August 4, 1829

From the Diaries

The Dowager Grand Duchess sent me over some beautiful aqua-
tints by Claude Lorrain to look at. At half past eleven Her Highness
dropped in and permitted me to select and keep one of the three.

◇◇◇◇◇

Garden House, August 6, 1829

Ottilie came toward evening. Then Walter came. He was very unhappy because he had won nothing at the shooting gallery. Wolf
sympathized with him. The women, too, took his part and a lively
and amusing scene ensued.

◇◇◇◇◇

Garden House, August 16, 1829

Toward evening came Ottilie and Herr Henry Crabb Robinson and Walter.

August, 1829

Henry Crabb Robinson's Diary

John Flaxman, 1755-1826, distinguished British sculptor and draughtsman.

. . . I told Goethe that I had brought him Flaxman's lectures on sculpture. He accepted the gift very courteously and spoke with the highest respect of Flaxman's illustrations of Homer. I promised to bring him that book in the evening. . . . Since we were invited to stay for dinner, we went to pay our respects to Frau von Goethe. I chatted very agreeably with her. Goethe calls her Crazy Angel, and I know precisely what he means. Take, for example, her curious reception of me which, I hope, was not ironical. She said she had been waiting for me for twelve years. But she was very cordial and said again and again, that I must come back and read English to them. . . . Her three children all resemble their great ancestor, the little girl of three strikingly so. . . . That evening he was friendlier than I could account for. He wanted to know exactly when I was leaving. He insisted that I stay several days in Weimar, because he had so many things to ask me and he saluted me with a kiss when I left. Here are some of the subjects of our conversation.—I asked him what he knew of Burns.—He doesn't know "The Vision." I pointed out to him certain coincidences in this poem with his Dedication.— Goethe asked me about the taste for German literature in England. I told him about a number of translations and the sudden turnabout in the *Edinburgh Review.* He was happy to hear how far his fame was spreading.—He spoke contemptuously of Ossian saying, no one had observed that Werther talks of Homer while he had his reason and fell in love with Ossian only after he had lost it. I mustn't neglect to record that Goethe, although his face has the wrinkles of an old man, has the voice of a man with sound lungs and youthful energy. He will be 80 in a matter of weeks. His hearing is slightly impaired but his memory is still good. There is no symptom of decay.

Weimar, October 1, 1829

From the Diaries

Little Wolf clings to me. His latest joke is to drink liquids through a straw.

◇◇◇◇◇

Weimar, October 12, 1829

Read all evening. On the floor little Wolf built a town of blocks and peopled it with all kinds of tiny dolls.

◇◇◇◇◇

Weimar, October 15, 1829

Dined alone. Alma played in the room all by herself for about an hour. Then Walter came in, singing and dancing, in his most farcical mood.

November 1, 1829

To Zelter

. . . If one wants to leave posterity something useful, it had better be in the form of confessions. One must present oneself as an individual with his thoughts, with his convictions. From all this, those who come after us may select what suits them and what may remain of general validity. . . .

Craigenputtock, Dumfries, November 3, 1829

Carlyle to Goethe

. . . Six years ago, I should have reckoned the possibility of a Letter, of a Present from Goethe to *me*, little less wondrous and dreamlike than from Shakespeare or Homer. Yet so it is: the man to whom I owe more than to any other—namely, some measure of spiritual Light and Freedom—is no longer a mere "airy tongue" to me, but a Living Man, with feelings which, in many kindest ways, reply and correspond to my own. . . .

My wife bids me say that she intends to read your entire Works this winter; so that, any evening, when the candles are lit, you can fancy a fair Friend assiduously studying you "far over the sea"; one little light and living point, amid the boundless Solitude and Night.

November 9, 1829

To Zelter

. . . I, too, went to hear Paganini. . . . To experience what is known as enjoyment which, in my case, is something that floats between the senses and the understanding, I seem to lack the basis in respect of this pillar of flame and cloud. . . . If I were in Berlin I would attend the evenings of chamber music. Of all instrumental music that kind was always most comprehensible to me. . . . It's extraordinary the way people, especially women, talk about the Paganini recital. It is as though they were uttering confessions. . . .

What I would very much like to know is, whether you have good news to tell me of the excellent Felix. I take the greatest interest in his fortunes.

December 6, 1829

Eckermann

Today after dinner Goethe read me the first scene of the second act of *Faust*. I rejoiced in his youthfully creative energy and in the terseness of the execution. "The conception is so old," said Goethe, "and I have meditated on it so much for fifty years that now, of course, there is far too much material and rejection and cutting are always difficult operations. The invention of the whole second part goes back quite as far as I tell you. But it may be to its advantage that I did not write it until now, when my insight into all mortal affairs is so much clearer. I am like a man who started out in youth with a great deal of small change in silver and copper. In the course of a long life he exchanges these coins for ever more valuable ones, so that in the end the fortune of his youth lies before him in the form of golden ducats."

◇◇◇◇◇

December 16, 1829

"In the end," Goethe said, "all is good and all is equal, whether classic or romantic, provided only that one uses the various forms skillfully and betrays one's excellence through them. And you can also make a fool of yourself in both and then again one is as ridiculous as the other."

⬦⬦⬦⬦⬦

December 20, 1829

"It is odd," I said, "that men of conspicuous talent, above all, poets, have such feeble constitutions."

"The extraordinary thing which such people bring forth," said Goethe, "presupposes a delicate organization to make them sensitive to rare perceptions and able to hear the heavenly voices. Now in its conflict with the world and its elements, an organization of that kind is easily disturbed and wounded. Unless, like Voltaire, they combine delicate sensibility with extraordinary toughness, continuous ill health is likely to be their portion. Schiller was sick the whole time, too. When I first met him I didn't believe he would live four weeks. But he was not without a certain toughness. He kept going for many years and could have gone on longer had his way of life been more wholesome."

Weimar, December 20, 1829

From the Diaries

The usual presents of stationery etc. from the Grand Ducal Chancellory. Doctor Eckermann at dinner. Re-read *The Vicar of Wakefield*, remembering my earliest impressions. The influences on us of Sterne and Goldsmith. The high ironic humor of both, the former tending to formlessness, the latter mobile within the discipline of form. Afterwards Germans were persuaded to believe that formlessness and humor are the same thing.

1830

January 3, 1830

Eckermann

"Faust," Goethe said, "is wholly incommensurable. All attempts to bring it closer to the mere understanding are vain. Nor must it be forgotten that the first part proceeded from a measurable inner darkness within the individual. Yet this very darkness attracts people and they take trouble over it as over all insoluble problems.

January 10, 1830

This afternoon Goethe read me the scene in which Faust descends to the realm of the Mothers. The new, unheard-of subject matter, as well as the manner in which Goethe recited the scene, moved me strangely. . . . It seemed very mysterious to me and I was impelled to ask him for an interpretative word. . . . He turned great eyes upon me and repeated the line:

The Mothers! Mothers! 'Tis so strange a sound!

"I can tell you nothing more," he finally said, "than that I found a passage in Plutarch according to which the ancient Greeks spoke of certain deities as the Mothers. This detail I owe to tradition; all the rest is the product of my imagination."

January 17, 1830

We spoke of *Le Rouge et le Noir* which Goethe considers Stendhal's best book. "Yet I cannot deny," he added, "that several of his female characters are somewhat too romantic. Nevertheless, these characters, too, bear witness to acute observation and psychological insight, so that the author may well be forgiven some improbabilities of detail."

January 29, 1830

To Zelter

. . . *We* fight for the perfection of a work of art, independently and in its own nature. Those others think of its effectiveness in the world. A true artist takes no thought of that, as little as does nature when she produces a lion or a hummingbird. . . .

As jest and superfluity let me say in addition, that I used every effort in my *Elective Affinities* to bring to a close the true, inner catharsis as purely and perfectly as possible. But I never imagined on that account that a handsome man could be cleansed through my story of looking lustfully at the wife of another.

Weimar, January 31, 1830

From the Diaries

My daughter came to show herself to me in her elegant dancing frock. Little Wolf entertained himself and me in various ways. That night the temperature stood at 15¼ degrees below 0. [*Goethe used the Réaumur scale which is here recalculated in terms of Fahrenheit.*]

February 14, 1830

Eckermann

At noon on my way to Goethe, who had invited me to dine, I was informed that the Dowager Grand Duchess Louise had just died. My first thought was how it would affect Goethe at his age. I entered the house with some apprehension. . . . I came into the dining room with these thoughts, but I was not a little surprised to see him sitting very cheerfully and vigorously at table with his daughter-in-law and his grandchildren, eating his soup as though nothing had happened. We spoke of indifferent things, when all the chimes of the town began to ring. Frau von Goethe looked at me and we began to talk in loud tones so that the knelling might not touch and shake his soul, for we thought that he would feel as we did. But his feelings were not like ours; his soul was in a different mood. He sat among us like a being from a higher sphere, impervious to mortal ill. Doctor

Vogel was announced. He sat down with us and told us the details of the passing of Her Highness. Goethe listened with the same tranquility and composure. Doctor Vogel departed and we continued our meal and our conversation. . . .

February 14, 1830

Soret

I found him with Eckermann. He was deep in his bottle of wine. He seemed excited and talked emphatically. "Well," he said, as he caught sight of me, "come and sit down. The blow has fallen. We need no longer fight against cruel uncertainty. We must go on doing the best with our lives that we can."
I pointed to the manuscripts in front of him and said: "There are your friends and comforters; it is work that keeps us erect and young."
"Ah, yes," said Goethe, "so long as it is day, we will not hang our heads. One need not yield, so long as work holds out. But the night, the great night is coming in which all work will cease."

Weimar, February 18, 1830

From the Diaries

The burial of the Grand Duchess Louise took place at 4 o'clock in the morning. I was given the details. Afterwards by little Wolf, too, who had watched the procession with the family from the upper windows. I took a drive with Ottilie in order to discuss troublesome matters.

March 5, 1830

Soret

. . . We spoke with regret of the departure of a charming young woman, whose presence had been enjoyed by the society of Weimar for several months. . . . It was Mlle. von Türckheim, the granddaughter of Lili Schönemann. "How I regret," said he, "that I did not see her oftener. . . . When I hear you speak of the girl who is leaving with such warmth, you awaken very old memories of mine and I seem to be living again in another age and close to her who was the first woman I loved profoundly and sincerely. Perhaps she was the last, too. Interests of this kind, which took hold of me later, were very superficial compared to that love. The continuation of my autobiography was prevented by the delicacy which kept me from saying publicly, what I would so gladly have said. But whenever I took up my pen to write her for permission, I felt restrained by hesitations of another kind. Never in my life was I so close to happiness as with her. I loved her as much as she did me. No obstacle would have been unconquerable—and yet I was not able to marry her." . . .

March 8, 1830

Soret

Wolf is his grandfather's favorite. I often find him in the room. Walter, who is less ingratiating, is definitely neglected. The poor boy hasn't the art of being as affectionate as his younger brother. August von Goethe said to me today, while he was petting Wolf: "Every night Wolf takes Grandpapa to his bedroom and helps him off with his stock." Wolf seemed tired and I asked him why he didn't go to bed. "Oh no," the child cried, "it isn't 9 o'clock yet and I must first take Grandpapa to bed."

March 16, 1830

Eckermann

This morning Herr von Goethe came to see me and informed me that his long-planned journey to Italy had been decided upon. His father was granting him the necessary funds, but he desired me to accompany him. We were both very much pleased and began to discuss our preparations.

When I walked past Goethe's house at noon he beckoned me from the window. I ran up the stairs to him. He was in the front room, very gay and lively. He began at once to discuss his son's journey. He approved it thoroughly, thought it most sensible and was glad to have me go along. "It will do you both a great deal of good," said he, "and especially your education will profit by it."

March 31, 1830

Eckermann

Dined with Goethe. He spoke first of all of his son's journey and
warned me that we were to have no great illusions about its success.
"A man usually comes back just as he went," he said, "indeed, we
must be careful not to return with ideas unsuitable to our situation.
Thus I came back from Italy with the vision of beautiful flights of
stairs. Obviously I ruined my house by insisting on such stairs, which
caused all the rooms to be smaller than they need have been. The
chief thing in life is to learn to govern oneself. If I were to yield to
all my impulses, I would be quite capable of ruining myself and
everything about me."

April 19, 1830

To an Admirer

I have been ever attentive to gain some significant advantage from
what was hostile to me. One is instructed concerning men and the
world by learning to have an insight into the why and wherefore of
their opposition, whether it is inspired by right or wrong, by conviction or mere malice, whether it is secret or open, underhanded or
brutal. In a word, I gradually learned how it is both with me and
with others. Yet in the end the whole matter ceased to interest me;
for it was always a repetition of the same thing under various
guises. . . .

Weimar, April 20, 1830

From the Diaries

My son submitted to me the final budget for his journey.

◇◇◇◇◇

Weimar, April 22, 1830

My son has said farewell and set out with Eckermann.

April 23, 1830

Soret

Goethe's son and Eckermann left for Italy yesterday. Today I dined with His Excellency. No one else was present except Frau von Goethe. When I came in he asked me how I was in Italian. I replied in German. We continued our conversation in that language. But his use of Italian pointed to his preoccupation. In the further course of my visit he avoided mentioning his son's departure.

April 24, 1830

Recollections of Genast

> Wilhelmine Schröder-Devrient, 1804-1860, an opera singer of high repute. It is clear that Goethe, accustomed to the simpler lyrical patterns of the earlier songs of Beethoven and those of Zelter, did not grasp the *Durchkomponieren* of the Romantic composers, that is, the progressive interpretative adaptation of the musical composition to the poem as a whole.

I hastened to Goethe to ask him, whether he would receive Mme. Schröder-Devrient. He said he would be happy to make the acquaintance of an artist, of whom he had heard so much that was excellent. . . .
Next day he received her most charmingly. Among other things she sang him the Schubert setting of his "Erlking." Although he was no friend of songs strophically *durchkomponiert*, the highly dramatic interpretation of the incomparable singer moved him so deeply that he took her head between his hands and kissed her on the forehead and thanked her warmly for her magnificent performance. Then he added: "I heard this composition once before and it did not please me at all. But sung as you sing it, it creates a visible image of the whole."

May 21, 1830

Felix Mendelssohn to His Parents

. . . Goethe asked me to come and dine at once. I found him externally unchanged, but at first very silent and not sympathetic. I think he wanted to see how I would take it and that depressed me and I was afraid things might go on this way. Then, luckily, the talk turned upon the Women's Clubs in Weimar and a quite crazy publication which the ladies issue. Suddenly the old gentleman grew merry and began to tease Ottilie and her sister. . . .

After dinner he suddenly said: "Now, my good children, my pretty children—what you must do is to make merry, for you are a little mad anyhow." At that moment his eyes were like a somnolent old lion's. Then I had to play, and he said how strange it was that he had heard no music for so long. The art seemed to have developed, and he knew nothing about that development. He wanted me to give him an account. He said that he and I must have a sensible talk.— Then he turned to Ottilie: "I suppose you have made your arrangements. But that will do you no good. I am issuing the command that you serve tea here today, so that we can all be together."—Ottilie asked whether that wouldn't make it too late for him, since he had made an appointment for Riemer to come and work with him late that afternoon. He said: "You let your boys off from their Latin this morning, so they could hear Felix play; you might let me off from my work, too, for once." . . .

◇◇◇◇◇

May 25, 1830

Last night Goethe gave a party and I played all evening. . . . The recital was over at 10 but, of course, I staid on and we danced and sang and cut capers until midnight. The old man always retires to his room at 9, and the minute he is gone the fun begins. . . .

I dine with him daily. He asks me an hundred questions. After we have eaten he is cheerful and communicative. We usually spend an hour alone in his study then, and he speaks uninterruptedly. It is a great joy. . . . In the evening he has invited people on several occasions, which is very rare nowadays, so that most of the guests have not seen him for long. Then he makes me play and pays me compliments, among which "quite stupendous" is his favorite. Today he invited a great many of the beauties of Weimar because, as he puts it, I must meet young people. . . .

◇◇◇◇◇

June 6, 1830

. . . I told Goethe that I would have to leave. He fell quite silent. After dinner he drew Ottilie into the window niche and said to her: "You make him stay." She did her best to persuade me, walking up and down with me in the garden. But I was firm and said I must stick to my determination. Then the old gentleman himself came and said that it was so foolish to hurry; there was so much he had still to tell me and so much that he would still like to hear. . . .

On the last day he gave me a page of the manuscript of *Faust* and wrote on it: "To my dear young friend, Felix Mendelssohn, the delicate and powerful master of the piano, in cordial memory of these happy days of May, 1830."

June 7, 1830

To Zelter

This morning at half past nine, the sky being clear and the sunshine radiant, the excellent Felix set out together with Ottilie and Ulrike and the children for Jena. He has been here for two weeks. His stay was delightful and he edified us all by his perfect and admirable art. . . . His presence was especially beneficial to me, since I found that my relation to music has not changed. I hear it with pleasure and reflective sympathy and love its historical aspect. For how can one understand any phenomenon, if one does not penetrate its historical development? . . . And so again Felix made everything vital to me from the period of Bach on, again playing Haydn and Mozart and Glück and giving me an adequate idea of the great contemporary technicians. Finally he helped me to feel and understand his own productions. He leaves with all my blessings. . . . Give my sincerest greetings to the excellent parents of the remarkable young artist.

Weimar, June 24, 1830

From the Diaries

The Lodge of St. John today celebrated the fiftieth anniversary of my becoming a Mason.

July 8, 1830

To Zelter

I suppose I have already told you that my son went South with Doctor Eckermann toward the end of April. His diaries up to Milan and
from there to Venice display a very good insight into practical matters and a thoughtful activity in the attempt to understand and make
friends of both people and things. The great advantage to him and to
us, which may arise from this journey, is that he become more conscious of himself, that he discover his true nature, which he could
not so clearly conceive amid our simple and limited conditions.

Eckermann to Goethe

During our second stay in Milan, to which city we returned from
Venice, I came down with a fever, so that I was quite ill for a number
of nights and lay there wretchedly for a week without any desire for
nourishment. In these lonely and unhappy hours I could not but
think of my manuscript [*the first volume of the* Conversations] and it
made me restless to realize that it was not clearly formed and could
not be used. I recalled that I had scribbled many passages in pencil,
neither legibly nor well expressed. . . .
Without betraying anything of this, I talked to your son about my
physical health. He realized that it would be dangerous for me to
drag myself on through the hot summer of the South, and we agreed
that, if I were not better by the time we reached Genoa, he would
leave it to me whether I had not better return to Germany. . . .
I was happy to make that choice and so on Sunday, July 25, at 4
o'clock in the morning we embraced each other in farewell on a
street in Genoa. . . .

September 3, 1830

To August

I now have your official leave of absence to the end of the year actually in my hands. I hope it will reach you in Rome, unless wretched
demons try you with new obstacles. . . .
There is nothing to say to one who has entered the Eternal City. If

he feels reborn, then he *is* so, and a longer stay will result in all possible good. Any other remark would imitate the rhetoric of Polonius, a part I have never undertaken to play. . . .

The celebration of my birthday was quite lively. I decided not to run away this time. Why should one shun kindness and affection? Friends and well-wishers whom I rarely see came to see me, including our gracious Lordships. The gifts were splendid and included a well-wrought silver punch bowl from Frankfurt friends, as well as 24 bottles of precious vintages. . . . There were magnificent cushions and window hangings, far too costly to be used in comfort. . . .

<><><><><>

September 17, 1830

I have your excellently continued diaries up to August 28 and I commend you for them. . . .

What can I tell you about ourselves? Nothing happens in our house or at the Court or in the city, which does not logically follow from world conditions. . . . Excesses against the governments have taken place, whether with good reason or with ill, in Brabant and other localities. In Leipzig houses were taken by storm, in Dresden the court house was burned and the police archives destroyed. . . . Russia and Austria, following the example of Prussia, have recognized the King of the French. . . . It is to be hoped that all these troubles will end profitably and fairly for all the parties concerned.

<><><><><>

September 30, 1830

. . . Now I have your excellent journal letters up to Monday, September 13 in complete good order. . . .

May all go well with you and all these excellent preparations augur the best for your arrival at Rome, where we may now imagine you to be. . . . Ottilie remains true to her various duties, including her editorial ones, nor does she cease on gala days to busy herself with the selection of innumerable hats. The boys are sociable and well tempered; they make progress in music; the fate of their other studies we cannot yet predict. The little girl is amazingly clever and somewhat self-willed, but her interest is easily deflected and her companionship quite charming.

Weimar, October 9, 1830
From the Diaries

Continued to read Terence and admired the infinite delicacy of the
theatrical urbanity with which rather scabrous subjects are treated,
as well as the shapely dialogue so well adapted to the size of the
theatre and the distance of the spectator from the actor.

William Makepeace Thackeray to George Henry Lewes

The great novelist, 1811-1863, wrote this reminiscence to the husband
of George Eliot, G. H. Lewes, 1817-1878, who was preparing to write
his well-known *Life of Goethe*.

In 1831, though he had retired from the world, Goethe would nevertheless kindly receive strangers. His daughter-in-law's tea-table was
always spread for us. We passed hours after hours there, and night
after night with the pleasantest talk and music. We read over endless
novels and poems in French, English and German. My delight in
those days was to make caricatures for children. I was touched to
find that they were remembered, and some even kept until the present time; and very proud to be told, as a lad, that the great Goethe
had looked at some of them.

He remained in his private apartments, where only a very few privi-
leged persons were admitted; but he liked to know all that was happening, and interested himself about all strangers. . . . Of course
I remember very well the perturbation of spirit with which, as a lad
of nineteen, I received the long-expected intimation that the Privy
Councillor would see me on such a morning. This notable audience
took place in a little antechamber of his private apartments, covered
all round with antique casts and bas-reliefs. He was habited in a
long gray or drab redingote, with a white neckcloth and a red ribbon
in his buttonhole. He kept his hands behind his back, just as in
Rauch's statuette. His complexion was very bright, clear and rosy.
His eyes extraordinarily dark, piercing, and brilliant. I felt quite
afraid before them and recollect comparing them to the eyes of the
hero of a certain romance called *Melmoth the Wanderer*, which used
to alarm us boys thirty years ago; eyes of an individual who had made
a bargain with a certain Person, and at an extreme old age retained

these eyes in all their awful splendor. I fancied Goethe must have been still more handsome as an old man than even in the days of his youth. His voice was very rich and sweet. He asked me questions about myself, which I answered as best I could. I recollect I was at first astonished, and then somewhat relieved, when I found he spoke French with not a good accent.

Vidi tantum. I saw him but three times. Once walking in the garden of his house in the Frauenplan; once going to step into his chariot on a sunshiny day, wearing a cap and a cloak with a red collar. He was caressing at the time a beautiful little golden-haired granddaughter, over whose sweet fair face the earth has long since closed, too.

Weimar, November 10, 1830

From the Diaries

At nightfall Chancellor von Müller and Doctor Vogel came to convey to me with all possible delicacy the fact that my son died in Rome on the night between the 26 and 27 of October.

Eckermann

On November 20 I was traveling between Nordheim and Göttingen. I got to the latter city by nightfall. At the table-d'hôte, the inn-keeper, being told that I was from Weimar and was on my way back, remarked with a certain complacency, that the great poet Goethe had been visited by a tragic misfortune in his old age. The host said he had read it in today's paper. My feelings at this piece of news are easily imaginable.

. . . My greatest anxiety was, of course, that Goethe at his great age would not be able to survive the pangs of paternal grief. And what impression, I asked myself, will my arrival make—I, who departed with his son and who come back alone! Amid such thoughts and emotions I reached the Post House at Weimar at 6 o'clock on the evening of November 23. . . . I went to Goethe's house at the first possible moment, seeking out Frau von Goethe first. I found her already in deep mourning, but calm and composed. There was a great deal that we had to say to each other. I then went down the flight of stairs to Goethe. He stood there erect and firm and took me into his arms. . . .

November, 1830

Müller to Rochlitz

His son died of a stroke quite suddenly in Rome on October 27. You
can easily imagine how bitter was the task of conveying this tragic
message to the venerable father. But he received it with great composure and resignation. *"Non ignoravi, me mortalem genuisse!"*
[*"I knew that I had begotten a mortal!"*] he cried, the while his eyes
filled with tears.

November 21, 1830

To Zelter

Nemo ante obitum beatus [*Call no one happy before his death*]—
such is the proverb which has figured so largely in history. Actually
it means nothing. If one were to express the matter with greater pre-
cision the saying should run: Expect trials to the very end.
You, my good friend, have not lacked such trials; neither have I, and
it seems indeed as though fate were convinced that we were not put
together with nerves and veins and arteries and the derivative organs,
but with wires. . . .
And the very strange and significant aspect of this trial is that I will
now have to begin to carry and drag onward all those heavy burdens
which I hoped at once or, certainly in the New Year, to have renounced and transferred to one younger and more vigorous than
myself.
All that can sustain me is the great concept of duty. My prime care
must be to retain my physical equilibrium. All else will take care
of itself. . . .

Weimar, November 25, 1830

From the Diaries

Went to bed at 9. Walter came from the theatre and told me the
story of the play. Fell asleep but was awakened shortly after 10 by a
hemorrhage. Doctor Vogel was summoned and bled me at once. Improved.

◇◇◇◇◇

Weimar, November 27, 1830

Quite well all day. The Grand Duchess sent me a jar of compote.

◇◇◇◇◇

Weimar, December 1, 1830

Ottilie read to me from the Encyclopaedia after dinner.

December 2, 1830

To the Willemers

From the enclosed you will see, my dearest friends, that after parting and suffering nothing remains for us to do but to think of pleasant things again, if not for ourselves, then for others. So my next task is to make Christmas as festive as possible for my grandchildren in their own sense. . . .

December 14, 1830

To Zelter

. . . My son's not coming back weighed on me very heavily and sorely in more ways than one. I tried to be absorbed by work. . . . I forced myself to continue the fourth volume of *Poetry and Truth* and succeeded so well that the volume could be printed as it stands. . . .

Thus I continued for four weeks and there is no doubt that the repressed grief, added to the intellectual exertion, caused that physical catastrophe for which the body was prepared. . . . An artery in my lung burst and the loss of blood was such that, had not medical skill intervened at once, my last line of all would have been written. . . .

December 27, 1830

To August Kestner

When I think of you in Rome it brings back to me vividly the dread and doubt in which I passed the eight months that are now over. My son traveled in order to recover himself and his earlier letters were consoling and encouraging. . . . He broke his collar-bone between Genoa and Spezia. That immobilized him for four weeks. But this, as well as an accompanying affection of the skin, so unbearable in the great heat, he bore with manly good humor. . . . His letters from Naples on ceased, I must confess, to please me. They exhibited a certain sense of haste and a morbid exaltation. . . . A quick trip to Rome could no longer soothe the excitation of nature. . . . Let me assure you once more that I appreciate to the fullest extent all the helpfulness and kindness shown my son by his Roman friends during the few days of his sojourn, as well as their arrangements subsequent to his demise.

Weimar, December 27, 1830

From the Diaries

I gave the coachman the key to the woodshed and had him bring wood for all fireplaces into the house. Then got the key back.

◇◇◇◇◇

Weimar, December 28, 1830

News came that on December 21 the great revolutionary crisis in Paris was over.

◇◇◇◇◇

Weimar, December 30, 1830

Read Walter Scott's *Letters on Demonology and Witchcraft*, evidently written in order to destroy a prevalent superstition.

1831

January 10, 1831

To Adele Schopenhauer

. . . And so our August did not come back. If the mind and character of the survivors are to be equal to such events, as is demanded of them, the body cannot help reacting in a certain way and following up a moral crisis with a physical one. And so I was, to all appearances, my dear girl, ankle deep in the Lethean stream. But I did

not reach the bark of Charon. This being so, nothing is left me but
to begin all over again and to play once more the troublesome rôle
of a German head of a family.

Weimar, January 27, 1831

From the Diaries

The last batch of my works arrived from the binder's. My copy is
now complete and in order. Assigned certain copies to friends. At
noon Ottilie came; she and I went through all the gossip of the city
which revealed all kinds of novelistic material. Arranged the 40 volumes of my works in a row and regarded them with grateful and
appreciative pleasure. Had not expected to live to see them.

❖❖❖❖❖

Weimar, February 10, 1831

A young man was sent me whom I hired to be our cook. Discussed
the various arrangements. Vulpius got rid of our old cook with a
small indemnity. Now that I'm rid of this burden I can go on to
important work.

❖❖❖❖❖

Weimar, February 12, 1831

Bravely and happily took in hand the completion of *Faust.*

❖❖❖❖❖

Weimar, February 14, 1831

Doctor Eckermann and little Wolf dined with me. We all joked
about the improvement in the cooking.

February 17, 1831

Eckermann

"People usually think," Goethe said laughing, "that a man must
grow old to have good sense. The truth is that, as the years go on,
one must make an effort to remain as intelligent as one used to be.
Man changes with the epochs of his life, but it cannot be said that he

gets any better. In certain things his judgment can be as sound at
20 as it is at 60." . . .
I asked after *Faust* and its progress. "It grips me every moment,"
said Goethe, "and I think of it and add inventively to it daily. I
have had the manuscript sheets of the second part stitched, so that
I may have a tangible object to look at. I have blank pages where the
fourth act is missing. There is no doubt but that the contrast of these
to the completed pages acts as an incentive."

March 20-22, 1831

To Boisserée

. . . Of myself I can say, that I cannot sufficiently revere that gracious manifestation of the moral order of the world, which permitted me to recuperate physically and spiritually in a manner that
meets the needs of the moment. . . . Under these circumstances, I
am impelled to close in seriousness and jest with a curious reflection. No man can defend himself against religious emotions. But
most men find it impossible to deal with these in their own souls.
Hence they seek to make proselytes. The latter is not my way; the
former I have successfully attempted, but I have found no faith or
dogma, from the beginning of the world on, to which I could give
my entire assent. Now in my old age I learn of the existence of a
sect called Hyspistarians who, dwelling amidst heathens and Jews
and Christians, declared that they were ready to value, to admire, to
honor whatever they learned to be the best and most perfect thing,
and to give it their adoration, since, being the best, it must sustain
a close relation to the Divinity. Suddenly, then, there came to me a
glad light out of a dark age. I felt at once that I had always tried to
qualify as a Hyspistarian.

March 22, 1831

Eckermann

"Niebuhr was quite right," said Goethe, "when he predicted the immediate approach of a barbarous period. It is here now; we are in the
very midst of it; for what is barbarism except man's failure to acknowledge the excellent?"

◇◇◇◇◇

March 25, 1831

Goethe showed me an elegant green armchair which he had caused to be bought at an auction the other day.

"I will use it not at all or little," he said. "These kinds of comfort are really not for me. You don't see a sofa in my study. I sit on my old wooden chair and have had a higher back to lean my head against added only recently. To be surrounded by comfortable and luxurious furnishings seems to cancel my mental activity and to reduce me to the passive enjoyment of ease. Except insofar as one has been brought up among them, handsome rooms and elegant appliances are fit for people who neither think nor want to think."

Weimar, April 1, 1831

From the Diaries

Went through the monthly bills and tabulated them.

◇◇◇◇◇

Weimar, April 6, 1831

Drove down to the Garden House. Ate by myself there and reflected on all necessary affairs.

May 2, 1831

Eckermann

Goethe delighted me with the information that he had succeeded in very nearly completing the beginning of the fifth act of *Faust*.

"The motifs in these scenes," said he, "are more than 30 years old. They are of such significance that I never lost interest in them, but so difficult to execute, that I was afraid to try. Through all kinds of ways and means I have now made myself fluid. With some good luck I will now go on to the end."

May 15, 1831

"When a man is over 80," Goethe said, "he has hardly the right to count on longer life. He must reckon daily with being no longer on earth and must seek to put his house in order. As I informed you the other day, I have appointed you editor of my posthumous works in my will. Now, today, I have set up a kind of little contract, which I want you to sign.

June 1, 1831

To Zelter

Do continue, my dear friend, to send me from time to time some sheaves from that rich harvest to which you were assigned. For I am wholly confined, so to speak, to the innermost garden of a cloister in order, to put it briefly, to finish the second part of *Faust*.

June 6, 1831

Eckermann

Goethe showed me today the beginning of the fifth act of *Faust*, which had hitherto been lacking. . . .
"The *Faust* of the fifth act," said Goethe, "is to be conceived of as exactly 100 years old, and I am not sure but what it were well to indicate that definitely."
We then talked about the close and Goethe called my attention to the following lines:

> Forever is from evil won
> This scion of the spirit:
> Who to the end strives nobly on,
> May our redemption merit.
> And if the Love that is on high
> Mark him from where its grace is,
> The heavenly hosts toward him will fly
> With welcome on their faces.

"In these verses," said he, "is the key to Faust's redemption. In Faust himself there exists to the end an ever higher and purer activity, which the eternal love comes to meet. This harmonizes entirely with the religious concept, according to which we are not saved entirely through our own efforts but through the addition of Divine Grace." . . .

June 18, 1831

To Ulrike von Pogwisch

Let me tell you first about the children who at this very moment are tumultuously playing about me in the front rooms and so making their existence very evident.

Walter, who certainly has musical talent, seems to have been given a sunstroke by a female singer from Leipzig who was here. He composes arias which he would like to hear sung by her. . . .

Little Wolf continues to stick to his grandfather. We have breakfast together and spend most of the day together. It is the theatre that entrances him. He writes tragedies and comedies and collects playbills. . . .

The little girl is charming. She is a born little woman and is quite incalculable even now. She sustains a very pleasant and amiable relation to her grandfather. . . .

So here, my dear girl, is a truly grandfatherly letter. . . .

July 29, 1831

To August Kestner

. . . As to the few things that my son left behind, I leave their expedition entirely in your hands. . . .

To proceed to the matter of the monument, may I express my deep emotion at the kind solicitude of friends in Rome and at the offer of Herr Thorwaldsen [*the great Danish sculptor, 1770-1840*] which I accept with a gratitude for which I have no words. . . . I am enclosing the inscription for the monument which, I hope, will meet the approval of experts:

Goethe, Fil. Patri. Antevertens. Obit.
Annorum. XL. MDCCCXXX.

(Goethe, the son, preceding his father, died at the age of 40. 1830.)

August, 1831

Eckermann

During these weeks Goethe had completed the lacking fourth act of
Faust, so that in August the entire second part lay bound before him.
To have reached this goal, after which he had striven for so long,
made him supremely happy. "Whatever of life remains to me," said
he, "I can regard purely as a gift from now on, and it really does not
matter whether I accomplish anything more or not."

1831

FAUST (Part II, Act V)

This Last Conclusion

Yes, to this truth my heart is dedicated,
This last conclusion wisdom drew:
For him alone freedom and life are fated
Who daily conquers them anew.
And though the sea still threatens, active here
Will men and children live their valiant year.
If such I could behold and be
With a free people on a soil as free—
Then to the moment transitory
"O fair one, linger," I could say,
Nor could the traces of my earthly story
Be by the aeons swept away.

Ilmenau, August 28, 1831

To Frau von Levetzow

To avoid elaborate celebrations of my birthday, I have gone to the
country. Here, my very dear friend, I contemplate that glass which
points back to so many years and brings to mind the most beautiful
of hours. After so many strange and sad blows of fate which I have
suffered and which, doubtless, engaged your sympathy, I turn once
more to you and your loved ones, requesting news and expressing the
assurance, that my sentiments have undergone no change.

Ilmenau, August 28, 1831

From the Diaries

Bright sunshine, though the sky is cloud-flecked. Arose at 5. Breakfasted with little Wolf, while Walter continued his morning nap. The city band serenaded me. Fifteen little girls dressed in white brought a poem and a wreath on a cushion. Herr von Fritsch, who had driven over last night. . . . At dinner Fritsch and the children. . . . Toward evening a brief storm, with lightning, thunder and rain. After nightfall the miners' band serenaded me. Before that a messenger, bearing gifts, had arrived from Weimar.

Late August, 1831

Recollections of the Inspector of Mines at Ilmenau

Goethe arrived toward evening with his two grandsons and servants and took lodgings at the Sign of the Lion here in Ilmenau. An entirely clear sky promised the most beautiful weather. Immediately upon his arrival he sent me a message, asking me to call on him. . . . I went to see him early in the morning. . . . His two grandsons, accompanied by his valet, had already gone on an excursion to the mountains and were not to return until noon. After various inquiries he asked me whether one could comfortably drive up the Kickelhahn Mountain. He was desirous of seeing the curious little hunting lodge he had seen there years ago. He asked me to accompany him. And so we drove up the forest road in the fine summer weather. . . .

Comfortably we reached the highest point of the mountain. He descended from the carriage and enjoyed the magnificent view. He was delighted, too, with the fine growth of the forest, and exclaimed: "If only my good Karl August could have seen all this once more!" Then he asked, whether the little hunting lodge was not quite near here. "I can go on foot. Let the carriage wait until we come back." Vigorously enough he made his way through the tall bilberry bushes to the well-known hunting lodge which had been built of logs and rude boards. A steep stairway led to the upper storey. I offered to give him my support. With youthful cheerfulness he declined. "You mustn't think that I can't climb that stairway alone; I can do it very well." As he entered that single upper chamber he said: "There was a time when I passed a whole summer week in this room with my valet and at that time I wrote a little poem on the wooden walls. That is what I would like to see once more, and to see, whether I marked the date beneath." I led him at once to the south window of the chamber. To its left the penciled writing was clearly visible:

> O'er all the hill-tops
> Is quiet now,
> In all the tree-tops
> Hearest thou
> Hardly a breath;
> The birds are asleep in the trees:
> Wait; soon like these
> Thou too shalt rest.   September 7, 1780

Goethe re-read the verses and the tears flowed down his cheeks. Slowly he drew forth a gleaming white handkerchief from his dark-brown coat and dried his tears and said in a gentle tone of deep emotion: "Wait; soon like these thou too shalt rest." He fell silent and gazed for another moment through the window at the sombre pine forest and then turned to me and said: "Now let us go back." Down the steep stairs I again offered him my help. But he replied: "Don't you believe that I can go down the stairway? I can do it very well. But walk in front of me so that I need not look down." . . . I accompanied him back to his inn. On the way he spoke many precious and powerful words to me. . . .

September 4, 1831

To Zelter

During the six most brilliant days of the whole summer I was away from Weimar, having taken my way to Ilmenau, where I was so active in earlier years and which I had not seen in so long. . . . In the perspective of the many years there appeared before my vision both the lasting and the perishable. I was cheered at the thought of what had succeeded and I realized that failures are forgotten and their pain is quenched. The human beings here lived as they had always done, each in harmony with his kind, from the poor charcoal burner to the wealthy manufacturer of porcelain. . . .

September 7, 1831

To Reinhard

I want to emphasize the fact to you that I succeeded in completing the second part of *Faust*. . . . It was during the second half of August. Since there was nothing more to do, I sealed up the manuscript, in order to withdraw it from my eyes and from any possibility of further preoccupation. Let it, at the right time, increase the specific gravity of future volumes of my works. It is my wish that it reach you at some fortunate hour. Expect no interpretation. Similar in this respect to the history of man and of his world, the solution of a present problem does but give rise to a new one that must be solved in its turn.

October 5, 1831

To Zelter

Every evening Ottilie reads to me from Plutarch's *Lives*. We do it after a new fashion. First we read the lives of the Greeks, remaining thus in one region, with one nation, attentive to a single mood of thought and aspiration. When we're through with this part, we will proceed to the Romans and read that series of lives. We omit his comparisons and await a purer impression by comparing the two groups to each other. For three months I have again not looked at a newspaper. . . . Thus I learn of the beginning of whatever happens and of its outcome, untroubled by the doubts that lie between.

Weimar, October 11, 1831

From the Diaries

I am continuing to read Balzac's *Le Peau de Chagrin*. . . . It is an admirable work in the newest fashion. It is distinguished by the fact that it passes back and forth, both powerfully and tastefully, between the impossible and the unendurable and, using the inexplicable as a means, delineates very logically the strangest sentiments and events. Much more that is good could be said about this in detail.

◇◇◇◇◇

Weimar, November 7, 1831

A very strange day to me on which in silence I commemorate my 56 years of life and activity in Weimar.

November 24, 1831

To Boisserée

When I sealed up the completed manuscript of *Faust* I didn't, I confess, feel altogether comfortable. I could not but remember that the friends whom I esteem most and who agree with me best, will not soon have the pleasure of spending some hours on these seriously meant jests and thus learn of what stirred my mind and soul so long, until at last it assumed its right form. Even as a poet, who does not like to hide his light under a bushel, it was a desperate thing to deny myself the comfort of immediate sympathy for my work. My consolation must be that precisely those, whose judgment I most value, are all younger than I. They will enjoy what has been prepared and conserved for them in memory of me.

December 1, 1831

To Wilhelm von Humboldt

If I may turn to you with the confidence of old, I would like to confess that, at my age, everything assumes a more and more historical character. It seems indifferent to me whether a thing took place in past times and far lands or at this moment under my eyes. Indeed, I seem to become ever more a part of history to my very self. . . .
Of my *Faust* there is both much and little to be said. . . . Through a mysterious psychological development, which probably deserves closer study, I believe myself to have attained a kind of production which, though completely conscious, brought forth what I can myself still approve, though I shall never be able to swim in this river again —a thing, indeed, which Aristotle and other prosaic minds, would ascribe to a kind of madness.

Weimar, December 2, 1831

From the Diaries

Planning our supply of firewood for the winter, I bought some from a local peasant at a very reasonable price. Reading just for entertainment in order to distract my mind from more serious reflections. Later in the day Ottilie read me from Plutarch again. How different the aspect of ancient history, especially that of the Greeks, in 1831 from its aspect sixty years ago.

Weimar, December 17, 1831

Went through all the kitchen accounts. Considered everything and decided on everything. Later Ottilie read me from Plutarch again, to the great annoyance of little Wolf who had been to a performance of Mozart's *Abduction from the Serail* and who wanted to tell us all about it.

Weimar, December 25, 1831

The children came to me early, well contented with their Christmas presents.

1832

January, 1832

Recollections of a Russian Statesman

I set down Goethe's words as they remained in my memory. "Fame, my dear Count, does nourish the soul magnificently. It fortifies and uplifts the mind and refreshes the heart. Man's feeble nature craves its delight. But he who has been long famous ends by despising fame. Public opinion makes idols of men and blasphemes gods: it celebrates the faults which make us blush and jeers at the virtues which are our pride. I assure you that fame is as much of an affront as infamy. For 30 years I have been fighting down my disgust in this matter. You would understand me if for a few weeks you could watch the

daily stream of foreigners who come to admire me, many of whom
have never read a line that I have written. This is true of nearly all
the Frenchmen and Englishmen. And most of those who have read,
have not understood. The meaning and significance of my works and
of my life is the triumph of the purely human. . . . In view of all
this, I am willing to admit with certain reservations, the truth of
your assertions that Germany has never understood me. There ob-
tains among the German people a spirit of sensual exaltation, which
is wholly alien to me. Art and philosophy are torn asunder from life;
their character is abstract and they are far removed from the sources
in nature which should nourish them. . . . I hold life to be more
precious than art." . . .

February 9, 1832

To Marianne von Willemer

The delicious candy you sent has arrived safely. What is odd enough
is that the upper layer has aroused the sweet tooth of your aged
friend. . . . As a rule, I am satisfied at table with the very simplest
things and with but little of those. But, of course, I have to think of
my family and of my guests. Consequently, I would beg you to send
us a reasonable quantity of chestnuts. . . . Another thing occurs to
me. If the cold weather continues, a couple of hog's head cheeses
ought to be easily transportable. While my mother lived I received
these things regularly at the proper time.

February 10, 1832

To Marianne von Willemer

I am trying quite earnestly to use the time still granted me for the
purpose of going through the infinite mass of papers which are piled
up about me, in order to classify them and to decide what is to be
done with them. Among these I find certain radiant documents
which remind me of the fairest days of my life. Some of these have
always been kept separately. They are now wrapped and sealed.
A package of this kind is before me with your address on it. I am
tempted to send it to you at once, to anticipate the accidents of life.
I would ask you to promise to keep it unopened until an hour not
yet determined upon. Documents of this kind give us the glad feeling
that we have indeed lived.

February 17, 1832

Soret

At 5 o'clock this afternoon I found Goethe all alone lingering at the dinner table. He was, as was his custom, finishing his bottle of wine. He wasn't sleepy yet and in a mood to talk.

He said: "How far would the greatest genius get if he insisted stubbornly upon producing everything out of his unassisted inner resources? What would remain of genius if you robbed it of the capacity of utilizing whatever struck its attention, of taking marble from one place and metal ore from another, and use these to construct its edifice? . . . What am I myself? Just what have I done? I have assembled and put to use everything I ever saw, heard, observed. My works have drawn their nourishment from a host of different people—the ignorant and the wise, the brilliant and the stupid, children and mature men and aged ones; all came and afforded me an insight into their thoughts, capacities, hopes, their entire way of being. I have often harvested what others have sown and my work is that of a collective being which bears the name of Goethe." . . .

He spoke last of all of his son—of the latter's travels, his irresponsible levity, his death. He gave me intimate details quite freely and philosophically, which surprised and interested me at the same time. . . .

Weimar, February 27, 1832

From the Diaries

Began to read an interesting pamphlet which describes the opening of the railroad between Liverpool and Manchester.

March 10, 1832

To Zahn

It was at this time that Walter Scott set out on his last journey in search of health. It was hoped that he would come to Weimar.

It was written in the stars (I use this figure of speech to describe one of those events for which there are no words) that my son, who was the source to me of so much joy and care and hope, before he reached his resting place near the Pyramid of Cestius should, on his para-

bolic course through Italy, have found so many sympathetic friends.
. . . I know very well how much of this we owe to your influence and
so I would acknowledge with appreciation not only your tireless,
purposeful activity but also your steadfastness of good will toward
those who have engaged your affection. . . .
If you are still able to reach Sir Walter Scott, do assure him that he
would find himself thoroughly at home among us, not only as the
author of so many significant works, but as one whose nobility of
thought we admire. . . . My good daughter, who returns your kind
greetings, desires, if it is at all possible, to convey her regards to the
unmarried daughter of Sir Walter Scott who accompanies him and
to assure her of the most cordial reception among us.

March 11, 1832

Eckermann

On this Sunday the conversation turned to the subject of those great
men who, before the time of Christ, had lived among the Chinese,
Indians, Persians and Greeks, and that the power of God moved them
even as it did the great Jewish figures of the Old Testament. And so
we came to the question how it was with the evidence of God's influence through the great personalities of our present world.
"To hear people talk," said Goethe, "you would be inclined to think
it to be their opinion that God had retired to utter stillness since
those days of old, that man was forced to stand on his own feet alone
and do the best he can without God and the daily breathing of God
through him. In religious and moral matters God's influence is
grudgingly admitted. Matters of science and of art are accepted as
purely mortal and the mere products of human forces.
"But let someone try to bring forth by the mere human will and mere
human strength works worthy to vie with the creations of a Mozart,
a Raphael, a Shakespeare. I know very well that these three are not
the only ones. In all the realms of art admirable spirits have been
active and have produced equally perfect things. Insofar as they did,
they also transcended the common run of human nature and were
as divinely inspired as those three.
"Look about you in the world! God did not withdraw after those
well-known six days of creation. Rather is He as continuously among

us as on that primal day. To construct this clumsy world out of simple elements and to let it roll year in and year out beneath the rays of the sun, would have been a crude enough jest, had it not been for the Divine Plan to found upon this material substructure the nursery for a whole world of spirits. Thus God continues to work through the higher natures, in order that the lower ones may attain to the level of the higher."

Goethe fell silent. But I preserved his great and goodly words in my heart.

Weimar, March 16, 1832

From the Diaries

Indisposed. Stayed in bed all day.

March 17, 1832

To Wilhelm von Humboldt

It is now sixty years since the conception of *Faust* arose clearly in my youthful soul—somewhat less elaborately the further development of the poem. Gently the plan and intention accompanied me through the years. From time to time I completed the most interesting passages. Thus gaps occurred in the second part which had to be filled and combined with the rest with an equal measure of interest. There arose, needless to say, the difficulty of attaining by an act of the will what should have arisen from the involuntary workings of nature. It would not have been well, had this not been possible after so long a life of active reflection. I am, at all events, not at all afraid that it will be possible to distinguish between older and newer passages, the later and earlier ones, when the whole is submitted to the kindly attention of future readers.

Undoubtedly it would have given me infinite pleasure to communicate these very earnest jests to my many excellent, deeply appreciated, far-scattered friends, while I am still alive. But the day in which we live is so absurd and confused that, according to my conviction, my honest and long efforts to build this strange structure would have been ill-rewarded. Driven upon a barren shore, they might have lain there like ruined wreckage and have been soon covered by the sands of the dunes. Confused doctrine leading to confused action rules our world, and I have no dearer purpose than to heighten what is in me and remains of me and to concentrate my very special character, even as you, my excellent friend, seek to do in the fortress in which you live. . . .

Forgive me for this belated sheet! Despite my isolation, there is rarely an hour in which I can call these mysteries of existence vividly to mind.

1832

FAUST (Part II, Act V)

Song of Lynceus, The Watchman in the Tower

Oh destined for seeing
And stationed for sight,
The tower is my being,
The world my delight.

My vision embraces
The far and the near,
Sidereal spaces,
The wood and the deer.

The grace of creation
My vigil did bless,
And in my elation
I pleased me no less.

Eyes happily ranging,
All that you have seen,
Though fortune was changing,
How fair it has been!

March 22, 1832

The Last Day

From: K. W. Müller: Goethe's Last Literary Activity and Death. Jena, 1832.

At 6 o'clock in the morning he asked to be helped out of his arm-chair and took the few steps from his bedroom into his study. Here, where she had stayed all night, he came upon his daughter-in-law.

Teasingly he said to her: "Aha, little woman, did you come down as early as all that?" But he suddenly felt weaker again and went back to his armchair in the bedroom.

Although the physicians had been certain that there was no way of saving him from the repressed catarrhal fever, the friends assembled in the front room were unwilling to accept this painful prognosis, especially as the barometer had been rising. They knew by experience what a powerful influence the condition of the air always had on Goethe's health. The patient himself spoke hopefully a little later to his daughter-in-law. . . . April, he said, had its storms, but it had beautiful days, too, and he would recover his strength in the presence of nature. He besought the physician to give him no more medicine, seeing that he was feeling better. But as the sun rose his condition grew markedly worse and his strength decreased. The room had been left in darkness in order to soothe him. But he said: "Let in more light. The darkness is disagreeable." . . .

Toward 9 o'clock he asked for some wine and water. When it was brought him he drew himself up and grasped the glass firmly and emptied it. . . . Next he called in his secretary and, supported by him and his valet, he stood up. He asked what day of the month it was. Being told it was the 22nd, he said: "So spring has come; it will be easier to recuperate." He sat down in his armchair again and seemed to drop into a gentle slumber. . . .

A little while thereafter he asked to have cold fowl for breakfast. It was brought to him. He took a bite of it and said he was thirsty. The valet handed him a glass of wine mixed with water. He took only a swallow of it and asked: "You haven't put sugar into the wine, have you?" He then ordered the menu for dinner and also for dinner on Saturday. On that day his physician was supposed to dine with him and he wanted his friend's favorite dish to be served. . . .

Thereafter his mind seemed to dwell on Schiller. He saw a sheet of paper on the floor and asked why Schiller's letters were so carelessly treated. The paper had better be picked up. Then he said to his valet: "Open the blind of the other window, so that more light may come in!" These are said to have been his last words.

As speech became more and more difficult, but his impulse to communicate persisted, he began to draw letters in the air with his hands. . . . Gradually his strength decreased and his arm fell and in the end he made signs on the lap robe, which covered his knees. . . .

His fingers began to turn blue and so his eyeshade was taken off and it was found that his eyes were breaking. His breathing became more difficult but there was no death rattle. Without the slightest sign of pain he leaned himself comfortably against the left side of his armchair, and that heart which had created a whole world and sustained and nourished it, had ceased to beat.

EPILOGUE

Friedrich von Müller to Bettina von Arnim

He died the happiest death, conscious, serene, with no presentiment of his passing to the last breath, wholly free of pain. It was a gradual, gentle sinking and extinction of the flame of life. There was no struggle. His last request was for light. . . .

Recollections of a Friend of Ottilie

He died in Ottilie's arms. His breathing ceased so quietly and gently, that she was not aware of the moment of his death and believed that he was still resting after life had ceased. He was cheerful to the end. During his last hour he still said to her: "Little woman, give me your little paw!" And she did hold his hand until his final breath.

Eckermann

On the morning after Goethe's death a longing overcame me to see his mortal vesture once again. His faithful valet opened the room for me. He lay like one asleep. Deep peace and firmness reigned upon the features of his sublime countenance. Behind the mighty forehead the thoughts still seemed to stir. For a moment I desired a lock of his hair, but reverence prevented me from cutting it off. Unclothed the body lay, wrapped in a white sheet. The valet opened the sheet and I was amazed by the perfection of his manly form. A perfect human being of great beauty lay before me and for a moment I was tempted to forget that the immortal spirit had fled. In the great stillness I laid my hand upon his heart. Then I turned aside and gave vent to my tears.

> *When the recurrent and unhalted*
> *In endless repetition flows,*
> *The universe, the thousand vaulted*

451

Wheels powerful on itself to close,
Then life streams forth from all creation,
From suns and stars on heaven outpoured,
And impulse, struggle, aspiration
Are endless peace in God our Lord.

THE END

BIBLIOGRAPHICAL NOTE

Since this book, though meant primarily for the general reader, is bound to fall into the hands of many scholars, the sources are herewith given. Whatever occurs in these volumes will be found under the proper date in the following works:

Goethes Werke. Herausgegeben im Auftrage der Grossherzogin Sophie von Sachsen. Weimar. 1890. 145 vols.
  Abteilung I. Poetische, biographische und kunstwissenschaftliche Schriften.
  Abteilung II. Naturwissenschaftliche Schriften.
  Abteilung III. Tagebücher.
  Abteilung IV. Briefe.
  (Generally known as the "Weimar edition.)

Der junge Goethe. Neue Ausgabe in sechs Bänden besorgt von Max Morris. Leipzig. 1910.

Goethes Gespräche. Gesamtausgabe neu herausgegeben von Flodoard, Freiherr von Biedermann. Leipzig. 1909. 6 vols.

Gespräche mit Goethe in den letzten Jahren seines Lebens. Johann Peter Eckermann. Zürich. 1948.
  (This is the latest and best edition, being volume 24 of the *Gedenkausgabe* of Goethe's Works in process of being issued.)

Briefwechsel zwischen Goethe und Schiller. Jena. 1905. 2 vols.
  (Despite its unmentionable editor, this edition has the advantage of containing in an appendix the correspondence between Goethe and Charlotte Schiller.)

Goethes Briefe an Frau von Stein nebst dem Tagebuch aus Italien und Briefen der Frau von Stein. (Cotta) Stuttgart und Berlin. n.d. 4 vols.

Die Briefe der Frau Rath. Herausgegeben von A. Koester. Leipzig.
1923. 2 vols.

Goethes Ehe in Briefen. Herausgegeben von H. G. Gräf. Frankfurt-
am-Main. 1921.

Briefwechsel zwischen Goethe und Zelter. 1834.
Briefwechsel des Grossherzogs Karl August mit Goethe. Herausgegeben von H. Wahl. Berlin. 1915. 3 vols.

Briefwechsel zwischen Goethe und Marianne von Willemer. Herausgegeben von Th. Creizenach. Zweite vermehrte Auflage. Stuttgart 1878.

Correspondence between Goethe and Carlyle. Edited by Charles
Eliot Norton. London. 1887.

Sämtliche Werke. Arnim, Bettina (Brentano) von. Berlin. 1920-22.
7 vols.

Briefe der Freunde. Das Zeitalter Goethes im Spiegel der Freund-
schaft. Herausgegeben von Ernst von Schenck. Berlin. 1937.

Charlotte von Stein. Von Wilhelm Bode. Berlin. 1920.

Goethe und Marianne von Willemer. Von Bernhard von Brentano.
Zürich. 1945.

INDEX

Stendhal, de (Henri Beyle), ii, 418

Sterne, Laurence, i, 67

Stieler, Johann K., ii, 396

Stieler portrait, ii, 396

Stock, Jakob, ii, 159

Stolberg, Christian, Count, i, 115, 134, 279

Stolberg, Friedrich, i, 118, 119, 125, 279, 362, 395

Stolberg, Henriette, i, 118

Stolberg, Katharina, i, 119, 279

Stolberg, Sophie, i, 395

Stolberg-Stolberg, Countess Auguste zu, i, 111-12, 113, 121, 122-23, 126, 152, 166; ii, 322

Strassburg, i, 45, 203

Strassburg, University of, i, 61

Stuttgart, i, 208

St. Valentine's Day, ii, 400

Suetonius, i, 280

Summer Night, i, 23

Supplementary Confessions, see Confessions

Suppressed Stanza, ii, 222

Susquehanna River, ii, 377

Swiss Journey, i, 118-20, 212, 213; ii, 13-19

Szymanowska, Maria, ii, 326, 327, 342-43, 345, 346, 347

Talismans, ii, 230

Talleyrand, Perigord de, ii, 160-61

Tanner's Mill, ii, 227, 240, 241, 242, 243, 247, 250

Tartuffe, ii, 375-76

Tasso, i, 226, 227, 232, 233, 242, 329, 337, 345, 349, 354, 362, 366, 370, 374; ii, 142, 188, 198, 271, 405

Teniers, David, ii, 402

Teplitz, ii, 179, 181, 182, 202, 214

Testament, ii, 407-08

Textor, Anna M., i, 51

Textor, Johann J., i, 255

Textor, Johann Wolfgang, i, 3, 51

Thackeray, William Makepeace, ii, 428

Theodore, Prince Karl, i, 129

Theory of Colors, ii, 175, 215

Thirty Years' War, ii, 313

Thorane, Count, i, 10

Thuringian Forest, i, 250

Tieck, Ludwig, ii, 47

Tiefenort, i, 248

Tiefurt, i, 212; ii, 85, 227; theatre in, i, 247

Tischbein, J. H., i, 319, 320, 328

Today and Forever, ii, 284

To Hafiz, ii, 223

Tom Jones, ii, 23

To Ottilie Von Goethe, ii, 269

Torbole, i, 314

To the Moon, i, 177

To the Rising Moon, ii, 402

To the United States, ii, 301

To Ulrike, ii, 327, 328, 331

Translation, poems, i, xiii, 126; ii, 48

Trebra, Friedrich von, ii, 218, 283

Trier, i, 391

Tristam Shandy, i, 67

Troilus and Cressida, ii, 359, 372

Tübingen, ii, 16, 19

Turandot, ii, 72

Türckheim, Bernhard F. von, i, 109

Türckheim, Frau von, see Schönemann, Lili

Tyrol, i, 313

Ultimate Aspiration, ii, 225

Undine, ii, 216

Unger, Freidrich G., i, 443

United States, ii, 285, 293, 300, 375

Vanerstrass, D., ii, 50

Vega, Lope De, ii, 366

Veit, David, i, 401, 420, 432

INDEX TO FIRST LINES